The Wider Western Europe

The Wider Western Europe
Reshaping the EC/EFTA Relationship

edited by
HELEN WALLACE

Pinter Publishers, London and New York
for
The Royal Institute of
International Affairs,
London

First published in Great Britain in 1991 by
Pinter Publishers Limited
25 Floral Street, London WC2E 9DS

British Library Cataloguing in Publication Data
A CIP catalogue record for this book is available from the British Library
ISBN 0 86187 069 7

Library of Congress Cataloging-in-Publication Data
A CIP catalog record for this book is available from the Library of Congress.

Typeset by Best-set Typesetter Ltd.
Printed and bound in Great Britain by Biddles Ltd.

Contents

List of Figures

List of Tables

List of Abbreviations

ASEAN	Association of South-East Asian Nations
BCM	billion cubic metres
BIS	Bank of International Settlements
CAP	Common Agricultural Policy
CDU	Christian Democratic Union (Christliche Demokratische Union)
CEN	European Committee for Standardization
CENELEC	European Committee for the Coordination of Electrical Standards
CEPT	European Conference of Postal and Telecommunications Administrations
CFP	Common Fisheries Policy
CMEA	Council for Mutual Economic Aid
Comecon	see CMEA
Coreper	Committee of Permanent Representatives
COST	Cooperation in Science and Technology
CSCE	Conference on Security and Cooperation in Europe
EAP	Environmental Action Plan
ECJ	European Court of Justice
Ecofin	Council of Economic and Finance Ministers
ECSC	European Coal and Steel Community
ECU	European Currency Unit
EEA	European Economic Area (renaming in 1990 of EES)
EES	European Economic Space
EMCF	European Fund for Monetary Cooperation
EMS	European Monetary System
EMU	Economic and Monetary Union
EP	European Parliament
EPC	European Political Cooperation
EPO	European Patent Organization
ESA	European Space Agency
ETUC	European Trades Union Confederation

EUREKA	European Research Agency
FAO	Food and Agriculture Organization
FTA	Free Trade Agreement
GATT	General Agreement on Tariffs and Trade
GSP	General System of Preferences
IBRD	International Bank for Reconstruction and Development (World Bank)
IEA	International Energy Agency
ILO	International Labour Organization
IMF	International Monetary Fund
MFN	most favoured nation
MTN	Multilateral Trade Negotiations
N&N	Neutral and Non-aligned
NORDEK	Nordic Economic Organization
NTB	Non-Tariff Barrier
OECD	Organization for Economic Cooperation and Development
OEEC	Organization for European Economic Cooperation
OPEC	Organization of Petroleum-Exporting Countries
QR	quantitative restriction
SAD	Single Administrative Document
SEA	Single European Act
TBT	Technical Barrier to Trade
UNECE	United Nations Economic Commission for Europe
UNEP	United Nations Environment Programme
Uniscan	economic cooperation by UK and Scandinavia (est. 1949)
VSTF	very short-term financing facility
WEOG	West European and Other States Group
WEU	Western European Union

Contributors

Esko Antola, University of Turku
Carl Hamilton, University of Stockholm and Swedish Institute of International Affairs
Michael Klein, University of Vienna
Olav Knudsen, Norwegian Institute for International Affairs
Gunnar Helgi Kristinsson, Icelandic Commission for Security
Finn Laursen, European Institute of Public Administration
Paul Luif, Austrian Institute of International Affairs
Janne Haaland Matlary, Norwegian Institute of International Affairs
Thomas Pedersen, University of Aarhus
Elfriede Regelsberger, Institut für Europäische Politik
Martin Saeter, Norwegian Institute of International Affairs
Richard Senti, University of Zurich
Carl-Einar Stålvant, University of Stockholm and Swedish Institute of International Affairs
Jens Thomsen, Danish Ministry of Economics
Helen Wallace, Royal Institute of International Affairs
Friedl Weiss, London School of Economics and Political Science
Wolfgang Wessels, Institut für Europäische Politik
Per Magnus Wijkman, EFTA Secretariat

Preface

When several years ago we at this Institute started to work on the new relationship between the European Community (EC) and the members of the European Free Trade Association (EFTA), we were told by several people who worked inside the EC (including some in the UK) that the topic was neither interesting nor important. They were wrong. We stubbornly persisted and have found ourselves grappling with questions that touch the fundamentals of the European integration process. How large can the EC become without losing its ability to deliver effective economic policies? Or compromising its essential political goals, whatever those are? Can or should the EC develop new forms of partnership with its various European neighbours that are less than full membership but sufficient to be worth it for those other partners? Can this be done without undermining the political coherence of the EC or destroying its delicate institutional balance?

We little knew at the outset of this work on the wider Western Europe just how important these questions would become. This volume is essentially only about West European integration and the scope for reconciling the different attitudes to integration and supranationality which had initially kept the EC and EFTA so separate and so distinct in their approaches. The dramatic reversal of a different European division between East and West, has meant that those same questions about European integration have now to be applied to a much wider canvas. The efforts of the EC and EFTA countries to grapple with these difficult but vital issues have proved an invaluable intellectual exercise, which at least helps to clarify some of the options for Europe as a whole.

This volume has been a long time in the making. From this institute we have, with our partners at the Institut für Europäische Politik in Bonn, developed a rich network of friends and partners across Western Europe. Many of them have contributed chapters to this volume, but many others inside and outside governments in 18 countries and inside both EC and EFTA institutions have encouraged us in our endeavours. We are grateful to them all and owe them all sincere appreciation for what they have taught us about Europe. I hope that the many individuals who have helped will not mind if I do not name each of them. Special thanks are due, however, to Thomas Pedersen, now of Aarhus University, who worked at this Institute in 1988 at an early stage of the project, to Michael Klein for his help with parts of the manuscript and to my colleagues here at Chatham House who have done much of the laborious work as we have proceeded.

The project would not have been possible without financial assistance from many sources, both direct and indirect. These include the Austrian Bankers' Association, the Danish Institute of Foreign Policy, the (British) Department of Trade and Industry, the Gatsby Charitable Foundation, IBM (Europe), and the Stifterverband für Deutsche Wissenschaft. The other institutes associated with this project have been the Austrian Institute of International Affairs, the Danish Institute of Foreign Policy, the Finnish Institute of International Affairs, the Icelandic Commission for Security, Institut für Europäische Politik in Bonn, the Norwegian Institute of Foreign Policy and the Swedish Institute of International Affairs.

Royal Institute of
International Affairs,
August 1990

Helen Wallace

1 Introduction

Helen Wallace and Wolfgang Wessels

On 17 January 1989 Jacques Delors chose the moment of his second investiture as President of the European Commission to identify the challenge of the wider Western Europe as a priority for the European Community (EC). For four decades the patterns of West European collaboration have been both intense and dispersed. Initially only six countries chose the radical EC experiment, but now they have become twelve countries, committed to a far-reaching exercise in economic and political integration. Indeed, the credibility of their economic ambition, at least as regards the creation of a single market by 1992, is proving seductively compelling to the remaining West European countries, as yet outside the EC fold. For these other Europeans face difficult choices: to try to join fully in the Community's endeavours; to keep at a respectable, but watchful distance; or to forge a new relationship. For the members of the EC the choices are no less difficult: the old debate between 'deepening' and 'widening' remains a dilemma, both because the 1992 goal is in itself extremely ambitious and because they are committed by the Single European Act (SEA) to creating a European Union, so much more than a single market.[1]

For the EC the issues have become a good deal more challenging as a result of the dramatic changes in Central and Eastern Europe during 1989. The debate is no longer about the future shape of Western Europe, but about the future shape of Europe. The EC has been enlarged, as what had been the German Democratic Republic was amalgamated with the Federal Republic of Germany. The EC has acquired a role of tutelage vis-à-vis Central and Eastern European countries set on reform and it has to be assumed that these will apply to the EC for special relationships and eventually membership. Although the detailed configuration of the resulting scenarios for the development of the EC remains shadowy, it is clear that some rather fundamental choices will have to be faced about the scope, character and scale of European integration.

The dialogue between the EC and the members of the European Free Trade Association (EFTA) started as an apparently self-contained set of discussions in Western Europe, but it is now caught in the web of the wider transformation of Europe as a whole. This makes the practical business of the EC-EFTA dialogue look comparatively straightforward. Yet it renders more strategic the choices for the EC about the new forms of partnership that may lie ahead and it forces the members of EFTA to look at their European policies in terms far broader than they have hitherto preferred. What is crystal clear is that the status quo is not a durable option for either group.

It should also be recalled that three groups of European countries are currently in the process of reappraising their relationships with the EC: the members of EFTA; the Mediterranean 'orphans', to use Delors' term; and the East Europeans. Beyond them, on the EC's southern borders, are the other Mediterraneans, not European, but linked by history and geography to the fortunes of the EC. Further afield the partners and competitors of the Europeans watch closely to assess the outcome of the 1992 experiment within the EC and the way in which it chooses to handle the realities of interdependence without compromising the central integrationist ambitions. This volume focuses on the evolving EC-EFTA relationship, while recognizing the impossibility of separating this from the broader European and global picture.

Cooperation and reappraisal

The EC-EFTA relationship is not a new question. Its history is rooted in the postwar debates and traumas about European reconstruction. That history remains a potent force in shaping basic attitudes, in particular in segregating the adventurers willing to pursue some form of European Union (however vaguely defined) from the cautious pragmatists, preferring limited functional cooperation. In the early 1970s, as a consequence of the first enlargement of the EC and the first 'defections' from EFTA, a series of free trade agreements was established between the remaining EFTA members and the EC. These were prudent and restrained on both sides. Both Austria and Sweden looked at the option of applying for full EC membership, but drew back. Norway was compelled by its 1972 referendum to pull back from the EC to the EFTA camp. Since then quietly, undramatically and pragmatically a number of bridges have been constructed to take account of the implications of both economic interdependence and the relative similarities of political values and affiliation, but, quite deliberately, neither group of countries sought to undermine the special character of the other. Yet by the early 1980s it was becoming evident that the loose relationship was insufficient.

The Luxembourg Declaration of April 1984 was the first solid evidence of a shared concern to push the EC-EFTA relationship beyond the free trade area and *ad hoc* cooperation, involving EFTA as an organization in the process. The resulting joint commitment to create a 'European Economic Space' (EES)* – yet another new, albeit vague, term of European art coined to identify a changing pattern of interdependence – was proof of the concerns of politicians and the shifting entrepreneurial dynamics. The subsequent publication by the European Commission of the 'Cockfield' White Paper on the completion of the internal

*Renamed in 1990 'European Economic Area' (EEA). We have retained the earlier term, as still being – at the time of writing – more familiar.

market injected a new sense of urgency into the discussion, as the EFTA members came to appreciate the extent of the Community's ambition and its seriousness of purpose.

Determined efforts have been under way since then to give substance to the EES and the interwoven commitments to strengthen EC-EFTA cooperation. Most of the pressure has come from the EFTA side; most of the terms have been set by the EC, its agenda and working methods. There have been solid, if undramatic achievements. But there has been frustration on both sides. On the EC side, the dialogue has mostly been in the hands of the Commission, set within the strict and orthodox guidelines of the rapidly expanding *acquis communautaire* (the corpus of Community legislation and commitments), with only occasional interventions by the Council of Ministers and the EC member states. On the EFTA side, the impetus has come from the member states, with considerable attention and energy, in the hands of trade ministers and their officials, but drawing on an enlarging political constituency of interest. The EFTA Secretariat has played a more modest role of support, necessarily so, given the deliberate limitations of the Stockholm Convention.

Thus the relationship has been asymmetrical in terms of power, procedures, political attention and ambition. The conduct of this new dialogue now consumes some 90% of EFTA's attention and is the primary focus of the foreign economic policies of the member governments. For the EC the dialogue has been interesting, but not exciting, taking its place in a multicoloured patchwork of external policies, but never taking priority over the internal agenda. In any case, the EC and its members have been able to take their EFTA partners for granted, assuming them to be friendly, sympathetic and pliant. The EFTA economies provide by far the largest market for the EC, more than those of the USA and Japan, as the representatives of EFTA repeatedly remind the EC.

EFTA has had no real nuisance value for the EC; nor has it presented a need for the more sharply focused strategies that characterise the EC's links with the US and Japan. EFTA members do not ask the EC for resource transfers or special adjustments, unlike the Mediterraneans. Nor do the EFTA countries raise the large systemic issues implied in the new and still tentative relationship with Eastern Europe. At the practical and operational level EC-EFTA cooperation runs relatively smoothly and the negotiating process is without political dramas.

However, in the period since the Delors initiative to upgrade the EC-EFTA debate there has been an evident shift of gears and reappraisal of goals and methods. Since 1984, a 'High-Level' Contact Group had been the vehicle for pursuing the 'Luxembourg process', supported by a myriad of technical working groups. But it had cumbersome procedures, which in practice did not facilitate sharply focused agendas or consistent 'productivity'. Once the EFTA Summit of March 1989 had welcomed the new initiative of the EC, the Community and EFTA embarked on the 'Delors-Oslo process', with a much more strategically defined agenda and a compact set of contact groups, four to cover the four freedoms (the movement of goods, of services, of capital and of people) and a fifth to define the overarching and institutional issues. Their efforts led to a Commission Communication on how the EC might proceed, endorsed by the Council in November 1989, and a joint affirmation by EC and EFTA ministers on 19 December 1989 to proceed from exploratory discussions to full negotiations on the establishment of the EES. In the process, EFTA was strengthened as a collective vehicle for expressing and pursuing the interests of its members to an extent unimaginable at the time when Delors challenged EFTA to a real dialogue.

The limits of pragmatism

To the attentive observer it had been evident for some time that the disjointed dialogue was likely to prove inadequate. Some EFTA governments wanted to run more quickly than others, as the widely previewed Austrian application for full EC membership in July 1989 indicated. None of the others has yet ventured so far and some would not, except in a context radically different from what could be envisaged in the short-to-medium term. But all of the EFTA governments and the economic actors within them have become, to differing degrees, increasingly impatient with the EC. The Luxembourg process had been too slow and had too low a profile to force a quickening of the pace of substantive output. For the EC, too, it became increasingly apparent that it needed to rethink its relationships with its wide range of partners and thus to re-evaluate the links with EFTA and its members. The speech by Jacques Delors to the European Parliament thus marked the first public sign of a new phase in the EC-EFTA relationship.

The positions of EC member governments – the 'stepmothers', in the current idiom of the practitioners – have been less clearly defined, though there is an emergent debate in at least some EC capitals and in the European Parliament. This last point is particularly important, since the EP will have to endorse any new structure for the EC-EFTA relationship and will not do so, unless it is persuaded of the merits of the case. MEPs, like their counterparts in the national parliaments of the EFTA countries, will be vigilant as regards the form and not just the practical substance.

The debates are proving difficult. Each participant has key interests at stake. Neither for the individual governments, nor for the EC and EFTA is the spectrum of choices yet fully visible. A range of options hovers around the negotiating table; even the long exploratory dialogue throughout 1989 did not crystallize the issues into clear and structured patterns. This makes it especially difficult to gauge either the real offer that the EC might make or the likely reactions in the EFTA countries at the parliamentary and popular levels. Later in this volume the shapes of some potential options will be delineated and individual chapters will touch on these in relation to particular policy issues or country perspectives.

It has, however, been striking just how far the EC and EFTA have moved to break new ground in terms of what might be thinkable and even feasible. Some of the possible contours of a reshaped partnership that are being publicly mentioned by the participants in the dialogue would have been unimaginable even a few months earlier. In private, many of the participants have been still more adventurous. But the question of what might be practicable or mutually acceptable cannot be answered in parochial isolation. The EC-EFTA dialogue does not take place in a vacuum. The wider context has to be seen in sharp relief, if we are to comprehend both why the dialogue matters and what the political and economic stakes are for the members of both groupings. Nor is it by any means a foregone conclusion that negotiations between the two groups will be successful.

A context of secular change

The truth of the matter, after all, is that all West Europeans currently face a context of rapid change, both economically and politically. On almost every relevant policy dimension, transformations of process and substance are running beyond the ability of policy-makers to keep pace. The EC-EFTA dialogue should thus not be seen as a minor adjustment of the inherited structures of West European cooperation. There are far bigger issues at stake: namely, the role of the West European mixed economy (with its inherited social and political features) within the global economy; the unpredictable, but crucially important, evolution of the relationships between Western and Eastern Europe; the need to take account of Western Europe's 'backyard' around the shores of the Mediterranean, with its challenging mix of cultures and affiliations; and the broader political and security context, shaped so heavily and for so long by the influences of the USA and the USSR. The traditional distinction and dialectic between the tight-knit EC model and the loose-knit EFTA model were embedded in the several 'givens' of the international economic and political system of the post-war period. Few of those givens can any longer be taken for granted.

The global economy is undergoing a systemic transformation. Markets are now predominantly global for the main goods and services produced and consumed by West Europeans. Competition is fierce from across the Atlantic and across the Pacific and much of the competition is already played out on European soil by foreign-owned companies selling into, distributing to and producing within Western Europe. Competition among indigenous European firms is also increasingly strong, however circumscribed by surviving national preferences and 'favorite son' policies. West Europeans no longer have illusions that they can stop the economic world and get off. Even if neither the EC nor EFTA had been invented long before, by the mid-eighties some form of intra-European management would have had to be found, to oversee the necessary economic and industrial adjustments.

However, global markets have not found global leadership. It has become commonplace to argue that American hegemony has been eroded, to be superseded not by a new hegemony, but by a creaking set of international institutions, supplemented by a mix of *ad hoc*ery and bilateral understandings. West Europeans can neither rely on their erstwhile American patron nor be assured that their own combined influence will be enough to safeguard their interests. But as yet West Europeans as a whole lack the capability to combine forces in order to seek to shape the international economy to their liking. The EC plays a key role in international trade matters, but not (yet) in macro-economic and monetary matters, as its limited impact in Western economic summits indicates. The

EFTA countries have no common trade policy, let alone the ability to work with the EC on a structured basis. Nor have EFTA foreign ministers operated as a group, except tangentially, in the new dialogue with the EC.

Yet regionalization of the international economy may be the plausible scenario for the next decade; that is to say, we may witness the emergence of three economic blocs – American, Pacific and European – not necessarily formally structured, but at least shaping the patterns of economic entrepreneurship and political leverage. The scenario is sufficiently compelling to deserve serious attention.

But what would be the composition and texture of the European bloc? The question is as pertinent for the other West Europeans as for the EC and its members. Part of the explanation for the urgency with which the EC is pursuing its 1992 goal is to position the EC as strongly as possible for whatever may follow at the global level. EFTA members wish to be part of the 1992 endeavour, but this must surely imply some potential impact on their relations with the rest of the world.

So far EFTA has stuck precisely with free trade arrangements, but deliberately eschewed a coordinated, let alone common, trade posture. EFTA has had no role as such in international economic and monetary management, though EFTA members have, of course, played a modest part as individual countries. Yet they have key interests at stake in the new international political economy and its European dimension. EFTA countries would, for example, be the first casualties of a rampantly protectionist EC and must be concerned to ensure that no (new) fortress walls are constructed. EFTA interests could be squeezed in a tough confrontation between the EC and either the USA or Japan or both.

The interaction of trade and macro-economic developments also means that we must expect to see linkages between different issue areas become more important and policy interdependencies increase. There will be little predictably comfortable space for free riders to occupy, and unilateral adaptation to the actions of powerful neighbours is not necessarily an attractive strategy. And if the scenario of regional blocs has force, then the EC too will have to think through the consequences of what this might imply for its evolving relationships with its neighbours. Greater European leverage might be achieved with a wider base. The current Uruguay Round in the GATT is already beginning to press some of these questions on to the European agenda, but the underlying issues spread much wider.

The entrepreneurial dynamics of Western Europe are already running ahead of politicians and policy-makers. Indeed, both the 1992 process and the renewed EC-EFTA dialogue are arguably the product, rather than the cause, of a secular shift in European business behaviour. For something like a decade it has become evident that many European entrepreneurs (with those from EFTA countries among the most active) have been engaged in a process of adaptation, restructuring and repositioning to take account of the new forces of competition. Not all of this process has been easily visible – the activities of larger firms have been more obvious than those of the small and medium-sized enterprises – and the results of the process will still take some time to work their way through, from the level of corporate reappraisal to real impacts in the market place. But already the contours of the industrial map of Western Europe are changing, in terms of patterns of investment, location, production, alliances, mergers and acquisitions. The process involves adjustments by indigenous European firms, both within Europe and elsewhere in the world. But it has also engaged the attention of firms owned outside Europe.

Three secular trends are relevant to the EC-EFTA dialogue. First, EC firms have an increasingly direct interest in ensuring that they have the firmest possible base in Western Europe as a whole, both to secure a solid home market and to attack global markets. Few entrepreneurs in the EC will want to see a – for them artificial – distinction between the EC and EFTA territory. But of course, if the distinction has uncomfortable legal and commercial consequences, EC firms will give priority to maintaining their EC footholds. Secondly, those entrepreneurs from the EFTA countries with the scale and resources to do so are moving to ensure that they maximize their presence within the EC market. On the one hand, this increases the business pressures on EFTA governments to align the policy framework to the actual industrial map; on the other hand, the firms in question will continue to act by hedging their bets, thus in practice draining industrial inputs from their original home bases. Thirdly, the behaviour of foreign-owned firms is increasingly focused on ensuring that they are on the right side of whatever lines are drawn by EC legislation and practice. Commercial logic argues for treating the whole of Western Europe as a unity, but prudent judgements by the corporate strategists often point in a different direction. We are thus faced with a paradox: the commercial logic for creating a European Economic Space is impeccable; but corporate prudence will prevent its achievement, unless the guarantees are copper-bottomed.

Eastern Europe has for several decades been locked into a political and economic freezer. Around the edges of that freezer the various countries of Western Europe have sat pat on the consequences of the post-war settlement, bemoaning many of the consequences, but settled into a fairly predictable pattern of relationships, some aligned, others neutral, some active in East-West trade, others rather passive. The relative stability of the status quo in some ways conveniently kept on ice some of the awkward questions for West Europeans. As the ice begins to melt, those questions will begin to demand answers. The beguilingly simple answer, that change in Eastern Europe, both political and economic, is welcome, does not, however, provide practical prescriptions for action. East European expectations of opportunities and support will be high. West European responses will be more hesitant, not least because of the difficulty, yet importance, of defining their European identity.

It will be difficult for West Europeans, preoccupied with the forces of competition in the already highly developed market economies, to divert their energies towards the economic exchanges sought by their East European partners. Along the central spine of Europe the dilemmas will be especially difficult, that is, for those countries which, for reasons of history, geography and politics, have closer economic and social ties with Eastern Europe. Yet it is clear that over the next couple of decades, if 'perestroika' bears fruit and if the reform movements become embedded, some new patterns of economic interaction are likely to emerge. It would be rash at this stage to predict how this might impact upon the EC-EFTA relationship, except to note, first, that the EC will find itself under continual pressure to upgrade its arrangements with East European countries and, second, that some EFTA countries, most obviously Austria and Finland, will have particular interests in the outcomes.

Political and security factors will play a crucial role in setting the environment within which the EC-EFTA relationship develops. For those EFTA countries which lie at the intersections of Eastern and Western Europe, the fundamental attributes of the post-war settlement, stable for the past forty years, may be altering. Relaxation in Eastern Europe will have political as well as economic consequences, not only for the members of both alliances, but for those who have stayed outside the military confrontation. Neutrality used to be set in a firm context of alignment. Perhaps it still is, but in ten years' time? Or twenty? It is not going to be easy to gauge whether neutral status will become all the more important, precisely in order to facilitate evolution, or whether it will become redundant, as the old alignments soften. In any case, continuing uncertainty about the future patterns of East-West relations in Europe is likely to be accompanied by the preservation of prudent security arrangements by the aligned West Europeans. Relaxation in Eastern Europe may well be matched by continuing efforts to develop a West European security identity. On current probabilities, this is likely to be expressed through several different fora – the Atlantic Alliance, the Western European Union (WEU) and European Political Cooperation (EPC), an evolution which the words of the SEA leave open.

Part of the explanation for this lies in the changing character of transatlantic relations. West European members of NATO derive two main lessons from the recent history of their defence relations with the US. First, after the experience of USA-USSR negotiations, prudence suggests that some European security interests differ from those of the Americans and that it is natural, if sometimes uncomfortable, that Americans should give priority to their perceptions of their own interests. Secondly, most West European experts on security matters see American perceptions of their security interests as changing towards a different balance between their European commitments and their other regional concerns. Quite how this shift will affect the US-European relationship is less clear. But at the very least it has to be assumed that the redistribution of the burden between the US and the Europeans will impose a heavier responsibility on Western Europe. This potential shift again strengthens the incentives for reinforcing not only a collective security identity, but the means to provide greater self-reliance in military organization and procurement. And at this point security provision comes back to both economic capabilities and political aspirations, thus within the sphere, however loosely defined, of the EC and EPC.

Two important points must be specified as far as EC-EFTA relations are concerned. So far in the history of the EC, any member has had to be a full participant in both the EC and EPC; and the instruments available to pursue external policies have been derived from both frameworks. The adoption of the SEA makes this link even more clear than it implicitly was before. The section on EPC alludes to a kind of division of labour between EPC, WEU and NATO, but leaves open the question of the extent to which EPC, and therefore the Community framework broadly defined, might eventually play a more active part in the development of a West European security identity. But four of the members of EFTA are neutral countries, although each casts its neutral status in a different form. Indeed this has been a primary (though not sole) reason in the past for rejecting the option of applying for full EC membership. Whether this particular circle can be squared, and if so how, is of course one of the central issues in the EC EFTA relationship.

Scenarios for Europe

Given all of these factors of change, it becomes peculiarly difficult to predict the likely patterns of organized collaboration within Western Europe. Both analysts and practitioners face an intellectual and operational challenge in sorting out the range of possibilities to project or to advocate. At one end of the conceivable spectrum is a continuation of a pattern broadly resembling the status quo, that is to say, the persistent division of Western Europe into an EC and an EFTA grouping, though perhaps with some changes of membership at the margins. This is in many ways the most straightforward scenario, since conservatism and inertia always have their powerful advocates and no change means no radical re-evaluation of assumptions. There will also always be a constituency of those whose vested interests lie in more of the same. Yet there are distinct costs attached to the status quo, if, as has been argued above, there is an increasing lack of congruence between the existing pattern of cooperation at the level of governments and the changing deep structures of the West European economy. Few would any longer hold to the precise status quo as a real possibility.

At the other end of the spectrum lies the possibility of a single primary framework for West European collaboration. The old tussle between the EC and the EFTA models might after thirty years be resolved with the eventual predominance of one model. But which of the two would prove the more robust? And would either prove sufficiently seductive to remove the accumulated doubts of the past? The logic of events and experience suggests that many policy issues, political values and economic interactions transcend the distinction between the two groups. However, vigorous though the EC-EFTA dialogue may have become, there is nowhere any serious advocacy of a wholesale merger. On the contrary, one of the striking features of the enlarged EC, including both the defectors from EFTA and the new adherents from the Mediterranean, is just how widely shared is the collective commitment to an enterprise that goes beyond the Treaty of Rome's original prospectus. Whatever is implicit in Mrs. Thatcher's rousing exchanges with Jacques Delors, it is not an attempt by the British to rewrite the history of the 1950s. Moreover, keen though one or two EFTA members might be to become *de jure* or *de facto* members of the EC, it seems improbable that the whole of EFTA will be absorbed painlessly into the EC in the short-to-medium term. Nor, though it has become fashionable to talk of pan-European integration, is it really plausible that both EFTA and the EC should lose their identities and characteristics within a new Europe-wide organization, at least not in the short-to-medium term.

The odds must therefore favour some form of intermediate pattern and the weight of the evidence suggests that the parameters will be set by the character of the EC, a point to which we shall return. But it should first be emphasized that in the absence of any formal change in the EC-EFTA relationship, there will in all probability be some underlying shifts. Amongst the more plausible is the emergence of a 'multi-speed' Europe. Here some care must be taken with the terminology, since the phrase 'two-speed' (sometimes 'two-tier') was coined originally at the time of the series of applications for EC membership from Mediterranean and less developed candidates. The phrase gained some further credibility from the soul-searching of those 'footnote' countries (Britain, Denmark and Greece) which were hesitant about the process which led to the SEA. Thus in the Dooge Committee Report, which preceded the SEA, a number of reservations were entered by these 'footnote' countries. The Dooge Report is an interesting piece of political history, but not a legal text. That debate is broadly resolved in so far as all EC members have ratified the same SEA text.

It is perhaps possible to envisage a two-speed Western Europe, with the EC as the faster group integrating politically as well as economically and the erstwhile Eftans in a second group defined by the new EES. Indeed there might be some changes in the composition of the two groups and it is a moot point whether EFTA as such would survive as the collective vehicle of the second group or become redundant. This would imply a clear EC core of countries, committed to economic and political integration (whatever its ultimate shape), surrounded by a group of neighbours, presumably both the EFTA group and the other Mediterranean Europeans, being pulled along by the propulsive forces of integration, but more slowly. Thus the countries moving at the more hesitant pace would have their agenda largely set by the EC, but reserve the right to maintain a separate identity and to eschew the stricter disciplines of the EC.

Another variation on this theme would be the less clear cut pattern of 'variable geometry', already after all a feature of the EC. This model works with the grain of economic and political diversity, by admitting degrees of differentiation in the application of common legislation and envisaging the possibility of some arenas of cooperation in which not all take part; that is to say, following the analogy of the European Monetary System, in which not all EC members play a full part. In some respects the EFTA members are already following this model, by seeking ways in which they can be closely associated with some, but not all EC policies and legislation. Involvement in the 1992 programme would be sought, but there would be no entanglement with the common agricultural policy. Cooperation in research and development would be pursued, whether through the EC programmes, Eureka, the European Space Agency or the patchwork of other, more *ad hoc*, arrangements. Nor on this formula is it necessary for all EFTA countries to have the same intensity of involvement with the EC. Such a pattern would be flexible and open-ended, but essentially discretionary and without solid foundations, except in pragmatism.

In either of these two variegated models it will be increasingly important to link the evolution of Western Europe to the developing shape of pan-European cooperation and convergence. In the transitory vocabulary of the new European architecture, some form of association will have to be found between Central and East European countries on the one hand and the West Europeans on the other. It is highly questionable whether the same basic framework could accommodate all European countries in the short-to-medium term; but the new patterns of West European collaboration will perforce shape expectations to the East and may well set many of the parameters within which subsequent convergence may occur. It is for these reasons that some see the EES as a framework which will have to be stretched; and that notions of multi-speed Europe or a Europe of concentric circles have become both respectable and seductive.

The dynamics of the European Community

A crucial factor will be the dynamics of the EC itself. If the 1992 goal is more or less achieved, the EC is likely to pursue vigorously a number of other economic and political objectives, since 1992 is only part of the integration story. It is improbable that the whole of the 1992 agenda will be completed to time: alignment of indirect taxation and the full dismantling of internal borders will almost certainly prove elusive. In the meantime, other areas of policy activity could well be intensified, as, for instance, in the monetary field. But 1992 success, especially if accompanied by economic and monetary union, could well pull the EC further away from its less integrationist neighbours.

If, on the other hand, the 1992 goal should not be achieved substantially, the internal repercussions for the EC would be grave and the pain engendered by the continuing need for economic adjustment would be severe. In such circumstances, the EC would not be a generous partner. Failure by the EC to achieve the more difficult target of European Monetary Union (EMU) as the next policy goal, would perhaps make the EC less overwhelming for the limited integrationists of EFTA, but would also make it less robust.

At this stage, the former scenario for the EC looks the more probable. It should, however, be noted that several key issues lie on the 1992 table: first, how far 1992 will rest on *deregulation* or rather on European *reregulation*; secondly, what kind of social dimension will be developed; and, thirdly, what kind of external trade policy stance the EC will adopt. Each of these issues is of considerable importance for the EFTA countries.

But irrespective of the eventual outcome of the 1992 process, there are other dynamic factors at work. The EC has a robust profile in relation to the rest of the world. It operates with increasing confidence and assurance internally and externally. This is reflected in the growing resonance of EC activities at the level of political attention and public opinion. There are forces of political propulsion: the impact of the Commission, the regular use of majority voting in the Council of Ministers and the emerging influence of the European Parliament on at least some of the EC's activities. The policy scope of the EC is continually being enlarged. If the differences between the EC and EFTA were already striking in the late fifties, the contrast is now palpable.

There is, however, a second large question looming ahead of the EC, namely the character of its *finalité politique*. On this point the debate within the EC is extremely difficult to read for those inside the EC, let alone those who seek to interpret it from outside. Differences of goal and of emphasis within the EC will not be resolved quickly. The EC will not all of a sudden be transmuted into a fully integrated political entity. But the supporters of movement in this direction have the capability to edge the debate forward and, in particular, to exert their influence against dilution of the EC. The old dilemma of 'deepening' versus 'widening' has not been forgotten. Ideas being trailed for the Intergovernmental Conference(s) planned for the second semester of 1990 include many proposals for a quantum jump in political integration. The concept of 'political union' may not be clear-cut, but it is firmly on the EC agenda. This leads some in the EC to seek to delay enlargement, and others to wish to deal with enlargement first. For the EFTA countries 'deepening' of the EC, and the implied reinforcement of supranationalism, would make EC membership harder to accept. Moreover, the increasingly vigorous debate about a European security identity and collective provision for defence, combined with the codification of EPC, has given a quality to the debate about political integration which was not discernible even five years ago. As always, any prudent appraisal of the EC must work from the assumption that in the last resort the EC will look to its own declared goals and policy interests.

But partners matter

All these cautions notwithstanding, the EC cannot afford to be introverted. It is already clear that the declared ambitions of the EC are taken sufficiently seriously elsewhere for every important partner of the EC to be rushing to improve its relationships with it. Not only EFTA and its members, but the US, Japan, the other OECD countries, the Mediterraneans, both European and non-European and the East Europeans are seeking revised arrangements, not to mention the rest of the world. It will be an awesome task for the EC to handle all of these requests and to make its various arrangements reasonably consistent. There are real problems of overload and of priority. In all probability this will induce the EC to try to simplify and to aggregate, rather than to deal with each individual case on its merits or by special bilateral means. Group-to-group arrangements, of which the EC now has considerable experience, look a more sensible way of proceeding. The EC-EFTA relationship and the EES look to be a simpler target than any of the others: economic interdependence is already high, political kinship is well established, and shared values are deeply embedded. But the EFTA partners may not matter enough to compel the EC to depart from its orthodoxies in managing partnership arrangements.

The rest of this volume explores the plausibility of these propositions by reference to countries and to some of the issue areas. The targets of analysis are all moving and the pace at which the unthinkable becomes yesterday's news is fast, so all conclusions are liable to be confounded by events. However, as will become clear, to refashion the EC-EFTA relationship is no easy task.

Notes

1. This chapter draws heavily on Helen Wallace and Wolfgang Wessels, *Towards a New Partnership: the EC and EFTA in the Wider Western Europe*, Occasional Paper No. 28 (Geneva, EFTA Secretariat, March 1989); and on Helen Wallace's introductory paper in J. Jamar and H. Wallace (eds.), *EEC-EFTA: More Than Just Good Friends?* (Bruges, De Tempel, Tempelhof, 1988).

2 EC-EFTA Relations: An Historical Outline

Thomas Pedersen

The history of the EC-EFTA relationship has shaped the perceptions of the 18 national governments which are currently engaged in negotiations aimed at creating a European economic area. It also provides some analogies and lessons from which today's decision-makers may learn.

It seems quite clear that the main impetus behind EFTA's current interest in a dialogue with the EC is economic, much as it was in 1958, when there was widespread fear in the non-EC countries of being excluded from a dynamic EC venture. Fear of trade policy discrimination is still the crux of the matter – though not the whole story.

Of course, much has also changed since 1958. Most importantly, the EC of 1990 is quite a different creature from that of 1958, and far more impressive. Moreover, decision-makers from the two groupings can look back on a common experience which has shaped today's pattern of EC-EFTA interconnections. What we must ask ourselves is, first and foremost, how big the changes have been; and whether the changes that have taken place since the 1950s make it more or less likely that the current exercise in EC-EFTA bridge-building will succeed.

The evolution of EC-EFTA relations

Four phases can be distinguished in the evolution of EC-EFTA relations.

1956–58: *abortive multilateralism*. It starts with the Maudling Plan to establish a wider free trade area, and ends with the breakdown of the talks.

1959–72: *separation* (not to be confused with divorce) which starts with the formation of EFTA and ends with the enlargement of the EC by the entry of the UK, Denmark and Ireland.

1973–1983: *pragmatic bilateralism*, marked by the negotiation and implementation of the bilateral free trade agreements between the EC and the EFTA countries.

1984– : a period of *combined bilateralism and multilateralism*. It is characterized both by an intensification of bilateral contacts and by the establishment of a multilateral dialogue, reminiscent of the free trade area framework of the 1950s, though more ambitious. What is striking and new about this phase, however, is the reintroduction of elements of multilateralism into the EC-EFTA relationship.

Abortive multilateralism

It is worth dwelling for a moment on the experience of the 1950s, because it was in many ways crucial in the history of EC-EFTA relations. The Organization for European Economic Cooperation (OEEC) had been created in the 1940s as a broad framework for economic reconstruction and collaboration within post-war Europe. The 'Congress of Europe' had been held in the Hague in 1948 with delegates from 16 European countries and resulted in the establishment in 1949 of the Council of Europe, within which attempts were made to form a broad integrated Europe.

However, already at the Hague meeting a split within the West European family had been apparent. The so-called 'unionists' favoured a community of states; the 'federalists', gathered in the European Movement, were intent on going beyond the traditional intergovernmental cooperation to create supranational institutions. Owing to this lack of consensus, the Council of Europe was soon reduced to near-impotence. In 1951 Paul-Henri Spaak laid down the presidency of the Council Assembly in protest.[1]

Discussions on the European Coal and Steel Community (ECSC) had started in 1950. Jean Monnet, together with other 'Europeanists' in France who were working to bring about integration, had tried in vain to recruit the UK, to which many looked for leadership after World War II. At least a part of the government of the Fourth Republic appears to have also been interested in cooperation with the UK in the field of nuclear technology, where the British had a clear lead.

The UK and France were indisputably the chief actors in this drama of the 1950s. A core of European countries led by France had more ambitious plans for European integration than the other OEEC countries. The French wanted to stabilize Franco-German, and thus European, relations through supranational economic integration. The French and the Germans had complementary economic interests and both in their different ways saw a unified Europe as the way to political rehabilitation on the international stage.

After the failure of the Pleven Plan for a European Defence Community in 1954, the UK's refusal to participate in the ECSC negotiations and the British withdrawal from the Messina Conference in 1955, the Six became determined to create an integrated economic organization without British participation.

While the UK had inched closer to the continent through the Western European Union (WEU) initiative in 1954 and the negotiation of an association agreement with the ECSC that same year, it was still not prepared to join a new supranational organization. The UK also paid scant attention to the EEC project and apparently had some difficulty in taking it seriously.[2] Besides, it probably underestimated the strength of purpose among the Six – especially that of France – to move towards a common market during 1955–56.[3]

Membership of a European customs union would also have represented a major obstacle to British imports from the Commonwealth. British agriculture was in no need of protection; the UK much preferred to collaborate within the OEEC framework, where it could build on the close links with the Scandinavians, reflected *inter alia* in the UNISCAN mechanism set up in 1949. Finally, and probably decisively, the UK did not want to see the creation on the Continent of a French-led political entity from which the UK was excluded.

Contrary to British expectations, the Six succeeded in agreeing on a treaty of economic collaboration, helped along by strong American support and spurred on by a wish to reassert Europe's self-respect after the humiliation of Suez. When it became clear that an economic community of Six would materialize, the UK reaction was to propose the creation of a wider free trade area in Western Europe.

The Six and particularly France had, however, no intention of jeopardizing the EC. France regarded the EC not only as a way to control the Federal Republic of Germany but also as a means of enhancing France's international standing, which could outweigh the UK's advantages in this respect after the war.

France was well aware that several of the ECSC members to a large extent shared Britain's views on economic integration. The creation of a wider free trade area might have tempted those EEC member states which had liberal trade policies to shirk their responsibilities towards their less liberal partners. Why accept the obligations of the EC, if almost the same benefits could be obtained from membership of the free trade zone?

There was thus undoubtedly a very real risk that the EC would 'dissolve like a piece of sugar in a cup of tea', as a perceptive EC negotiator put it at the time. In a larger and less formalized grouping, the UK would be able to continue playing a leading role. The Six could be forgiven for harbouring the suspicion that the UK proposal for a large free trade area was meant to harm the EC.

Consequently the EC, led by the French, refused to discuss in parallel the opening of the Common Market and the free trade area, demanded by Britain. The dominant forces among the Six wanted first to set up the EC, and then to make suitable arrangements with the rest of Europe, most probably in the form of association agreements. Moreover, the French and Italian economies were in a rather bad state at the time, and the protectionist French and Italians realized that the Maudling Plan would involve further liberalization, on top of painful adjustments to the EC customs union.

As just mentioned, British economic thinking met with a good deal of sympathy in several ECSC countries. The Netherlands and the FRG, especially, had a strong liberal tradition. West German industry was not delighted at the prospect of operating within a small, inward-looking European market. However, the British proposal paradoxically made it easier for the Netherlands and the FRG to ratify the Treaty of Rome, since the prospect of a wider free trade area made the drawbacks of the EC seem bearable.[4] Besides, Chancellor Adenauer consistently gave priority to political considerations and was somewhat suspicious of British intentions: and this proved decisive.

As it happened, the wider free trade area was not to materialize. Compromises were sought, but the UK could not countenance the abandonment of tariff autonomy and did not regard the formulation of a common external trade policy as a necessity. The French, for their part, made it increasingly clear that they were basically opposed to a European free trade area. In November 1958 the Maudling negotiations were suspended.

The British seem to have counted on President de Gaulle, who had taken power in May 1958, to block the integration of the EC. Much to their and others' surprise, de Gaulle accepted the Treaties of Rome and soon showed himself capable of making the Community into an instrument to further French interests.

The period of separation

After the collapse of the free trade negotiations, the UK and six like-minded countries in Western Europe formed with the Stockholm Convention in 1960 the European Free Trade Area (EFTA), as a reaction to the EC. The original members were the UK, Sweden, Norway, Denmark, Austria, Switzerland and Portugal. Finland became an associate member in 1961.[5]

The negotiations on the formation of EFTA progressed with remarkable speed.[6] The Seven could build on their OEEC experience of coalition-making, and early consultations between industrialists had prepared the ground. Besides, the Nordics had for the past ten years been engaged in fruitless discussions on a Nordic Customs Union: the main problem had been Norway, which feared competition from the strong Swedish industry, and being a young nation, formerly dominated by Denmark and later tied to Sweden, protected its independence with great vigour.[7] Though this did not bode well for Nordic participation in more ambitious European integration, it nevertheless meant that a lot of collaborative groundwork had been done within one subgroup of EFTA countries.

The original idea was that the EFTA grouping would strengthen the hand of the member states in their negotiations with the EC,[8] which were widely expected to continue. To most of its members, EFTA was clearly a second best: Austria went on hoping till the last moment for a resumption of negotiations with the EC.[9]

Denmark was the least enthusiastic about EFTA and campaigned vigorously for the wider free trade area. At that time Danish exports were overwhelmingly agricultural and their main destination was the UK and the FRG. EFTA was a non-solution for Denmark, because it would, as government circles put it, 'draw an iron curtain between our main customers'.[10] The ideal solution for Denmark was, and remains, a wider European cooperation. Only after the UK and Sweden had made agricultural concessions, and the FRG had acknowledged that Danish membership of EFTA would not be regarded as an unfriendly act, did Denmark join the association.

EFTA also served the UK's political interests. Britain wanted to demonstrate to the EC that it was possible to create a free trade area; and it had an interest in tying the rest of the OEEC countries to itself, thus preventing them from seeking membership of the EC. Greece and Turkey had already asked for association with the EC in June 1959, Greece obtaining associate status in 1961.

Little more than a year after the signing of the Stockholm Convention, the UK changed its policy and applied for EC membership, much to the satisfaction of the Danes and the dissatisfaction of other EFTA countries. This is not the place to dwell on the exact causes of that change, but it should be pointed out that Britain's European options had narrowed down considerably by 1961. The UK stood outside the Franco-German dominated EC; the free trade plan had collapsed. The British reaction had been to pin its hopes on the OEEC, where it had hitherto played a prominent role and could use the emergent EFTA grouping as a pressure group.

The EC Commission and France, having had to suffer continuous criticism from a majority within the OEEC, reacted with great tactical skill. Jean Monnet estimated that if the OEEC could be adapted to incorporate the USA, the positive American attitude towards the EC would neutralize the attacks of the Seven. The USA had its own good reasons for wanting to be present in the evolving economic system of Western Europe: the UK could hardly object to a strengthening of Atlantic ties. Thus in 1960 the OEEC was reorganized and transformed into the Organization for Economic Cooperation and Development (OECD) with the USA and Canada as full members.[11] The UK was left with EFTA, a politically heterogeneous grouping, of limited value to a big European power such as Britain and, in any case, not a permanent solution.[12]

Most importantly, the British government had become increasingly convinced that the EC was going to succeed and that therefore Britain had better join.[13] The fact that in May 1960 the Six had been able to decide on an acceleration of their customs union and a further lowering of external tariffs had made a great impression.

Britain's early 'defection' profoundly changed the atmosphere within EFTA, and the British imposition in 1964 of an import surcharge on third countries including EFTA did little to improve relations with EFTA;[14] from that moment, bilateralism was clearly the order of the day.

Denmark, as expected, followed suit and applied for membership of the EC on the same day as Britain, so demonstrating the degree of Danish dependence at the time on British market policy. Ireland had already applied a week before the UK. Norway took more time to react, but submitted its application in April 1962. That same year Sweden, Switzerland and Austria asked for association with the EC, subject to neutrality reservations.

In January 1963, De Gaulle blocked the British accession, for reasons partly to do with the British relationship with the US and Macmillan's choice of an American nuclear weapons system.[15] The refusal came as a shock to the Macmillan government. Association negotiations with other EFTA members were also broken off. There had been an attempt by the EEC to separate negotiations with the UK from arrangements with the other applicants. Originally, negotiations were opened with all four applicants (that is, Britain, Ireland, Norway and Denmark). The negotiations broke down; next, de Gaulle appears to have offered full membership to Denmark alone. Significantly, the Danish government rejected the idea of independent entry and kept in close touch with the British.[16]

In 1967 Britain renewed its application, again followed by Denmark, Norway and Ireland. The EC Commission submitted a favourable opinion, but for the second time, De Gaulle vetoed the British application, and so Denmark and Norway again turned their attention to the development of Nordic cooperation.

From 1968–70 a plan for the creation of a Nordic economic organization (NORDEK) was discussed at Denmark's initiative. It proved impossible, however, to bridge the gap between the Danes, for whom NORDEK was basically a tactical device (meant to strengthen EFTA's bargaining power vis-à-vis the EC), and Finland, for which NORDEK was a very serious matter. A political dimension having been added to the EC with the Davignon Report on political cooperation, and the Werner Plan, it was important for the Finns that there should be a clear demarcation line between the EC and NORDEK.[17]

That same year, Sweden submitted an 'open' application for EC membership, asking for 'extensive, close and durable relations in a form compatible with continued pursuit of Swedish neutrality'.[18] For Sweden's dynamic export economy, a Nordic economic community had limited attraction. In 1970, the Swedish Social Democratic government reaffirmed relations with the EC as its long-term goal. No doubt, France's withdrawal from the military structure of NATO had been interpreted by some Swedes as suggesting that the EEC's external politics might not interfere with Swedish neutrality, with possible implications for the EC's external posture. The Swedes were soon to be disappointed, however. The EC's adoption of the Davignon Plan, along with the implications of the Werner Plan for monetary sovereignty, effectively killed the discussions on a possible Swedish accession. However, Sweden did not give up its hopes for a far-reaching economic deal with the dynamic EC and launched a proposal for a customs union between Sweden and the EC.

In 1969, after the resignation of de Gaulle, the EC Council of Ministers finally resumed consideration of the applications, submitted by Britain, Denmark, Ireland and Norway, and the first three of these became members of the EEC from 1 January 1973.

Pragmatic bilateralism

Shortly after the accession of the UK, Denmark and Ireland, and the withdrawal of Norway, following an adverse referendum result, negotiations started on bilateral agreements with the remaining EFTA members. Britain and Denmark had insisted on the condition that no new trade barriers should be erected between them and the other EFTA countries. They had also committed themselves to working within the EC to achieve a West European free trade system,[19] and this led to the signing on 22 July 1972 in Brussels of bilateral free trade agreements (FTAs) between the EC and Austria, Iceland (which had become a member of EFTA in 1970), Portugal, Sweden and Switzerland. Finland had to postpone signing its agreement with the EC pending successful termination of negotiations on Finland's cooperative arrangements with the CMEA and the USSR. Norway, having failed to become a member, had a similar free trade agreement.

The FTAs established a free trade area of 16 countries, embracing both the enlarged EC and the EFTA. The agreements, which took effect on 1 January 1973, followed the same general pattern, but displayed some variations to suit the special interests and needs of individual EFTA countries. Providing for the gradual elimination of tariffs for industrial products and a number of processed agricultural goods, the agreements stipulated a general transitional period of four and a half years. For the so-called sensitive products, the transitional period was extended to 1980 and for paper products, until 1984. The timetable for removal of tariffs was basically the same as for the then acceding EFTA countries. All the FTAs, except the Finnish, contained an evolutionary clause, keeping the door open for an expansion of cooperation.

The special provisions and political consequences of the individual FTAs can be summarized as follows:

Austria signed an interim agreement in addition to the main agreement, authorizing a 30% tariff cut on all industrial products as early as 1 October 1972 and including a 5% cut on sensitive products, also ahead of schedule. This agreement was a reflection the particularly close relations between Austria and the EC. Austria had hoped for a further agreement on agriculture.

Norway signed a FTA with the EC in May 1973 after the nation had rejected full membership in a referendum. The agreement contained special provisions for fisheries and provisions restricting access for sensitive products, in particular aluminium and other metals. Fish fillets and frozen prawns were subject to tariffs lower than the normal EC ones.

Sweden was hit by some restrictions on the export of special steels and on the whole considered the agreement less than ideal. Having been prepared to enter a customs union with the EC, the Swedish government stressed the evolutionary clause in its comments on the outcome of the negotiations.

Finland was particularly concerned about the EC's insistence on longer transitional periods for paper products and retaliated by imposing its own restrictions on EC products, covering 30% of trade in industrial products.

Switzerland added to the agreement a separate accord on watches and clocks, plus a protocol on foreign workers in Switzerland. The Swiss had wanted a more comprehensive agreement, covering, *inter alia*, the service sector, insurance, technical barriers to trade and questions of rights of establishment. They had also been interested in acquiring some influence on the EC decision-making process.[20]

Iceland, like Portugal, was given specially favourable arrangements to protect its weak industry. Iceland was also given concessions on fisheries, which covered 80% of its exports, but were made dependent on a mutually satisfactory settlement of the fishery limits dispute with Britain. This dispute was eventually settled in June 1976 and tariff reductions were able to take effect in July of the same year.

The implementation in the 1970s of the bilateral free trade agreements on the whole went smoothly. The loss of Britain and Denmark caused some demoralization within EFTA, while the intensified bilateralism further weakened its internal cohesion. In 1977 Portugal 'defected', applying for membership of the EC. That same year – probably in reaction to the Portugese step – an EFTA summit was convened on the initiative of the Austrian Chancellor Kreisky, with the object of strengthening EFTA's cohesion and giving it a kind of coalition role vis-à-vis the EC. The EC reaction to the EFTA invitation was positive, but no definite steps were taken. With the Portugese and Spanish membership applications pending, the EC had enough on its hands.

At the end of the 1970s, the EFTA countries showed themselves in one or two cases to be capable of acting collectively, for instance in setting up an industrial development fund for Portugal; but these were occasional flashes of light on a darkening horizon.

A new multilateralism

In the 1980s, bilateralism has continued to be a prominent feature of EC-EFTA relations. A slow but steady political upgrading has taken place: thus, with most EFTA countries, of the two annual meetings of the mixed commissions stipulated in the FTAs, one has been raised to political level since 1981 (that is, the EC is represented by the Commissioner for External Relations). In 1986 the EC concluded framework agreements on technological cooperation with all EFTA countries except Iceland.

However, a multilateral element has been added to the EC-EFTA relationship. A multilateral EC-EFTA dialogue was initiated at a joint ministerial meeting in Luxembourg in April 1984: the first meeting at ministerial level between the EC and EFTA. It had a dual purpose: it celebrated the successful implementation of the free trade agreements between the EC and the EFTA countries, but also offered the ministers an opportunity to look ahead and identify new common tasks. Once tariffs and quantitative restrictions on trade had been removed, EFTA had fulfilled its main function and was seeking a different role, in new forms of collaboration with the EC.

Although it is important to bear in mind that this initiative originated mainly with EFTA, changing EC attitudes played a part in ensuring that the idea got off the ground. The Swedish Minister of Trade, Mats Hellström, suggested the idea to Claude Cheysson, the French Foreign Minister, during a routine meeting in 1984, but was quite surprised by Cheysson's positive response. The reason for this was partly French electioneering, in the run-up to the elections to the European Parliament, in which grand European plans tend to cut a lot of ice; and partly a more profound change in French attitudes to European integration.

In his opening statement at the Luxembourg meeting, Claude Cheysson, speaking on behalf of the EC as President of the Council of Ministers, indicated the EC's willingness to engage in a dialogue with the EFTA countries, with a view to establishing a European Economic Space (EES). He went on to outline four areas in which the EC and EFTA should expand their cooperation:[21]

(1) research and development;
(2) industrial cooperation through such measures as a truly free internal market;
(3) common action at the international level, with special emphasis on appropriate reaction to 'the international monetary disorder';
(4) cooperation with regard to the third world.

The general concept underlying all of Cheysson's suggestions was that Western Europe had to face up to the challenge from the USA and Japan in the field of high technology and industry, as well as in monetary policies. The same global concept was shared by both President Mitterrand and Jacques Delors, the President of the European Commission, as reflected in many of their statements and writings.[22] The French emphasis on the need to assert European interests more forcefully at the international level struck a responsive chord in most EFTA governments, with the possible exception of the Swiss. In the context of an increasingly competitive international economic environment and the international debate about incipient 'Euro-sclerosis', the Western European governments felt a need to draw closer together.

On the EFTA side, there was some concern lest the complexity and magnitude of trilateral problems between the EC, the USA and Japan should preoccupy Brussels to such an extent that economic collaboration within a wider Western framework was lost sight of or not accorded a high enough priority. Moreover, in the early 1980s, the EFTA countries feared that growing internal divergences and economic problems in the EC might lead to an outbreak of protectionist tendencies that would hit third countries hard and endanger EC-EFTA economic cooperation.[23]

Within the European Commission and EC member states there was an awareness of the increasing importance of trade and economic interpenetration between the EC and EFTA. During the 1970s EC-EFTA trade had gained in importance, compared with EC-USA and EC-Japan trade; in the period 1972–86, trade between the EC and EFTA had quintupled. Today more than 25% of total EC exports go to EFTA countries (more than the USA and Japan together) and 60% of total EFTA exports are destined for the Community.[24]

In the face of keener competition from the USA and Japan, the calls for a 'European', that is, more collective and, in practice, protectionist solution to the EC's problems, became louder, not least in France. The snag was that because of the FRG's close links and substantial trade with Switzerland, Austria and the Scandinavian countries, a 'European option', to be acceptable to the FRG, had to be defined to include these countries.[25]

At the Luxembourg meeting, the EC and EFTA governments committed themselves to creating a dynamic European Economic Space, encompassing the EC and EFTA. Significantly, this was the first time that the EFTA countries appeared jointly and in a multilateral framework with the EC. The resulting dialogue gained immensely in importance by the endorsement by the Community in 1985 of the European Commission's White Paper programme on the internal market, which created apprehension among EFTA countries that they might be facing new trade discrimination at the EC's external borders.

Since the mid-1980s, a pragmatic, multilateral dialogue with a broad and open-ended agenda has developed between the EC and the EFTA countries. It covers most, if not all, of the internal market agenda, as well as areas such as research and development, environment and education. This new collaboration clearly goes far beyond the areas covered by the Stockholm Convention. It confronts EFTA with a major challenge of adaptation: will EFTA be able to strengthen its administrative apparatus and political cohesion, thereby turning the EC-EFTA relationship into a kind of inter-regional cooperation?

What has not changed: two ideas of integration

After World War II, there was a general willingness to overcome economic nationalism, which had cost Europe so dear. Most European governments also realized the necessity of establishing a closer European collaboration than had existed before the war. But the concepts of integration differed widely within Western Europe. As we have seen, there were two closely interlinked major issues at stake. First, political integration: should the new structures of West European cooperation include supranational institutions and the transfer of sovereignty? Secondly, economic (or trade) integration: should it take the form of a customs union or of a wider free trade area?

Arguably, a certain degree of supranationalism is the logical corollary of a customs union: but the distinction between the two kinds of integration should be maintained. The point to stress is that the motivation behind the EC was not only, probably not even mainly, economic and that political integration was the chief bone of contention. The six countries which were founder members of the EC shared ambitious political goals and were prepared to accept more infringements of their national sovereignty for the sake of European unity than the other European countries.[26]

These divergences in the attitude to national sovereignty and supranationality can probably to some extent be explained by differing historical – and particularly wartime – experiences. The opponents of the federalist model, the UK, Sweden, Denmark, Switzerland, etc., had either not been significantly affected by the war, or had come out of the war victorious, with a political system and a foreign policy line that retained considerable prestige and legitimacy.

Five of the six founding countries had suffered a painful occupation: they had less to lose from making concessions on sovereignty. Besides, all of them had, more than other West European countries, suffered the effects of large-scale war, the consequence of rampant nationalism; they therefore had a stronger incentive for seeking a model of integration that broke radically with the traditions of the European nation-state. It was no coincidence that the resistance movements, which gained considerable political influence in post-war Europe, were among the most ardent supporters of supranational integration.

On these criteria, Austria should belong to the 'federalist' group and does, in fact, display the most positive attitude to supranationalism of all the EFTA countries. One might argue that Austria has always been strongly predisposed towards supranationalism, bearing in mind that in the not too distant past, it formed part of a multinational entity, the Habsburg Empire. Only today, however, in the context of the new *détente*, can this integrationist sentiment be freely expressed.

Britain also suffered the effects of large-scale war (and had gone through the nightmare before), but its territory was never occupied, and, more importantly, Britain came out of the war an indisputable victor. Denmark appears to be an intermediate case, but even so, had for the second time avoided being turned into a battlefield, and had also managed, for most of the wartime, to retain some control over the state apparatus. Most importantly, along with Norway, Denmark had sided with the victorious allied forces.

As for Sweden and Switzerland, they could in the 1950s look back on quite an impressive foreign policy record. No traumatic experience had given them any reason to review their traditional form of interconnectedness with the rest of Europe or to question the validity of their traditional form of political organization.

Thus the victors or half-victors emerged from the second world war psychologically prepared to reform but not to revolutionize European collaboration. As Jean Monnet has put it, the price of victory was the illusion that it was possible to keep what one had without having to change.[27] This was particularly true of Britain, the one unambiguous European victor. The very national instability and democratic fragility that caused the Six to opt for supranationality, made the Anglo-Nordic countries in particular want to protect their democratic stability and keep at a certain distance from the rest of Western Europe. It was also feared that the high standard of living and social welfare system of the Scandinavian countries might be difficult to uphold within a European economic union.[28] Finally, Finland and Norway were both 'young' nation states and as such, probably shared, and still share, a strong wish to preserve and defend their national freedom of action.

I am not arguing that in the 1950s, only the Six had the political will to strengthen European collaboration. The rest of the Western European countries were also eager to forge new European links: but their concept of integration was overwhelmingly economic and functional, and they were less prepared to pool national sovereignty and to make short-term sacrifices for the benefit of long-term European political construction.

Other historical factors also played a part in propelling the Six towards forming a (partly) supranational community. The Benelux countries had had positive experiences with their own customs union. The former success of the German states in forming a *Zollverein* offered an analogy, perhaps even a model, which served to calm the FRG's anxieties about entering a supranational community. Moreover, the FRG had little to lose at the time from joining the EC and could be argued to have gained sovereignty by becoming a member of the Community.

Like Germany, Italy had undergone a process of unification in the nineteenth century, but whereas Germany had taken the functionalist road to unification, starting with economic integration, political unity had come first in Italy. The current integration policy of the two countries can thus be traced back to experiences with national unification in the last century.

In the course of the last 30 years, these divisions have undoubtedly become less absolute, partly due to the accession to the EC of two former EFTA countries, one of which is a major European power which still tends to regard European integration primarily in functional terms. One can observe a certain convergence of outlook between the EC and EFTA as far as integration policy is concerned. The six founder-members of the EC have developed into respectable democratic states and the living standards of the original Six and the EFTA countries have drawn closer. However, the southern enlargement of the EC has made it more heterogeneous, perhaps reawakening EFTA fears that membership of the EC would lead to an erosion of *l'acquis social*, their social welfare systems.

While EFTA has come to terms with its limitations of size and cohesion in an increasingly challenging, international environment, the EC has introduced certain adjustments to its original, partly supranational structure. The 1970s saw the establishment of the European Monetary System (EMS), participation in which was, in the event, defined flexibly, the so-called 'variable geometry'; while in the field of research and development, wider European ventures such as the

Cooperation in Science and Technology (COST), the European Space Agency (ESA) and the European Research Agency (EUREKA) have been set up.

Nevertheless, the long-term political objectives of the EC retain very considerable support within the Community. The adoption of the Single European Act (SEA) and the accession of Spain and Portugal show that the Community is regaining momentum. Increasingly, membership of the EC requires a political willingness to sacrifice parts of formal national sovereignty. This has implications for the EFTA countries. It means that most EC members are likely to be unwilling to make concessions to EFTA countries beyond a certain limit. It is considered important that the difference between association with and membership of the EC should not be blurred.

The EC and EFTA thus constitute entirely different organizations, a reflection of deep-seated differences in the way European integration is regarded. It is worth stressing that from the very beginning, EFTA was seen, at least by some of its members, less as a political goal in itself than as an instrument to strengthen the EFTA countries' bargaining position vis-à-vis the EC and, more specifically, to establish a broader European cooperation.

What has changed: a stronger EC in a tougher world economy

Arguably, one of the most important preconditions for a strengthening of the EC and an improvement in EC-EFTA relations was Britain's coming to terms with the EC and French acceptance of a European role for Britain. In the course of the last two decades these preconditions have largely been met.

For years EC-EFTA relations seemed largely to be the continuation of Franco-British rivalry by other means. The EC had given France a prominent role in Europe, which it saw no reason to place at risk. Only at the end of the 1960s did France feel economically and militarily strong enough in relation to the UK to allow British entry into the Community. France had observed with some apprehension that the FRG had not only expanded economically but had also engaged in a new *Ostpolitik*. Gradually it came round to the view that there was a need for a British balancer within the Community, though France's relations with the FRG would still be privileged.

Even though Britain entered the EC in 1973, like Denmark it did so somewhat hesitantly and without a solid domestic consensus on EC policy. In the 1970s, France and the original community governments could be forgiven for suspecting the UK of wanting to 'dilute' the Community. It is thus unlikely that France (or Italy) would have accepted a wider West European collaboration in the 1970s.

However, the 1980s have brought a considerable change in British EC policy. As Françoise De La Serre points out in a recent study, the UK has come to see the EC as a means of optimizing the economic and political resources of a major power such as Britain.[29] De La Serre even talks about a qualitative change in British EC policy, in the direction of a positive commitment to the further development of the EC. The Labour Party has also adopted a more positive attitude to the EC. Both the UK and Denmark have to a significant degree solved their domestic EC problem. These changes have influenced their relations with major EC partners and indirectly had a positive effect on EC-EFTA relations.

In the 1980s, the EFTA countries had to come to terms with the fact that their erstwhile fellow-members have increasingly emerged as 'normal' EC members, and that consequently it is no longer wise to try to rely solely or even mainly on these countries to defend the EFTA point of view within the EC.

British and Danish entry into the EC changed the EC-EFTA relationship in yet another respect: it then became even more apparent that EFTA did not have the size or the political clout to make it a credible alternative to the EC, and this probably had a beneficial effect on EC-EFTA relations. The Southern enlargement of the 1980s further underlined the centrality of the EC in the European integration process, making evident what had been a reality for a long time, that the EC was the motive power in the wider European integration process.

Whereas in the 1970s and early 1980s the EFTA countries could afford to sidestep the issue of their future relationship with the EC, pointing to signs of 'Euro-sclerosis', the new EC dynamism has from the mid-1980s forced the EFTA countries to rethink their role in Europe. The planned completion of the internal market confronts the EFTA countries with a major challenge. For the EFTA countries, the relationship with the EC is becoming more important. True, the more successful the EC is in its endeavours to create a 'European Union', the harder it becomes to develop closer ties with the EC without jeopardizing the credibility of neutrality. On the other hand, a stronger EC is also one to be taken more seriously.

Furthermore, a learning process has taken place in EC-EFTA relations. The bilateral free trade agreements of the early 1970s proved to be success stories in a modest way, paving the way for new joint ventures. It is sometimes forgotten that the fairly smooth liberalization of EC-EFTA trade took place against the backdrop of a recession and protectionist trends in the OECD economies of the 1970s. Given the growth of non-tariff barriers to trade in the late 1970s, the implementation of the FTAs was a considerable accomplishment, which indicates the uniqueness of the EC's relationship with EFTA.

The most important change affecting EC-EFTA relations has probably been the toughening of the international economic climate in the 1980s. The challenge from the new growth centres in East Asia has created an incentive for Western Europe to close ranks. Also important has been the relaxation of East-West tension.

The interaction of the EC and EFTA

So far, we have dealt with EC-EFTA relations mainly from the perspective of individual member-goverments. However, the history of the relationship can also be perceived as a case of interaction between regional subsystems.[30] Karl Kaiser has formulated a number of helpful hypotheses regarding the interaction of such systems.

Of particular relevance is what Kaiser calls the 'postulate of alternative opportunities'. It holds that comprehensive regional subsystems (like the EC) weaken other regional subsystems if (a) they hurt the interests of members of other regional subsystems; (b) they are reasonably strong and offer rewards for participation; and (c) participation in or access to the benefits of the comprehensive subsystem is an option that is reasonably open to individual members of the other subsystem.

It would seem that the EC-EFTA relationship meets all three conditions. The EC has weakened EFTA, because it offers great enough rewards and is sufficiently open to make direct participation through membership, association or special arrangements a reasonable alternative for some of EFTA's members – without, however, being so open as to make possible the overall settlement between Western Europe's two trading groups that EFTA has been seeking.

As Kaiser points out, there are two options open to the regional subsystem whose interests are being hurt. It can strengthen its own subsystem; or its members can individually seek accommodation with or participation in the other subsystem, with the effect of weakening their own system. It is an interesting question whether the first option is a realistic one for EFTA, given its geographical and political heterogeneity.

If confronted with economic pressure from the EC beyond a certain point, EFTA might just possibly be able to increase internal cohesion. But to what extent? Historically, as we have seen, whenever the EC has deepened integration, EFTA or the Nordic subgroup has responded by attempting to increase its internal cohesion – so far, however, with limited success. The point to stress is that the EC has been a 'threat' to EFTA, not because it has been closed or inward-looking, but precisely because it has been reasonably open and prepared to concede participation in the benefits of the system.

One precondition for such relative openness is, of course, that the rewards must be there to be shared. The successful EC integration in the 1960s gave the EC the necessary leeway to offer the Northern applicants attractive deals, to accommodate the accession of a major country like Britain and to negotiate the FTAs with the rest of EFTA. Following the same logic, the fate of EFTA can be expected to depend to a large extent on the fate of the internal market programme and the shape of the international economy in the 1990s.

The EC has thus had a very large impact on the evolution of EFTA. Has EFTA (as distinct from the policies of individual EFTA countries) influenced the EC ? Probably only to a very limited degree. No doubt every cooperative venture has a potential 'demonstration effect', but that of EFTA has been almost non-existent, given the limited nature of its objectives. Still it is probably fair so say that EFTA has, as Per Kleppe has put it, served as a training ground for prospective EC members.[31] This is particularly true of Denmark, for which the rebirth as a 'European' country has been a slow and painful process – and one that has not always been seen as an entry into a higher sphere.

Notes

1. Pierre Du Bois, 'Les enjeux européens des années 50' in *EFTA from Yesterday to Tomorrow* (Geneva, EFTA, 1987), pp. 18f.
2. For an interesting analysis of the decision-making process leading up to the British departure from Messina, see Simon Burgess and Geoffrey Edwards, 'The Six plus

one: British policy-making and the question of European economic integration, 1955' *International Affairs*, 3 (1988).

3. Toivo Miljan, *The Reluctant Europeans* (London, Hurst, 1977), pp. 119, 124.
4. Pierre Gerbet, *La Naissance du Marché Commun* (Paris, Editions Complexe, 1987), p. 127.
5. Barry Turner and Gunilla Nordquist, *The Other European Community* (London, Weidenfeld & Nicolson, 1982), pp. 130f.
6. Paul Luif, 'Die Entstehung der EFTA' in *EFTA from Yesterday to Tomorrow*, p. 70.
7. Turner and Nordquist, *The Other European Community*, pp. 109f.
8. For details of the national considerations and multilateral discussions leading to the formation of EFTA see Miljan, *The Reluctant Europeans*, pp. 143f.
9. Luif, *Die Entstehung der EFTA*, p. 69.
10. Christian Thune, 'Denmark, Europe and the creation of EFTA' in *EFTA from Yesterday to Tomorrow*, pp. 74f.
11. Gerbet, *La Naissance due Marché Commun*, p. 139.
12. The UK's lack of enthusiasm for EFTA is emphasized in Clive Church, 'Great Britain's European policy' in *EFTA from Yesterday to Tomorrow*, p. 36.
13. Michael Charlton, *The Price of Victory* (London, BBC, 1983) p. 252.
14. *EFTA from Yesterday to Tomorrow*, p. 114.
15. See the interviews with high-ranking decision makers from that time in Michael Charlton, p. 256.
16. Miljan, *The Reluctant Europeans*, p. 175.
17. Miljan, *The Reluctant Europeans*, p. 104.
18. Carl-Einar Stålvant, 'Nordic policies toward international economic cooperation' in Bengt Sundelius (ed.), *Foreign Policies of Northern Europe*, p. 124.
19. Hans Mayrzedt, 'EFTA and the EC' in *EFTA from Yesterday to Tomorrow*.
20. Paul Luif, 'Neutrale und Europaische integration', *Österreichische Zeitschrift für Politikwissenschaft* 2 (1987) p. 126.
21. *Agence Europe*, 9–10 April 1984.
22. François Mitterrand, *Reflections sur la Politique Extérieure de la France* (Paris, Fayard, 1986); and Jacques Delors and Philippe Alexandre, *En Sortir ou Pas* (Paris, Grasset, 1986).
23. Karl E. Birnbaum in Loukas Tsoukalis (ed.), *The European Community: Past, Present and Future* (Oxford, Basil Blackwell, 1983), p. 196.
24. Herman de Lange, 'Taking stock of the EC/EFTA dialogue' in J. Jamar and H. Wallace (eds.), *EEC-EFTA: More Than Just Good Friends*? (Bruges, De Tempel 1988) p. 311.
25. Wolfgang Hager, 'Little Europe, wider Europe and Western economic cooperation' in Tsoukalis (ed.), *The European Community*, p. 171.
26. For an analysis of the attempts to create a European Defence Community, including a Political Community, see Roy Pryce, *The Dynamics of European Union* (London, Croom Helm, 1987).
27. Quoted from Michael Charlton, *The Price of Victory*, p. 307.
28. Miljan, *The Reluctant Europeans*, p. 82.
29. Françoise De La Serre, *La Grande-Bretagne et la Communauté Européenne* (Paris, Presses Universitaires de France, 1987) p. 216.
30. Karl Kaiser, 'The interaction of regional subsystems', *World Politics*, 21, no. 1 (1968), pp. 85–107.
31. Per Kleppe in *EFTA from Yesterday to Tomorrow*, p. 132.

Part I
The Policy Issues

3 European Security in Transformation

Martin Saeter

The problem

The Luxembourg Declaration of 1984 on the European Economic Space (EES) ushered in a new stage in the participation of the EFTA countries in the process of integration in Western Europe, a process centred on the European Community. This took place just at the time when the EC itself was about to open a new and dynamic phase in its own development, characterized by the combined strategy of the Single European Act (SEA) and the internal market.

In trying to evaluate the security implications of what could be called the EES approach, it is important to bear in mind that the adaptation of the EFTA countries to the dynamics of EC integration constitutes only a small part of the process of structural change taking place in Europe in connection with EC developments. Through the coordination of security policies within the framework of European Political Cooperation (EPC), the Community is gradually becoming a centre of gravity at the security level as well. Of much greater importance from a general European security point of view than EC-EFTA relations is the changing relationship between the Community and the countries of Central and Eastern Europe, because this alters the primary structures of the East-West bloc division in Europe. But because the EC-EFTA relationship also involves the question of neutrality, it too has to be seen in connection with developments at the more general East-West level. Taken as a whole, the European integration process has now reached a stage where it has an increasing impact on existing security frameworks and structures, not only in Western Europe but in Europe as a whole, including both East-West, Soviet-East European and Atlantic dimensions. European integration does not imply a break with existing security structures, rather their gradual transformation. In 1988 the top political EPC institution, the European Council, officially described the integration process as 'irreversible': this is probably correct. The emerging new structures seem to be at least as coherent as those they are replacing, the main difference being that they are not linked to the old bloc division of Europe but to a perspective of organized all-European cooperation, with the EC as a dynamic core element. In short, this is the essence of the 'Europeanization' dimension.

The following discussion is built on the assumption that the EES approach must be seen in the light of internal EC developments, changes in East-West relations and the all-European orientation of EPC. It further assumes that the present long-term trend will continue. Should this turn out to be wrong, then the prospects for the EES approach would also probably be fundamentally different. Of course, one cannot exclude the possibility of such discontinuities. But the EES approach makes up part of the process of change and simply has to be evaluated against this dynamic background. It would be wrong to apply a static view, and futile to try to guess what might happen if present trends change in unforeseeable circumstances. There is therefore no better way of arriving at a realistic assessment of the security implications of the EC-EFTA relationship than to try to gain as much insight as possible into the character and orientation of the European integration process as a whole.

For the EFTA countries, adapting to the EC process means accepting being linked through the Community to the changes taking place in the wider European context. It would be illusory to think that these countries, individually or collectively, could significantly alter the character or course of this larger process, although they no doubt can help to influence it. It would be equally illusory to assume that the policy of adaptation could be carried on without raising questions of security, because the process is contributing to changing European security structures in general, whether the EFTA countries intend it or not.

It is logical, therefore, when analysing the security implications of possible relationships between EC and EFTA countries, to start with the changes that are taking place in the European security environment as a whole, regardless of the form EC-EFTA relations may have. In the context of what seems to be the dominating trend in EC developments concerning European security, we will try to see if, to what extent, and in what sense one or another form of EC-EFTA relations might make a difference to the individual EFTA countries, the EC integration process as such, East-West relations and the developing European security system. Other chapters in this volume consider the specific situation of individual EFTA countries in greater depth.[1]

Historical basis

The security role of the European Community has to be seen in the context of the security motives and strategies of the main member states, the institutionalization of security policy at Community level, and interactions with the international environment.

In fact, security considerations have always been crucial to the integration strategies of the main members. Divergencies at this level largely explain the pattern of integration in Western Europe since World War II.[2] *Great Britain* gave priority to the containment of the Soviet Union both through NATO and through organizing West European economic and political cooperation on as wide a geographical basis as possible, but without any kind of supranational institutionalization, thus making it possible to include neutral countries (as in the OEEC, the Council of Europe, EFTA). *France* on the other hand, seeking to regain its status as a great power and also trying to secure a foundation for lasting peace with Germany, took the initiative in establishing a much closer Western European union, with the explicit purpose of binding the emerging West German state to a common West European framework, economically, politically and militarily. In addition to the Coal and Steel Community (ECSC), there were the abortive French proposals for a European Defence Community (EDC) and a European Political Community. The *United States*, also seeing the need for an integrated framework for West German rearmament but relying more on Great Britain than on France, favoured an integrated NATO as the primary framework for European security. The Western European Union (WEU), which was established in 1954 on British initiative after the failure of EDC and EPU, became in practice a sub-organization of NATO without much influence. The *Federal Republic of Germany* had no choice but to accept NATO integration as the way to obtain a more equal status and a formal basis on which to build its position on the national question. But Chancellor Adenauer made it no secret that he preferred a federal European solution.

These outcomes reflected the postwar constellations of power and interests and had a long-term, decisive impact both on European security politics in general and European integration policies more specifically. Priority was given to the institutionalization of the bloc division of Europe under superpower hegemony. West European integration schemes became limited to the functional approach, i.e. to a bottom-up strategy starting with economics and not including 'high politics'.

For exactly the same reason, France under de Gaulle tried to weaken, and as far as possible to sever, the links between European integration policy and NATO. De Gaulle rejected the British free trade area approach, because he thought this would be inadequate as regards the German question and would also be likely to strengthen Anglo-American dominance at France's expense. Instead, he presented a plan for a political union in the EC of a confederal kind (the Fouchet Plan, 1961), but this failed. He made British membership of the EC conditional on its loosening of the 'special relationship' with the US, and vetoed the application when he did not succeed in convincing the British government. He refused to accept supranationality in the EC as long as the Community was firmly inside the NATO framework, in the end withdrawing France from the integrated NATO structure. He blocked the development of EC institutions until other members accepted his demand for the right of veto. And perhaps most importantly, he successfully engaged himself in developing a special relationship between France and the Federal Republic of Germany, outlining a common strategy of detente, entente and cooperation with the Soviet Union and other Eastern bloc countries as the basis on which to solve the national German problem.

The experiences of the late 1960s told the West Germans that without France there could be no West European integration, and that without a kind of 'Europeanization' of European politics there could be no progress as regards the German national question. This recognition contributed decisively to the 'new deal' of the Hague Summit of 1969, which envisaged EC development as the centrepiece of a larger European system of cooperation, in a way that seems at least as valid today as it was then.

The Hague breakthrough had several elements of great significance for future security relationships in Europe. First, it was closely coordinated with President Nixon's strategy of transition 'from an era of confrontation to an era of negotiation' in the East-West relationship. Second, it built on a French-West German understanding achieved by de Gaulle and Federal Chancellor Kiesinger in spring 1969 according to which France promised to support the West German policy of detente and negotiation with the Eastern bloc countries through NATO coordination, while the Federal Republic declared its readiness to support the development of a politically more independent EC. Third, agreement was reached on the conditions for enlarging the Community to include Great Britain and other applicants: new members had to accept existing treaties as well as the plans and general aims already adopted for the further development of the Community, including European Political Cooperation (EPC). Fourth, the Hague communiqué defined detente and understanding between the peoples of 'the whole Continent' as a primary task of the Community.

Compared with the original motives and strategies of the main advocates of integration, this new platform represented significant readjustments. The more status quo-oriented, 'Atlantic' approach of Great Britain and the United States was modified so as to make possible a 'Europeanization' of the EC process more along French-West German lines. On the other hand, France consented to a continued role for NATO both as an integrated organization for defence and as a forum for the coordination of policies of detente and negotiation with East countries, without, however, changing its decision to stay outside the alliance. Perhaps most importantly, the establishment of EPC on a confederal – not supranational – basis took place in accordance with French preferences. Taken together, this then made up the basis on which the Federal Republic of Germany defined its new Ostpolitik in the perspective of an all-European peace arrangement (Friedensordnung), implying a 'Europeanization' of the German question both at the EC level and at the level of the Conference on Security and Cooperation in Europe (CSCE). The goal of national reunification was in practice subordinated to the policy of European integration and East-West rapprochement. Only on the basis of an integrated and strengthened Western Europe cooperating closely with the Eastern bloc countries within the framework of the all-European CSCE was there any hope of a lasting solution for Germany, whether as one state, some kind of confederation between two sovereign states or even a European federation.[3]

EC-EFTA relations in the broader European context

The position of both EFTA and its member countries changed radically in consequence of these historic events. Whereas it had been an organization led by the British in their rivalry with France and the Brussels Commission, after 1973 EFTA became a periphery of the EC, linked to it through free trade agreements aimed at establishing one common free trade area.

Security was not an explicit part of the rearrangement. Implicitly, however, important security considerations were involved. In the East-West context, EFTA until 1973 had been linked to the British Atlantic-oriented status quo approach. After 1973 not only Great Britain and Denmark, as new EC members, but also the remaining EFTA countries, became ever more closely linked to the dynamic process of EC integration. The rest of the EFTA countries could no longer look to British leadership in their European and market policies.

With the benefit of hindsight, the implementation of the free trade treaties between the remaining EFTA countries and the EC in 1973 can be seen to mark a major step in the evolution of the EES strategy of today. The process of incorporation of the EFTA countries into the EC economic and political orbit was already established. Plans for making the EC an economic and eventually a political union had already been adopted, though not yet as explicitly as in the SEA of 1985. And the development of a framework for closer cooperation between the Community and the East European members of the CMEA was already being seriously considered in formal contacts between the two sides.

In the absence of greater East-West rapprochement, it is difficult to imagine how the neutral countries could have joined in the EC-dominated process of integration in the way that they have, without any adverse effects worth mentioning on their relations with the Soviet Union.

Thus, since 1970 EC-EFTA relations have been part of the expanding process of *Europeanization*, which is characterized by parallel sub-processes at several levels, mutually reinforcing each other in the development of regional European decision-making frameworks and gradually freeing themselves from superpower hegemony and the politics of blocs. The most important of these sub-processes are: the development of the EC proper, the intra-German rapprochement, EC-East European cooperation, Soviet perestroika, and the CSCE process. The latter is to be regarded as a common all-European framework of interaction, including both superpowers.

It will be the overall 'balance' between developments at these levels that decides the viability, scope and speed of the Europeanization process. And it will be this same process of Europeanization that will determine the continuously changing international security framework to which the EFTA countries will also have to adapt their policies.

EC

Of these four levels, the EC level is clearly the most dynamic, and the one which at the present stage influences the situation of the EFTA countries most directly. From a security point of view, the strengthening of the EFTA countries' relations with the EC contributes to linking them into general community dynamics. As already mentioned, the Community process inevitably contributes to changing existing international economic and political structures, not only in Western Europe but also at the Atlantic level, in East-West relations and globally. The close cooperation between France and West Germany within the Community contributes crucially to counterbalancing the Atlantic, East-West and all-European elements of security politics both in the community itself and in the wider context of Europeanization. These aspects will increasingly have to enter into the security considerations of the EFTA countries as well.

FRG-GDR

The second level, that of intra-German rapprochement, represents what are perhaps the most decisive linkages between the 'old' and the 'new' security structures in Europe. The West German strategy of multilateralizing the German national question within the framework of an all-European peace order was built explicitly on NATO defence policy, on EC integration and policy coordination, on the so-called Eastern Treaties and on the CSCE perspective of an all-European peace order. At the same time, the dynamics of Ostpolitik acted as a strong driving force in promoting EC integration as well as East-West agreement in the context of the CSCE. For the EFTA countries, the intra-German rapprochement is of special relevance because it forms a crucial link between several of the most important levels of Europeanization: between NATO and the Warsaw Pact, the EC and NATO, the EC and CMEA, the EC and the Soviet Union, the EC and CSCE, etc. By observing developments in the relationship between the two German states, the neutral EFTA countries formed a better picture of their own prospects in the East-West context. And, in view of West Germany's strengthened position within NATO, Norway and Iceland, also NATO members, began to acquire clear indications on the direction in which alliance policy was moving. Since the events in the GDR of autumn 1989 and the rapid moves towards German reunification, this dimension of the new European security relationships has become the centrepiece of the transformed context with which the EFTA countries have to come to terms.

Perestroika

Since 1985 the dramatic catalyst of the Europeanization process has been that connected with Soviet perestroika and the 'New Thinking'. The new Soviet policy of interdependence and cooperation with the West might be regarded as a positive Soviet response to the EC's Europeanization approach and Ostpolitik. It necessarily has far-reaching effects on East-West relations in Europe as a whole, not least on the situation of the smaller East European countries and the neutral countries. Faced with the prospect of an unwinnable arms race with the USA and with tremendous internal economic and political problems, the new Gorbachev leadership undertook a radical reconsideration of how to reconcile its role as a global power with participation in the regional European process. In many respects, Gorbachev's idea of a 'common European house' resembles Brandt's concept of a European peace order. They both build on cooperation and interdependence instead of on military confrontation. Successful perestroika is seen as a precondition for an effective Soviet policy of interdependence within the framework of the CSCE, whereas the strengthening of the CSCE is regarded as a means to a viable compromise with the United States on the role of nuclear weapons and the overall strategic balance. As far as Europe is concerned, this means, among other things, following up the Stockholm Conference in the direction of arms control, disarmament and confidence building in Europe as a whole (from the Urals to the Atlantic, including the adjacent sea areas).[4]

Perestroika also allows for greater decentralization within Eastern Europe and in the Soviet Union itself as regards forms of cooperation with the EC and other countries in the West. It is now even possible to imagine the Baltic republics playing more independent roles within the larger European system of cooperation. This relaxation of Soviet control in Eastern Europe also creates new prospects for EFTA in relation to the Eastern bloc states, to which we will return below.

EC-Eastern Europe

The first important expression of the restructuring of East-West relations in the direction of all-European cooperation was the framework treaty between the EC and the CMEA signed in Brussels in June 1988. It made possible bilateral treaties between the EC and the different CMEA states. It not only reflected the asymmetry between the two organizations, but also to some degree institutionalized this asymmetry as part of the larger process of Europeanization, breaking with the structures of bloc division.

Like the EFTA states, the East European states through their bilateral treaties and new links with the Community are likely to be increasingly influenced, economically as well as politically, by the Community process of integration.[5] This prospect is of course of fundamental significance for the policy orientation of other European countries, especially the neutrals. At the practical level, for example, the EFTA countries will have to decide how to formalize their future relations with the East European countries. Should they opt for a joint EC-EFTA basis? Or should they extend their bilateral treaties with the EC to include these relations? Or should they approach the East European countries unilaterally? Could questions like these be dealt with within the framework of the EES? Could the EES perhaps be extended to include CMEA countries and the Mediterranean 'orphans', so that EC-EFTA, EC-CMEA and EC-Mediterranean relations were defined as different but interlinked sets of concentric and dynamic arrangements?

CSCE

The need to balance out asymmetries in the transition from bloc structures to all-European structures is what makes the CSCE so important as an overarching framework for negotiation, confidence building, cooperation and institution building. The Europeanization perspective presupposes parallel asymmetrical changes at several levels and in several fields. A downgrading of the structures of military confrontation is in itself an asymmetrical task, both for geographical and political reasons; so is the corresponding replacement of these structures by cooperative structures transcending the bloc division of Europe. This is what the Europeanization process is about. To make possible a military retrenchment by the superpowers – which will necessarily change the US position more fundamentally than the Soviet one – a West European centre of gravity is required which is strong and independent enough to provide the basis for an asymmetrical restructuring of European security. Since 1969, the EC has –

through the coordination of the CSCE policies of its member states and above all through the Ostpolitik – increasingly engaged itself in this direction. And since 1987, the all-European trend based on the above-mentioned processes has become the dominant one in European politics, as illustrated by the revival of the superpower dialogue on arms control and disarmament linked to the CSCE, by the EC-CMEA treaty and the intensified Soviet-West European dialogue, by the Soviet-West German treaty concluded during Gorbachev's visit to Bonn in mid-June 1989,[6] and by the new-found independence of Central and East European countries. Of course, this trend to Europeanization is not unambiguous in every respect. But it seems probable that it will continue and become further strengthened, because any attempt to reverse it would probably imply more risks than gains for the protagonists.

Future relations

The comprehensive process of Europeanization dealt with above cannot be said to be dependent on the policies of the EFTA countries in any decisive way. Both politically and economically, these countries will have to adapt to the changes taking place in the EC and in East-West relations. They are part of the process whether they like it or not. And the character of the international framework in which they operate will determine the range of options open to them.

From a security point of view, there seems to be a clear difference between the two NATO members, Norway and Iceland, on the one hand and the neutrals on the other. Closer relations between the EC and the two former countries would probably have only a marginal impact on security structures in Europe; there would, then, seem to be no serious external constraint on their freedom of choice as to their strategy towards the EC. They can opt for membership if they like: no one would interpret it as a change in their security policies. And they would have every reason to expect a positive response from the Community. Or else they can continue their present strategy of building their policy towards the EC on their free trade treaties and on EFTA coordination within the framework of the EES.

EFTA's neutral countries are in a different position. As European countries, they also have the formal possibility of applying for full EC membership. A move in this direction, however, was, at least until recently, bound to be considered as implying a potential change in the prevailing East-West power structures in Europe, of which the neutrality of some countries was an important element. This did not necessarily mean that the possibility of applying for membership was ruled out. Indeed, the old grounds for maintaining neutrality have been dramatically eroded in recent months. But in practice, to be realistic, such a structural change has to be accommodated to the larger international context in a way that is acceptable to the main protagonists in East-West relations. The case will be roughly similar for other relations between the neutral EFTA countries and the EC, whether they go through a coordinated and common EFTA approach or bilaterally within the framework of the EES. In an international context characterized by the trends towards Europeanization described above, the whole question boils down to whether stronger participation by the neutral countries in the EC integration process is compatible with the general aims of the all-European policies pursued by the main participants.[7]

The process of Europeanization seems bound to have the effect of widening the neutral countries' room for manoeuvre in their relations with the EC. Progress in the establishment of all-European frameworks of cooperation will tend to reduce the significance of blocs in general and that of military alliances in particular. The above-mentioned asymmetrical character of the EC-East European relationship opens up the prospect of increasingly close cooperation. This, together with increased independence of the EC in its relations with the USA on the one hand and increased cooperation between the EC and the Soviet Union on the other, means that participation by the neutral countries in the EC integration process does not necessarily imply taking sides between the two alliances in Europe. In any case the Warsaw Pact has already lost credibility as a military alliance. And to the extent that the EC process has proved itself to be a driving force behind all-European cooperation in the framework of the CSCE, and is recognized as such by the Eastern bloc countries, participation in the EC process by the neutral countries also means participation in an all-European system of cooperation. An orientation of this kind does not violate the general security aims of neutrality. The neutrals have been constantly active in their efforts to strengthen the CSCE. To the extent to which the main EC participants in EPC coordination make their primary security interests dependent on the success of such *common* forums of all-European cooperation, the question for the neutrals is not whether they should participate, but *how* they can most effectively participate in such a development.

Given the above-mentioned perspective of asymmetrical reconstruction in Europe, the position of the neutral countries is bound to change. In parallel with the establishment of ever closer cooperation between the Eastern bloc countries and the EC in an increasing number of fields, neutrality will probably become of less significance as regards the question of EC membership.

The question whether there is some limit beyond which the neutrals cannot go as regards integration with the EC can only be answered through the process of Europeanization itself and will depend primarily on political judgment. Of crucial importance for such a judgment will be the character of the future institutionalization of security policy within the EC/EPC, the outcome of the East-West negotiations on arms control and disarmament, Soviet policy towards the other East European countries, and Soviet-EC relations. Provided the Europeanization process continues along the lines mentioned, the development in the first of these areas – the formal inclusion of security into the EC process – will probably give the neutrals the best guidance as to their options towards the Community.

What makes this question especially difficult for the neutrals is the fact that the EC perspective on how to organize security is still somewhat ambiguous. This is illustrated by the existence of divergent priorities in the continuing debate on the role of the WEU. Whereas France and West Germany see WEU as a potential extension of, and a supplement to, EPC in the context of an all-European restructuring, there are other member states such as Great Britain which would perfer to keep WEU as a subsystem of NATO, implying the survival of the two alliances in Europe.

It seems clear that only the former, more 'independent', approach is compatible with the Europeanization perspective. In such a perspective, the WEU could well be used as an instrument of EPC in speeding up the internalization of security into the Community decision-making process and thus in strengthening both EC independence and East-West rapprochement.[8]

On the other hand, using WEU as a means of strengthening a European NATO pillar or as an *alternative* to including security into EPC would be contradictory not only to the all-European perspective but also to the main trend in the EC since 1970, which has been to make the community ever more inclusive.

As regards the neutral countries, a 'NATO pillar' approach on the part of the EC to the WEU question would in all likelihood exclude them from Community membership, whereas a stronger all-European EC profile would no doubt tend to reduce the significance of neutrality as a constraint on possible membership.

Neutrality cannot thus be regarded as an absolute hindrance to membership, provided that the all-European orientation of the Community process becomes more or less irreversible. Of course, as long as the most important EC members themselves define NATO as their main security instrument, the compatibility of neutrality with EC membership remains a controversial question for Austria, Finland and Sweden, because their position as neutrals has hinged on the East-West division of Europe. On the other hand, whereas NATO is a more specific and static kind of organization, the process of Europeanization has a general and dynamic character and so is of great importance. The Austrian application for EC membership evidently anticipates a continued process of Europeanization.

Seen in an East-West context, EC membership for neutral EFTA countries would unavoidably mean a change in both the image of the Community and their own status. Given the nature of the Single European Act and the Community integration process in general, it is difficult to see how the EC could possibly accept any 'neutrality reservations' on the part of such new members. On the other hand, on joining the EC a neutral state would have the opportunity to influence the orientation of the Community in questions related to European security. And the fact of accepting a new member implies a willingness on the part of other community states to take their new partner's foreign policy and security interests into consideration in the process of coordination. The character of EPC is such as to make flexibility possible in this respect. It seems clear, however, that a rearrangement of this kind is only possible if it is compatible with the new security configuration of Europe and is acceptable to the main protagonists.

Of decisive importance in this connection is the relationship between the EC (or main EC countries) and the Soviet Union. As long as the EC continues the above-mentioned ambiguous position between an 'independent' EPC approach and a 'NATO pillar' approach, Moscow must be expected to resist any formal change in the status of the neutral countries. However, as its reactions to the Austrian approach to membership show, the Soviet attitude to this question seems to be conditional upon developments within the EC itself, in Soviet-EC relations and in East-West relations in general.[9] Because such a prospect means a change in the regional balance of power in favour of the Community and at the cost of Soviet control over the other East European countries, it seems reasonable to conclude that changes in the 'real' situation will have to precede any change in the formal status of neutral countries. This means in practice that the EC will have to demonstrate convincingly that Community membership for neutral EFTA countries is inseparably linked to a strategy of establishing a wider European system of cooperation to succeed the old bloc politics. Given the present trend towards rapid East-West rapprochement in Europe, the security policy restrictions on EC membership for the neutrals may be considered irrelevant by 1992, which is the earliest date that the Community has said it will be ready to consider new applications.

Possible alternative choices: the security implications

Within the framework of the EES approach, there are several different possibilities for establishing closer relations between the EFTA countries and the EC. The three most interesting at present are those mentioned by the President of the Commission, Jacques Delors, in his speech of 17 January 1989 to the European Parliament:[10]

(i) a continuation of the present 'essentially bilateral' approach, restricted more or less to the free trade sector;
(ii) a 'two-pillar' approach, implying a strengthening of EFTA both as a forum for coordination of the policies of the member countries towards the Community and as an instrument for negotiation with the Community and for the implementation of common rules, norms and principles;
(iii) a strengthening of the EES to make it an institutionalized joint decision-making framework (which does not necessarily imply a strengthening of EFTA); Delors envisaged 'a system based on Community rules, which could be extended – in specific areas – to interested EFTA countries and then perhaps, at some date in the future, to other European nations'.

Two further possibilities of a more radical kind must also be considered:

(iv) a strengthening of EFTA, explicitly aiming at EC membership for EFTA countries at the end of an appropriate transitional phase;
(v) an extension of the EES to include not only EFTA but also Yugoslavia, Malta, Cyprus, Turkey and those Central and East European countries that would be prepared to participate in it on certain agreed conditions. Such an arrangement could encompass both bilateral treaties between the EC and the participant non-member countries and multilateral framework treaties linking the other three groupings to the Community and to each other.

These five approaches clearly have different security implications, but the differences need not be very great. Option (i) seems at first glance to be the most compatible with the former status quo as regards European security, but is – realistically speaking – likely to develop into option (iii) in parallel with the EFTA countries' adaptation to the internal market. It is difficult to imagine how these countries could be detached from the general EC process of integration in the way suggested by option (i). If they were, however, the result would be an increasing split between the Community and the rest of Europe, which no doubt would also make the security positions of the EFTA countries more vulnerable. The result would probably be greater pressure on them to choose between membership and non-membership; this would be likely to cause domestic instability in some countries, especially Norway.

A strengthening of EFTA institutionally (ii) could perhaps serve as a means of formally distinguishing between economic and political affairs in such a way as to make it easier for the neutral countries to continue their participation in the European integration process. But such a distinction could only be illusory, at least in the longer-term perspective of EC integration, because the spill-over effects of economic integration do not stop where politics begins. One could also turn the argument around, saying that to the extent that such an arrangement really did contribute to preserving the credibility of neutrality, it would probably tend, in an unacceptable way, to undermine the credibility of the alliance membership of Norway and Iceland. It is also difficult to imagine how any Norwegian government could accept any EFTA solution which excluded EC membership as a future possibility. Nor would it be possible to make a formal distinction between allies and neutrals, excluding the latter from becoming EC members. For one thing, Austria is already applying for membership. In addition, any attempt at exclusion would be regarded by the neutrals as an unacceptable kind of discrimination, and by the Eastern bloc countries as a signal that the EC wants to hold to the constraints of the old politics of blocs for the foreseeable future. This would have negative repercussions on the EC policy of closer relations with the Central and East European countries.

Some of the problems connected with option (ii) might be easier to solve if one went a step further, stating that the goal should be EC membership for all EFTA countries (option (iv)). There are, however, two vital preconditions which would then have to be met. First, the EFTA nations would each have to choose this goal independently – and not all of them could possibly be expected to do so quickly. Second, the road to EC membership for neutral EFTA countries would in some way or other have to be cleared with the great powers, i.e. with the Soviet Union. EC membership for neutral EFTA countries cannot be looked upon in isolation from the wider East-West context. For these reasons, option (iv) means both too much and too little.

Options (iii) and (v) are left. Basic to both is a dynamic conception of European integration, with the EC as the centrepiece. Further integration means the extension of the EC system to include more European countries – not just the EFTA ones. This trend seems likely to continue, regardless of formalities. The main difference between the two options concerns the role of EFTA as an organization and the degree to which the EC-EFTA relationship should be formally – maybe also institutionally – tied to the all-European framework.

According to option (iii), there would in reality be no need to strengthen EFTA as an organization, because the member countries would have to adopt EC rules and regulations anyway. The discriminatory political effects of non-membership, however, would be bound to increase in parallel with the strengthening of the Community as the real decision-making centre for the integration policies of the EFTA countries. And the growing dependence of these countries on the Community would tend to make the question of neutrality more acute over time unless counterbalanced by concurrent East-West or all-European measures.

Building on the logic of (iii), option (v) envisages extending the EES, potentially to the whole of Europe. It ascribes to EFTA an explicit role as part of a common all-European system of cooperation, in principle comprising the Mediterranean 'orphans' and the Central and East European countries. This conception is compatible with Gorbachev's idea of a 'common European house'. It builds on the notion of both the EC process of integration and the all-European process of cooperation and rapprochement, seeing them as irreversible trends. The EES strategy would be to try to link the EC and the all-European levels, with the aim of counterbalancing the different conflicting elements through multilateral policy coordination.

In this perspective, the role of EFTA could be to function as a transitional and 'preparatory' framework for European countries – including the Eastern ones – aspiring to full EC membership or, at least, to full participation in the EC internal market, including the customs union. EFTA's treaty obligations and institutions would have to be revised accordingly. There would have to be permanent close policy coordination both at and between the different levels of organization, including the CSCE.

Option (v) would be in line with the dynamic perspective of Europeanization dealt with above. Such a comprehensive conception seems to be required in the longer term in order to reconcile the process of integration with the differing security policy interests of the parties concerned. Option (i) can be dismissed at once as not attractive to anyone. Options (ii) and (iv) are both clearly insufficient. Option (iii) describes what is taking place today, but will probably sooner or later have to be broadened into something like option (v) if the Europeanization process is to be continued. The situation in Europe today seems to favour such comprehensive multilateral rearrangements.

Notes

1. See also K. Möttölä and H. Patomäki (eds), *Facing the Change in Europe. EFTA Countries' Integration Strategies* (Helsinki, The Finnish Institute of International Affairs, 1989).
2. The following description of the integration strategies of the main actors is based, *inter alia*, on M. Saeter, *Europa – politisch. Alternativen, Modelle und Motive der Integrationspolitik* (Berlin, 1977).
3. For an analysis of the Europeanization strategy of the FRG, see M. Saeter, *The Federal Republic, Europe and the World* (Oslo, University Press, 1980), pp. 41–58.
4. These questions are dealt with more thoroughly in Martin Saeter, 'New Thinking, Perestroika and the Process of Europeanization', *Bulletin of Peace Proposals*, 1 (1989), pp. 47–57.
5. For an interesting Hungarian view on EC-EFTA-CMEA relations, see Andreas Inotai, 'EG, EFTA und Comecon', *Europäische Rundschau*, 2 (1989), pp. 35–47.
6. Text (in German) of the common Soviet-West German declaration, reproduced in the governmental *Bulletin*, 61 (15 June 1989), pp. 542–4.
7. For a more comprehensive treatment, see Paul Luif, 'Neutrale in die EG', *IWP*, 11 (1988).

8. A very clear statement of such a view was presented by Undersecretary of State (Bonn) Helmut Schäfer in his speech to the Parliamentary Assembly of the WEU in Bonn on 11 November 1987 *Bulletin*, 126 (1987), p. 1075.
9. See Paul Luif, 'Neutrale in die EG', pp. 182–4.
10. Text of speech in *Europe Documents*, 1542/1543 (23 January 1989), p. 9.

4 Foreign Policy: Towards a Dialogue?

Elfriede Regelsberger

Increasingly, EC governments seek 'to speak with one voice' on issues of international politics and are obliged to coordinate with EC activities in the attempt to create a 'European foreign policy' (Art. 30, 1 SEA). How, then, do the EFTA countries impinge on this process of European Political Cooperation?[1] Do the EFTA countries want to be associated with EPC? Can or should the intensification of economic relations be kept separate from the field of political cooperation?

Foreign policy cooperation is completely outside the usual definition of the EC-EFTA dialogue. It is therefore not directly affected by the debate on 1992, or linked to the discussions on the European Economic Space, or the more structured partnership envisaged in the Delors speech of January 1989. So far any link with EFTA countries on foreign policy questions has been of limited interest to the Twelve. Yet such a prospect has high salience for some EFTA countries, though for others almost none. In any case everything is in a state of flux due to the radical changes in Eastern Europe and their impact on both the Twelve's Ostpolitik and the relationship of the individual EFTA countries with the Soviet Union and Eastern Europe.

Multilateral cooperation on matters of foreign policy between the twelve EC governments on the one side and the EFTA member states on the other does take place, but in a rather subtle manner. It operates through the traditional diplomatic links between individual EC member states and the EFTA countries, and also through the political debates within the Council of Europe, particularly its committee of ministers. Issues of foreign policy are also raised informally during the 'high-level talks' which individual EFTA countries (e.g. Austria) have established with the European Commission.

The 'political dialogue' between the two groups has no contractual basis and is only loosely institutionalized. Not surprisingly, it is very difficult to understand and analyse for those not directly involved. The process is more a by-product of the EC countries' efforts to 'speak with one voice' in international politics than a clearly designed EPC policy towards the EFTA countries. No collective aim to achieve some sort of 'common foreign policy for Western Europe' exists. Some EFTA governments are eager for the closest possible association with the Twelve because they feel the EC's search for a 'European foreign policy' has a real and direct impact on their own foreign policy; but other EFTA governments disagree.

The notion of a 'political dialogue' is a recent development within EPC. It reflects EC governments' desire not merely to react to international events, but to 'shape' them: hence 'the High Contracting Parties shall organize a political dialogue with third countries and regional groupings whenever they deem it necessary' (Art. 30, 8 SEA). From the perspective of the Twelve, contacts with the outside world serve various purposes. First, the results of consultations within EPC have to be brought to the attention of the international community, particularly to those most directly concerned. In claiming to contribute to the peaceful settlement of conflicts in the world, the Twelve address those governments or political forces involved in international conflicts (e.g. in the Middle East, southern Africa or Central America) and those who infringe the basic principles of international law and order (e.g. human rights, use of force, state-supported terrorism).

Second, political dialogue is an essential vehicle for the EC and its twelve members in the search for a 'consistent' (Art. 30, 5 SEA) external position. It is intended to be a means of fostering cooperation in various fields of common interest between the EC/Twelve and other groups of states (e.g. ASEAN or the Gulf Cooperation Council), thus promoting regional stability and reducing tensions and intra-regional conflicts (e.g. in Central America). Third, a political dialogue with selected third countries and groupings may permit wide-ranging consultations with important partners, in particular with the United States, but also other 'like-minded' countries such as Japan or Norway. The aim here is twofold: first, to inform important partners about EPC in order to avoid misunderstandings and clashes of interests; and second, to promote a united, or at least coordinated, external position for the West, thus meeting international challenges more adequately and strengthening Europe's voice through coalition-building.

Relations between the Twelve and the EFTA countries belong to this latter category of dialogue with 'friendly and allied' states. They are primarily a product of the 1980s, apart from the various rounds of multilateral negotiation in the earlier days of the CSCE and the less successful experiences of concertation within the United Nations. The extent of political dialogue in recent years is due mainly to EPC's 'qualitative leap': this has attracted more attention from those in EFTA who had previously tended to ignore it. Even the greatest sceptics had to admit that the collective diplomacy of the EC governments had become a factor in world politics worthy of consideration. Despite all the weaknesses of a consensus-based and primarily 'declaratory' approach, EPC has attracted the attention of an ever-increasing number of third countries, both within Europe (Austria, Sweden, Soviet Union, Yugoslavia) and elsewhere (China, Japan, Canada, not to mention the parties of the Arab-Israeli conflict).

EPC is primarily intended to be a means for collective response to international crises. Second, it accommodates EC member states' desire to gain/regain weight internationally and to play a political role consistent with the Community's status as an economic giant. Thus political dialogue proves to be an attempt to establish international peace and security through economic, political and cultural cooperation on the basis of equal partnership, in line with conceptions of Europe as a 'civilian power'. This has clearly been interpreted by the Twelve as implying an emphasis mainly on crisis regions in other parts of the world, rather than on their immediate neighbours in Western Europe. Western Europe in general and the EFTA countries in particular do not figure on the EPC agenda, except in those situations where Western democratic values and principles might be at stake (as in the case of the unsuccessful *coup d'état* in Spain in 1981 or the generals' seizure of power in Turkey in 1980). Other bilateral conflicts between EPC participants, such as Northern Ireland or Gibraltar, are by definition excluded from EPC and not dealt with by the Twelve.

So, if issues related to the EFTA countries are raised at all, they usually concern the various political dialogues (see below). Uncontested as these issues are among the Twelve in general, decisions can be taken easily and implemented quickly, provided the acting EPC presidency is sufficiently attentive. Due to increased demands from third countries for political dialogue during the 1980s, the Twelve face considerable problems in fulfilling their many obligations for consultations with third countries and groupings. Giving these political dialogues adequate attention becomes an almost unbearable burden for smaller EC member states when holding the presidency. So far the EFTA countries have not suffered from EPC's limited resources from the narrow perspective of procedural arrangements, but it is open to question whether the potential for cooperation in some policy areas, such as East-West relations, the Middle East or South Africa, has yet been sufficiently exploited. This is astonishing, given how far values are shared by Western Europe as a whole and the efforts undertaken by West Europeans to have them acknowledged in international politics.

Past experience and constellations of interest

Among the Twelve

EPC dates from the early 1970s: the then six EC members wanted to give a new impetus to the process of political unification, partly because of the forthcoming enlargement of the Community. They also sought to substitute for the decreasing international influence of the traditional European powers. As the EC had become the world's biggest trading bloc, the Europeans should also, they felt, contribute to the maintenance of international political order and peace.

The initial aim was to establish a process of mutual information, exchanges of views and, 'where it appears possible and desirable', common action in the highly sensitive field of foreign policy.[2] The results were uncertain and success by no means guaranteed. EC governments consequently remained preoccupied first and foremost with national considerations. They paid less attention to the possible impact of their joint declarations and actions on their neighbours in Western Europe; nor did they contemplate collaboration with these neighbours on issues of common concern. The EC countries' primary outside interest was the United States, especially when Washington advised them to assume 'global', not merely 'regional', responsibility.[3] The then Nine's intention in 1973 'to strengthen their links . . . with the Member Countries of the Council of Europe' did not reach the stage of implementation.[4] Neither side felt the need to go beyond the arrangements already signed on economic cooperation between the EC and EFTA countries. Norway, however, found itself in a very vulnerable position and particularly regretted the distance from the Nine. When, after a very short involvement (January–September 1972), Norway had to leave EPC following its people's vote against EC membership, it found itself cut off from the emerging 'heart' of foreign policy formulation in Western Europe. The entry of Denmark into the EPC 'club' somewhat helped to compensate for Norway's isolation. Nevertheless, sitting at the negotiating table is quite different from being a mere recipient of information on the results of debates within the EPC.

The Copenhagen government has been the most fervent supporter of a close association between EPC and the Nordic countries on account of its intimate relations with its Nordic partners, which form part of Denmark's national identity and are a constituent element of Danish foreign policy.[5] Denmark holds very similar views to its Nordic neighbours on a great number of international questions (e.g. North-South issues, the apartheid regime, human rights). Since these views are quite often compatible with the *acquis politique* of the Twelve,[6] Denmark's position is generally comfortable. But when divergences arise, the Danish government has to try to reconcile its two loyalties in order not to distance itself too far from its EPC partners.

Within EPC circles Danish participants understand their role as that of 'bridge-builder' between Nordic attitudes and those of the Twelve. The nature of foreign policy and the need to respect both national sovereignty and EPC principles mean that Denmark cannot be authorized to integrate Nordic policy into EPC or vice versa. But it can and does act as a channel of reciprocal information and sometimes also as a mediator (e.g. in the CSCE).

Denmark again underlined the importance it attaches to Nordic cooperation during the recent negotiations over the Single European Act.[7] When signing the Act, Denmark unilaterally declared that the provisions of the EPC treaty did not 'affect' the country's participation in Nordic cooperation on foreign policy. Furthermore, the Danish government, strongly supported by the Norwegian authorities which were the driving force behind the scene, tried to loosen the strict parallelism between EC membership and participation in EPC during the debate on the SEA. It did not succeed. Art. 30, 1 SEA, explicitly states that the 'High Contracting Parties' are members of the EC. All that the European partners were willing to accept was a separate declaration indicating the Twelve's readiness to intensify cooperation with the members of the Council of Europe and to include Finland (which at the time was not a member of the Council of Europe) among the other democratic states in Western Europe.

Since then the Twelve have kept their promises and established or intensified contacts with a number of countries in Western Europe (e.g. Norway, Austria, Cyprus, Malta) who wish to be associated more closely with the Twelve in the 'political' field. The political dialogue has grown largely in response to the wishes of third countries, not at the Twelve's initiative.

After Denmark, the Federal Republic of Germany had traditionally shown the greatest interest in developing political dialogue. This might be attributed to the personal interest of Herr Genscher in strengthening European foreign policy, through specific forms of cooperation (e.g. with ASEAN and the Contadora countries or the United States). But other elements of political dialogue in recent years (e.g. with Malta, Cyprus) might provoke questions on the need for such a commitment from EPC, given the limited importance of small countries in Western Europe compared with other of the Twelve's partners and the enormous organizational burden of all these dialogues, particularly for the EPC presidency, given the Twelve's numerous existing obligations. German enthusiasm for creating additional contacts between EPC and third countries may reflect a strong desire for clear-cut 'structures' and 'rules' to govern the external relations of EPC, as well as a certain compulsion to 'invent' something new during their term of office in the presidency of EPC. German diplomats would, however, argue that the quest for political dialogues is more than image-making. They recall their government's general commitment to strengthen Europe's weight internationally and they interpret the promotion of EPC relations with third countries as a means towards this end.

A glance at the history of EPC's contacts with third countries suggests that the EFTA group has received rather low priority. For the Twelve, the need for coalition-building seems to lie elsewhere, with the United States and Japan, particularly when common action (e.g. sanctions) in a particular international crisis is being considered (e.g. South Africa 1985–6, the US-Libyan affair of 1986 and Syria's involvement in international terrorism). The reason for giving priority to the major alliance partner and world power is quite obvious. The opening to Japan results from its participation in the Seven Power Summits and its endeavours to develop a more active foreign policy. The omission of the EFTA countries from EPC diplomacy until recently is all the more astonishing given their immediate geographical proximity and, even more importantly, their shared values and convergence of views on a large number of international issues. It may be attributed to the lack of cohesion in the group of EFTA countries, which makes them less attractive partners for EPC. However, it is also connected to the difficulties being encountered by the Twelve in their search for an identity in the world in general and in (Eastern and Western) Europe in particular. The definition of a comprehensive Ostpolitik to respond to Mr Gorbachev's proposals involved a long series of discussions at ministerial and directorial level in EPC, with hot disputes over the final wording of communiqués. It took the EC governments from 1985 until the end of 1988 to reach consensus on the guidelines of policy towards Eastern Europe,[8] while different views persisted as to the timing of the European Ostpolitik and the substance of specific proposals.[9] Thus if a common denominator is so difficult to find and fragile in nature within EPC, neither the time nor the inclination exists to develop the *acquis politique* further in collaboration with other (i.e. in particular the remaining West European) states.

The situation has been different in the various rounds of negotiations within the CSCE where the mediating role of the Neutral and Non-Aligned Countries proved indispensable for the whole process of East-West relations. It also proved helpful to the EC governments, most of which give the issue high priority. It is in this area that cooperation between the two caucuses is the furthest advanced. The negotiations during the Vienna follow-up conference gave further evidence that coalition-building could cut across groups and produce mixed constellations comprising countries from inside both the EPC and EFTA circles. This observation, made by participants at the Vienna conference,[10] once again shows how historical ties, geography or other factors create very distinct interests which make it rather difficult for the Twelve to form one identity in foreign policy.

Among the EFTA countries

It is difficult to give an overall assessment of the EFTA countries' attitude to EPC. Austria and Norway greatly desire to join EPC or at least to be associated with the Twelve as closely as possible. But Sweden, Switzerland, Finland and Iceland are less interested in any closer association with the Twelve's foreign policy cooperation. Factors such as NATO membership or neutrality and other aspects of the countries' national foreign policies are also decisive.

Let us start with *Norway*, a partner of the Twelve in NATO which has been aiming at quasi-membership of EPC ever since it had to abandon the idea of becoming a full member of the EC. Norway is most acutely aware of what it loses in international standing by its non-participation in EPC when it sees other countries in Western Europe reap the benefits of collective foreign policy-making. When EPC extended its sphere of interest in the 1980s to fields of paramount importance for Norway – such as East-West relations and European security – its fear of isolation increased still further. The reactivation of WEU in consequence of EPC's limited potential in security and defence (Art. 30, 6 SEA)[11] intensified this fear. Norway strongly deplores the fact that a European Ostpolitik is being developed in which it cannot participate to any great extent although the all-European dimension ranks high in Norwegian foreign policy. Norway finds itself in a dilemma: it supports a stronger European influence on US policy and shares the views of the Twelve but it is excluded from the intra-European concertation process. Another item on the EPC agenda – the Middle East – is also of interest to Norway, which participates in the UN peacekeeping forces there. It would favour some sort of concertation and perhaps even EPC backing for its role.

Through constant activism the Norwegian government has managed to achieve a privileged status vis-à-vis EPC. It has access to the consultations of the Twelve, not only after decisions have been taken but even prior to EPC debates. Of course, from the Twelve's point of view, Norwegian perceptions are only one of many elements to be taken into consideration. For Norwegian foreign policy, however, this advanced form of association with EPC offers enormous benefits.

Iceland, the second NATO partner within the EFTA group, has hitherto almost totally ignored EPC, an understandable attitude given the country's limited interest in international affairs. It has been said elsewhere[12] that Iceland views developments in the EC and EPC with 'unease'. Thus the country may sooner or later have to modify its position, while minimizing the consequential constraints. Iceland might increase its interest in EPC so as to counterbalance to some extent its relationship with the United States. But as this is mostly based on security and defence issues the potential of EPC from Iceland's point of view, and the attractiveness of Iceland as a dialogue partner for the Twelve, seem rather limited.

The remaining four EFTA countries share a general interest in the Twelve's actions and statements, an interest which is perhaps least in the case of Finland and greatest in the case of Austria. Apart from Austria, the principle of neutrality has hitherto fostered caution; or at least their dialogue with EPC has been presented to domestic public opinion as cautious avoiding any step that might be interpreted as a sign of affiliation to or even identification with the Twelve.

Austria has undertaken a remarkable shift in its policy towards the EC, culminating on 29 June 1989 in a formal application for EC membership. This is motivated overwhelmingly by economic considerations: there have been no arguments that a close association with or even an entry into EPC is essential to preserve or even enlarge the country's scope of foreign policy and international influence. On the contrary, advocates of Austrian membership of the EC actually tone down the importance of EPC, rating it as a 'non-binding mechanism of information and consultation' in which participation in the debate on European security is optional.[13] More cautious and realistic voices recognize, at least implicitly, the incompatibilities between the *acquis* of the Twelve and neutralist Austrian positions on international questions.[14] On the other hand, there is already a remarkable convergence of views and it may be supposed that the definition of Austria's neutrality is open to modification. But this remains mere speculation until the EC responds to the Austrian bid to enter the Community.

Austria pays close attention to the Twelve's policy within the CSCE, this having been judged as very pertinent to developments in East-West relations, in particular at times of deterioration in the overall climate. On the fringe of the negotiations, the Austrian delegation usually keeps in close contact with EC representatives, the presidency being the first, but not the only, addressee. Other EPC activities (e.g. concerning human rights, the Middle East) have been viewed with some scepticism, particularly in periods of socialist government in Austria.

The more EPC has enlarged its scope of activities and intensified its concertation procedures, the more worried Austria has become about the declining importance of other multilateral forums and the correspondingly reduced scope for its participation. The Vienna government was one of the most vigorous protesters against the 'isolationist' approach of the EC-European delegations at the UN during the 1970s. It urged EPC participants to pay more attention to aligning their views with other members of the Western group and even attempted to encourage concertation among the non-EPC countries as a counterweight to EPC. Interestingly enough, it was also an Austrian initiative which led to the reconsideration of the relationship between the EC and the Council of Europe in the early 1980s, an initiative taken because Austria observed a constant shift of activities of a political nature from the circle of the then Twenty-one to the Ten/Twelve.

In the context of Austria's recent rapprochement with Brussels, it also decided to seek closer association with EPC. Austria enjoys a reputation as an important 'bridge' between Eastern and Western Europe which could be useful for the Twelve's Ostpolitik. This is why they gave a positive response to Austria's request to institutionalize the already existing informal contacts.

Austria's move towards an institutionalized political dialogue in 1988 would be incompatible with both *Swiss* and *Swedish* policy. Neutrality, and a concomitantly independent foreign policy (open only, if at all, to multilateral cooperation with the Twelve, e.g. in the UN and in the Council of Europe), has led these two countries to maintain a certain distance from the EC until recently. The principle of 'proximity' practised in the EC-EFTA relationship[15] seems not to be acceptable in the sphere of foreign policy. Even a mention of any interest in what is happening in EPC is avoided. Instead, in the Swedish case, official and semi-official statements[16] and documents underline the incompatibility of neutrality and membership in a system of foreign policy coordination.[17]

In daily diplomatic practice, however, the situation looks somewhat different; despite solemn declarations that it is not possible even to discuss issues of foreign and security policy with EC representatives,[18] this is precisely what is done every day in diplomatic life in Western Europe. Since 1987–8 both Swedish and Swiss diplomats have sought closer links with EPC, albeit on an informal basis. The information EFTA countries receive via the presidency about EPC is greatly valued by their diplomats. To go further, towards visible solidarity with the Twelve, would, of course, be different and is not implied in Swedish or Swiss approaches to EPC. Since 1986, when EPC was given an institutionalized basis, it has become more difficult for neutral countries in Western Europe to be 'associated' with it, since their public opinion is very sensitive about strict adherence to the principle of neutrality.[19]

At first sight, neutrality seems to require greater distance from EPC for Switzerland than for Sweden. Official Swiss voices, if they are heard at all, show interest in strengthening the Council of Europe in matters of common political concern such as human rights and other democratic values.[20] Since 1987, however, the Twelve have also been approached bilaterally by both. Even in Berne there is growing interest in receiving the latest news from EPC through individual channels of communication.

Finland's neutrality, together with its obligations under the Treaty on Friendship, Cooperation and Mutual Assistance with the Soviet Union, constitute an even greater obstacle to association with EPC. Until 1988 the government felt neither the need nor the desire to take any steps in this direction.[21] From the Finnish perspective, challenges to their foreign policy come from the need to develop economic relations with other European states. Finland is keenly interested in multilateral economic cooperation and favours a strengthening of EFTA vis-à-vis the EC, provided it is still able to preserve its 'independent power of decision'.[22] It is only recently, in the course of the country's general move towards closer political links with Western Europe, that the Finnish attitude to the Twelve has become more open: during the German presidency the Finnish government even went so far as to ask for – occasional – contacts with the EPC spokespersons.[23] Finland's entry into the Council of Europe in May 1989 automatically opens the door and offers additional contacts with the foreign policy cooperation of the Twelve. Given continuing detente in East-West relations, Finland is finding it both easier and more attractive to take more interest in EPC.

Given the very distinctive conditions and traditions determining the foreign policies of the individual EFTA countries, the potential for a common West European approach by the Twelve and the Six is limited. Of course both sides hold the same views on the fundamentals of international politics and on many international developments. But it is quite different to translate this common assessment into joint action. The Twelve, willing to proceed in this direction, have been anxious to achieve tangible results. The EFTA countries do not feel collective diplomacy between themselves to be imperative; those interested in closer relations with EPC prefer to seek them on a unilateral basis.

The network of cooperation

It follows from the very different approaches of individual EFTA countries towards EPC and from the responses of the Twelve that the network of co-operation is diffuse and complex, varying from the very informal to the institutionalized. Two main categories can be distinguished: the multilateral and the bilateral.

The group-to-group approach

The outstanding example of multilateral cooperation is the political dialogue between the Twelve and the non-EC countries of the Council of Europe. Representatives from the EFTA countries, together with the other non-EC members of the Council of Europe, meet their counterparts from the EC on a regular basis to discuss matters related to EPC.

The concept of such consultations, designed to supplement the exchange of views which already takes place in the Committee of Ministers of the Twenty-three, is of Austrian origin and dates back to 1982–3. It was a reaction to the Genscher-Colombo plan of 1981, subsequently transformed into the Solemn Declaration on European Union of 1983. It was an expression of a growing concern within the Council of Europe that the body was being deprived of its competences by EPC and an EC with ever-enlarging scope. The then Ten responded favourably to the request of their West European neighbours to intensify the relations between the two bodies, including a regular exchange of views on EPC-related issues.

Meetings at both ministerial level – on the fringe of the committee of ministers' sessions – and senior official level were agreed upon during early 1983 and introduced during the Federal Republic's presidency.[24] Since then regular six-monthly gatherings have taken place with the foreign ministers of the Ten/Twelve or their deputies, while at the level of political directors contacts exist between the group of non-EC Council of Europe members and the EPC Troika, i.e. the acting President of the Twelve, supported by a colleague from both the preceding and succeeding presidencies. Occasionally meetings of experts (e.g. on the CSCE) take place.

Once again at the initiative of the German government, these informal gatherings were supplemented by a special ministerial session of the then Twenty-one in early 1985.[25] Foreign Minister Genscher, President of the Council of Europe Ministeral Committee at the time, sought to allay anxieties among the non-EC participants. At least symbolically, this meeting was meant to bridge the gap between the Council of Europe and the EC,[26] a gap which was to widen after the Dooge and Adonino Committees were established by the European Council of Fontainebleau in 1984 to draft proposals for EC institutional reform and a People's Europe. In 1989 another attempt was made to increase reciprocal information and understanding between the representatives of the two organizations. On the occasion of the fortieth anniversary of the Council of Europe in 1988 foreign ministers had decided to extend contacts, with regular meetings between the President of the Council of Europe Ministerial Committee and the President of EPC, the former being assisted by the Secretary General, the spokesperson for the Twelve being accompanied by the President of the EC Commission. This new format was inaugurated in Paris, then the capital of the EPC presidency country, with overwhelming French participation, including French Foreign Minister Dumas, French Commission President Delors and French Secretary General of the Council of Europe Mme. Lalumière; Norwegian Foreign Minister Mr Stoltenberg spoke on behalf of the 23.[27]

Discussions between the two groups have focused on selected international political questions of common interest, notably East-West relations but also developments outside Europe, in Central America, South Africa and the Middle East for example, and North-South relations in general. They comprise a *tour d'horizon* by each side; details of the internal EPC process are not revealed but its results are reported. From their debates on international politics in the Council of Europe, EFTA representatives may well be aware of divergencies among the Twelve, and may thus be better prepared than other third countries to assess the Twelve's common foreign policy realistically. Out of consideration for the sensitivities of the neutral partners, the debates do not end in common declarations or joint action. Where a convergence of views exists it is revealed through the final communiqué of the official ministerial sessions of the Council of Europe, while the meetings described earlier are informal and kept confidential.

Another aspect of group-to-group cooperation, albeit much looser, operates in the UN framework (the Swiss being excluded owing to their abrogation of UN membership), where both the EPC and the EFTA countries belong to the Western European and Other States Group (WEOG).[28] This is said to be unsatisfactory, principally owing to the large size of the Western group, but also because the EC Europeans tend to focus consultations exclusively on themselves.[29] This is not surprising, since the EC member states' primary consideration is their wish to present themselves as a unit at UN consultations, with other Western countries' concerns ranking second. As is well known, it is not guaranteed that the Twelve speak with one voice in the UN forums: the voting pattern of EC countries between 1985 and 1988 reveals a more than 50% rate of disagreement (e.g. on the question of Palestine,[30] South Africa, disarmament); there has been only a marginal improvement in subsequent years.[31] It would be wrong to blame Greece for being the sole *enfant terrible* blocking unanimity. France and the United Kingdom must also be mentioned, as well as Denmark which is often tempted to vote against the EPC majority, not only when it holds another view but also because it wishes to be seen to close ranks with its Nordic friends.

Within the CSCE context EFTA does not exist as a group. It is split between those who are part of the N&N group and those belonging to the Western caucus through their membership of NATO. On the EPC side, Ireland holds a special status as well. This very specific mixture of the eighteen countries and the maintenance of their positions and status runs counter to a group-to-group approach in the sense described earlier. This is not to say that EC governments prefer to go it alone rather than speak with one voice, least of all in formal sessions of the negotiations. But they are not against 'playing different cards' or closing ranks at a given moment with partners outside EPC. As noted earlier, coalition-building in the CSCE may cut across the established caucuses, depending on congruences of interest or the role each government wishes to play.

Another extension of the group-to-group formula is directly related to daily EPC business: after each ministerial meeting of the Twelve (at least three each presidency) and each meeting of the Political Committee (monthly) the EPC presidency gives briefings to 'friendly and allied' states. It has become a habit to inform privileged third countries belonging to the Atlantic Alliance or at least sharing the same Western democratic values on the major results of EPC. This is done by the spokesperson of the Twelve in the capital of the country holding the presidency, usually with the European Correspondent (i.e. the head of the Western Europe and EPC desk in the Foreign Ministry) or the Political Director convening a meeting with diplomats from the embassies of the countries in question. The Twelve's addressees may differ depending on their interests in the given subject, also on their actual physical presence in the presidency country, which tends to be reduced in the smaller EC member states (e.g. Ireland or Portugal). Another factor to be considered is the 'philosophy' of individual presidencies, which may offer special treatment to special partners, such as individual rather than collective briefing (in the case of the USA); another factor is the personal resources at the disposal of the Twelve's spokesperson.

Usually, representatives from the EFTA countries find themselves with diplomats from other Council of Europe countries (Turkey, Cyprus, Malta) and from Japan, Canada, Australia and New Zealand. Gatherings of this sort, with a considerable number of participants, not necessarily those closest to EPC, must of course be rather formal and are often criticized as providing inferior-quality information to the allegedly privileged EPC partners. It is no surprise, then, that other, i.e. individual, channels of communication with EPC should be significant. Apart from Iceland, all EFTA countries enjoy such additional contacts.

The bilateral approach

Each EFTA member's association with the Twelve varies according to the importance it attaches to EPC. The Swiss and Swedish approaches are similar, but different from those of Austria and Norway. Iceland has so far been satisfied with the multilateral contacts.

Sweden generally uses informal channels to seek supplementary information on EPC policies, via its embassy in the country holding the presidency and/or its mission in Brussels. Contacts usually take place between embassy staff and senior officials participating in EPC at working group level. Since 1987 exchanges of information have also been held at directorial level. These meetings, once every six months, usually in the capital of the presidency country, have to be seen as a step towards institutionalized political dialogue, even though no formal agreement exists. Neither side wishes to reveal too many details of the nature and quality of these contacts. Sweden carefully avoids any act that might be interpreted as a move away from neutrality; the Twelve are anxious not to create precedents for other third countries and do not wish to open their internal consultations to outside interference.

The Swiss government has adopted a similar approach. Since 1987 the Political Director of the presidency has met her Swiss counterpart twice in Berne to explain the priorities on the EPC agenda. As with Sweden, any impression of institutionalization is carefully avoided and information on the dialogue is, to say the least, scarce.

The same is broadly true for *Austria*, even though (since April 1988) the country has enjoyed an institutionalized bilateral political dialogue with the Twelve. During the German presidency it was agreed in an exchange of letters to hold regular consultations, preferably at ministerial level, between the Austrian Foreign Minister and the EPC President, if possible once every six months. The first consultation took place in Athens under the Greek presidency in late 1988, the second in Vienna with the Spanish Foreign Minister speaking on behalf of the Twelve. According to ministerial decision, gatherings between Austria and EPC may also be held at directorial level.[32] In fact since 1988 biannual consultations of the Political Directors precede or follow those of the foreign ministers. Such gatherings usually offer an exchange of views on international topics of mutual interest without, however, leading to an agreed policy or joint action. They are highly appreciated by the Twelve's partners, because such contacts heighten the international profile of third countries. In addition, Austria seeks contacts with the Twelve in Vienna, where diplomats from the presidency country meet representatives from the Austrian Foreign Ministry at irregular intervals.

As would be expected, *Norway* has the most sophisticated network of contacts with EPC. It is a mixture of recently (1988) formalized practices and *ad hoc* procedures. Biannual meetings between the Norwegian Foreign Minister and the President-in-Office, preferably at the beginning of each presidential term, have been supplemented by similar ones at directorial level since autumn 1988. After repeated attempts during the 1980s the Oslo government managed to formalize this privileged status, during the 1988 German presidency. The diplomatic notes exchanged in April 1988 may be understood as some sort of recognition of Norway's difficult position as a member of NATO which is, nevertheless, excluded from consultations within the EC.

In addition, informal access at the working group level has a long tradition in the Norwegian-EPC relationship. It offers at least insights into the substance of EPC and the internal consultation process of the Twelve, prior to the final decisions being taken in EPC. Occasionally Norway may even be able to influence EPC policy. The Norwegian government is also eager to establish regular links with the Twelve in Oslo. These could take the form of gatherings between the resident ambassadors of the Twelve and the Norwegian Political Director. Occasionally the Norwegian Foreign Minister accepts the EPC presidency's invitation for a working lunch.

Future prospects

At a time when structures in the EC, Western Europe and East-West relations are undergoing fundamental changes, a prognosis as to the future shape of the EFTA-EPC relationship is difficult. In the short term, both the Twelve and the EFTA countries appear to be happy with the existing mixture of bilateral and multilateral concertation. From past experience with other group-to-group relations,[33] one may assume that the Twelve would favour linking consultations on international politics with the 'Six' to talks on EC-related issues, at least when the foreign ministers are themselves involved. During the EC-EFTA ministerial session of December 1989 ideas of this kind were launched. They were received with benevolent caution, nothing more.[34] In view of the fundamental changes in Eastern Europe and their impact on the EC and EPC, it may be more likely than not that political consultations between the Twelve and the EFTA countries will gain a new momentum. The group-to-group approach, with the format 12:6, would be the necessary complement to the new EC-EFTA partnership, to be established only in addition to the already existing bilateral and multilateral forums described above. Such a new political dialogue would increase the existing burden on EPC of managing all the Twelve's external obligations. However, the proposed Intergovernmental Conference to deal with institutional questions (in addition to that dealing with economic and monetary union) may produce some reforms of the management of EPC.

Notes

1. On European political cooperation in general, see A. Pijpers, E. Regelsberger and W. Wessels (eds), *European Political Cooperation in the 1990s. A Common Foreign Policy for Western Europe?* (Dordrecht, 1988); W. Weidenfeld and W. Wessels (eds), *Jahrbuch der Europäischen Integration 1980–1988/1989* (special sections on European political cooperation) (Bonn, Europa Union Verlag); F.G. Jacobs (ed.) *Yearbook of European Law* (Oxford, 1982 onwards) (special sections on European political cooperation); Ph. de Schoutheete, *La Coopération Politique Européenne* (Brussels, 1986); R. Rummel, *EPZ-Erfolgsformel für gemeinsame westeuropäische Aussenpolitik? Entwicklungsmöglichkeiten der Europäischen Politischen Zusammenarbeit auf der Basis der Einheitlichen Europäischen Akte* (Ebenhausen, 1987).
2. This is the careful wording of the Luxembourg Report of 27 October 1970, the first political commitment and basic document upon which EPC was established. Since the Single European Act of 1986 the main principles and procedures of EPC are laid down in Art. 30 of the Single European Act.
3. B. Kohler, 'Euro-American Relations and European Political Cooperation', in D. Allen, R. Rummel and W. Wessels (eds), *European Political Cooperation: Towards*

a Foreign policy for Western Europe (London, 1982); H.G. Krenzler, 'The Dialogue Between the European Community and the United States of America – Present Form and Future Prospects', paper presented at the Annual European Policy Unit Colloquy, European University Institute, Florence, 1988.

4. de Schoutheete, *La Coopération Politique*, p. 153.
5. See N.J. Haagerup and C. Thune, 'Denmark: The European pragmatist', in C. Hill (ed.), *National Foreign Policies and European Political Cooperation* (London, 1983), pp. 106–20.
6. Ibid., p. 112.
7. C. Bo Bramsen, *EF-pakken og det udenriqspolitiske samarbejde (EPS)* (Copenhagen, 1987), p. 34; J. De Ruyt, *L'Acte Unique Européen, Commentaire* (Brussels, 1987), pp. 226, 249.
8. See point II.5 of the Declaration on the EC's international role, European Council, 2–3 December 1988, Rhodes.
9. Perhaps most obvious in the FRG's strategy of 'openness' and British resistance to concessions to the Soviet Union (e.g. in the case of the Soviet proposal on a human rights conference in Moscow presented at the CSCE follow-up meeting in Vienna).
10. Cf. H. Schneider, 'Über Wien nach Gesamteuropa? Der KSZE-Prozess nach dem dritten Folgetreffen', *Integration*, 2 (1989), pp. 47–60.
11. For details, see G. Bonvicini, 'The Political and Institutional Aspects of European Defence', *The International Spectator*, 2 (1988), pp. 108–16; P. Tsakaloyannis, *Western European Security in a Changing World: From the Reactivation of the WEU to the Single European Act* (Maastricht, 1988).
12. See G.H. Kristinsson's chapter in this volume.
13. W. Hummer and M. Schweitzer, 'Das Problem der Neutralität. Österreich und die EG-Betrittsfrage', *Europa-Archiv*, 17 (1988), pp. 501–10.
14. See P. Luif's chapter in this volume.
15. V.B. Tscharner, 'Die Europäische Gemeinschaft auf dem Weg zum grossen Binnenmarkt', paper presented at the Aargau Chamber of Commerce, May 1988.
16. See the speech by the Swedish Prime Minister during his visit to the Federal Republic in 1988: J. Carlsson, 'Schweden in Europa', *Europa-Archiv*, 12 (1988), pp. 323–30.
17. Schwedisches Institut, *Tatsachen über Schweden. Die schwedische Aussenpolitik* (Stockholm, 1986). See also C. Hamilton and C.-E. Stålvant's chapter in this volume.
18. According to the Swedish Foreign Minister in 1987; see R. Wolff, 'EG-Schweden: Mehr als nur ein Flirt?', *EG-Magazin*, 5 (1988), pp. 14–15.
19. See also C.-E. Stålvant and C.B. Hamilton, *A Swedish View of 1992*, RIIA Discussion Paper 13 (London, 1989), p. 31.
20. See the speech of Swiss Secretary of State E. Brunner, 'Die Stellung der Schweiz in der heutigen Welt' (Bonn, 1984, manuscript), p. 9.
21. These were the words of the Finnish Prime Minister according to *Agence Europe*, 17 July 1987.
22. Speech of the Finnish Prime Minister, 3 September 1987, published in *Yearbook of Finnish Foreign Policy 1987* (Helsinki, 1988), pp. 57–60.
23. C. Trojan, 'The European Political Cooperation and the EFTA', speech at the Alpbach Conference, 5–8 July 1988, p. 10.
24. E. Regelsberger and W. Wessels, 'National Paper on the Federal Republic of Germany', in C. O'Nuallain (ed.), *The Presidency of the European Council of Ministers* (London, 1985), pp. 73–100.
25. See the report of the Colombo Commission prepared by former Italian Prime Minister E. Colombo who chaired a Committee set up by the Council of Europe Parliamentary Assembly in 1984 to consider relations between the Council of Europe and

the EC in the broadest possible perspective. The report was published in *Agence Europe*, 19 June 1985.

26. See the speech of H.-D. Genscher given to the Parliamentary Assembly of the Council of Europe, 30 January 1985, published in *Bulletin of the Press and Information Office of the Federal Government*, 1 February 1985.
27. *Bulletin d'informations*, 13 July 1989.
28. See B. Lindemann, *EG-Staaten und Vereinte Nationen* (München, 1978), p. 204.
29. Ibid.
30. At the UN Special Session on Palestine in Geneva in December 1988, the Twelve took a major step towards greater cohesion when they unanimously rejected recognition of the Palestinian State just proclaimed by the Palestine National Council.
31. E. Regelsberger, 'EPC in the 1980s: Reaching Another Plateau?', in Pijpers, Regelsberger and Wessels, *European Political Cooperation*, p. 48; K.-D. Stadler, 'Die Zusammenarbeit der Zwölf in der Generalversammlung der Vereinten Nationen in den achtziger Jahren', *Europa-Archiv*, 7 (1988), pp. 181–90.
32. Trojan, 'European Political Cooperation', p. 10.
33. E. Regelsberger, 'The Dialogue of the EC/Twelve with Other Groups of States', in *The International Spectator*, 4 (1988), pp. 252–69.
34. See the vague wording of point 8 of the Joint Ministerial Declaration, *Agence Europe*, 23 December 1989.

5a Economic Interdependence
Per Magnus Wijkman

The term European Economic Space (EES) seemed beguilingly straightforward when first coined in connection with the Luxembourg Declaration by EFTA and EC Ministers in 1984. It reflected the reality of strong economic interdependence between the Community and its EFTA neighbours, each group being the major trading partner for the other. But it lacked concrete and substantive goals. As a result five years of steady progress on a case by case basis in the Luxembourg follow-up could not keep pace with developments in the EC after it launched its programme for the single market. Nor could it satisfy enterprises in EFTA countries which, as the single market emerged, pursued European-wide strategies through mergers, acquisitions and new establishments in the EC.[1]

It was thus necessary to define the substantive content and institutional framework of the EES to give EFTA-EC cooperation direction and pace. In June 1990 formal negotiations started between the European Community and the six members of EFTA plus Liechtenstein to do precisely this. These negotiations were triggered by a speech which the President of the EC Commission, Jacques Delors, gave to the European Parliament on 17 January 1989 in Strasbourg. President Delors suggested two options for intensified cooperation between the EC and the EFTA countries:

> ... We can stick to our present relations, essentially bilateral, with the ultimate aim of creating a free trade area encompassing the Community and EFTA; – or, alternatively, we can look for a new, more structured partnership with common decision-making and administrative institutions to make our activities more effective and to highlight the political dimension of our cooperation in the economic, social, financial and cultural spheres.

By speaking of common institutions President Delors held forth the prospect of a quantum leap in EC-EFTA relations. However, it was to prove easier to propose than to achieve. For one thing the leap was of an inherently political nature, requiring decisions at the highest political level. At the same time, it involved a number of down-to-earth issues. It was necessary to clarify what policy rules must be common to the EFTA countries and the EC in order for them to constitute a single market. In particular is an EES customs union necessary in order to integrate the economies of the EFTA and the EC into an extended single market? In his speech, President Delors appeared to assume that this was the case, since he went on to say:

> The single market is first and foremost a customs union. Are our partners prepared to abide by the common commercial policy that any customs union must apply to outsiders? Do they share our basic conceptions? The single market also implies harmonization. Are our partners willing to transpose the common rules essential to the free movement of goods into their domestic law, and, in consequence, accept the supervision of the Court of Justice, which has demonstrated its outstanding competence and impartiality? The same question arises in connection with state aids and the social conditions of fair competition directed towards better living and working conditions.

President Delors' speech was received as a major political initiative. It was, however, not without ambiguities. Thus, it appeared to some – not only on the EFTA side – that Delors was offering the EFTA partners, if they shared the basic conceptions, inter alia the chance to participate in deciding the policies and rules of an EES customs union and in their supervision. It appeared to others – not only on the EC side – that Delors was asking the EFTA countries to abide by such rules as the EC might decide. At first sight it might appear difficult to find a middle course between these two positions. That would be a premature conclusion.

This chapter presents some considerations on the substance and the institutions of the EES which indicate that there is indeed a middle ground of options. Following Delors, it compares the basic principle of a customs union with that of a free trade area as an organizing principle for a common market encompassing goods, services, capital and persons. These basic principles are respectively the application of common policies and autonomous policies towards third countries. One key question is to what extent lack of common external policies would restrict the free movement of goods, services, capital and persons *within* the EES. Another key question is whether, as Delors appeared to imply, existing bilateral arrangements are sufficient in the case of an expanded free trade area, whereas a customs union requires common institutions. The chapter concludes that the essential elements of a single, common market can be realized without common external policies, but that it nevertheless requires common institutions, albeit of a different scope and nature from those implied when common external policies are involved as in a customs union.

The EES designed as a free trade area

Free movement of goods, services, capital and persons would be achieved within the EES *while members' retain decision-making autonomy vis-à-vis third countries*. Thus, barriers to free movement within the EES would have to be abolished as far as is possible in the absence of a common external policy.

How closely can markets be integrated in this option? Can the substantive cooperation implied be based on essentially bilateral relations or are common administrative and rule-making institutions necessary?

Free movement of goods

Since 1973 the movement of industrial goods within the EES has become free from tariffs and quantitative restrictions as a result of the bilateral free trade agreements that each EFTA country has with the Community. By 1984 all such restrictions had been completely abolished.[2] However, numerous non-tariff measures still affect trade in industrial goods and free movement does not extend to non-industrial goods. Thus, considerable scope exists for intensifying EFTA-EC cooperation in this field so that trade between EFTA countries and the EC can take place on the same conditions as those between the EC countries. In addition, two important areas were not covered, namely anti-dumping and anti-subsidy measures.

Important non-tariff measures are differences in standards and certification procedures (technical barriers to trade), and the public procurement practices of central and local authorities. Discriminatory public procurement can distort trade flows. Common rules and legal institutions would be necessary to ensure that an economic operator has equal possibilities to complain about discriminatory public procurement practices wherever they occur in the EES. Without uniform rules uniformly applied, firms in different countries of the EES will not be able to compete on equal conditions for public contracts.

Government measures against unfair trade practices (countervailing duties, anti-dumping measures) can in themselves constitute unjustified barriers to trade.[3] Anti-dumping and anti-subsidy measures are not used within the EC. Instead Community institutions have strong powers to oversee and enforce the rules of Community competition policy and state aids so that trade within the EC is not distorted. It would be logical to extend this principle to the whole EES. This would require the EFTA countries and the EC to apply a common competition policy vis-à-vis trade flows within the EES. Common policy rules would, in turn, have to be administered and enforced by common bodies to ensure their consistent application over the whole EES. Thus, common rules and institutions would be necessary even within an improved free trade area. This would require major systemic changes by the EFTA countries.

Free movement of services

Effective market access in services requires not only free cross-border trade but also free establishment for service producers. In the past effective market access has been prevented by the existence of national regulatory regimes for various service sectors both in the EC and in various EFTA countries. This has often included effective limitations on, or outright prohibition of, foreign establishments. Examples include financial services, where governments grant establishment rights, and transport services, where governments award traffic rights.

However, the EC is in the process of achieving free intra-Community establishment for services based on the principles of mutual recognition and home country control subject to common minimum standards. This is the basic principle embodied in the Second Banking Directive and is being extended to other areas.

If this principle were applied on a reciprocal basis also in EFTA countries it would constitute a major extension of EFTA-EC cooperation by establishing a single market for services encompassing the EES. By employing the principle of mutual recognition of national systems rather than the principle of harmonization of national regulatory regimes the need for common EES institutions would be reduced. Some common institutions for surveillance and enforcement of minimum rules would nevertheless be required. They would, however, be institutions for the administration of existing rules rather than for deciding new common rules. The end result might be de facto harmonization of regulatory regimes, but this would be the outcome of 'competition among rules' as firms and governments adjusted to the new situation.

As in goods, the EES parties would not conduct a common policy vis-à-vis third countries in this option. Therefore, the right of free establishment would have to be limited to institutions originating in EES countries. This would require a system of 'rules of origin' for e.g. financial institutions, so that a third country bank establishing itself in an 'open' EFTA country would not automatically have the right to move freely into other countries in the EES.

Free movement of capital and persons

If all participating countries liberalize capital movements on an *erga omnes* basis there is no need for common institutions. But if they want to have binding commitments and control over the use of safeguard measures in this context there would be such a need. Free movement of persons is not a necessary corollary of a free trade area, but there is nothing to stop participating countries making access to each other's labour markets easier by relaxing national rules.

Implications

This first option is the traditional approach used in EFTA-EC relations, as exemplified by the bilateral free trade agreements. It extends EC-EFTA cooperation within the EES to new areas while maintaining autonomy in policies vis-à-vis non-EES countries. It does not require comprehensive change in the relationship, but systemic change is needed in specific areas. Therefore, this option limits but does not eliminate the need for common institutions.

Internal border controls will continue to be necessary owing to the lack of common external policies. The question is whether their existence segments the single market encompassing all EES countries and whether their costs are an important consideration. Border controls need not segment markets – except in such cases where this is precisely the political objective (e.g. to prevent free trade in agricultural goods). On the contrary, they are necessary to ensure equal conditions of competition within the EES by offsetting internally the effects of different external policies. This involves a cost, which, however, is likely to be small. Because of their geographic characteristics, most EFTA countries cannot separate EES-internal border controls from what would be external border controls. These external controls will still be required and can also serve to provide the limited EES-internal controls that will be needed. For some purposes, spot checks inside borders can even replace controls at the border. Thus, the cost of limited internal border checks is unlikely to be an important consideration. Nevertheless, work to make border controls less costly in terms of time and money should continue (simplification of border formalities and of rules of origin).

Thus, also in the absence of a common external policy, equal conditions of competition are possible throughout the EES at little additional cost. However, this will require some common institutions both for industrial goods and for services. In industrial goods, the bilateral approach of the Luxembourg process is insufficient. In services and capital movements, coordination – but not harmonization – of regulatory regimes is necessary. Common institutions are necessary to manage sets of rules jointly determined at the outset. However, they have primarily an administrative rather than of a rule-making function. This is an important distinction.

The EES designed as a customs union

The second option involves applying common policies towards third countries, as in a customs union, the EC's historically preferred method of integration. Free movement of goods, services, capital and persons would be realized within the EES as in the first option, but in addition members would harmonize policies vis-à-vis third countries. Key questions here are whether a customs union is sufficient for a single market, in the sense of abolishing internal border controls, and what kind of institutions it requires. Consider first the substantive implications of this option.

Industrial goods

The EC and the EFTA countries would have to harmonize their policies vis-à-vis third countries in at least the following major respects: tariff measures, non-tariff measures, safeguard measures (including grey-zone measures) and measures against 'unfair trade' practices such as dumping and subsidies.

The parties in an EES customs union would have initially to harmonize their tariff rates, and thereafter *keep* rates harmonized. This applies both to rates generally applied (most-favoured-nation rates) and to lower rates applied toward a particular country or group of countries (preferential rates). In practical terms this means that the EFTA countries and the Community would have to agree on a substantially common tariff schedule.[4] In accordance with GATT rules, the common tariff regime cannot on the whole be more restrictive than the pre-union regimes. In practice, the common tariff schedule for industrial goods would approximate some average of the EC's and the EFTA countries' current rates, about 4.2% and 3% respectively.[5] If this were an import-weighted average, the EES customs union would have an average rate of about 4.0%, implying a minor reduction by the EC and a significant increase by the EFTA countries.

The adjustment would be least for the Nordic EFTA countries since their average tariff rates on industrial goods are close to the EES weighted average.[6] A major reduction, on average, would be required by Austria (from 5.7% to 4%) and a major increase by Switzerland (from 1.9% to 4%). In all EFTA countries, significantly greater adjustments would be required in some individual commodity groups.[7]

Thus, all EFTA countries other than Austria would have to raise their tariffs on average. If these rates are bound, GATT rules give other GATT members the right to ask for compensation. When determining what compensation is reasonable, the tariff reductions by the EC and by Austria are to be taken into consideration. A one-sided adjustment of EFTA countries' rates to the existing levels of the EC would result in reductions only by Austria.

The EES customs union would also have to apply a common set of rules for preferential tariff treatment. EFTA countries provide preferences to developing countries under the generalized system of preferences (GSP). These systems differ from country to country within EFTA but characteristic of them is that each national system treats all developing countries equally. Some EFTA countries give MFN treatment to CMEA countries. The Community has a more varied system of preferences. It gives the APC states preferential treatment through the Lomé Convention. In addition, it has preferential arrangements with a number of non-European Mediterranean States and association agreements with Turkey, Cyprus and Malta. In some of these, the EC enjoys preferential treatment. The EC system can be characterized as a hierarchy of preferences determined by historical and geopolitical considerations. Adjustment of EFTA countries' preferential systems to the EC's would involve a major revision of EFTA countries' trade policies toward developing countries.

The EFTA countries and the EC would also have to employ the same safeguard measures vis-à-vis third countries (including those under GATT's Article XIX and grey-zone measures). The EC countries, individually and through the Community, are major users of such measures, surpassing on some counts the United States. They have used them primarily against non-European exporters in the form of 'voluntary' restraint arrangements in a number of fields for protectionist reasons. The EFTA countries have used these instruments much more sparingly. Adoption of the EC's current safeguard policies would therefore constitute a significant policy shift for the EFTA countries.

Control over these instruments remains in the hands of member governments in many cases and is made effective through Article 115 of the Treaty of Rome which allows EC members to retain internal border controls. According to the White Paper this control will be transferred to the Commission. The pace and ultimate scope of the transfer is as yet somewhat unclear.

The EFTA countries and the EC would also have to apply the same measures against alleged unfair trade practices by third countries. Anti-dumping and anti-subsidy measures are currently Community instruments: cases against third countries are filed by the Community and not by member states. The EC has used these instruments increasingly actively. Most EFTA countries have used these instruments more sparingly than the Community. Also in this respect a customs union might require a significant policy shift for the EFTA countries.

Services

The distinction between a free trade area and a customs union can be applied to services as well as to goods. Liberalization of services involves free establishment as well as free cross-border trade in services. The main issues concerning a common policy against third countries in services are then connected with the rights of establishment vis-à-vis third countries. In financial services, for instance, the Community is expected to grant the right of first establishment of subsidiaries to third country banks, insurance companies and security dealers on a reciprocal basis. This same policy would have to be applied also by the EFTA countries against third countries in this 'customs union' approach.

Implications

Adoption of the common policies towards third countries within the customs union model involves two steps. First, current policies must be subjected to a one-shot harmonization. Thereafter, common policies towards third countries must be continually formulated and implemented. The outcome of the immediate harmonization is rather predictable. The EFTA countries would have to align themselves to EC policies concerning tariffs and non-tariff measures vis-à-vis third countries. These policies are on the whole more protectionist than the EFTA countries' current policies. An EES customs union would therefore involve non-negligible welfare costs in the short run for most EFTA countries. In addition agreement must be reached on how to distribute the tariff revenues of the customs union among the participating states.

The policy outcomes of the accompanying rule-making processes are less predictable. They depend partly on what influence EFTA countries would have in the formulation of the EES's future policies. Major issues are at stake here. An EES customs union must continuously formulate common positions within the GATT on trade disputes and on negotiations in future GATT rounds. It must decide how to use safeguard measures and measures against unfair trade. The institutions of a customs union have decision-making functions as well as administrative functions. In this respect, there is a significant difference in kind between this option and the first.

A member of a customs union loses exclusive control over commercial policy variables. In exchange, it gains some control over its partners' policies through the common rule-making institution. This is the purpose of shared sovereignty. Thus, an EES customs union would necessarily dilute present Community members' rule-making power, but it would also extend this power to the EFTA countries' policies. Each EFTA member faces a similar dilemma in sharing sovereignty with its EES partners. It loses exclusive control over its own commercial policy but gains an influence over their policies. Each party must judge whether this simultaneous dilution and extension of its rule-making powers strikes an appropriate balance of advantage. An important consideration will be whether a new member shares basic conceptions with a sufficiently large group to influence decisions.

A customs union encompassing all goods is necessary to abolish the need for border controls within the EES. However, it is not sufficient. Governments must maintain a capacity to check EES internal trade flows, if they wish to maintain autonomy over politically motivated trade embargoes or to maintain significantly different rates of indirect taxes.

Conclusion

The pairing of common institutions/customs union and bilateral arrangements/free trade area is too simplistic. A larger number of combinations of substance and institutional arrangements is available. An EES common market characterized throughout by equal conditions of competition can be achieved both without common external policies and with. In both cases, common institutions would be necessary. There is no escape from common institutions if the EES is to be a functioning, single market.

However, these institutions are of a somewhat different character in the two options. Without common external policies, the institutions can be of an administrative nature to a larger extent. Their task is to implement and manage rules or regulatory systems agreed upon at the outset. In most cases the effectiveness of these rules requires that they are stable and not subject to continual revision. Economic operators need credible and stable rules.

Common external policies require in addition common decision-making institutions. Policies towards third countries cannot be predetermined at the outset and thereafter administratively implemented. By their nature, they require a continuous stream of policy decisions. Common rule-making by the parties of the EES poses fundamental questions of principle to EC and EFTA countries.

It will be no easy matter for any party to add up the costs and benefits of the substantive content and the institutional framework. In terms of substantive content, both sides must weigh the benefits of reducing (but not completely eliminating) the need for internal border controls in a customs union type arrangement against the welfare costs and benefits of aligning to EC-dominated common external policies. For the EFTA countries this is likely to constitute a net cost, for the EC a relatively small net benefit.

In terms of institutional framework, both sides must assess the political costs and benefits of sharing sovereignty. Both sides are likely to perceive the necessity for common administrative institutions in the EES. Sharing power in common rule-making institutions is much more difficult. At present, it seems as though it would be more difficult for the EC to make the offer to share rule-making in EES matters with EFTA countries than for the latter to accept such an offer. The EC appears to prefer a system where it decides and EFTA abides. This is unacceptable on the EFTA side. At the moment, therefore, it looks as though the substantive content of the EES will lie in those areas where common institutions can be limited to having primarily administrative functions.

Notes

1. J. Leskelä and S. Parviainen, *EFTA Countries' Foreign Direct Investments* (Geneva, EFTA Occasional Paper 34, 1990).
2. The fact that a free trade area already exists in industrial goods suggests that President Delors was using the concept in a generic rather than specific sense.
3. See J.M. Finger, 'Anti-dumping and Anti-subsidy Measures', in J.M. Finger and A. Olechowski, eds. *The Uruguay Round: A Handbook for the Multilateral Trade Negotiations* (The World Bank, Washington DC, 1987).
4. The GATT requirement in Article XXIV is that members apply 'substantially the same duties and other regulations'.
5. J. Herin, *Rules of Origin and Differences between Tariff Levels in EFTA and the EC* (Geneva, EFTA Occasional Paper 13, 1986).
6. In Switzerland, the average level of tariff protection would have to be raised from the current 1.9% to about 4%. Austria would have to reduce its average level of industrial tariff protection from about 5.7% to about 4%.
7. In Austria the structure of protection is more uneven than in other EFTA countries or in the Community. While a lower and more uniform tariff protection would bring allocative advantages to the Austrian economy, major restructuring would follow in some industries.

The author alone is responsible for the views expressed in this chapter.

5b Extending the EES to Services

Michael Klein

The EFTA countries have highly sophisticated economies with well over half of their civilian employment in the service sector, although – relative to most EC countries – the primary sector, which includes agriculture, fishery and forestry, is also quite prominent.

Four – Finland, Iceland, Norway and Sweden – are net service importers, with Sweden, the second largest economy, importing the most. Norway's deficit, in comparison with the similar-sized Finnish economy, is low, because of its relatively high earnings in the transport sector through its merchant fleet. The volume of Norway's service flows are comparable with those of Sweden, even though its economy is only half the size.

Of the two surplus countries, Switzerland, the largest EFTA economy, derives its substantial credit balance in services mainly from investment income, followed by travel earnings. Austria's surplus is based on its tourist industries. Austria is most dependent on services as a revenue earner, with almost half of its income derived from trade comprising invisibles. For each of the three, services account for 16% or so of national income. Thus for Austria, Switzerland and Norway, trade in services is very important, while for Iceland, Finland and Sweden, each averaging around 20% of trade dependence in services, the invisibles category does not warrant the same special attention. For these three, invisibles make a relatively low contribution to national income, an average of 8%.

EC actions in the services sector obviously have a major impact on EFTA economics. Consequently, it is important for them to keep to a minimum potential discrimination as a result of the 1992 process. As liberalization within the EC process continues, the problems for third parties of securing equal market access grow. For most services, market access is achieved by free establishment as well as free cross-border trade. Authorization and supervision within the EC will be based largely on home-country control and mutual recognition, subject to commonly agreed minimum standards so as to ensure consumer protection and avoid systemic risk. It has been suggested by the Commission that the principles governing EC service liberalization could be extended to cover countries outside the Community.[1] EFTA countries have been closely following the developments within the EC, and most of them have already adopted provisions of relevant EC directives, or are planning to do so. This creates the basis for even closer EC-EFTA cooperation and is a step towards a European-wide financial market. Against the background of the international work done within the Cooke Committee, under the auspices of the Bank for International Settlements (BIS), on bank supervision and the consistency of the Basle Concordat with the EC directive, the Commission's suggestion was only logical.[2]

The 'rules of origin' principle, applied to financial institutions, has the advantage of minimizing the need for a common policy towards third countries. EFTA countries would not be required to change their existing policies dramatically, while EC policy seems not to be aimed at creating a 'fortress Europe'. By encouraging foreign, i.e. EFTA, financial service providers to compete within the Community, the Commission hopes to create an environment which fosters efficiency and innovation so as to take on the Japanese and US challenge. The EFTA countries are expected to follow this 'enlightened' approach by allowing, in return, access to their domestic markets by EC financial institutions. A single licence would then enable a financial institution to take up business anywhere within the EES, where, because of the differing national legal frameworks, conduct of business would most probably be applied on a host-country basis. Despite the current integration and liberalization drives, there will probably be no major effect in the banking sector on how the business is done, except that it will be conducted at a more competitive pace especially at the retail end. In the insurance sector, however, the changes will be significant and there is likely to be more 'competition among rules'.

A prerequisite for a unified European market in services is the liberalization of capital transactions. Most EFTA countries still operate a restrictive exchange-rate regime. With the abolition of most intra-EC capital regulations by July 1990, the onus is now on the individual EFTA members to do likewise.

There are two differing approaches to the abolition of barriers to trade in services. The vertical one envisages that specific barriers to trade be dealt with and negotiated away separately. Proponents of a horizontal strategy seek to establish common rules and principles as regards service trade with which all parties have to conform. There are some fears that in practice individual deals may tend to produce convergence on standards, increasing the vulnerability of the whole system. Which approach will predominate only time will tell. There can be no doubt, however, that a unified European service market which removed existing inefficiencies would give additional impulses to sustained economic growth and thus be in the interests of both the EC and EFTA.

The EC-Switzerland agreement on insurance

One concrete example of EC-EFTA cooperation in services is the insurance agreement signed on 1 June 1989 between the Commission and the Swiss authorities, the result of 13 years of negotiations. These started in 1976 on a Swiss initiative, as a reaction to the directive on insurance agreed by the EC in 1973, and were also in line with OECD efforts to promote liberalization.[3] The Swiss economy is very closely intertwined with the EC: Swiss foreign direct investment within the EC amounts to 25 billion Swiss francs, generating employment for some 350,000 EC citizens. About 25% (some 750,000) of the Swiss working population are foreign, of which 600,000 are from the EC. In total, therefore, almost one million EC citizens are employed by Swiss companies. In terms of foreign trade patterns in goods and services, as well as direct investment flows and the resulting employment, the economic integration of Switzerland with the EC is in fact more extensive than that of Ireland or Greece. This economic potential gives Switzerland a strong negotiating position.

With the adoption of the 1989 insurance agreement, the Swiss authorities have shown that concrete results can be reached with the EC (often more uncompromising with third countries) without having to consider the membership option. The agreement, which covers non-life insurance, stipulates equal access by Swiss and EC insurance companies to each other's markets. Firms are given the right of establishment and, to the extent that this is already possible within the EC, the right to do business across borders. In addition, the agreement abolishes the obligation of having to transfer funds in national currency into the respective markets, which would otherwise have been required as a guarantee for company solvency because supervisory rules and regulations from outside the EC were not recognized by the authorities of EC member states. This solvency guarantor obligation had not only been discriminatory but also represented an additional cost to companies, vulnerable to unforeseeable exchange-rate movements.

The insurance agreement was close to adoption in 1982, but it failed because of an EC veto. The Commission was concerned that, given the binding form of the agreement, it would be unable to develop future insurance policies independently. The Swiss would have acquired an indirect say in Community legislation. The Swiss suggested in the spring of 1988 the insertion of a 'flexibility' clause, by which the parties would, in the event of new developments, enter into new negotiations to reach appropriate agreements. If no consensus could be reached, the agreement would after six months automatically become invalid. For this reason the clause has also been labelled a 'self-destruct' clause.[4] The agreement can be seen from the Swiss point of view as an insurance for the future, since Swiss companies will, by virtue of their common market status, not be discriminated against. This special bilateral deal was very important for Switzerland. The insurance sector is both prominent in the Swiss economy and dependent on foreign markets. The insurance sector provides employment for about 40,000 people in Switzerland, but in a small and highly saturated national market. The Swiss insurance density is among the highest in the world, making up 16% of real disposable income; it ranks first in importance for the domestic consumer, ahead of housing and food. The lion's share (75%) of total insurance expenditure is made up of mandatory social insurance contributions, with private insurance taking the rest.

The extent and importance of foreign involvement for the Swiss insurance sector is easily demonstrated: the Swiss share of world GDP in 1982 was 1.1%, whereas its share of world insurance business was almost double at 2.1%.[5] Two of the ten biggest European insurance companies are under Swiss control (Zürich Versicherung and Winterthur), as is Schweizer Rück, the second largest reinsurer in the world. Because of the limited domestic market, economies of scale can be achieved only by international, particularly European, trade. For a country with few natural raw materials, this insurance income makes a particularly welcome and positive contribution to the balance of payments. In 1986, more than 50% of the total premiums were collected abroad, with 40% originating in the EC. In life insurance, over 90% of foreign premiums were collected in the EC, while for non-life and reinsurance business the figure is 50%. In volume terms, the EC share is larger than the domestic one.[6] The Swiss would have had much to lose if they had been left on the margins of the legal harmonization process within the EC. While legally incorporated and duly authorized third-country insurance subsidiaries are given EC status, this is not automatically the case for agencies and branches. The purpose of the agreement was thus to ensure that Swiss institutions, under a reciprocity condition, would be put on an equal footing with their EC competitors in each other's markets.

One of the main lessons emerging from this Swiss exerience is that the EC must get its own house in order, and have finished its internal legislative process, before any outside agreements can be reached. It is revealing, too, that the EC used as its legal basis for the negotiating process Article 29 of the 1973 directive,[7] i.e. secondary Community law, while the Swiss side used the evolutionary clause of the FTA. It may, therefore, be argued that outsiders should be encouraging the current integrative drive within the EC in the interests of a wider European economic cooperation. This agreement could perhaps be a model for other areas of services, where EFTA countries could be given the opportunity of access to the EC market on the basis of reciprocity in the common market, thus helping to build an EES. Until EC policy is agreed and consequently a negotiating basis is established, the EFTA countries can best serve their industries by actively following relevant EC activities, and analysing their possible consequences for their domestic markets.

A cognate case arose between the Norwegian government and the EC on transport issues, because the Norwegian merchant fleet is comparable with the Swiss insurance sector as far as its national economic importance and foreign market dependence goes. There were in 1988 a series of informal contacts between the Norwegian government and the EC about maritime transport, but no formal direct talks. The EC was still engaged in trying to establish its own policy goals in the field.

Services thus offer scope for the EC approach of mutual recognition to be extended to a wider grouping, once the EC has itself achieved agreement internally on the key issues and provided that it has enough interest to work for an agreement. In the Swiss-EC insurance case, the field of economic integration pushed the negotiations forward to an agreement. Even so it look a long time, it is a complex document and it is vulnerable to any major shift in EC policy. This would suggest that there may not be scope for countless issue-specific bilateral deals between the EC and individual EFTA countries.

Notes

1. Sir Leon Brittan, speech in Copenhagen, 31 August 1989.
2. *The Financial Times*, 1 September 1989.

3. Code of Liberalization of Current Invisible Operators and Code of Liberalization of Capital Movements, both adopted by OECD on 12 December 1961.
4. *The Financial Times*, 27 July 1989.
5. Estimates from O. Jenni, 'The Swiss insurance market in the world context', *Schweizerische Versicherungswirtschaft*, 1984.
6. Dr Charles Wyniger, 'Die schweizerische Assekuranz und der Europäische Binnenmarket für Versicherungen', in *Versicherungkurier*, February 1989.
7. Article 29 states: 'The Community may be means of agreements concluded pursuant to the Treaty with one or more third countries, agree to the application of provisions different to those provided for in this Title, for the purpose of ensuring, under conditions of reciprocity, adequate protection for insured persons in the Member States.' *Official Journal*, 05L228, 16 August 1973.

6 The Monetary Dimension

Jens Thomsen

Norway and Denmark were members of the European Community snake almost from its inception in 1972. Sweden became a member in March 1973 but left in 1977, while Norway stayed in until 1978. Sweden left because it feared that the close link with the Deutschmark (DM) would lead to a low rate of exchange vis-à-vis the dollar. Norway, however, decided to leave for political reasons, fearing that the European Monetary System (EMS) would be a back door to integration into the European Community. Switzerland once applied for membership of the snake, but was not accepted.

In the period since the creation of the EMS the Austrian Schilling has followed the DM very closely, making Austria a *de facto* but not a *de jure* EMS member. Austrian interest rates have similarly been closely linked to German rates. (see Figs. 6.1 and 6.2.)

The Swiss authorities have not followed a strategy of the Austrian kind on the DM, although monetary policy may be corrected in the event of a large movement in the DM rate. In practice the Swiss franc has not fluctuated widely in relation to the DM since the beginning of the 1980s. Swiss interest rates have followed German rates, though not as closely as the Austrian rates (see Figs. 6.2 and 6.3).

In the 1980s Sweden, Norway and Finland based their policies on currency baskets, which resulted in considerable fluctuations in relation to the EMS. Since the large devaluation of the Swedish krone in 1982, the Swedish government has emphasized that it would not pursue an active exchange rate policy any further (see Figs. 6.4 and 6.5). Iceland is not discussed in this chapter.

Associate membership of EMS

The decision establishing the EMS allows for association agreements (Art. 5.2): 'European countries with particularly close economic and financial ties with the European Communities may participate in the exchange rate and intervention mechanism. Participation will be based upon agreements between central banks; these agreements will be communicated to the Council and the Commission of the European Communities.'

No country has applied for association, although Norway and Austria made inquiries on the terms in 1989. In autumn 1978, when the EMS was first dis-

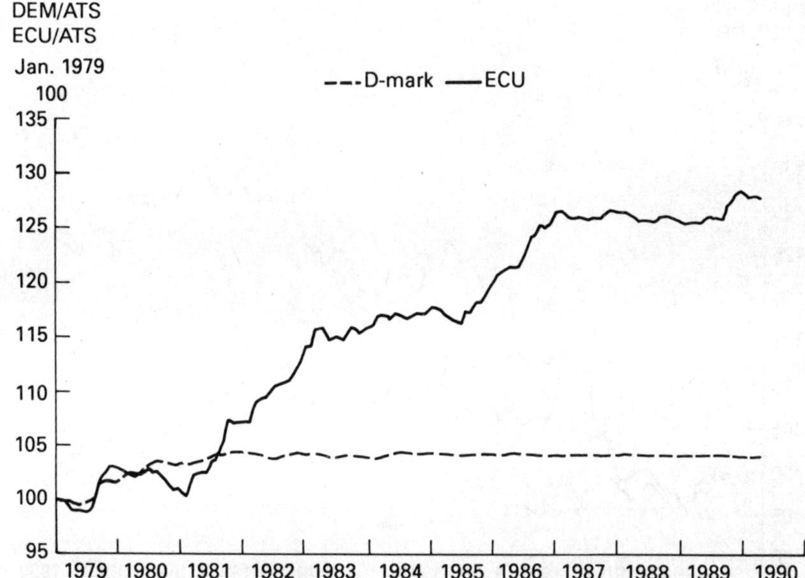

Fig. 6.1 D-mark and ECU vis-à-vis Austrian schilling

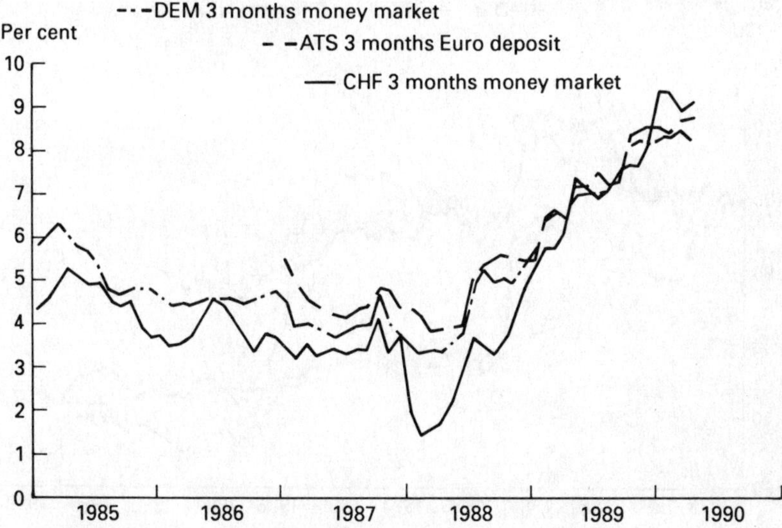

Fig. 6.2 Interest rates

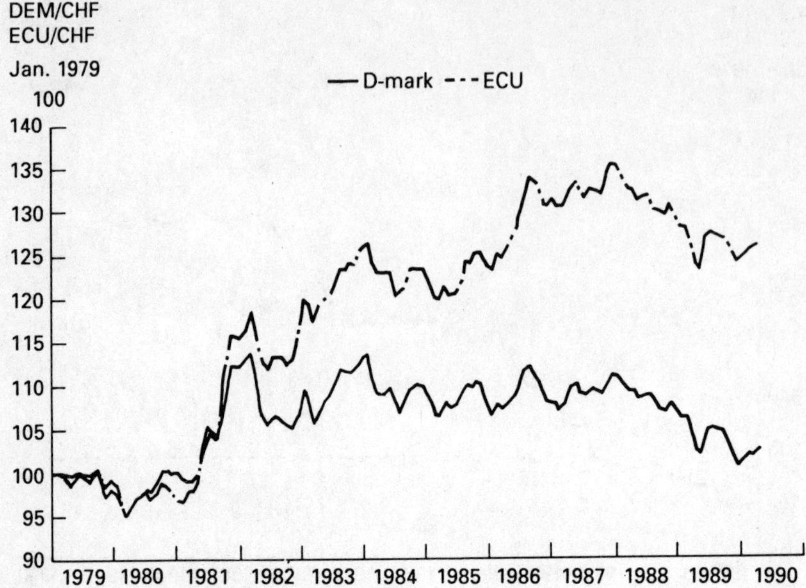

Fig. 6.3 D-mark and ECU vis-à-vis Swiss francs

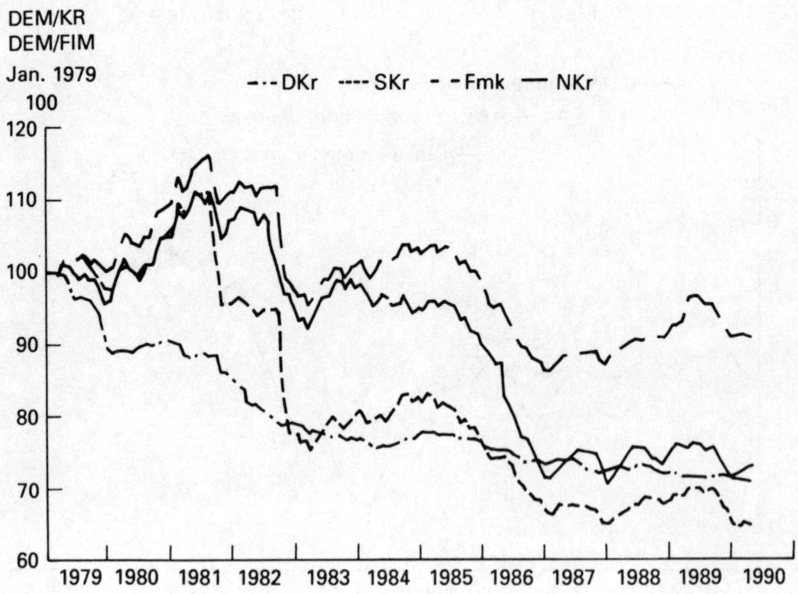

Fig. 6.4 D-mark vis-à-vis Nordic currencies

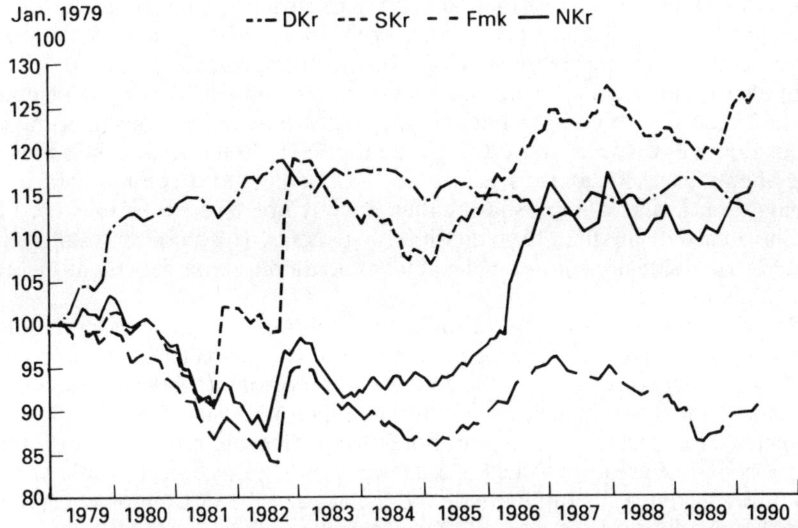

Fig. 6.5 Nordic currencies vis-à-vis ECU

cussed, Norway was expected to apply, but decided not to, mainly for political reasons. The number of countries eligible as associate members is probably small. It is of course difficult to foresee the exact terms of association, but the association agreements under which Sweden and Norway were linked to the snake could be taken as a model. An alternative could be that the third country establishes a central rate and a fluctuation band vis-à-vis the ECU or against an ERM currency (e.g. the DM). Only the third country would defend these margins by unlimited interventions. The EC central banks could make very short-term credit facilities available. The EMS has, however, extended well beyond the central bank agreements of 1979 to become an essential part of the Community fabric. This makes the snake model less relevant. The fact that the EMS is discussed during meetings of Ecofin (Council of Ministers of the Economy and Finance), not during special meetings restricted to EMS (formally exchange rate mechanism (ERM)) members as was the case for the snake, could complicate the institutional arrangements. Furthermore, the revised convergence decisions have strengthened the surveillance procedures in the context of stage one of the EMU. How to involve the associated countries in this process is an important question. The discussions take place in Ecofin, in the monetary committee, in the economic policy committee and in the committee of governors. It is unlikely that associated countries could participate in the ordinary meetings of Ecofin, although meetings between Ecofin and the associated countries could be envisaged. Adjustments of bilateral central rates are subject to a common procedure comprising all countries participating in the ERM and the Commission. The realignment meeting is not a Council meeting. This procedure would probably enable associated countries to participate.

Associated currencies would have to participate in the very short-term financing facility (VSTF), a network of credit lines where each central bank makes its own currency available to the other central banks in order to finance compulsory intervention at the margins. Even if immediate settlement could be envisaged, the VSTF is an integral part of the intervention mechanism; any association will therefore have to include the VSTF. In the snake, the VSTF arrangements were bilateral in nature and not subject to a ceiling after 1976. During their snake membership neither Norway nor Sweden was covered by the short-term or medium-term credit arrangements. The medium-term credits related to the EMS are conditional and it would therefore be difficult to include non-EC members.

EMS members deposit 20% of their gold holdings and 20% of their dollar reserves to underpin the European Currency Unit (ECU). These ECUs can be used for transactions between the monetary authorities of the EC. The aim of this arrangement is primarily to mobilize gold holdings. Since the Scandinavian countries have relatively small gold holdings, participation in the arrangement would not be of great importance; it anyway poses no technical problems.

Non-EC currencies could in theory be included in the ECU; in practice, however, this would not be acceptable for political reasons. The ECU is also used for other EC purposes. A country may be a member of the EMS without its currency being included in the ECU, so this does not need to create any problems. Spain was an EMS member from June to September 1989 without the peseta being included in the ECU.

In 1985 the EC Council decision on the EMS was amended to empower the European Fund for Monetary Cooperation (EMCF) to grant non-EC members the status of 'other holders' (Art. 2): 'The Fund is also empowered to grant to the monetary authorities of non-member countries and international monetary institutions the status of "Other Holders" of ecus as referred to in Article 1 and to fix the terms and conditions under which such ECUs may be acquired, held and used.' Switzerland, Norway, Austria, Malta and the Bank of International Settlements (BIS) now have the status of 'other holder'. Some of the 'other holders' possess official ECUs issued by the EMCF but only limited amounts.

Economic and monetary union

Discussions about economic and monetary union started in the Community in the late 1960s. In 1969 the Hague Summit called for such a union. Monetary instability, which had been experienced in 1968 and 1969, was seen as a danger to the Customs Union and to the Common Agricultural Policy. The Werner Report of 1970 established a blueprint for economic and monetary union. In 1971 the Council adopted a resolution on the realization of the EMU by stages. The resolution expressed the political will of member states to establish it within ten years. But by early 1974, in the wake of the first oil crisis, it had become impossible for the Council to effect a painless transition to the second stage of the EMU.

The snake remained. It was envisaged as a 'snake in the tunnel' to reduce margins between EC currencies from ±1.5% to ±1.2%, while the margin to the dollar remained ±0.75%. The decision to establish the snake was, however, taken after the Smithsonian agreement of 1971 which had widened the intra-EC margin to ±4.5%. The snake limited this margin to ±2.25%. For a brief period in spring 1972 the snake included all nine EC countries and Norway, and from 1973 to 1977 it also included Sweden. However, by 1978 only the DM, the Benelux currencies and the Danish and the Norwegian krone remained in the snake.

EMS

In 1979 the European Monetary System was established. It was based on the principles of the snake, especially the parity grid and the obligatory intervention at the margins. The credit arrangements were increased and the central banks contributed 20% of their gold and dollar reserves against the ECU. The resolution on the EMS stated that: 'we remain firmly resolved to consolidate, not later than two years after the start of the scheme, into a final system the provisions and procedures thus created. The system will entail the creation of the European Monetary Fund.'

The European Council did not discuss the specific features of a European Monetary Fund. It could have been a kind of a regional IMF, a European central bank or a combination of the two. After long technical discussions no political support was available for such a major step. Discussions on the European Monetary Fund stopped in 1982.

The EMS has performed better than expected when it was negotiated in 1978. Aggressive devaluations, like those of Sweden and Australia after the second oil crisis, have been avoided. Several studies support the view that the EMS seems to have reduced the variability of intra-European exchange rates. Inflation rates have, however, only decelerated in line with those of other OECD countries. Gros and Thygesen (1988) discuss the performance of the EMS. Three EC members (Greece, Portugal and the UK) are outside the exchange rate mechanism of the EMS, the members of which remained at eight until the entry of Spain in June 1989.

The rules of the EMS were included in the central bank agreement of March 1979. Minor amendments were adopted in 1985 and 1987, mainly relating to the financing of intervention. The basic operating features – the intervention obligation at the margin, the availability of unlimited very short-term finance facilities for intervention at the margin and the principle that adjustments of central rates are subject to mutual agreement – have remained unchanged.

The Single European Act adopted in 1986 inserted a new article, Art. 102A, in the treaty: 'In so far as further development in the field of economic and monetary policy necessitates institutional changes, the provisions of Article 236 shall be applicable.' Art. 236 stipulates the procedure for amendment of the EEC treaty.

The Delors Report

In 1988 discussions on the European Monetary Union started again. Memoranda were submitted by the German foreign and finance ministers and by the French and Italian finance ministers. The French memo stressed that no single country should assume responsibility for establishing economic and monetary targets. The German foreign minister stressed the need for an independent European central bank (the German model). At the European Council in Hanover in June 1988 the Delors Committee was set up to review the means whereby monetary union might be achieved. It reported in April 1989. Since no country is at present associated to the EMS, the Delors Report does not consider forms of association.

The formal arrangements for a European central bank would have to take into account the nature of European cooperation, but also recognize that it is impossible to decentralize monetary decisions under a system based on irrevocably fixed exchange rates. Under such a system changes in interest rates, reserve requirements and interventions in third currencies cannot be delegated to the participating central banks. At present interest rate decisions are in practice taken by the Bundesbank. In 1988–9 German interest rate changes were usually followed immediately by similar changes in the Netherlands, Belgium, France, Denmark, Austria and Switzerland.

The Delors Report stresses the importance of an independent system of central banks: independent of instructions from national governments and Community authorities, their overriding objective should be the stability of the value of money. Strict limitations on granting credit to public authorities should apply. Although it is not discussed in the Delors Report, non-EC central banks could in theory be members of a European system of central banks.

The Delors Report envisaged in stage one a new procedure that would strengthen economic and fiscal policy coordination, this being the responsibility of the Ecofin Council.

The Community has only a very limited budget, at present equivalent to 1% of Community GNP. This percentage will probably rise, but not by more than 1–2 points. In federations like Canada, the USA and Australia the share is about 20%, in Germany 30% and in Switzerland 10%. The role of the individual EC members would be much more important than that of the individual states, provinces, länder or cantons within these federations.

Agreement on fiscal policy coordination will be difficult to achieve. The Delors Report proposed that the Council should have the authority to impose constraints on national budgets to the extent to which this proves necessary to prevent imbalances. This aspect of the Delors Report has been criticized and the considerable difficulties in establishing budget constraints have been emphasized (House of Commons 1989). In line with the United States and Canada, it has been proposed not to introduce binding rules for budget policies and not to give a Community guarantee that member states in financial difficulties will be bailed out; it has also been proposed to restrict member states from creating money to finance budget deficits. Under such circumstances, any possible association of EFTA countries with the proposed monetary union would not encounter the problems posed in a system with binding budget rules.

Sweden, Norway and Finland have higher inflation rates than Germany. Membership of the EMS could, however, help to stabilize prices, as the EMS would be an anchor for expectations. Switzerland and Austria already have very low inflation rates (see Fig. 6.6). In the 1980s the Swedish and the Finnish

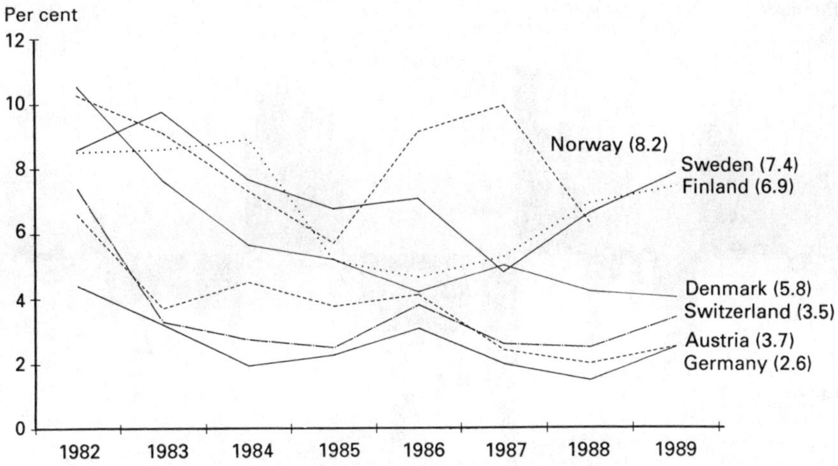

Note: Norway 1982–8; mainland Norway only, Numbers in brackets illustrate the average annual growth rate during the period.
Source: OECD, *Economic Outlook*, and *Statistisk sentralbyra in Norway*.

Fig. 6.6 GDP-deflator, 1982–9: annual growth rates

balances of payments were generally in deficit, while the Swiss showed a large surplus. The Austrian external account was in approximate equilibrium and Norway had large surpluses or deficits depending on the price of oil (see Fig. 6.7).

In Europe the mobility of capital, goods and labour is clearly lower than in the USA. The single market will help to increase mobility by reducing barriers. However, after 1992 some barriers, e.g. language, will remain. Under the existing EMS exchange rate adjustments are already few and small. It is therefore important to promote other measures to increase mobility.

For all the five EFTA countries mentioned above, EC purchases of their exports are quite high and their economies can be considered as open (Table 6.1). Petroleum products account for a large proportion of Norwegian exports, which consequently have a higher degree of specialization than those of other EFTA countries. There are some restrictions on factor movements between EFTA and the EC which do not exist in the EC. The bilateral agreements do not, for example, include free movement of labour. A separate Nordic agreement allows for free movement of labour between the Nordic countries.

The decision to free movements of capital requires EC member states to abolish all restrictions on such movements within the Community. Member states have in practice discriminated against outsiders to only a very limited degree. All the EMS members have agreed to liberalize their remaining capital restrictions, most of them by July 1990, with Spain and Ireland to follow by December 1992. While Austria and Switzerland have long had liberal rules on capital movement, the Nordic non-EC countries have traditionally been

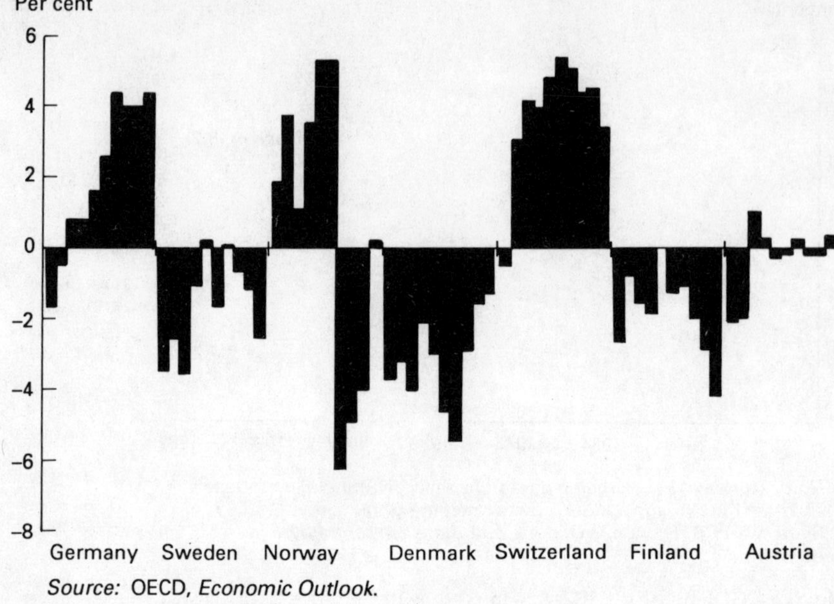

Source: OECD, *Economic Outlook.*

Fig. 6.7 The balance of payments as percentage of GDP, 1980–9

Table 6.1 Structure of trade in Denmark and the EFTA countries

Country	*Imports from* *EEC* %	*Imports from* *EFTA* %	*Exports to* *EEC* %	*Exports to* *EFTA* %	*Exports as % of GDP*
Denmark	51	24	50	25	32
Sweden	56	17	52	20	32
Finland	44	19	44	20	25
Norway	46	24	65	16	36
Austria	68	7	64	11	36
Switzerland	71	7	56	7	36

restrictive. Recently, however, they have reversed their policies, setting in train a process of rapid liberalization. The right of establishment is not covered by the agreement between the EC and the EFTA countries. But here too a more liberal attitude now prevails in both groupings than previously.

As a result of all these developments over the last decade or so the economic policies of the EFTA countries do not differ greatly from those of the EMS countries. The association of EFTA countries with the EMS should therefore neither be too difficult for any of the former nor create economic problems for the latter. For the moment the EC countries are engaged in discussions of the Delors Report and of the future of monetary cooperation within the Community. They have agreed to start the first stage of EMU on 1 July 1990, and an intergovernmental conference on the economic and monetary union will begin in December 1990. In a period of intensification of European monetary cooperation, it is more difficult to find a workable solution to a request for association. However, it is also in the Community's interest to extend the zone of monetary stability to other European countries.

References

Committee for the Study of Economic and Monetary Union (1989) *Report on Economic and Monetary Union in the European Community* (Brussels).

Gros, D., and Thygesen, N. (1988) *The EMS, Achievements, Current Issues and Directions for the Future*, CEPS paper no. 35 (Brussels).

House of Commons, Treasury and Civil Service Committee (1989) *The Delors Report*, HC 341 (London).

Svensson, L.O. (1989) *Finansiell integration, resursfördelning och penningpolitik in Svensk Ekonomi och Europaintegrationen* (Stockholm).

Thomsen, J. (1990) *Det europæiske monetære samarbejde* (Copenhagen).

Thygesen, N. (1987) 'Is the EEC an Optimal Currency Area?' in Levich, R., and Sommariva, A. (eds), *The ECU Market* (Lexington).

7 The Consequences for EFTA of the Internal Energy Market

Janne Haaland Matlary

This chapter analyses the possible consequences for EFTA countries of the internal market in energy under two scenarios: membership; and adaptation without membership. The first section outlines the energy structures of EFTA countries, comparing and contrasting them. The second section analyses the EC Commission's proposals for an internal market in energy. The final section attempts to show how the different EFTA countries may fare under the scenarios of membership versus adaptation.

Energy in the EFTA countries

The EFTA countries form a heterogeneous group in the energy sector as elsewhere. Norway stands out as the major energy producer and exporter of the group, whereas all the others are dependent on imports to a large degree. Austria imports almost all its gas from the USSR, while Switzerland relies on nuclear energy to offset dependence on oil imports. Finland also relies on the Soviet Union for all its gas and oil imports in a counter-trade arrangement. Sweden is in a transition period, probably moving away from nuclear energy which was banned as a result of a referendum in 1981. Iceland imports its oil from the Soviets in exchange for fish. All the countries have energy policies, and none of them relies primarily on market forces to solve energy problems.

In the following outline of the most important features of each country's energy picture, special attention is paid to import dependencies, the use which is made of different fuels and the organization of the energy sector.[1] These factors are particularly relevant to the proposals for an internal market in energy in the EC.

Austria

A great deal of energy is transported through Austria, especially natural gas going from the USSR to Western Europe. Austria thus has an important role as a transit country. It was until recently completely dependent on the Soviet Union for gas. However, in winter 1987 the public gas company ÖMV contracted to purchase 1 BCM from Norwegian Statoil. This will mean a diversification of Austrian gas imports by about one-third, from the early 1990s. However, the issue of transportation has not yet been resolved. The gas will have to be transported through the network owned by Ruhrgas. Ruhrgas and Statoil have been negotiating over the issue of transportion.[2]

Austrian national production of energy is declining. Hydroelectric power is the main domestic source of energy, covering 70% of demand for electricity and 25% of total demand for energy. Oil makes up around 36% of demand for energy, gas 16% and coal about 20%. All oil and gas is imported. The 1986 energy plan aims to reduce dependence on oil imports by conservation and energy switching. Total demand for energy is not expected to rise significantly in the foreseeable future. Imports are expected to decline to 56% of total energy requirements by the year 2005, in contrast to a 63% import dependence (total gas and oil) in 1985 when dependence on oil imported from OPEC countries was 46%, while COMECON countries supplied 72% of coal, 24% of oil, 98% of natural gas and 49% of electricity.

Price controls for natural gas and electricity are set by the *Länder* governments. Prices of diesel oil and petrol are regulated. An official licence is required for the export and import of oil and coal.

The Austrians have recently adopted stringent measures on conservation and the protection of the environment. Emissions from oil refineries and power plants are strictly controlled; so are automobile emissions. Ordinary petrol is unleaded.

Switzerland

Switzerland is the EFTA country with the most market-oriented energy sector. However, dependence on energy imports and energy security are important factors shaping policy. Energy prices are not regulated, and the cantons have a large degree of autonomy in energy policy. This makes a national energy policy difficult. Referendums in 1983 and 1984 rejected a transfer of authority over energy to the federal government.

Environmental and conservation issues have become prominent in the national energy debate in the recent years because of damage to forests. Nuclear energy is also under review in the aftermath of the Chernobyl accident. However, energy security remains the foremost concern.

Oil import dependence was reduced from 64% in 1973 to 48% in 1986 as a result of fuel switching, with large increases in nuclear energy and a smaller increase in the use of coal. Gas is increasing from its modest share of about 5% of total energy demand. Switzerland has sufficient emergency stocks of oil and oil products to cover more than a three-month period, and coal for a six-month period. It is planning emergency stocks of gas. Food and raw materials are also part of of this comprehensive security system.

Solid fuels make up only a small part of energy consumption, about 5%, whereas oil represents more than 48%. The share of nuclear energy is around 18%, hydroelectric power 27% and gas 5%.

Sweden

Sweden's nuclear programme was abandoned by referendum in 1981. It comprised two nuclear plants which are still in existence. The search for substitute forms of long-term energy has not yet been completed, but gas will probably be the main choice for electricity generation. Hydroelectric power constitutes 30% of electricity production; oil provides about the same amount. Coal, oil and gas requirements come entirely from imports, two-thirds of the oil coming from the North Sea and the rest from OPEC countries. Oil imports are thus well diversified; conservation and fuel switching are expected to reduce oil imports. The government has traditionally had a great deal of control over energy policy and planning, and this continues.

Finland

Finland relies on oil and gas imports from the USSR, in addition to domestic coal and timber. The natural gas network has been extended to Helsinki and could be further extended to the west of the country, if a pipeline were to be built under the gulf of Bothnia to transport gas exports to Sweden. Finnish energy imports are counterbalanced by exports of other goods. The Finns are very anxious to increase their exports, which would mean a higher volume of energy imports from the USSR. This one-sided dependence on Soviet energy imports would pose a problem for Finland in today's EC which, like the IEA, regards diversification of import sources and reduction in import dependence as major goals. However, imports provide less than 50% of primary energy consumption, including gas, oil and coal.[3] The trend is to substitute gas for oil, and to increase the share of nuclear energy in electricity production.

Iceland

Iceland exchanges its fish for oil from the USSR under a barter agreement. However, the share of oil in energy consumption is relatively low, being confined to the transportation sector. For domestic heating, the country relies on geothermal power (hot springs), which, together with hydroelectric power, provides 95% of electricity. This makes up almost 50% of energy use.[4]

Norway

Norway is a net exporter of oil and gas, and is self-sufficient in electricity, which is generated by hydropower. It is therefore in a very favourable position compared to other EFTA countries. The major issue is not to procure energy, but to sell it: as natural gas gradually takes over as Norway's main export, it is bound to sell the majority to the EC countries. Today, petroleum makes up 50% of total exports, including offshore goods and services. Norway therefore views its relationship to the EC internal energy market as of the utmost importance. The ability to sell gas in the next century is crucial in view of recent predictions by the Norwegian Petrolum Directorate that oil resources will be seriously depleted in about fifteen years' time.[5]

The consequences for Norway of an internal energy market in the EC are thus very different from those of the other EFTA countries, and are discussed separately below.[6]

Most EFTA countries share a heavy reliance on imports of oil and, to a lesser extent, other fuels such as gas. Three countries stand out in their energy dependence on a single main source of oil and/or gas: Austria, Finland and Iceland. Norway differs from the other EFTA members in being a net energy exporter. All countries except Switzerland have a strongly centralized national energy policy. Environmental concerns loom large in the national energy debate in all EFTA countries; a concern with the risks inherent in nuclear energy is even evident in Switzerland which relies more than the other EFTA countries on market variables to determine its energy mix. Austria's only nuclear plant, Zwentendorf, has never been put into operation because of political protest. The two nuclear plants now in operation in Sweden are to be dismantled and the entire nuclear programme abolished.

Thus in their energy sectors EFTA countries have little in common apart from anxiety about the risks of nuclear energy and pollution from coal and automobile emissions.

Energy policy in the European Community

Energy policy in the EC has traditionally been rather insignificant, despite the fact that two of the three original EC treaties, the ECSC (European Coal and Steel Community) and Euratom, both concerned energy.[7] Based on the 'lowest common denominator' among member states with widely different interests, EC energy policy has not amounted to much. Expressed in 'guidelines', it has been confined to suggestions to member governments on energy conservation, import dependency, research into renewable sources, etc. These guidelines, usually valid for a five-year period, represent compromises between national energy policies.

The concept of the single market presents the energy field with an entirely new challenge. The often monopolistic national energy sectors will have to deregulate, and national energy policies will have to follow suit, as energy markets are opened up. Thus the task of the EC Commission is challenging indeed, since European energy markets are considered to be some of the most difficult to change, usually being characterized by heavy government control in the form of strong national energy policies. This is why energy was originally left out of the single market concept, only to be added as late as 1988.

This chapter is primarily concerned with the natural gas sector, although other aspects of the energy market are occasionally discussed. There are a number of proposals within the single energy market regarding natural gas.

These range from highly 'free market'-oriented proposals to very political ones. Throughout the deliberations over the single market in general, there is a potential conflict between the *deregulation* of markets – the push for more market and less politics – and the call for a *reregulation* – where political reordering of markets results, or could result, in more political control. This is perhaps partly a question of national political style – the British want a *laissez-faire* market, the Germans a *geordneter Markt* and the French more *dirigisme* – but there are undoubtedly major differences of opinion as to what role the EC should play in the future single market itself: should the Commission be an active watch-dog or a laid-back observer once the work of reordering is done? In practice, the tension between 'more politics' and 'more market' is evident in the discussion over how the EC can ensure that, for example, the right to transport gas in third-party pipelines obtains in reality. Some opt for a controlling bureaucracy in Brussels; others balk at this idea, fearing that it will lead to even more political intervention and bureaucratic delays.

In the case of the single energy market, this tension is very acute because some energy issues are suited to a market solution, while others require a political solution. Energy dependence is a political issue but also a commercial one, while there are political differences between being 50% dependent on Soviet or Algerian gas or on a West European source: in other words, commercial diversification will usually not take account of the political factors inherent in the geopolitics of energy. Hence, there will be forces within the EC that will argue that a single energy market cannot take account of problems of energy dependence, and that the Commission must therefore have an energy policy for the Community akin to that of a nation-state. Although the rapprochement between East and West has made dependence on Soviet gas less politicized, the issue may soon come to the fore again.

Thus, different issues have different impacts on the energy sector. For instance, the security-of-supply issue is less vital now than it was five years ago, despite the Soviet energy blockade against Lithuania. The environmental aspects of energy use have, however, come to the forefront of EC energy policy. Concern for the environment is rapidly being translated into a demand for the substitution of coal with gas or nuclear energy, and for the introduction of petroleum taxes. These are *political* issues that will limit the free market movement of energy and therefore typify the 'interventionist' approach. An EC proposal for common carriage and price transparency, on the other hand, typifies the move towards 'more market'.

Thus, it is not primarily security-of-supply issues that will motivate demands for 'more politics'. It is rather the propelling of environmental issues onto the EC agenda. There is already special provision for environmental factors to be considered in all legislation concerning the single market. This is laid down in the SEA, paragraph 130, which calls for a 'high standard' of protection.

Natural gas has always been a political question at the national level. R.S. Price defines three factors: health and safety concerns; economic concerns; and national security concerns.[8] He cites instances of policy-making guided by these three categories throughout the gas trade, in Japan, the USA and Europe.

An 'inventory' of EC proposals relating to natural gas can be summarized as follows:

'More market' proposals:
Harmonization of indirect taxation, price and investment transparency, competition for public procurement, common carriage, integration of grid.
'More politics' proposals:
Security of supply: integration of grid, but nothing on the diversification of supply (but guidelines for 1995 are currently under review).
Environment: reduction of coal subsidies (but 1975 directive limiting the use of gas in power stations upheld by Commission), limits on combustion plant emissions, standards for small vehicle emissions.

Measures that pertain to the single market as such may also have a direct bearing on energy policy. Foremost among these are the directives on VAT harmonization and public procurement. On the former issue there is as yet no agreement; on the latter the energy sector as a whole was at first included in the directive, then later excluded,[9] because 'public entities must open to Community competition the markets related to their infrastructures, the construction of networks and supplies in general, but for the present these rules do not cover energy supplies themselves.[10] France wanted all energy supplies to be included in the directive, while others wanted them to be dealt with in the general context of the single energy market. The Council agreed that energy must be fully included before 1995, the latest date for the completion of the single market. The public procurement directive also covers *private companies with exclusive rights*. Thus this very far-reaching directive is not to be immediately applied to the energy area in order to facilitate the transition to competition for monopoly companies which, as mentioned earlier, typify the sector.[11]

The 'more market' proposals that fall within the responsibility of the energy directorate have been introduced as a package: price transparency in the electricity and gas sectors was the subject of a communication in March 1989,[12] and common carriage proposals for gas and electricity were put forward at the same time,[13] along with plans for the monitoring of large investments in the energy sector.

The proposals for open access both envisage two stages: first, grid owners will be allowed access to other grids; later, third parties will be included. Further changes are expected in 1993. According to the Commissioner for Energy the long delay before these changes become effective is necessary for the industry to prepare itself. Requests for transit will have to be given to the Commission, which will supervise to ensure that they are granted within a month of notice being given. If no contract appears after a year of negotiations, the Commission can open legal proceedings. This could mean invoking the Treaty of Rome, paragraph 86, or Article 90, which allows the Commission to take action against state-owned monopolies that distort market conditions. The Commission will set up expert panels to settle commercial and technological disputes, such as what is grid spare capacity and what price is fair. Each group is expected to have two panels, one representing the Commission, the other interest groups in the sector.[14]

Energy investments above a certain amount might have to be reported to Brussels, under a draft directive,[15] intended to facilitate competition and ensure that investment is rational from a Community perspective.[16] The Commissioner for Competition Leon Brittan initially opposed the directive on the grounds that it would lead to greater bureaucracy. Under the directive countries would screen the investment reports of their neighbours and could make them the object of proposals for change, a provision designed to avoid national decisions that counter development towards the single market. The Energy Commissioner states that 'we want to introduce a line of Community investment thinking.'

Common carriage is a new issue: transmission systems for natural gas extend all over Continental Europe. Most of them are owned by national and regional gas companies, with the following important exception. The pipelines for importing Soviet and Norwegian gas to the Continent are controlled by the German gas company Ruhrgas. Soviet gas enters through Waidhaus in Czechoslovakia and goes through Austria.[17] Norwegian gas going to Spain and Italy has to pass through the grid owned by Gaz de France.

Two disputes have arisen over Rurhgas's refusal to transport third-party gas. First, when Statoil sold gas in the order of 1 BCM to Austria in 1987, Ruhrgas refused to transport it.[18] Insisting that it is not a third-party transporter, Ruhrgas wanted to buy the gas from Statoil and resell to the same company after transporting it to the Austrian border. This dispute has not yet been settled. It should be added that the German government has no legal right to impose third-party transportation obligations on its companies.[19]

The second case arose from Rurhgas's refusal to transport third-party gas for Bayerngas, the local company of Bavaria, which had contracted to buy Algerian gas and needed to transport it through Ruhrgas's network. It made a complaint to the EC Commission about Ruhrgas's refusal to transport the gas, claiming that it constituted an abuse of a dominant market position. The dispute was finally settled in private between the two companies.[20]

So far there has been relatively little debate as to whether the EC single market should include legislation providing for common carriage in gas transportation. Both producers and transporters share an interest in retaining the present market structure, which allows long-term stability and predictability. An introduction of common carriage in some form or other would entail uncertainty and risk. Would it lead to a gas spot market? Who would be in control? What would be the role of the transporters? Potentially, it could mean more competition and less cooperation among those involved in the gas market, something which could lead to lower prices and related problems for a high-cost producer like Norway. A great advantage of Europe's present gas market structure is that it ensures the long-term stability essential for gas supplies.

But is the introduction of common carriage in Europe really possible? In an examination of the issue of common carriage in the US and Europe, Uffe Bundgaard-Jorgensen pinpoints three factors which make progress towards common carrier rules in the EC appear likely: there is the political will to bring gas transportation into line with the internal market philosophy; there is an interest on the part of the large producers, Norway and the USSR, in expanding the market for gas in large volumes in the future; and there is consumer interest in gas for environmental reasons if the price is low enough.[21] Gas will probably be used in power generation on a large scale in Europe in the future,[22] because of concern about acid rain, potential problems with nuclear plants, and the fact that large supplies of gas are available from Troll, possibly northern Norway, and from the USSR. Algeria is also conducting a more market-responsive price policy, and will rely increasingly on gas exports in the future.

It would thus seem that the EC's current effort to establish a truly free market in the transportation sector including the natural gas transportation sector, coincides with long-term market developments in Europe. Whereas both producers and consumers may have an interest in expanding the market for gas, for example in the area of power generation, the transport companies do not expect increased profits to come from transporting low-cost gas. They certainly see no advantage in being subjected to legislation introducing common rules for tariffs.

EFTA and the Internal Energy Market

There are four possible modes of development for the internal market in energy and EFTA's relations with the EC. First, the internal market proposals may be implemented and EFTA countries may become members of the EC. Second, the internal market may be achieved, but with EFTA countries remaining outside. Third, the status quo may continue; that is EFTA countries may remain outside the EC and the internal energy market may not materialize. Finally, the internal energy market may be partially achieved, with EFTA countries adapting to it to varying degrees.

As members, Austria, Finland and presumably Iceland would have to diversify their oil and gas imports. Austria is already doing so by buying some of its gas from Norway. However, this issue apart, there is no clear-cut discrepancy between EC energy policy, as it exists today in the form of objectives or proposals for an internal energy market, and the present energy structures and policies of the EFTA countries. The questions of common carriership and price transparency affect energy exporters much more than they do importers.

The more specific proposal for common carriage would, if adopted, affect gas suppliers and purchasers especially. Detailed questions cannot yet be answered, for example on the conditions for access to the gas grid, and the status of the transport companies vis-à-vis gas suppliers and purchasers, as they are still being debated within the EC. There has been some speculation that the American experience of common carriage will be applied in Europe, but this seems very unlikely. In Europe, the question of the security of gas supplies is and will remain vital. So far the transport companies have been the guarantors of supplies by virtue of buying the gas as it enters the pipeline, thus making it possible to calculate the number of days of gas supply in the case of an emergency, political, technical or otherwise.

In the present structure of the European gas market, take-or-pay contracts, often running over 25–30 years, have ensured a degree of security of supply to the domestic consumer. This security could very well be threatened if common carriage in a radical form were introduced.

In the USA, there has been much debate over how radical a concept of common carriage should be. The transport companies have lost ground in their arguments against common carriage, and there seems to be an emerging consensus that a free market in gas should be instituted. Hitherto, producers have had access to pipelines under specific conditions only. However, the American experience must be seen within the context of the process of deregulation of the gas industry, and cannot be compared directly to the European experience.[23]

Thus the first scenario assumes only the *principle* of common carriage in Europe, with the specification that it will not be applied as radically as in the US. There would be open access to pipelines for gas destined for markets other than the domestic consumers' market – for power generation in industry and the like. A new market for gas, perhaps mainly a spot market, would then develop in Europe.

In this first scenario, it might be assumed that Norway will become a *de facto* or *de jure* member of the EC for the purpose of the energy market. This assumption is made because Norway will, in any event, have to adapt to the EC single market, including its energy sector. My second assumption in this scenario is that adaptation would mean full reciprocity between the EC and Norway, which in turn would require Norway to offer the EC countries the same conditions for free market access that the EC offers Norway.[24] The major advantage of membership is that Norway would participate in the EC discussions and decisions on energy. As a member, Norway would automatically benefit from the establishment of common carrier obligation in the transportation of gas.

If the first assumption on the establishment of an internal energy market is realized, but with Norway a non-member, access to the gas transport system would depend on the general relationship between the country and the EC and how the trade between the two was organized.

The third scenario assumes that the efforts to create an internal energy market fail, given how well the structure of the European gas market is entrenched and how far it is supported by the industry. Under this scenario the question of whether or not Norway is an EC member appears somewhat irrelevant, because the implication is that the EC would have no real influence on the gas market. The only advantage of membership for Norway in this situation would be the opportunity to influence EC energy policy through talks with other importing countries on a regular, political basis in the EC Energy Directorate.

Returning to the other EFTA countries, all energy importers, more price competition and open access to transport networks would be generally advantageous to purchasers. The question of whether or not an EFTA country became an EC member would probably not matter, as energy prices would be non-discriminatory in a free market situation. However, the advantage of membership would be – as for Norway – the ability to influence the shaping of the internal energy market. It is paradoxical that although the internal market in energy implies as free a market as possible, energy remains an area of public policy concern, because it involves questions of supply security, import dependency, the environment, etc. Therefore not all aspects of energy policy will be left to market forces; some will continue to be subject to political and public policy consideration. The EFTA countries which remain outside the EC will have little chance to influence decision-making in this area.

In the area of energy, the interests of the EFTA countries are far too diverse to suggest a common EFTA approach to the EC. Norway's interests as an energy exporter will probably remain a predominant factor for many years and it will have to find its own approach to the EC on this basis.

Notes

1. The main source for the information on Austria, Switzerland, Sweden, Finland and Norway is contained in the most recent review of IEA countries' energy policies: International Energy Agency, *Energy Policies and Programmes of IEA Countries, 1987 Review*, (Paris, OECD, 1988).
2. Ruhrgas wants to buy the gas from Statoil and resell it to that company at the German-Austrian border, as it does not want to act as a transporter only. Today any national company which owns a pipeline can bar the transportation of other gas. The EC Commission has proposed that all transportation of gas be opened up in line with the principle of free transportation of goods and services central to the internal market philosophy. As discussed in detail later, this has met with opposition from the gas industry.
3. See *Finland and Energy 1988* (Helsinki, Finnish Ministry of Trade and Industry); *Energiakatsus*, 4 (1988); *Energiatilastot* [Energy Statistics] (Helsinki, 1988).
4. See the publications of Orkustofnun, the national energy authority of Iceland.
5. Speech by Petroleum Directorate head Farouk al-Kasim at the International Monetary Fund's Norwegian Month, November 1988, Washington, DC.
6. See Janne Haaland Matlary, *Norway's New Interdependence with the European Community: The Political and Economic Importance of Natural Gas Trade* (Oslo, Norwegian Institute of International Affairs, 1989).
7. For a history of early EC energy policy, see Nigel Lucas, 'Energy, the UK and the European Community', in Robert Belgrave (ed.), *Energy – Two Decades of Crises* (London, Gower House, 1983).
8. Robert S. Price, 'Government Policy and International Natural Gas Trade', *Journal of Energy and Development*, 11 (2) (Spring 1986).
9. 'Commission Drops Energy from Public Procurement Proposals', *EC Energy Monthly*, 9 (September 1989), p. 12.
10. 'Energy and Public Procurement', *Bulletin d'Europe*, 26 February 1990, p. 7.
11. *Proposal for a Council Directive on the Procurement Procedures of Entities providing Water, Energy and Transport Services*, COM (88) 377.
12. *Transparency of Consumer Energy Prices*, COM (89) 123.
13. *Draft Directive on Electricity Transportation*, COM (89) 336; *Draft Directive on Natural Gas Transportation*, COM (89), 334.
14. COM (89) 332; 'Commission Finalises Common Transit and Investment Legislation Proposals', *EC Energy Monthly*, July 1989.
15. COM (89) 322.
16. COM (89) 335.
17. Chapter 3, 'Gaswirtschaft', *Jahrbuch fur Bergau, Ol und Gas, Elektrizitat, Chemie* (Essen 1987/8).
18. 'Ruhrgas Holds Out Against Transporter Status', *World Gas Report*, 19 June 1987. See also 'Now Europe Faces Effort to Free Up Natural Gas Market', *Petroleum lutelligence Weekly*, 9 October 1987, which calls the conflict between Ruhrgas and Statoil embarrassing and the arrangements between transporters in Europe 'cosy'.
19. A possible exception may be if a company can show that there has been an 'abuse of the market', which allows the government to intervene under the Restrictive Trade Practices Act. However, this does not cover joint ventures for gas transportation, combined contracts for sale and purchase and stand-alone contracts agreed prior to

pipeline construction ('Survey of the Natural Gas Industry in Germany', *World Gas Report* (1984), p. 18).

20. 'Europe Faces Effort to Free Up Market'.
21. Uffe Bundgaard-Jorgensen, 'Will the Third Party Right for Transportation in Gas Transmission Networks also be a European Issue?', paper presented at the conference 'Natural Gas in the Nordic Countries', Gothenburg, 26 May 1988.
22. It appears very likely that the EC will change its current policy that gas may not be used in power generation.
23. The problem in the US has been that the price of gas has been regulated, then deregulation was attempted, with the result of even more artificial gas pricing. Today an attempt is being made to subject the gas sector to competition without constraints; this has led to many court cases over old contracts and price clauses which are completely unrealistic in a market with gas-to-gas competition. A good discussion of recent developments in both Europe and the US on common carriage is provided by Uffe Bundgaard-Jensen and R.J. Hopper, 'The Potential for Open Access Contract Carriage', international conference in Luxembourg, 4–7 July 1988. J.H. Matlary gives an overview of the American gas market and its institutions: 'Det amerikanske marked', *NUPI-Notat*, 397 (May 1988).
24. An EC-EFTA Dialogue Congress in Alpbach, Austria, June 1988, was a very good sounding-board for this issue. The conclusion from the discussion was clearly that EFTA countries would have to offer reciprocity if they wanted access to the single market. The Working Document *explicitly* states that a *common* policy towards non-members will be developed where the notion of reciprocity is central. In other words, no *à la carte* adaptation to the energy market.

8 Environment

Finn Laursen

This chapter discusses the place of environmental issues in the EC-EFTA dialogue since the Luxembourg Declaration (1984). This dialogue, which predates the EC's White Paper on the Internal Market (1985) and the Single European Act (1986), covers some issues not directly associated with the internal market, including some aspects of general environmental policy.

If environmental policy is broadly defined to include not only the natural environment but also the working environment and the safety of various products, then it touches many issues dealt with under the heading of technical barriers to trade (TBTs), which form an important part of the internal market. If, for instance, Switzerland sets higher emission standards for cars than the EC (or individual EC members), then producers within the EC will not be able to export their cars to Switzerland without raising their standards. Market integration, therefore, is very much linked to standardization and certification of products. This is one of the main reasons why EFTA countries are so anxious to find ways of adapting to the EC internal market procedures by 1 January 1993. The free trade in industrial goods achieved through the Free Trade Agreements (FTAs) between the EC and the individual EFTA countries should not suffer. Rather, free trade should be further expanded in the so-called 'dynamic European Economic Space' (EES) comprising the twelve EC and six EFTA countries.

Another reason for dealing with environmental policy at the international level lies in the very nature of many forms of pollution which do not respect national borders. This is especially true of air and water pollution, for which the most important sources are land-based; therefore it is not easy to distinguish between pollution of national origin and pollution of extra-national origin. Our natural environment, as it has often been said, does not respect national sovereignty.

The following sections deal briefly with the development of environmental policy within the EC and its 'constitutionalization' through the SEA. Next we shall consider in greater detail the role played by the environment in the EC-EFTA dialogue proper. As we shall see, little has happened so far in terms of concrete decisions or agreements. But a number of joint meetings and seminars on environmental problems have taken place, giving EC and EFTA environmental officials and experts the opportunity to exchange information and ideas.

The evolution of a Community environment policy

The Treaty of Rome did not foresee a common environmental policy. The issue was not really on the political agenda in the mid-1950s, except, perhaps, for river pollution and oil pollution of the seas.[1]

The first major comprehensive international conference on the environment was the UN conference in Stockholm in 1972, which, among other things, led to the establishment of the United Nations Environment Programme (UNEP). From this moment, the environment was recognized as an international issue.[2] At about the same time, the Community began to develop an environmental policy. The meeting of heads of state or government of member states in Paris on 19–20 October 1972 declared:

> ... economic expansion is not an end in itself: its first aim should be to enable disparities in living conditions to be reduced. It must take place with the participation of all the social partners. It should result in an improvement in the quality of life as well as in standards of living. As befits the genius of Europe, particular attention will be given to intangible values and to protecting the environment so that progress may really be put at the service of mankind.[3]

The Paris Summit, stressing the importance of a Community environmental policy, 'invited the Community institutions to establish before 31 July 1973 a programme of action accompanied by a precise timetable'. The Commission, which had in fact already prepared the first internal documents in this area, rewrote them and presented a draft Council resolution on an EC Environmental Action Programme (EAP) to the Council on 10 April 1973.[4] This first environmental action programme of the EC was adopted as a Declaration of the Council and of the representatives of the governments of the member states meeting in the Council on 22 November 1973.[5]

Although there is no explicit legitimation of an environmental policy in the Treaty of Rome, the declaration referred mainly to Art. 2, which mentions the harmonious development of economic activities and the improvement of the quality of life as objectives of the Community. Among the principles on which the new environmental policy would be based were the following:

(i) prevention of pollution at the source;
(ii) integration of environmental considerations into all planning and decision-making processes;
(iii) the 'polluter pays' principle;
(iv) promotion of international cooperation;
(v) establishment of appropriate levels of action (local, regional, national, Community, international);
(vi) coordination and harmonization of national programmes.

Educational activities to increase environmental awareness and the establishment of an environment information system were also envisaged.

The first EAP gave priority to combating pollution by certain substances considered especially dangerous, such as lead, sulphur, nitrogen oxides, asbestos, cadmium, mercury and pesticides. Various directives were worked out and adopted concerning the quality of surface waters, air quality standards, waste, chemicals and noise. As well as Art. 2, these directives were based on Arts. 100 and 235 of the Treaty. Art. 100 deals with the harmonization necessary to establish the Common Market. Art. 235 deals with actions not explicitly foreseen but necessary to attain the objectives of the Community. (Since the process of European integration was to be a dynamic one in which not everything could be foreseen from the beginning, Art. 235 was included to make it possible for the Community, on the basis of unanimous decisions in the Council, to increase the scope of integration without complicated amendments.)

The second EAP, covering the period 1977–81, continued the work begun by the first.[6] Achievements in this period included measures to monitor surface water quality standards, and to set quality requirements for waters capable of supporting freshwater fish and favourable to shellfish growth, and for water for human consumption.

The development of the EC's environmental policy continued with the third EAP, 1982–6. This period saw directives regulating the discharge of mercury, cadmium and titanium dioxide. Also, air quality standards were established as regards lead and nitrogen dioxide.

The Community is now implementing its fourth EAP (1987–92), which was adopted as a resolution by the EC Council on 19 October 1987.[7] Its priority areas include integration of the environmental dimension into other policies, dangerous chemical substances, reduction of atmospheric, water and soil pollution at the source, development of non-polluting technology, and international cooperation.

All in all, the scope of EC environmental policy had become impressive by the mid-1980s. One author has summarized the areas covered as follows:

> Water (with subtitles e.g. on drinking water, water standards for freshwater fish, bathing water, dangerous substances in water, detergents), waste (with e.g. toxic waste, disposal of PCBs, waste oils), air (e.g. smoke and sulphur dioxide in air, lead in petrol, lead in the air, pollution from motor vehicles), chemicals (e.g. preventing risks by testing, major accident hazards, pesticides and plant protection products), wildlife and countryside (birds and their habitats, whales, international conventions on fauna and flora), noise (noise from cars, buses and lorries, construction plant noise, aircraft noise).[8]

How effective all these policies are from an environmental point of view is of course another question.

The Single European Act and the environment

The Single European Act signed by the member states in 1986, and in force from 1 July 1987, introduced various changes in the EC treaties. Section II deals with provisions relating to the foundations and the policy of the Community. Subsection I deals with the internal market, and Subsection VII with the environment. Art. 100 A, paragraph 1, introduced the use of qualified majority voting for the achievement of the internal market. Art. 100 A (3), which deals with environmental questions in relation to the internal market, stipulates that the Commission 'in its proposals envisaged in paragraph 1 concerning health, safety, environmental protection and consumer protection, will take as a base a high level of protection'.

The new Title VII dealing with the environment in general established three objectives in Art. 130 R, paragraph 1:

(i) to preserve, protect and improve the quality of the environment;
(ii) to contribute towards protecting human health;
(iii) to ensure a prudent and rational utilization of natural resources.

Art. 130 also listed certain principles and factors to be taken into account.

The Community and the member states were to have concurrent powers in relation to the environment. The principle of subsidiarity was to apply: 'The Community shall take action relating to the environment to the extent to which the objectives . . . can be attained better at Community level than at the level of the individual Member States.' Externally, both the Community and the member states were to cooperate 'within their respective spheres of competence'.

For voting in the Council on the environment, the general rule is unanimity. However, on a matter related to the internal market, the rule is qualified majority (Art. 100 A). Conflicts about which voting rules to apply to environmental issues are inevitable. Some matters like product standards clearly come under Art. 100 A. But conflicting interpretations may be expected over many other matters.[9]

Finally, the SEA allowed member states to maintain or introduce more stringent measures of national protection than those adopted at Community level (Art. 130 T). This suggests fears on the part of some members that EC environmental standards would be set too low. The best example is Denmark who was finally persuaded to ratify by this environmental guarantee.[10]

The environment in the EC-EFTA dialogue, 1984–9

From Luxembourg to Interlaken

The joint EC-EFTA ministerial meeting which started the EC-EFTA dialogue took place in Luxembourg on 9 April 1984.[11] The joint declaration refers to various fields of mutual interest where pragmatic and flexible cooperation should be pursued. Broadening and deepening cooperation, in particular in research and development, was discussed. The declaration further called for intensified cooperation and/or consultations in fields such as transport, agriculture, fisheries and energy. Areas where consultations, contacts or exchanges of information were called for included working conditions, social protection, culture, consumer protection, the environment, tourism and intellectual property.

The concept of a European Economic Space (EES) was proposed for the first time without being given a clear definition. The environment was part of the concept, but was given low priority as an area where there should be 'consultations, contacts or exchanges of information'.

A joint meeting between EFTA ministers and the EC Commission took place in Vienna on 10 May 1985. The communiqué specifically mentioned further liberalization of trade and it was clear that the products area still had priority. The declaration did, however, also mention the 'urgent need to tackle pollution and other environmental problems'.[12] Three days after the meeting the Commission published the final version of a communication to the Council on the implementation of the Luxembourg Declaration. 'Economic policy coordination, contacts and consultations' between the EC and EFTA had increased steadily and were now going 'well beyond the field of trade to cover transport, energy, the short-term economic outlook, the environment and services'.[13]

The Commission suggested that increased cooperation with EFTA countries should be based on certain principles, including that '(c) No specific field should be excluded *a priori* for cooperation. The Community must, for example, also step up coordination with EFTA countries in fields such as transport or environmental policy, which of their nature cannot be limited by frontiers and are also issues of great concern to ordinary people.'[14]

As regards technical standards and rules with a possible environmental impact, cooperation already existed between the EC and the EFTA countries, notably through the European Committee for Standardization (CEN) and the European Committee for the Coordination of Electrical Standards (CENELEC). Both the EC and EFTA countries take an active part in the work of these bodies, also in devising joint technical standards and specifications for information and telecommunications technology products through the European Conference of Postal and Telecommunications Administrations (CEPT). Another facet of the drive to eliminate TBTs by the recognition of tests and certification became a more active concern within the EC through 'new measures aimed at ensuring genuine intra-Community mutual recognition of test results and certification'. The Commission favoured progress towards similar mutual recognition between the EC and EFTA.

In the area of environmental protection the Commission also mentioned regular contacts with a number of EFTA countries. The recent Council decisions on standards governing exhaust gases were seen as potential barriers to trade if no Europe-wide harmonization took place. Coordination of environment policy between the EFTA countries and the EC was thus needed to avoid new trade barriers.

At a meeting between EFTA ministers and the EC Commission in Reykjavik on 5 June 1986, as well as further trade liberalization, science and technology were emphasized. But the environment was again mentioned: participants agreed to work closely together in the organization of the European Year of the Environment in 1987. The environment was also mentioned at the Interlaken meeting between EFTA ministers and Willy De Clercq on 20 May 1987.[15] But no specific measures were proposed in the communiqué.

Although the 1984 Luxembourg Declaration had put the protection of the environment on the EC-EFTA agenda, practical steps appeared difficult. In 1985 EFTA parliamentarians had agreed that the environment could usefully be dealt with within EC-EFTA cooperation. The main argument for such measures was that many aspects of environmental protection have commercial and economic implications. As mentioned earlier, 'the differing deadlines, upper limits and standards for introducing catalytic converters for passenger cars' can become non-tariff barriers to trade.[16] However, one reason cited for delays on the environmental measures was the risk of duplicating the work of other international organizations such as the OECD, the Council of Europe, the Geneva Convention on Long-range Transboundary Air Pollution of 1979, etc.

For this and other reasons, exchanges of information, consultation, and similar non-binding procedures have become the predominant ones in the EC-EFTA dialogue on the environment. The first concrete step, cooperation within the European Year of the Environment, 1987, designed to bring about a better awareness among the general public of environmental matters, did not commit the participating countries to specific policies. A common EFTA-EC logo was, however, designed for the event.

On 12 December 1986 the Commission made various proposals to the EFTA experts on future cooperation. These included the comparison and possible harmonization of legislation, classification and labelling of existing and new chemical substances, and a strategy on atmospheric pollution, including the classification of forty-four different atmospheric pollutants according to the urgency of action needed. The Commission experts also suggested an exchange of views on nitrogen oxide reduction, type approval and coordination of instruments for measuring pollution, the marking and labelling of batteries with mercury and cadmium content, exhaust emission standards, environmental accidents and nuclear safety. Commission experts further invited comments and suggestions from EFTA experts on the fourth EC Environmental Programme (1987–92). But EFTA was apparently not ready. An EFTA official wrote: 'It is obvious that EFTA experts could not react immediately to such a large number of proposals and it will take some time to select priorities according to a common denominator amongst EFTA countries.'[17]

The Noordwijk ministerial conference

On 25–6 October 1987 the ministers responsible for the environment in the EC and EFTA countries, and the Commissioner for the Environment, Stanley Clinton Davis, met for their first conference on the environment at Noordwijk, the Netherlands. The Noordwijk conference gave priority to cooperation in five areas:

(i) *climatic change*: countering the greenhouse effect, caused by the production of carbon dioxide and other substances which tend to raise the temperature of the world's atmosphere;
(ii) *pollution of the atmosphere*: reducing sulphur dioxide and nitric acid emissions from large combustion plants; reducing car and lorry exhaust gases; making unleaded petrol more widely available;
(iii) *soil and ground-water protection*: cooperating in carrying out appropriate research programmes and formulating quality standards for soil and the environment as a whole;

(iv) *water protection*;
(v) *accidents affecting the environment*: working out common safety rules; introducing an early warning system.[18]

It was also agreed that senior environment officials should meet at least once a year, ministers as often as necessary.

Papers prepared for the conference outlined the problems in the five areas. The background papers referred to recent scientific projections for the first half of the twenty-first century: 'Model calculations show a temperature rise due to doubling CO_2 and other trace gas concentrations of 1.5–4.5 C as most probable. Such a temperature rise may cause a sea level rise of 20–140 cm. Combined effects of CO_2 increase, temperature rise and sea level rise will have great consequences for agriculture, water management, coastal defence, ecosystems and so on.'[19]

A section on European concerns went on to admit that

> . . . the EC and EFTA countries contribute substantially to the greenhouse effect. The 354 million inhabitants of our countries (i.e. 7% of the world population) are consuming 16% of world energy production and contributing 16% of global CO_2 emissions. Although real data are not available, it may be expected that the emissions of other greenhouse gases such as methane (CH_4), nitrous oxide (N_2O) and CFCs [i.e. chlorofluorocarbons] will be considerable too. Emissions of these trace gases are still growing due to burning fossil fuels and other industrial processes.[20]

The reduction of CFC emission had already been agreed internationally in the Vienna Convention (1985) and, more particularly, in the Montreal Protocol on Substances that Deplete the Ozone Layer (1987). It was felt that joint international action was now especially urgent on CO_2.

The central issue in respect of atmospheric pollution was acid rain, and the effects of acidifying substances like sulphur dioxide (SO_2), nitrogen oxides (NO_x) and ammonia (NH_3) and photochemical oxidants like ozone generated by reaction between volatile organic substances (VOC) and NO_x. The SO_2-protocol to the convention on air pollution adopted within the UN Economic Commission for Europe (Geneva, 1979) was a first step, but more were needed. NO_x was a candidate for 'precautionary measures in the shortest term possible'. Specifically it was suggested that 'an effective EC directive containing emission standards and reduction targets for large combustion plants could serve as an example and a stimulus for further efforts in ECE.'[21] On soil and water protection, one of the proposals was for the integration of environmental and agricultural policy. Reference was made to the reduction of oxygen in the North Sea, causing fish and shellfish in coastal waters to die. This was attributed to agricultural nutrients.

The statements at the conference by national ministers showed some differences in priorities. The Mediterranean countries were very concerned about soil erosion. The Nordic countries were especially concerned about acid rain. Some countries emphasized the need for more research (such as the UK), whereas others, especially the Scandinavian countries and the Federal Republic of Germany, called for immediate action. Still others were especially concerned about formalities: 'In order not to complicate the decision-making process, France believes that any meetings of the environmental ministers of the countries concerned should be of an informal character, so as to allow a pragmatic and flexible cooperation to develop in the spirit of the Luxembourg Declaration of 1984.'[22]

The declaration adopted by the conference was rather vague on most points. Since many of the environmental problems went across frontiers, strengthened cooperation between the EC and EFTA was said to be needed. New barriers to trade should be avoided. Existing multilateral and bilateral contacts should be strengthened. There should be an exchange of information on proposed legislation, etc. The need for further research in some areas was also mentioned.[23]

In response to the French concerns the conference adopted a general statement that the meeting 'had no formal character, as it was not based on any existing legal instrument'. Whereas some EFTA countries wanted to institutionalize the meeting, France and, to a lesser extent, some other EC countries opposed the idea.[24] The general statement also said that 'the strengthening of relations between EFTA and the EC should be undertaken while fully respecting Community rules and should be in line with the spirit of the 1984 Luxembourg Declaration, in order to avoid unnecessary procedural complications.'[25]

Commenting on the Noordwijk Declaration at a symposium organized by the College of Europe, Bruges, in 1988, L.G. Larsson, Director of the Department for Environment and Energy Questions of the Federation of Swedish Industries, said: 'The document contains a lot of words – for instance the word "cooperation" on almost every page – but only one figure. I welcome the initiative to reduce the sulphur dioxide to at least 30% by 1993. But this is only a first step.'[26]

Follow-up to the Noordwijk conference

Environmental cooperation, or at least discussion of environmental problems, has continued. The group of senior environment officials set up at Noordwijk met for the first time in Munich, on 25–6 April 1988. More than sixty experts from the EC and EFTA countries and the EC Commission and EFTA Secretariat discussed a number of issues, including emissions from cars, distribution of unleaded petrol, reduction of NO_x emissions, protection of the ozone layer, integration of environmental goals into agricultural policy, phosphates in detergents, and the transport of hazardous waste across frontiers. The achievements of the Second International Conference on the Protection of the North Sea, the ninth meeting of the Helsinki Commission (dealing with the Baltic Sea) and the fifth meeting of the contracting parties to the Barcelona Convention (dealing with the Mediterranean) were also noted.[27]

A discussion similar to the one on institutionalization at the Noordwijk conference took place on the question of the future work of the senior environment officials. The Commission and some EC countries preferred a pragmatic and informal approach. The Federal Republic of Germany and the EFTA countries preferred a more organized and formal one, including, *inter alia*, 'the setting up of joint groups of experts, the organization of meetings between representatives of the EFTA and EC missions in Brussels, and a structure for the exchange of information on proposed legislation between the EFTA countries and the Commission'. It was decided to follow the informal approach. According to the Spanish representative this would be in line with the decision at the Noordwijk conference.[28]

The Munich meeting of senior officials was followed by three seminars in 1988. The first, in Rome that September, was on heavy vehicles and related air and noise pollution problems. The note prepared by the secretariat after the meeting suggests a fair amount of disagreement among the participants: 'The Seminar could not agree whether future work in this special area is needed in the EFTA-EC framework or not.'[29] The Federal Republic and the EFTA countries saw such a need. France, the United Kingdom, Italy and Spain felt that common work should take place within the ECE in Geneva. The fact that the minutes of the meeting were only agreed after two hours of discussion also suggests disagreement.

The next seminar, at Ispra in November, dealt with climatic change. It seems to have been less conflictual, and 'participants found the discussion and exchange of views most useful. . . . Most participants invited the senior officials to consider an appropriate framework for the future cooperation between EEC and EFTA countries on the subject.'[30]

The third seminar, in Switzerland in December, discussed whether to ban phosphates in detergents. 'The debate was considered interesting and useful and was performed in a positive spirit. No negative interventions as regards EFTA-EC co-operation on the environment were made.'[31]

At the general political level there were no less than three joint meetings between the EC and EFTA in 1988, starting with a ministerial meeting in Brussels on 2 February, and continuing with meetings between EFTA ministers and Willy De Clercq of the Commission in Tampere, Finland, on 15 June, and in Geneva on 29 November.

The Geneva communiqué talked about 'considerable progress' in a number of areas, including the exchange of notifications on draft technical regulations. 'Good prospects for early progress' were seen in other fields. But a number of areas remained where cooperation should be strengthened, including environmental protection. Finally, exchanges of information would continue, or be initiated, in a number of fields including legislation on foodstuffs, veterinary and phytosanitary measures, and other questions concerning consumer protection.[32] This amounts to an admission that cooperation had to be strengthened in the environmental area. (Diplomatic language for admitting failure so far?)

A second meeting of senior environment officials took place in Vienna in February 1989. 'The main results of the meeting were the decisions to arrange seminars or workshops on the following topics: environment and agriculture, cleaner technologies, climate change and positive labelling.'[33] Spain, Italy and France underlined the informal nature of environmental cooperation. In contrast, the EFTA countries wanted the various meetings to be more policy-oriented. The reluctance of some EC countries thus continued to put strict limits on environmental cooperation.

Concluding remarks

At the beginning of 1989 the agenda of the EC-EFTA dialogue had expanded to include most issues relating to the completion of the EC's internal market. The environment had won a place on the agenda: various meetings to discuss it had taken place, but without producing concrete results in spite of numerous joint declarations from 1984 on. Despite the ministerial meeting in 1987 and its follow-up, these have so far largely remained at the level of rhetoric. Western Europe is still waiting for concrete achievements other than those of wider international agreements or conventions in which both EFTA countries and the EC (and EC countries) are parties.

The value of the continuing dialogue on the environment is therefore mainly at the level of exchange of information. The concern to avoid new technical barriers to trade is a powerful motive for attempting some *de facto* harmonization, even through unilateral national adaptation on the EFTA side. The Community side has been somewhat hesitant in this dialogue, partly because of the attitudes of the southern members and partly because of bureaucratic politics within the Commission. The EFTA side, which on average is more progressive on environmental issues than the Community side, has been the plaintiff in the dialogue. But EFTA's possibilities have been limited by the fact that there is no common environmental policy within EFTA. The fact that the Community's dialogue is with six countries, not a single organization, has contributed to making it more time-consuming and less productive than it could have been. Whether this institutional problem can be solved through the new prospects raised by the Delors speech to the European Parliament in January, it is too early to tell.

The joint EC-EFTA Declaration of 19 December 1989 on the opening of formal negotiations on the creation of a European Economic Space (EES), apart from referring to the achievement of the 'free movement of goods, services, capital and persons, on the basis of the relevant *acquis communautaire*', also mentioned the strengthening and broadening of cooperation in other areas, including the environment.[34]

The issue is thus still on the agenda, but nothing concrete has been decided.

Beyond the institutional problem – which in general will probably be the most difficult one in the forthcoming negotiations – the question of appropriate forums remains. If the six EFTA countries are to take part in the internal market of the Community, environmental issues affecting market access will clearly have to be addressed. But for some aspects of environmental policy wider forums will be more appropriate. For cross-frontier air pollution the UN Economic Commission for Europe, which includes East European countries, is clearly more appropriate. Sometimes smaller forums are more appropriate, as for the Baltic Sea. The Helsinki Commission includes the Soviet Union, Poland and the German Democratic Republic; if it did not, it could not be effective. The environmental issues which mainly affect the eighteen countries of the EES therefore must be defined. This means applying the principle of subsidiarity at the wider European level.

Once the issues have been delineated, common goals and an effective forum for decision-making and management must be established. This is the only way the countries concerned can reduce costs and achieve better management of the common natural environment.

Notes

1. Jesper Grolin, *The Politics of International Marine Pollution Control*, Occasional Papers No. 2 (Amsterdam, Institute for Global Policy Studies, 1985).
2. Lynton Keith Caldwell, *International Environmental Policy: Emergence and Dimensions* (Durham, NC, Duke University Press, 1984).
3. Quoted from Stanley P. Johnson, *The Pollution Control Policy of the European Communities*, 2nd edn (London, Graham & Trotman, 1983), p. 1.
4. For a good overview, see Ida Johanne Koppen, *The European Community's Environment Policy: From the Summit in Paris, 1972, to the Single European Act, 1987*, EUI Working Paper No. 88/328 (Florence, European University Institute, 1988).
5. OJ C 112 (20 December 1973).
6. Resolution of the Council of the EC and of the representatives of the governments of the member states meeting in the Council of 17 May 1977, OJ C 139 (13 June 1977).
7. Resolution of the Council of the European Communities and of the representatives of the governments of the member states, meeting within the Council of 19 October 1987 on the continuation and implementation of a European Community policy and action programme on the environment (1987–92), OJ C 289 (29 October 1987), pp. 3–6. See also 'Summary of the Statement by the EEC Commissioner for the Environment, Transport and Nuclear Safety, Mr S. Clinton Davis', in *Report, Ministerial Conference of EFTA and EC on the Environment, Noordwijk aan Zee, 25–26 October 1987*, p. 25.
8. Gert Nicolaysen, 'Environmental Policy before the Single European Act', in Jürgen Schwarze and Henry G. Schermers (eds), *Structure and Dimensions of European Community Policy* (Baden-Baden, Nomos Verlagsgesellschaft, 1988), pp. 111–12.
9. See for instance Francis G. Jacobs, 'The Protection of the Environment under the Single European Act', in Schwarze and Schermers, *Structure and Dimensions of the European Community Policy*, pp. 117–22; and Ludwig Krämer, 'The Single European Act and Environment Protection: Reflections on Several New Provisions in Community Law', *Common Market Law Review*, 24 (1987), pp. 659–88.
10. Uffe Ellemann-Jensen, *Da Danmark igen sagde ja til det fælles* (Copenhagen, Schultz, 1987).
11. EFTA, *The European Free Trade Association* (Geneva, 1987), pp. 105–6.
12. 'Meeting of EFTA Ministers and the EC Commission. Vienna, 10 May 1985', in EFTA, *Twenty-fifth Annual Report of the European Free Trade Association* (Geneva, 1986), pp. 49–51.
13. European Community, Commission, *The Community and the EFTA Countries: Implementation of the Joint Declaration Issued in Luxembourg on 9 April 1984*, COM (85) 206 final. Brussels, 13 May 1985, pp. 1–2.
14. Ibid., pp. 2–3.
15. *EFTA Bulletin*, 28 (2) (April-June 1987), p. 19.
16. Wolfgang Locker, 'EFTA and the Protection of the Environment', *EFTA Bulletin* 28 (3) (July-September 1987), p. 8.
17. Ibid., p. 9.
18. EFTA, *Twenty-seventh Annual Report of the European Free Trade Association* (Geneva, 1988), pp. 18–19.
19. 'Background-paper to the EC/EFTA-Conference, 25 and 26 October 1987, Doc. ECEFTA/PM/2 (def)', in *Report. Ministerial Conference of EFTA and EC on the*

Environment, p. 78.
20. Ibid., p. 79.
21. Ibid., p. 83.
22. 'Summary of the Statement by the Head of the French Delegation, Mr T. Chambolle', in ibid., p. 30.
23. The declaration is reproduced in J. Jamar and H. Wallace (eds), *EEC – EFTA: More Than Just Good Friends?* (Bruges, College of Europe, 1980), pp. 154–62. Also in *Agence Europe*, 4 November 1987.
24. *Agence Europe*, 26–7 October 1987, p. 7.
25. Jamar and Wallace, *EEC – EFTA*, p. 162.
26. L.G. Larsson, 'Comment', in Jamar and Wallace (eds), *EEC – EFTA*, p. 167.
27. 'EFTA and EC Cooperate for a "Greener" Europe', *EFTA Bulletin*, 29 (2) (April-June 1988), p. 17.
28. EFTA, 'EFTA-EC Co-Operation on Environment: First Meeting of Senior Environment Officials. Munich, 25 and 26 April 1988', Note by the Secretariat, Doc. EFTA/BR 8/88, 28 April 1988, p. 2.
29. EFTA, 'EFTA-EC Co-operation on Environment: Seminar on Heavy Vehicles and Related Air and Noise Pollution Problems, Rome, 19 and 20 September 1988', Note by the Secretariat, Doc. EFTA/BR 17/88, 29 September 1988, p. 3.
30. EFTA, 'EFTA-EC Co-operation on Environment. Seminar on Climatic Change. Ispra, 29 and 30 November 1988', Report by the Secretariat, Doc. EFTA/BR 31/88, 5 December 1988, annexe III, p. 2.
31. EFTA, 'EFTA-EC Co-operation on Environment: Seminar on the Prohibition of Phosphates in Detergents. Opfikon, 7 and 8 December 1988,' Report by the Secretariat, Doc. EFTA/BR 32/88, 14 December 1988, p. 2.
32. 'The Special Relationship between the EC and EFTA Countries Should Be Further Developed', *EFTA Bulletin*, 29 (4) (October-December 1988), pp. 4–5.
33. EFTA, 'EFTA-EC Co-operation on Environment. Second Meeting of EFTA-EC Senior Environment Officials. Vienna, 20 and 21 February 1989', EFTA/BR 7/89, 3 March 1989.
34. *Agence Europe*, 23 December 1989, p. 9.

Part II
The Attitudes of the Participants

9 Community Attitudes and Interests

Thomas Pedersen

This chapter looks at the EC-EFTA relationship from the viewpoint of the European Community.[1] It examines more closely the EC's common interests as well as the specific interests of the member states; the limitations to EC-EFTA cooperation as seen from Brussels; and the initial negotiating position adopted by the EC.

How the Community stands to benefit

In trying to identify the EC's common interests in relation to EFTA, a logical starting point might be the EFTA market. As is often pointed out, this market is very important to the EC; however, because access to it is often taken for granted, its importance is consequently underestimated.

As a trading partner, EFTA accounts for as much EC trade as Japan and the US. This trade is predominantly industrial – in other words, it is concentrated in the more advanced sectors of the economy. Moreover, EFTA is the only trading partner with which the EC is significantly in surplus. The external trade stance of EFTA countries has been quite liberal.

Of total Community trade with EFTA, West German trade represents about 40%, British trade some 15% and Italian and French trade each about 10%.

Of the individual EC countries, Denmark has the greatest interest in trade with EFTA. Almost 40% of Danish foreign trade is with EFTA countries, compared with 30% of West German trade, just over 20% of UK trade and slightly less than this in the case of France and Italy.

In economic terms, the EC and EFTA are more closely involved with each other than in the early 1960s and 1970s, in spite of Western Europe's comparatively low growth rates. Part of the explanation probably lies in the more 'European' business strategies adopted by West European firms in the 1980s. The ASEA-Brown Boveri merger is a case in point: it follows a long line of mergers and acquisitions in the EC by EFTA companies.

The EC's new growth strategy, combining promotion of technological innovation with attempts to achieve economies of scale through internal liberalization, makes the EFTA countries its natural partners. The EC's modernizing thrust focuses on technologically advanced industries, where EFTA economies are generally in a strong position (with Austria as a possible exception). Moreover, the creation of a European Economic Space (EES), as envisaged in the Luxembourg declaration, would make Western Europe much the largest Western market and would thus bring about benefits greater than those flowing from an internal market restricted to the EC.

Arguably, the international economic climate risks generating protectionism in a new guise. Bilateral measures are increasingly displacing multilateral solutions to trade disputes. There is thus a case to be made for the EC to strengthen its hand in international trade negotiations, both the bilateral ones with the US and the multilateral in the Uruguay Round and thereafter. Closer cooperation with EFTA countries could be valuable, as some EC governments recognize.

The Luxembourg Declaration states: 'Europe through closer cooperation will be better able to play a more important role in the world, especially through a strengthening of contacts as regards economic and monetary policy'. Closer consultations between the two groupings are envisaged within the General Agreement of Tariffs and Trade (GATT), the International Monetary Fund (IMF) and the World Bank, with a view to reaching 'reasonable solutions' and promoting an 'open and multilateral trade system'.[2] However, reaching a common EC position in trade negotiations has already been found difficult. A forum of 18 would be even more cumbersome.

Against this must be weighed the greater strength of the wider Western Europe. Already there are quite extensive EC-EFTA consultations within the framework of GATT and the Organization for European Cooperation and Development (OECD). There is some scope elsewhere for concerted EC-EFTA action on a case-by-case basis, for example, within the IMF and on issues of development and third-world policy.

In its first report to the Council on EC-EFTA relations, the Committee of Permanent Representatives (Coreper) drew particular attention to the importance of a common policy on international economic issues.[3] This interest is shared by most, if not all, EFTA countries, which lack clout in bilateral negotiations and are thus even more dependent than the EC on a functioning multilateral trade and monetary system: should this system be undermined in the years ahead, the EFTA countries might seek refuge under the wings of the EC.

The new EC member states, Portugal and Spain, undoubtedly constitute important markets for the more advanced EC economies, but they both need injections of resources for economic development and as yet offer relatively little in the way of research and development expertise. Cooperation with the advanced EFTA economies is seen in some EC quarters as a welcome complement to, or even compensation for, the Southern enlargement.

Finally, over the years the EFTA countries have developed a unique expertise in some areas: the 'welfare state tradition' in most of them might serve as inspiration to some EC governments, as well as to parties and trade unions, in attempts to add a social dimension to the internal market. During an official visit to Sweden in June 1986, Jacques Delors emphasized that Sweden had demonstrated an ability to create jobs and maintain full employment that should serve as an inspiration for the other European countries.[4] EFTA countries also have a positive contribution to make in fields such as environmental protection.

The attitudes of the member countries

Not surprisingly, the degree and the nature of the EC member states' interest in cooperation with EFTA vary considerably. Generally speaking, the FRG, the UK, Denmark and the Netherlands display the most positive attitude. There seems, however, to be a slight difference between the British stance on the one hand and the Danish and West German stance on the other. The UK seems to be anxious not to write a blank cheque for the EFTA countries, whereas Denmark and the FRG occasionally give the impression of being prepared to do exactly that. France has adopted an intermediate position between the northern group and the southern member states.

Federal Republic of Germany

For the Federal Republic there are both political and economic arguments in favour of expanding links with EFTA and its member countries. The FRG has by far the greatest economic interest in EC-EFTA cooperation. The strong, export-led Germany economy would profit from improved access to the advanced EFTA market.

As far as the political dimension is concerned, the Federal Republic has conflicting interests. There would be obvious advantage in facilitating Austria's accession to the EC; but were Switzerland and the Nordic EFTA countries to move faster in the direction of membership, this would not affect German interests adversely. At the same time it is recognized that Austrian accession might 'dilute' or at least delay the process of foreign policy and security cooperation.

There is, however, a wider East-West European dimension. Intensified collaboration with neutral EFTA countries also serves the Federal Republic's longer-term interest in promoting pan-European cooperation. The development of EC-EFTA relations cannot be separated from changes in the relationship between Eastern and Western Europe. The Federal Republic has strong interests in improving EC relations with Eastern Europe, and does so by promoting a more relaxed Soviet policy.

Thus several considerations spur the Germans on in their efforts to intensify cooperation with EFTA countries. A number of German decision-makers are open to the idea of a customs union between the EC and EFTA and/or an Austrian membership. However, other sections of opinion in the CDU-CSU coalition emphasize that an Austrian membership of the EC would endanger the new impetus towards political unification in the Community.

France

Attitudes to West European integration have changed during the 1980s, with indirect implications for the attitude to wider European cooperation. The socialist government of 1981–1986 learned the lesson of interdependence the hard way, in the dramatic failure of its attempt to implement a Keynesian reflationary economic policy on a strictly national basis. Consequently, French socialists have readjusted their policies to recognize the increased importance of West European integration.

Furthermore, the socialists and large parts of the centre-right believe that wider European collaboration in research and development is necessary to take on the Japanese and the Americans. The European Research Agency (Eureka) was proposed partly as an attempt to include the technologically advanced economies of EFTA in a drive to create an integrated, West European economy, strong enough to compete successfully with Japan and the USA.

French opinion, however, prefers this wider European collaboration to be based on ventures into variable geometry, while generally regarding the idea of enlargement with little enthusiasm. France is well aware that in terms of EC coalition politics it has little to gain from that sort of enlargement. Given Britain's and particularly the FRG's traditional ties to the EFTA countries, France's political position within the EC is likely to suffer from full integration between the EC and some or all EFTA countries. Norway might, however, for high politics reasons, be regarded as an exception. In 1987 France concluded an agreement on defence cooperation with Norway: Norwegian membership could therefore be regarded in Paris as a valuable contribution to the stabilization of the northern region.[5]

French policy towards EFTA is shaped to a considerable extent by more political considerations, both tactical and strategic. France foresees that unless the EC demonstrates a political will to cooperate with EFTA countries, these may choose to forge bilateral links with the FRG: to the French this is an unpalatable prospect. The cultural links with Switzerland are another factor impinging on France's policy towards EFTA.

France favours the internal market and gives qualified support to the EES idea, but stresses the need for 'real reciprocity' and tough bargaining in EC-EFTA relations. It should not be forgotten that France's trade policy incentive for greater commitment to EC-EFTA cooperation is rather limited.

There is a long-standing current of thought in the French elite – and, in a more radical version, on the left of the socialist party – that wants to see the completion of the internal market and the creation of the EES matched, if not by a West European protectionism, then at least by a tougher common commercial policy towards the EC's major international competitors.[6] The FRG is, however, unlikely to support this point of view, unless that 'European option' is defined so as to include the EFTA countries. It is probably fair to say that to the French, EC-EFTA cooperation is more a means than an end in itself.

Great Britain

Britain obviously opposes this line of thinking, given the current government's commitment to liberal trade policies; especially as the consequence of such strategy would be more frequent and probably more severe transatlantic trade disputes.

In the past, Britain cooperated closely with the Nordic EFTA countries in the field of trade. (The Uniscan framework of the fifties was a formal mechanism for this.[7]) Politically, there is a clear-cut case for Britain supporting wide-ranging EC-EFTA cooperation. Linking the Nordic EFTA countries to the EC, both politically and economically, has been seen as a way of stabilizing a region in which the presence of the superpowers has sometimes been strongly felt, and where East-West tensions in the Baltic continue to cause anxiety. Moreover, Norway has extensive foreign policy and security links with Britain.

The EFTA issue also touches on internal EC coalition politics. Britain has consistently been sceptical of the EC's official objective of creating a European Union: it generally prefers collaborative procedures to be flexible and pragmatic.[8] Given the prevalent opposition towards supranationalism within most EFTA countries, the accession of one or more EFTA countries could be viewed as being in Britain's interest.

It might then be tempting to argue that the creation of an EES would fulfil long-standing British policy objectives. One should not, however, overlook the developments in the European policy of the UK and the extent to which in recent years British opinion has come round to regarding some deepening of EC cooperation as according with long-term British interests. Nevertheless, there probably remains in some quarters a feeling of affinity with the Scandinavians.

As for British attitudes to specific EFTA applicants for membership of the EC, Norway, as indicated, would present few problems. Possible Austrian accession has, on the other hand, been regarded with considerable scepticism. Furthermore, it is feared that it might cause some counter-productive anxieties in Moscow. The prospect of an even closer German-Austrian association within the EC framework might be disturbing. Within EPC, Austria's membership could be expected to put a brake on plans for a strengthening of security cooperation; more generally it would tend to weaken what limited political cohesion has been achieved within the Community. The British have repeatedly questioned the compatibility of EPC membership with Austria's neutral status, in which Britain has a particular interest as a signatory of the Austrian State Treaty.

Italy, Spain, Portugal, Greece

The southern European governments, especially the Spanish and Portuguese, take the view that non-EC countries should not be allowed to reap the benefits of EC membership without accepting the costs, an understandable demand from recent and poorer adherents. They emphasize that in the absence of a willingness in EFTA countries to apply for membership of the EC, EC-EFTA negotiations must guarantee real reciprocity in all areas: economic and social cohesion is an integral part of the internal market package deal and consequently, if EFTA countries are to share in the benefits, they should also contribute to the reduction of regional differences in Western Europe.

The Spanish, Portuguese, Greek and in part Italian economies would have difficulty in facing strong competition from the technologically advanced EFTA economies. They also fear that, in the absence of an external trade policy shared by the EC and EFTA, non-European competitors would be able to take advantage of EC-EFTA liberalization agreements and enter the EC market through the 'EFTA back door'.

This North-South divide first became critical during the preparations for the February 1988 joint ministerial meeting between the EC and EFTA; the Spanish minister went so far as to threaten to veto the meeting itself.

The climate of tension in the relationship between Spain and EFTA becomes easier to understand if account is taken of earlier confrontations between the two parties in the course of negotiations about Spanish adaptation to the EC's free trade agreements with EFTA. Spain had demanded immediate and full access to the EFTA market, even though Spanish access to the EC market was not yet entirely free. From an EFTA point of view this amounted to discrimination against EFTA countries. Negotiations were broken off for three months. Eventually, Spain had to bow to pressure from its EC partners, which demonstrates EFTA's importance to the rest of the EC. However, the Spanish attitude appears to have mellowed somewhat, following the decision of the European Council, also in February 1988, to expand the EC's structural funds.

Politically, the southern EC members also fear that a more wide-ranging integration between the EC and EFTA might lead to a realignment of the internal power structure of the EC, in that the northern and central European groupings would regain the influence lost in the course of enlargement. This would be a particular concern if Norway applied for membership and were accepted along with Austria.

Enlargement to include any EFTA country is, however, complicated by the pending Turkish application to move from association to full membership (though this has been rebuffed for the present.) Turkey could be expected to add to the weight and demands of the southern European member states.

Italy and the Benelux countries have voiced another political concern: they are worried that the EC's own integration process might be diluted through closer association with countries mostly opposed to supranationalism. Only Austria appears to have no qualms about this.

The Spanish position deserves separate treatment, as Spain has so far adopted the hardest line in EC consultations with EFTA countries: it subscribes to the objective of creating an EES,[9] but insists that EFTA countries should make specific concessions to balance the benefits from increased participation in the internal market, and that these should take the form of contributions to cohesion.

One possibility is financial aid to the southern EC members, channelled through structural funds along the lines of the Portugal Fund. The Spanish government also draws attention to problems in the field of agriculture. The free trade agreements with EFTA countries do not cover agricultural produce; nevertheless, 26% of Spanish exports to EFTA are agricultural, compared with only about 7% of EFTA exports to Spain. Therefore, from a Spanish point of view, a necessary EFTA contribution to cohesion would be easier Spanish access to EFTA agricultural markets and fishing areas.

Spain wants the cohesion principle to be applied in all major areas of EC-EFTA negotiations, such as state aid. It has also suggested that EFTA countries might promote technological transfers to the southern EC countries (whatever that means in practical terms) or unilaterally shorten the transitional period for Spanish industrial exports to EFTA – a repetition of an old demand.

Denmark

Denmark has special links with the Nordic EFTA countries: it sees itself, and is to some extent perceived by the Nordic EFTA countries, as a 'bridge-builder' between the EC and the Nordic countries,[10] and though it cannot negotiate on their behalf, it is sometimes able to act as a 'political interpreter', helping to avoid misunderstandings between the two groups.[11]

The importance of the integration issue has, however, increasingly forced the Nordic EFTA countries to establish direct contacts with Brussels, where they all now have permanent missions. Even so, Denmark still plays an important role in the burgeoning Nordic cooperation on internal market issues and occasionally uses the Nordic caucus to bolster its own position in EC negotiations. As the only Nordic member of the EC, Denmark is somewhat lonely and so has a political interest in seeing other Nordic countries join the EC, since the effect would generally be to reinforce the Danish view in areas such as environmental protection and foreign policy.

There is also a more practical concern behind this position. Danes can today cross the border with Sweden without having to show a passport. If the frontiers between Denmark and the FRG were removed, Sweden would have to reintroduce passport control at the frontier with Denmark, unless it were prepared to accept the uncontrolled entry of EC citizens. Thus Denmark would be obliged to impose controls on fellow Nordic citizens in order to maintain strong external perimeters for the Twelve, unless wider-ranging EC-EFTA integration allowed the present border arrangements to be retained.

Denmark can thus be expected to act as the promoter of further EC enlargement to include EFTA countries. This became apparent during the negotiations on the SEA, when, urged by Denmark, the EC issued a declaration that the Community maintain an open attitude towards 'democratic, European countries outside the Community, particularly members of the Council of Europe'.[12]

It should be added, though, that some Danish politicians appear at times to be committed less to Nordic unity than to the preservation of Denmark's unique identity and profile within the EC. Right-of-centre parties in Denmark also occasionally invoke alleged internal market necessities as a means of justifying policies at variance with the Nordic 'welfare state tradition'.

Coalition politics

Looking at the EC as a whole, one can detect a certain convergence between British, French and German interests in relation to the EFTA countries. They share an interest in expanding cooperation, but the British and German attitude is more clearly positive than the French.

Efforts to place relations with EFTA higher on the EC agenda would be politically useful to Britain, in focusing attention on the considerable, but often neglected, common ground between Britain and the FRG: this shows the scope for further improvement of EC-EFTA relations. It must, however, be seen against the likely inclination of the French, Spaniards and Italians to insist that concessions to EFTA countries would have to be compensated for by a tougher EC stance towards other major international competitors.

In any case, given the foot-dragging from the southern EC members and France's pivotal position, France will have to be won over before the northern EC member states can achieve a breakthrough in their efforts to establish an EES. Greater willingness on the part of these states to defend the wider West European interests and to take account of the anxieties of southern members might be needed to tilt the balance.

Since the early 1970s the FRG has strengthened its position as Europe's most powerful actor alongside the Soviet Union. This has enabled it to pull the Community in the direction of more active European cooperation. The Franco-German rapprochement has calmed, though not removed, France's traditional anxieties as regards Germany, thereby giving Bonn more leeway. The continuation of the Franco-German pairing within the Community and the recent changes in Europe may push Britain into a new exercise in European coalition-building, in which EFTA could play an important role.

Stumbling-blocks on the road to cooperation

From the point of view of Brussels and the EC capitals, several factors hamper EC-EFTA cooperation.

First, granting EFTA countries a special status as trading partners risks negative reactions from other third countries. As early as 1971, the USA submitted a note to the EC warning it not to conclude trade agreements which discriminate against the US with countries unwilling to join the EC as full members.[13]

Secondly, far-reaching agreements with EFTA countries are bound to be unwelcome to associate countries. Turkey, which already has an association agreement with the EC with the promise of eventual membership, and the Maghreb countries, whose trade agreements and economic links with the EC are extensive, present particularly intricate problems. For example, it would be politically difficult for the EC to entertain an Austrian membership application without being prepared to enter into accession negotiations with Turkey. The EC will therefore have to justify the existence of a 'special relationship' with EFTA. This is one reason why political rhetoric and symbolism are so important in EC-EFTA relations.

Thirdly, the crowded EC agenda is a constraint. Until recently, the agricultural and budgetary issues facing the Twelve were so huge and urgent as to make it impossible for EC members to devote more than scant attention to the EC-EFTA issue. It is not certain how rapidly the internal market will be put into effect: and progress in EC-EFTA negotiations hinges on the progress made in implementing the internal market. But developments in Eastern and Central Europe have overtaken this important matter and now enjoy compelling priority. It will be very difficult for the EFTA countries to command the same sense of urgency.

Fourthly, membership negotiations are a tricky and time-consuming business. The Commission does not consider any enlargement prior to 1992 to be a practical possibility, mainly because the internal market programme claims much of the EC negotiators' attention. The SEA has given the European Parliament (EP) a voice in decisions on both association and accession agreements; and it takes time for the Commission to give an opinion on applications, for the Council to reach a common position, for negotiations to be conducted and for the national parliaments to ratify the eventual treaty. Moreover, the staff in the Commission's DG I assigned to the management of EC-EFTA relations are few and heavily burdened.

Lastly and more generally, there is much apprehension in a number of EC countries that the EC's own integration might be jeopardized by far-reaching EC-EFTA cooperation, or in the longer term, by the accession of one or more EFTA countries to the EC. The Community is still in the process of 'digesting' its two most recent members.

Karl-Heinz Narjes, at the time vice-president of the Commission, warned against further enlargement of the EC, pointing out that it is already reaching the limit of its decision-making capacity.[14] Enlargement generally brings new issues on to the agenda and requires tricky adjustments within all EC institutions.

But while wide-ranging EC-EFTA cooperation will surely change the nature of the EC somewhat, it need not necessarily make impossible the further progress of integration. Existing evidence indicates that the problems have been exaggerated. The introduction of majority voting has partly offset the negative impact of enlargement on decision-making. Within EPC Spain and Portugal have managed to adapt quite smoothly to *acquis politique*.

Even so, the interest of most EC members in developing the security consultations within EPC means that to be acceptable as candidates for membership, the neutral EFTA countries would probably at the very least have to adopt a flexible attitude to security discussions, such as displayed by the Irish; unless, that is, they were granted only the status of closer economic associates.

In the past, enlargement has generally been accompanied by efforts to deepen integration. This was the case in the early 1970s with the Werner Plan for economic and monetary union and again in the mid-1980s with the single European Act. In both cases, initiatives for a deepening of integration were taken concurrently with enlargement or after enlargement had been decided on.

Clearly, this partly reflects the need to work out a political compromise with the most ardent adherents of *approfondissement* within the EC. Enlargement may even tend to act as a spur to integration, in that it can be persuasively argued that the supranational institutions and mechanism must be strengthened[15], in order to prevent an administrative and political 'overload' resulting from the increase in the number of member states. In other words, enlargement creates a need for political side-payments to the federalists. In any case, past experience leads us to expect that a new round of enlargement will coincide with attempts to move the EC further towards some kind of European union.

The above constraints are powerful. In principle there is no strong case against enlargement, but to overcome these difficulties would test the skills and commitments of the Commission and of the governments in the two groups of countries. The creation of an EES with new structures and procedures would evade many of these constraints by avoiding the most stubborn political obstacles. But the EES is not an easy option either, as other contributors to this volume demonstrate.

Principles underlying negotiation

The EC's general negotiating position towards EFTA rests on four political principles:

(1) Integration within the Community has absolute priority.
(2) The decision-making autonomy of the Community must be safeguarded.
(3) Cooperation with the EFTA countries should be based on 'real reciprocity' in all areas.
(4) No area of cooperation should be excluded a priori.[16]

In the run-up to the joint ministerial meeting in February 1988, Spain tried but failed to introduce a fifth principle: that 'social and economic cohesion' should be applied in every area of cooperation.

The first principle derives from the fact that the EC has not yet fully achieved its original objectives, and so should avoid delays and distractions as far as possible. It can, in any case, be argued that in many respects, EC integration would benefit EFTA. The creation of a unified market of 320 million people opens up immense possibilities for EFTA companies investing directly in the Community area. For the larger EFTA-based companies, a solid market share in the EC is a precondition for taking on more powerful competitors in the world market.

As for the second principle, EFTA participation in the EC's decision-making process would add complexities to an already burdensome process. The EC has not been inclined to engage in full consultations with EFTA prior to EC decisions on new legislation, as this would give EFTA countries a *de facto* right of co-decision, and thus devalue membership.

It is, however, possible to envisage more modest steps towards association, short of actual participation in decision-making. It is hard to see why EFTA governments could not be granted a kind of observer status in certain issue areas, giving them the right to explain their country's position without actually taking part in decision-making. Trade issues and technological cooperation might be such areas, in view of the high degree of common interest. But it has become clear that the heart of the negotiations over the EES lies here.

'Real reciprocity' is a contentious principle, difficult to define in practice. There is no general agreement within the EC as to exactly what real reciprocity would constitute. It has so far proved almost impossible to calculate an individual member's benefits and obligations in relation to the EC. More importantly, it is much easier to calculate the effects of the removal of tariffs and quantitative restrictions on trade than the effects of eliminating specific, non-tariff barriers to intra-European trade.

It should be noted that, because of its very vagueness, the reciprocity principle can also be used as a means of exerting pressure on EFTA countries. It is, however, undeniable, that EC membership involves obligations and costs which EFTA countries are spared. What is also clear is that the difference between the legal enforcement mechanisms of the EC and EFTA creates a certain asymmetry which complicates the negotiation of EC-EFTA agreements.

Furthermore, for a long time EFTA countries enjoyed much the same trade advantages as EC members, simply because slow progress within the EC prevented its members from enjoying many of the advantages going beyond the freedom from tariffs and quantitative restrictions already shared by EFTA countries. However, the speeding-up of liberalization under the 1992 programme has made it much harder for these countries to keep in step or to avoid discrimination by the EC, whether intended or not.

It has been suggested that in order to achieve greater overall reciprocity and cohesion, EFTA governments might contribute financially to the EC's structural funds. Until recently, they were able to point to the fact that EC policy of redistribution were rudimentary. Since the European Council agreement of February 1988 on the Delors package the situation has changed and the political pressure on EFTA countries to make financial transfers is likely to increase.

In principle, all EFTA countries seem to accept the need for reciprocity. The Swedish Minister of Trade, Anita Gradin, in a speech to the Council of Europe on 19 November 1987, hinted that Sweden would be willing to consider some kind of participation in initiatives aimed at maintaining the cohesion of the developing EES[17] and this has been confirmed by high-ranking officials in the trade department of the Swedish foreign ministry. EFTA's own still extant fund for the industrial development of Portugal has been cited as a useful precedent. The Austrian government has also responded positively, though without going into detail as to contributions: in October 1987 Chancellor Vranitsky made it clear that – 'Austria would be prepared to engage in fair burden-sharing'.[18]

The issue of reciprocity is, however, more complex than is often realized. EFTA governments argue that if they contribute financially to the regional funds, they will want to participate in decision-making, and this is difficult to envisage, given that the EC does not want to give up its decision-making autonomy. 'It is like trying to square the circle', as one senior Swedish official put it.[19] The EC may not be prepared to let EFTA governments take part in decisions on the use of the EC's own structural funds. However, it would be difficult for EFTA governments to explain to their publics that they were paying out money without having a say in its use.

Funding directly from EFTA governments to the less prosperous regions of the EC, along the lines of the Portugal fund, has been regarded within the Commission as a more reasonable solution. But whatever the precise formula, some arrangement will almost certainly have to be found to satisfy both the southern Europeans and the European Parliament, especially now that the EC also has to carry a budgetary burden for Eastern Europe.

As mentioned earlier, the Spanish government proposed in 1988 that in addition to making a financial contribution to the less prosperous regions of the EC, EFTA countries should eliminate tariffs for certain agricultural products (such as oranges) and that Norway should give the Spanish fishing fleet greater access to Norwegian waters.[20] However, such an arrangement would probably have serious repercussions on relations with the Maghreb exporters of citrus fruit. 'This is not the time for the EC to be seen to punish Morocco', one Commission official commented tartly.

It should be added that some EC members, (for instance the FRG) point out that the Nordic EFTA countries also have their regional development problems. The cohesion debate in the EC-EFTA context is related to the general question of who will be the losers and who the winners in the emergent internal market.

The fourth principle, that no area of cooperation should be excluded a priori, is simply meant to indicate that the EC intends to adopt a flexible and open-minded attitude in negotiations with EFTA. Indeed, it is important to note that in agreeing to the Luxembourg Declaration of 1984, the 18 West European countries have entered into an open-ended commitment. New or 'flanking' areas are under discussion, for instance the environment, and they have in turn led to some broadening of the scope of EFTA.

Progress towards the EES

By 1988 it had become clear that there was a range of options for developing EC-EFTA relations, from modest extensions of the inherited pattern of interconnectedness to much more ambitious arrangements. Five main options could be envisaged:

(1) parallel, national adaptation on the part of the EFTA countries;
(2) cooperation: a mixture of multilateral and bilateral agreements;
(3) association: EFTA countries drawing closer to the EC to form a kind of 'outer circle';
(4) partial integration: the creation of a customs union encompassing both the EC and EFTA, including some or all EFTA countries;
(5) full integration: the enlargement option.

Initially a combination of options (1) and (2) was chosen. Varying combinations of multilateral, bilateral and national approaches were possible: the question was which approach to EC-EFTA cooperation was to be given priority in which issue area. Officials in the EC Commission emphasized that issues such as technical barriers to trade and public procurement lend themselves easily to multilateral bargaining, whereas in other areas, such as fisheries, services and energy, divisions within EFTA impeded a group-to-group approach.

On the face of it, autonomous adaptation on the part of EFTA countries is an attractive prospect, saving the EC Commission valuable time. The Commission has, however, had second thoughts about this approach, of which Austria and Switzerland have made enthusiastic use. The snag is that once EFTA products have been granted compatibility status, the EC might subsequently be expected to consult with EFTA countries before changing its own legislation. The Commission fears that in this way it might be conferring a right of co- decision on the Austrian and Swiss governments.

The multilateral approach has, as mentioned, already been tested in practice. The Commission and the EC member states are negotiating new multilateral conventions with EFTA.[21] The EC seems intent on exploiting to the full the advantages of efficiency inherent in the multilateral approach: however, there is no uniformity of views on the issue of multilateral versus bilateral procedures, nor is the multilateral approach straightforward. Some observers believe that the Commission prefers multilateral negotiations, because they enhance its own role, even though this seems to enhance the status of the EFTA secretariat as well, thus implying a misleading symmetry between the EC and EFTA. Others have the impression that the Commission as a whole is using divide-and-rule tactics, both promoting bilateralism and stimulating the membership debate in certain EFTA countries. This reflects differences of opinion within the EC.

There is now a stronger case for the multilateral approach, as the EFTA countries have, much to the EC's surprise, been able to achieve a surprisingly high degree of cohesion. However, the remaining divergences are still very considerable and are likely to preserve bilateralism as a prominent feature of EC-EFTA relations.

The EC is not in favour of enlargement prior to 1992, so a logical extension of the multilateral approach would be the conclusion of some sort of association agreement (option (3)) or, more ambitiously, the creation of a customs union (option (4)). The pressures have grown for 'rationalization' of relations; moreover, general foreign policy considerations relating to the future evolution of the European state system would seem to favour a flexible group-to-group approach.

The Community will probably regard the full enlargement option as a last resort, until the bulk of the internal market legislation is in place. In the medium and long run, its appraisal might well change, under the influence of pan-European integration. In any case, the Community will distinguish among EFTA members in terms of their relative attractiveness in terms of economic, political and security policy criteria. A few general observations may help to illustrate the point.

The accession of Norway, a NATO member, would raise the fewest problems. Norway occupies a vital strategic position within the alliance, geographically not very different from that of the FRG. It is also the EC's main supplier of gas, helping to diversify dependence on external energy supplies. Sweden has less to offer, both politically and in terms of security, but has a technologically advanced and generally very successful economy. Neither Finland nor Iceland would be likely to apply for EC membership except alongside their Nordic partners: hence the dowries they might bring have not been examined by the EC.

Austria's economy may not measure up to the Swedish, but it would be able to bring to the Community valuable diplomatic contacts, especially in Eastern European countries. Switzerland is, after Japan, the second largest market for EC exports. Switzerland and Austria are both important transit countries and so have a certain leverage over the EC, particularly in view of the plans for an EC without internal frontiers. The close German-Austrian relationship is likely to prove a two-edged sword. While Austria can count on some German support for its EC policy, the prospect of a strengthening of the German-speaking peoples' position in the EC is likely to cause antipathy in some quarters, a problem compounded by Austria's 'image problem'.

The neutral status of four EFTA members raises issues of principle for the EC: but it has no policy position and even Austria's formal application for full membership has not stimulated much open debate.

Conclusion

In December 1989 the EC and EFTA decided formally to negotiate on the formation of a structured EES. The decision followed the flurry of activity and preparatory discussions joined since Jacques Delors' speech of January 1989. But the future of EC-EFTA relations remains intertwined with several other developments:

(1) the extent and pace of the completion of the EC's internal market;
(2) the extent to which the northern EC members can mobilize the support of their fellow members for a more ambitious EC-EFTA partnership;
(3) further progress in the dialogue about burden-sharing;
(4) the internal political debate in the EFTA countries;
(5) the interaction of the EC-EFTA issue with the wider question of Western Europe's external trade policies;
(6) the scope and degree of permanence of the current changes in the Soviet Union, and the wider transformation of Central and Eastern Europe.

In principle, however, enlargement is possible, in the longer term. Norwegian accession is widely regarded as uncontroversial. Intermediate arrangements are being explored, but none is straightforward; and there are costs attached to a blurring of the distinction between association and full membership.

On the assumption that the major part of the internal market programme will be completed on schedule, a realistic scenario is that in about ten years' time Norway, Sweden and Austria will have joined the EC and the other EFTA members will be facing an excruciatingly difficult decision on whether to join as well. The debate on further enlargement is only just beginning: it is difficult to envisage such an enlargement taking place, except through the emergence of a two-speed Western Europe, at least as regards security and defence cooperation.

Notes

1. The research for this chapter included many interviews with officials who understandably wish to remain anonymous. They were an invaluable source of information and advice but bear no responsibility for this text.
2. Luxembourg Declaration of 9 April 1984.
3. Esko Antola, 'EFTA-EC relations after the White Paper', *EFTA-Bulletin* 3, 1987.
4. *Agence Europe*, 4 June 1986.
5. 'Franske militære vil trene i Norge', *Aftenposten*, 11 July 1987.
6. 'French cautious on opening up markets', *Financial Times*, 11 April 1988. This article quotes a report submitted to the French Foreign Ministry as saying that the opening up of the West European market needs to be matched by parallel measures towards the outside world, to safeguard the interests of European business.
7. Clive Church, 'Great Britain's European policy' in *EFTA from Yesterday to Tomorrow* (Geneva, 1987).
8. Helen Wallace,' with Adam Ridley, *Europe: The Challenge of Diversity*, Chatham House Paper No. 29 (London, Routledge, 1985).
9. Based on Victor Echevarria Ugarte, 'La cooperation CEE-EFTA: la posición española',

Boletín Economico de Información Comerical Española no. 2, 20–26 June 1988, p. 139.

10. Tove-Lise Schou, 'Danmark mellem Norden of EF', *Økonomi og Politik*, 1982/3; and Christian Thune, 'Denmark, Europe and the creation of EFTA' in *EFTA from Yesterday to Tomorrow*.
11. Jørgen Ørstrøm Møller, 'Konsekvenser for de nordiske lande af udviklingen i det økonomiske samarbejde mellem EF-landene', *Samfundsøkonomen*, March 1988.
12. 'Single European Act', *Bulletin of the European Community*: Supplement 3/1986.
13. Harto Hakovirta, 'The Nordic neutrals in Western Europe', *Cooperation and Conflict*, XXII, 1987.
14. *Der Spiegel*, 9 November 1987.
15. A similar argument is suggested in John Palmer, 'The scope for further enlargement of the EC' in J. Jamar and H. Wallace (eds), *EEC-EFTA: More Than Just Good Friends?*' (Bruges, De Tempel 1988), p. 279.
16. See COM (85) 206 final and COM (86) 298 final, Commission of the European Communities, Brussels.
17. Council of Europe Doc. CM (87) 216, Strasbourg.
18. 'Erste High Level Talks Ö/EG', *Resumèprotokoll*, Vienna, 15–16 October 1987.
19. Interview with Ambassador Ulf Dinkelspiel, 12 February 1988.
20. 'España pide compensaciones frente a la EFTA' *El País*, 26 January 1988.
21. Nikolaus van der Pas, 'Konzept und Realisierungschancen für eine Vertiefung der Beziehungen zwischen EC und EFTA' in R. Rack (ed.), *30 Jahre Danach: Neue Perspektiven für die Beziehungen der EFTA-staaten zur Europäischen Gemeinschaft* (Baden-Baden, Nomos Verlagsgesellschaft, 1987).

10 Austria
Paul Luif

Legal and constitutional barriers to union

Austrian foreign policy rests on two important legal pillars. One is the State Treaty for the Re-establishment of an Independent and Democratic Austria, signed on 15 May 1955 by France, the Soviet Union, the United Kingdom, the United States and Austria. This treaty includes several articles which have some relevance for Austrian integration policy. One important article forbids any union with 'Germany':

> *Article 4: Prohibition of Anschluss*
> 1. The Allied and Associated Powers declare that political or economic union between Austria and Germany is prohibited. Austria fully recognizes its responsibilities in this matter and shall not enter into political or economic union with Germany in any form whatsoever.
> 2. In order to prevent such union Austria shall not conclude any agreement with Germany, nor do any act, nor take any measures likely, directly or indirectly, to promote political or economic union with Germany, or to impair its territorial integrity or political or economic independence. Austria further undertakes to prevent within its territory any act likely, directly or indirectly, to promote such union and shall prevent the existence, resurgence and activities of any organizations having as their aim political or economic union with Germany, and pan-German propaganda in favour of union with Germany.

In the late 1950s, some specialists in international law, as well as politicians from the Socialist Party (SPÖ), thought that this article must forbid Austrian membership of the EEC, since West Germany had an overwhelming influence on the EEC's economic structure.[1] As membership of the EEC has been extended beyond the original six members, practically all lawyers and officials have agreed that for Austria to join the EC of Twelve would not constitute an 'Anschluss'.[2] The 'Germany' of the State Treaty is not West Germany; the Federal Republic (or a United Germany) is only one of twelve member states and does not have the final say in EC decision-making.

The State Treaty includes a few other provisions which could be of some small nuisance value if Austria should become a member of the EC:

Article 14: Disposal of War Matériel of Allied and German Origin

. . .

4. Austria shall not manufacture any war matériel of German design.
Austria shall not acquire or possess, either publicly or privately, or by any other means, any war matériel of German manufacture, origin or design except that the Austrian Government may utilize, for the creation of the Austrian Armed Forces, restricted quantities of war matériel of German manufacture, origin or design remaining in Austria after the Second World War.

. . .

Article 15: Prevention of German Rearmament

. . .

2. Austria shall not employ or train in military or civil aviation or in the experimentation, design, production or maintenance of war matériel: persons who are, or were at any time previous to 13th March, 1938, nationals of Germany; or Austrian nationals precluded from serving in the Armed Forces under Article 12; or persons who are not Austrian nationals.

Article 16: Prohibition Relating to Civil Aircraft of German and Japanese Design
Austria shall not acquire or manufacture civil aircraft which are of German or Japanese design or which embody major assemblies of German or Japanese manufacture or design.

. . .

Article 22: German Assets in Austria

. . .

13. Austria undertakes that, except in the case of educational, cultural, charitable and religious property none of the properties, rights and interests transferred to it as former German assets shall be returned to ownership of German juridical persons or where the value of the property, rights and interests exceeds 260,000 schillings, to the ownership of German natural persons. Austria further undertakes not to pass to foreign ownership those rights and properties indicated in Lists 1 and 2 of this Article (oil fields and concessions to oil exploration areas in eastern Austria) which will be transferred to Austria by the Soviet Union in accordance with the Austro-Soviet Memorandum of 15 April 1955.

These provisions of the State Treaty have to be 'reinterpreted' or concessions from Germany are needed because some of the above-mentioned provisions could hinder free trade with Germany.

The second legal pillar of Austrian external relations – the constitutional law on permanent neutrality – is of a much greater relevance for Austrian integration policy.

Article I
1. For the purpose of the lasting maintenance of her independence externally, and for the purpose of the inviolability of her territory, Austria declares of her own free will her perpetual neutrality. Austria will maintain and defend this with all means at her disposal.
2. For the securing of this purpose in all future times Austria will not join any military alliances and will not permit the establishment of any foreign military bases on her territory.

Article II
The Federal Government is charged with the execution of this Federal Constitutional Law.

This law was passed on 26 October 1955. Through notification to all nations with which Austria had diplomatic relations at the time, Austria's neutrality status became binding under international law. Neither Austria nor any other member of the international community of states can unilaterally interpret or alter its obligations; nor can Austria unilaterally abandon its neutral status.

Discussions on the compatibility of Austrian neutrality and membership in international organizations started almost immediately after the passing of the constitutional law. It was envisaged by the decision-makers in 1955 (and explicitly stated in the so-called Moscow Memorandum) that Austria would adhere to a neutrality 'of a type maintained by Switzerland'.[3]

In 1955, Switzerland was a member of the OEEC, but had joined – for neutrality reasons – neither the United Nations nor the Council of Europe nor the ECSC. In contrast, Austria, with the consent of the signatories of the State Treaty, joined the UN in December 1955. In April 1956 it even became a member of the Council of Europe.

Specialists in international law have explained this by distinguishing neutrality law from neutrality policy. *Neutrality law* includes all rights and duties inherent in the international status of permanent neutrality and agreed upon by the community of states. *Neutrality policy* is that part of the foreign policy of a permanently neutral state which enhances its status, especially the credibility of its neutrality. It is only indirectly influenced by neutrality law and depends on the free will and the political assessments of the neutral country's decision-makers. Membership of the UN and the Council of Europe was seen by the Austrians as compatible with neutrality law. The accession of Switzerland to the Council of Europe in 1963 and the decision of the Swiss government to join the UN – which was rejected by the Swiss population in a referendum in March 1986 – confirmed the Austrian decisions of 1955–56 that membership of both organizations would be compatible with neutrality law.

First approaches to the European Community

After Austria's achievement of full independence in 1955, some politicians, especially in the SPÖ, started to talk about possible membership of the ECSC. But it was soon realized that the Austrian (nationalized) coal and steel industry would lose from the competition from ECSC. The leading politicians from the conservative People's Party (ÖVP), especially Chancellor Raab, wanted to avoid any criticism from the Soviet Union. Therefore there was little discussion in Austria about joining the EEC when the Treaties of Rome were signed in March 1957,[4] though Austria would have had very good reasons for joining: of all the countries which formed the EEC and EFTA, Austria had the highest level of exports to the Six and relatively little trade with the EFTA countries.

Even the Freedom Party (FPÖ), which from 1964 onwards started to plead for EEC membership, at first wanted only an association agreement. Austria's economy was backward. The consensus among Austrian specialists in international law was that the membership of a neutral country would not be feasible. The Soviet Union was hostile to the EC. After the failure of the negotiations for a great free trade area, Austria joined EFTA, together with the other neutrals.

In mid-1961, the United Kingdom, the most important member of EFTA, applied for EC membership, along with Denmark, Norway and Ireland. The EFTA neutrals had to decide on their relationship with the EC. In informal discussions among civil servants and specialists in international law and at a ministerial meeting in Vienna (19 October 1961), Austria, Sweden and Switzerland tried to coordinate their actions vis-à-vis the Common Market. The neutrals agreed on the limits of this association which were laid down in three points.

First, as regards trade policy towards third countries, the neutrals wanted to preserve their freedom of action and their treaty-making power to negotiate and sign agreements in their own name.

Secondly, in case of war or grave international crisis, the neutrals might have to introduce their own trade measures or to refrain from taking part in embargoes directed against a belligerent, perhaps even going so far as to suspend some or the whole of the agreement of association or to withdraw from it.

Thirdly, the Treaty of Rome contains special provisions regarding war materials; it was stressed that, in addition, certain supplies (such as pharmaceuticals and vital foodstuffs) would have to be safeguarded, partly through the maintenance of domestic agricultural production.[5]

On 15 December 1961, the three countries sent letters requesting association under Article 238 of the EEC Treaty. When President de Gaulle vetoed the British request for EEC membership in January 1963, Sweden and Switzerland suspended their applications, whereas Austria continued its efforts to reach an agreement on its own.

The reason for going it alone – the 'Alleingang' – was the increased strength of the so-called 'reformers' in the ÖVP. They wanted to modernize and liberalize Austria through a close connection with the EEC. At the same time, the Socialists came to fear loss of influence in a more market-oriented economy and preferred the 'socialist' EFTA to the 'capitalist' EEC. When they lost the general election in November 1962, they had to agree to the 'Alleingang'.

In the 'special arrangement' (the term 'association' was avoided in the later stages of the negotiations) Austria wanted a *de facto* customs union with some elements of economic union.[6] This approach failed in June 1967, when Italy rejected any further talks until the conflict with Austria on South Tyrol had been solved. The underlying reasons for this failure lay in the hostility of the Soviet Union towards a closer relationship between Austria and the EEC; the sudden French aversion to any special arrangement; and the difficulty in finding appropriate institutional mechanisms.[7]

The implementation of Austria's 1972 free trade agreements on industrial goods with the EC and the ECSC brought no major problems. It was only in the mid-1980s, when the EC decided on the completion of its internal market, that new challenges appeared to Austria's relations with the Community.

Political responses to EC developments

As in the other neutral countries, the first reaction towards the new dynamics of the EC was that a new relationship would not be necessary. Foreign Minister

Gratz saw 'neither an economic nor a political reason to change our attitude'.[8] But in the opposition party, the ÖVP, powerful voices were already pleading for a closer relationship with the EC. In an important article, Andreas Khol, one of the party's younger foreign policy specialists, suggested a 'triple jump' towards Europe – from cooperation via association to union.[9]

The Austrian government's integration policy began to change, only in mid-1986, when a group of younger politicians from the SPÖ obtained important positions in the government. The new Chancellor, Franz Vranitzky (SPÖ), stated that Austria should seek a 'quasi-membership' of the EC. This trend was strengthened by the creation of the Grand Coalition government by the Socialists and the Conservatives. In its statement of policy (January 1987) it declared that intensifying Austria's relations with the EC was a 'central objective' of its foreign policy.

Under Vice-Chancellor and Foreign Minister Alois Mock (ÖVP) the Foreign Ministry conceived a 'global approach' for participation in the EC's internal market; through this, Austria would aim to play a full part in the internal market, in order to avoid the reproach of wanting only to 'pick the raisins out of the cake'. This approach would also improve the internal decision-making process. No part of Austria's economy would get any special treatment; otherwise, it was feared, the large protected sectors of the economy would try to resist any opening up and thus weaken the negotiating position vis-à-vis the Community. The agreements which were deemed necessary to ensure Austrian participation in the internal market could later be included in a new Treaty, which would replace the free trade agreements between Austria and the EC.[10]

During 1987 representatives of the EC made it clear to the Austrian government that only full members of the EC would play a part in making decisions about the internal market. Austria was facing a growing resistance to plans for participation in the internal market without being a member of the EC. So by the end of the year, such participation was being seen by the SPÖ-ÖVP government as only the next step in Austria's integration policy. It was decided to aim at more wide-ranging cooperation, to include the solution of the transit traffic problems, the securing of Austria's agricultural exports, participation in the technology programmes of the EC, enhanced cooperation in monetary matters, participation in citizens' Europe and an intensive dialogue with the European Political Cooperation (EPC). The option of EC membership at a later date was not excluded – provided that the EC fully respected Austria's neutral status.[11] Following some debates in the Cabinet, Chancellor Vranitzky announced on 5 July 1988 that the government would decide in 1989 on the EC question, and that this decision could include the possibility of an application for membership.[12]

In December 1988, differences of opinion on the urgency of application led to a quarrel about who should present the government's report to the parliament. Vice-Chancellor Mock wanted to present a short paper stressing the arguments for joining the EC; Chancellor Vranitzky wished to present a larger, detailed study which would also include a discussion of the problem areas. Finally, both parties agreed on a 'pause for reflection'.

Of the opposition parties, the FPÖ has since 1964 included a demand for EC membership in its programme. In contrast, the smallest and youngest party in the Austrian Parliament, the Greens, vehemently opposes it. The minuscule Communist Party (KPÖ) is also an outspoken adversary.

Since mid-1988, an opposition to EC membership has started to build up. Apart from the Greens, it includes people from the conservative camp (especially farmers and Catholic youth groups) and parts of the SPÖ's traditional left wing (such as the Socialist Youth), as well as some people from the mainstream of the party. The socialist mayor of Vienna has criticized the quest for EC membership on the grounds that 'they don't want us at the moment'.[13] The opposition's main arguments are:

- EC membership would endanger Austrian neutrality, since the EC would become a political and military union without room for neutrals.
- EC membership would give more decision-making power to the bureaucracy in Brussels, a shift hardly compatible with Austria's representative democracy.
- EC membership implies drastic changes in the political, economic, social and ecological situation of Austria.
- EC membership would make Austria's traditional role as a mediator between Eastern and Western Europe more difficult.[14]

Even harsher critical comments come from the tiny Communist Party. Elfriede Jelinek, a well-known writer and member of this party, called Austrian EC membership 'a more quiet, more "modern", but finally an almost more terrible "Anschluss"' than the one Austria endured in 1938.[15]

According to public opinion polls, between April 1987 and March 1989, support for Austria's EC membership fell sharply. This growing opposition carried costs for the Conservatives. In March 1989, they lost heavily in three provincial elections, for instance, some 16 percentage points in the Tyrol, and the ÖVP's all-out EC policy was seen by many as one of the main reasons for this setback. Alois Mock, spearhead of the faction that pushed for EC membership, had to resign as party leader and his place was taken by Josef Riegler, somewhat more restrained on EC matters.

Interested parties

The first important interest group to opt for full membership of the EC was the Federation of Austrian Industrialists. In a statement published in May 1987, the Federation made an 'urgent appeal to the federal government to do everything so that full membership in the EC can be accomplished at the earliest possible moment'.[16] Alternatives, such as an association according to Article 238 of the EEC Treaty, or a customs union, were rejected because they would not permit a comprehensive and equal participation in the internal market. This move was not a total surprise, since the Federation, which represents the bigger companies in the exposed sector of the Austrian economy, was always in favour of close connections with the EC.

A considerable reversal of policy occurred when on 9 December 1987 the governing body of the Federal Chamber of Commerce 'endorsed full participation in the great European market ... For Austria, this amounts to entry into the EC'.[17] The Federal Chamber seems to have been under pressure from the chambers of commerce of the western provinces, which since the mid-1980s had been stressing the importance of EC membership. Up to that time the Federal Chamber, dominated by small and medium-sized enterprises from eastern Austria, had always shown reluctance towards integration. In a memorandum, it admitted that the date for the achievement of EC membership depended not only on Austria but also on the EC, and recommended that Austria should use the period before accession in several ways:

- careful preparation of the talks and negotiations;
- agreements with the EC in various sectors, either bilaterally or with the other EFTA countries;
- economic policy measures to bring Austria nearer to the goal of membership and to strengthen the competitiveness of the Austrian economy.

According to the Federal Chamber, there were several areas of the Austrian economy where adjustments would be necessary (though measures should be implemented only after Austrian accession): among them were competition law, agricultural policy, monopolies and *Gewerbeordnung* (trade regulations).[18]

Since the beginning of the 1960s, representatives of Austrian agriculture had urged close contacts with the EC, but in the mid-1980s their position changed because agricultural prices in the EC did not rise as fast as the prices for the same products in Austria. However, in early 1988, the then Minister for Agriculture, Josef Riegler (ÖVP), stressed that Austria's huge trade deficit in agricultural products could be reduced only through EC membership. The most promising markets, southern Germany and northern Italy, remain completely inaccessible to Austrian products.[19]

In February 1989 a memorandum from the Presidents' Conference of the Chambers of Agriculture stressed that the 'historic decision' to enter the EC's internal market must be based on a national consensus, an important condition of which was a national balance of interests. Therefore, any considerable loss of income to the farmers would need to be compensated from public funds.[20]

The Austrian trade unions and chambers of labour always maintained a pragmatic attitude: when the business lobbies started to push for EC membership, the labour groups did not offer any marked opposition, but rather displayed a wait-and-see stance. Finally, after some six months of discussions, the Trade Union Council issued in July 1988 a 'cautiously positive' statement, identifying a list of principles to be agreed before membership application:

- Austria's permanent neutrality must be preserved.
- The expected increase in the growth rate must be used to expand incomes, employment and welfare.
- The priority of full employment must be accepted.
- The EC treaties did not justify any reduction of social standards.
- An active labour market policy was a requirement.
- The expected financial burden on the public budgets should be distributed in a socially balanced way.
- The trade unions must be included in all decision-making processes concerning European integration.[21]

The Council of the Chambers of Labour has also warned against using the integration process as a pretext for reducing the social standards. It criticized those groups which had already demanded EC membership and 'now clamour for billions of Schillings from public funds in compensation for maintaining their freely chosen positions'.[22]

The Delors initiative: Austria's response

In his statement of 17 January 1989 to the European Parliament, Jacques Delors, President of the Commission spoke on the EC's relations with other Europeans, especially the EFTA countries. On the one hand, he offered a more structured partnership between the EC and EFTA, with common decision-making and administrative institutions 'to make our activities more effective and to highlight the political dimension of our cooperation in the economic, social, financial and cultural spheres'.[23] On the other hand, he seemed to be referring to the Austrian aspirations to membership when he stressed that: 'the Community is ... on the way to becoming a political union entailing closer cooperation on foreign policy and security. The marriage contract is, as it were, indissoluble ... It is extremely difficult, within this all-embracing union, to provide a choice of menus.'[24]

A week later Jacques Delors underlined in an interview that the marriage contract provided for the creation of a 'political Europe' with a common foreign policy and a common defence. He did not believe that the Austrians would be ready 'to go the entire way with us'.[25]

In reply, Foreign Minister Mock pleaded for a continuation of the Austrian integration policy. Since Delors had not offered any alternative, the question of membership still remained.[26] The Socialist Party's foreign policy spokesman, Peter Jankowitsch, said that the Delors initiative reflected some 'nervousness' about Austria's foreign policy. Austria should maintain its bilateral approach, but also use EFTA as much as possible.[27] Chancellor Vranitzky was convinced that the EFTA countries would give Delors a positive answer.[28] Economic Minister Robert Graf (ÖVP) wanted Delors to explain his proposal to EFTA at its annual conference in June, but did not believe that it would work, because EFTA had no common economic policy. Austria should keep to its schedule and send its membership application to Brussels in mid-1989.[29]

Most commentators were convinced that the Delors initiative was intended to put a brake on Austria's EC ambitions.[30] Some even thought that he wished to strengthen the critics of Austrian EC policy, taking advantage of the recent quarrels in the Austrian government; but that this should not halt Austria's aspirations.[31]

The discussion caused by the Delors proposals, as well as by the EFTA summit in Oslo the following March and an informal meeting of EC and EFTA ministers in Brussels (also in March), did not alter the government's policy. As Alois Mock explained, he could not see a global resolution of EC-EFTA relations being achieved through multilateral negotiations. Austria, as a loyal member of EFTA, would participate in the EC-EFTA negotiations on the creation of a European

Economic Space, but this was no alternative to the bilateral approach which envisaged membership of the EC.[32]

The same attitude was expressed by the social partners, who jointly reported to the government on 1 March 1989. They thought that only membership could guarantee a comprehensive and equal participation in the internal market. They saw their future role as maintaining Austria's competitiveness, but realized that EC membership would transfer to Brussels large parts of their rights to industrial co-determination. They would have to adjust their influence on economic policy to the position Austria would take in the EC institutions, especially in the Council.[33]

Another important step forward was the decision of the Executive Committee of the SPÖ in April 1989 to agree (after some hesitation) to an Austrian application for EC membership. In its paper on this topic the SPÖ made some stipulations, such as the preservation of social standards in Austria and of the strict environmental protection laws. The paper stressed the importance for the Socialists of Austria's permanent neutrality and admitted: 'The SPÖ realizes that the maintenance of neutrality and membership are not directly compatible. But it assumes that they can be made compatible through the appropriate political will.'[34]

These stipulations were probably inserted to disarm critics inside the SPÖ. Some journalists observed that the paper seemed actually to exclude accession to the EC.[35]

The 'letter' to Brussels

On 17 April 1989 the coalition government reported to both chambers of parliament on the 'Future arrangement of Austria's relations with the European Communities', recommending an application by Austria for membership of the EC.[36] This report was scrutinized by parliamentary committees. There were still some differences between the ruling parties on the handling of the application: particularly as to whether the Chancellor (SPÖ) or the Foreign Minister (ÖVP) should coordinate the preparations for the forthcoming talks; and about the financial consequences of EC membership. After protracted discussions, a compromise was reached.

The accord will continue until the end of the negotiations. The agreement stresses the importance of Austria's permanent neutrality, but goes even further, by stating that 'the necessary political latitude for action must be preserved, so that Austria as a member of the European Community will be able to continue its policy of neutrality, a policy which is in the interest of the whole of Europe'.

Integration must not lead to a deterioration of social security or of the high standard of Austrian environmental and consumer protection. Austria's integration policy is to be coordinated through consensus between the Chancellor (SPÖ) and the Vice-Chancellor (ÖVP). The Foreign Minister (ÖVP) will be in charge of the negotiations with Brussels but will not supervise the internal Austrian coordination (as parts of the ÖVP had demanded). The expected costs of EC membership are not to be covered simply by cutting other budget expenditure (which means that taxes would be raised, if necessary).[37]

On 29 June, the Nationalrat, the lower (and more important) house of the

Austrian Parliament, discussed the government report. Representatives of the SPÖ, ÖVP and FPÖ called Austria's membership application a 'historic step'. The EC had become more pluralistic and so could accommodate neutrals. Austria was part of Europe and the European economy, with a 'clear and convincing position' on its role in European integration: not to participate in the internal market would make it an outsider and carry a danger of 'Albanization'. Increased trade with Eastern Europe would not be an alternative.

Some caution was expressed with regard to Austria's neutrality, particularly since the positive developments in Eastern Europe might prove to be reversible. It was also feared that Austria's foreign policy on sensitive issues might come under pressure for 'good behaviour', during the negotiations.[38].

The only opposition came from seven Green MPs (on the grounds of a threat to neutrality). The Nationalrat passed by a large majority a resolution giving the government a green light for making the application. Should the negotiations be successful, a referendum was envisaged.

On 4 July 1989, the Council of Ministers settled the final wording of the 'letter' which Foreign Minister Mock would present on 17 July in Brussels, asking for full membership of the EEC, ECSC and Euratom. The most important sentence was this:

> In making this application Austria proceeds from the assumption that it will maintain its internationally recognized status of permanent neutrality, based on the Federal Constitutional Law of 26 October 1955, and that also as a member of the European Communities, on the basis of the accession treaty, it will be in a position to fulfil its legal obligations deriving from its status as a permanently neutral state and to pursue its neutrality policy as a specific contribution to the preservation of peace and security in Europe.[39]

In the EC Council, the Belgian Foreign Minister, Mark Eyskens, vetoed a German initiative to change the agenda of the Council of 17 July and send the Austrian application immediately to the Commission. Belgium wanted first a discussion about Austrian neutrality and its compatibility with the political aims of the EC. In an interview, Eyskens even suggested that the EC should negotiate with Moscow about Austrian neutrality.

This move by a Christian Democrat Foreign Minister was criticized both by the Belgian Social Democrats, coalition partners in the government, and by the Austrians, in particular by the ÖVP and Foreign Minister Mock. Finally, 11 days after the delivery of the 'letter', all the EC governments agreed in a written procedure to send the Austrian application immediately to the Commission for its opinion. But the Council also declared that Austrian neutrality would be examined by the appropriate bodies with regard to the Single European Act, especially Article 30, point 5, which stresses that 'the external policies of the European Community and the policies agreed in European Political Cooperation must be consistent'.[40]

The Soviet Union's attitude

The Soviet Union, has been a keen (and often critical) observer of Austria's integration policy. In recent years its comments have been contradictory. Some officials have stated that neutrality would be compatible with full EC membership, so long as the EC did not embrace military matters. But by early 1988, Soviet comments had become more critical. On 16 May 1988 Gennady Gerasimov, the spokesman of the Soviet Foreign Ministry, said that the entry of Austria into the EC would contradict its status of permanent neutrality.[41]

After a visit to Moscow in September 1988, Foreign Minister Mock stated that the Soviets showed 'understanding' for the Austrian position.[42] However, according to the published minutes of his meeting with Soviet Foreign Minister Shevardnadze, the latter explicitly stated that the Soviet side

> ... does not understand the conclusion of the Austrian federal government that an EC membership of Austria is compatible with the status of permanent neutrality. The EC is an economic and political organization with military aspects....
>
> The EC is an organization with strong structures and internal discipline. As an EC member, Austria would have to accept majority decisions in political matters. A neutrality reservation would possibly not be sufficient safeguard for the status of permanent neutrality.... In the present circumstances, an Austrian accession to the EC would upset and alarm the USSR.[43]

A month later, Chancellor Vranitzky made an official visit to the Soviet Union. Afterwards, he was asked by a journalist if he 'had reduced the Soviet nyet, so to speak, from a hundred to ten per cent'. Vranitzky replied that the reduction was not to ten per cent 'but from a hundred to fifty, and that's already something'.[44] In a short comment, on the 'letter', the Soviet government acknowledged Austria's intention of solving its economic problems. It also expressed hopes that Austria would maintain its policy of neutrality.[45]

On 10 August 1989 the Soviet Union sent an *aide-mémoire* to the Austrian government, expressing 'concern' at the EC membership application and the expectation that Austria would heed its obligations under the State Treaty and the permanent neutrality law. The Austrian government was not particularly worried and did not send any formal reply.

It is clear that the Soviet Union would not invade Austria nor any other neutral country that abandoned its status in joining the EC without taking any precautions. The Soviets would have some economic leverage, as in suspending the supply of natural gas and breaking off trade relations. These inconveniences could perhaps be more easily overcome than the indirect consequences of Soviet reproach. Some EC member states might regard membership with a neutrality clause as giving the Soviet Union an opportunity to influence EC decision-making.[46] But recent developments in Eastern Europe make the Soviet position and its influence on the EC difficult to predict.

Internal reasons for Austria's choice

The process leading up to the Austrian application for EC membership seems to be a classic exercise in corporatist decision-making. Austrian foreign policy in the late 1970s and early 1980s was shaped by Chancellor Kreisky's 'global approach'. Helping to find solutions for conflicts in the Middle East and other parts of the world were deemed to be favourable to Austria's international status.

Kreisky stressed the importance of EFTA and the multilateral approach to the EC. About 1980, the opposition parties (ÖVP and FPÖ) began to criticize the Kreisky government for neglecting bilateral relations with the Community. The new SPÖ-FPÖ coalition government actively supported the multilateral rapprochement between the EC and EFTA which led to the Luxembourg ministerial meeting in April 1984.

In the mid-1980s, companies in western Austria started to press for EC membership. Trade with Western Europe has always been more important there than in the eastern provinces, where the trade with Eastern Europe used to be larger. In particular, the textile industry of Vorarlberg felt – in spite of the free trade agreements – increasing discrimination from the EC market. At the same time, younger MPs from the SPÖ and ÖVP spoke up for for a closer relationship with the EC, not excluding full membership.

Since 1945, industry in western Austria had grown much stronger than that of eastern Austria, whose economy had been weakened by the Russian occupation until 1955 and by the geographical position near the Iron Curtain. This change was instrumental in causing the Federal Chamber of Commerce to opt for EC membership in December 1987. This decision and the fact that early in 1988 EC membership was highly popular with the public, led the ÖVP, the junior partner in the coalition and closely linked with the Federal Chamber, also to plead for accession.

The trade unions were divided on the usefulness of EC membership. Some, such as the textile industry union, had obvious reasons for wanting it; others, such as the building industry union, feared increased competition and increased labour immigration and therefore opposed it. They compromised by opting for membership, under certain conditions, and this agreement made it almost impossible for the SPÖ to oppose joining the EC. The problems of nationalized industry and the precarious situation of the East European economies did not provide any viable alternative.

Economic pressures for EC membership

In November 1985 Austria's large state-owned industry was on the brink of bankruptcy and the federal government had to come to the rescue, but the already high budget deficit set limits for such intervention. The nationalized industry had to abandon one of its most cherished policies and to dismiss workers and employees on what was, for Austria, a massive scale. These problems were only one indication of the precarious state of the Austrian economy, which in the mid-1980s was growing more slowly than the economies of the other EFTA countries or than the EC economies taken as a whole.

In 1988 the Austrian economy recovered considerably and increased its growth rate; but this development came too late to have much influence on the Austrian decision about EC membership.

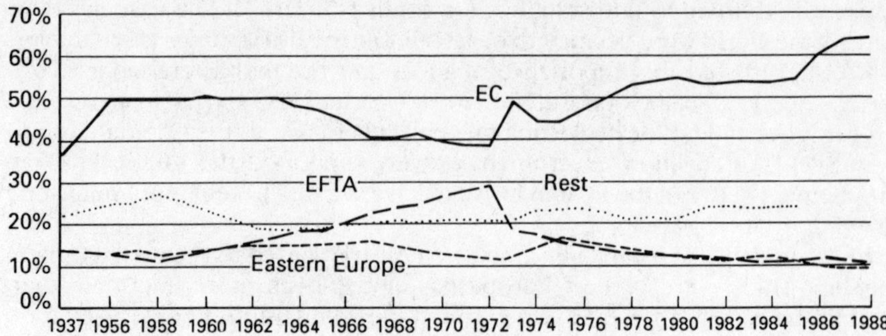

Sources: *Statistiches Handbuch für die Republik Österreich* and *Statistische Nachrichen*, various volumes, and own calculation.

Fig. 10.1 Austrian exports to selected groups of countries, 1937–88

When it comes to external trade, Austria has the highest percentage of exports to the EC of all the EFTA neutrals. Austria's exports have been highly sensitive to changes in the patterns of integration in Western Europe. Between 1959 and 1972, the percentage of exports to the EC decreased significantly. Since 1981 Austria's exports to the EC have increased substantially.

A closer look at Austria's exports shows (Fig. 10.1) that the alternative outlets – Eastern Europe and other countries – have lost importance in the 1980s. During the years between the World Wars, the proportion of Austria's exports going to Eastern Europe used to be much higher, amounting to almost one-third of the total. The changes now taking place in Eastern Europe could bring great opportunities to Austrian exporters at least in the long range view.

But exports are not the whole story; one aspect of Austrian external relations is the low presence of its companies in foreign countries. In the mid-1980s Swiss-owned companies in the EC countries employed some 350,000 persons; the number for Sweden is 160,000 persons and for Finland some 80,000. Exact data are not available for Austria, but in 1984 the number of people working for Austrian companies abroad was between 30,000 and 50,000.[47] The lack of internationalization is characteristic of the Austrian economic structure: hence Austrian companies are more dependent on exports than those of the other neutrals.

EC membership and public opinion

Fig. 10.2 shows the results of several polls between April 1987 and February 1990 which asked similar questions about EC membership.[48] They show a clear trend: the percentage of people in favour of Austrian EC membership remained

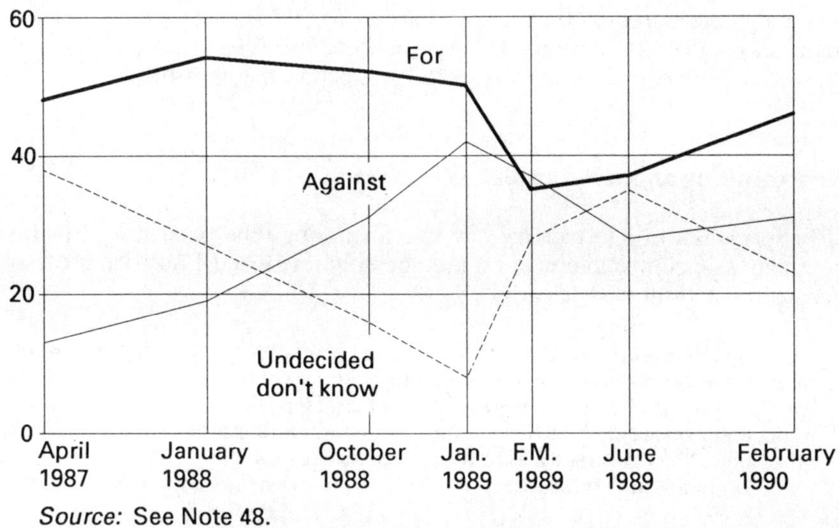

Source: See Note 48.

Fig. 10.2 Public opinion polls on attitudes towards EC membership in Austria

constant at about 50% until January 1989. Opposition to membership varied inversely with the percentage of undecided/don't knows. In the first half of 1989, the intense discussions on Austria's membership application sharply reduced the percentage of positive attitudes towards EC membership. The undecided/don't know share rose sharply. In a poll in February/March 1989, the opponents of accession actually had a small majority. After the letter to Brussels (July 1989), the percentage of Austrians in favour of membership increased again.

All polls show that the strongest opponents to EC membership are the farmers. The other occupational groups tend to be more in favour; the level of support for accession rises with the level of occupation or education. In October 1988 a poll had showed a comfortable majority of SPÖ, ÖVP and FPÖ supporters in favour of EC integration: the Greens and the Communists alone appeared to be at variance with the other political parties. Six months later the picture had changed: another poll showed that the majority of Socialists were now against EC membership. This change could have been brought about by criticism from some elements in the party, but it could also have been the other way round: some members of the party elite had sensed the increasing scepticism of the rank and file.

Clearly, public opinion has changed over the last two years – in the first half of 1989 even against the intentions of the political elite, where there has existed a more or less stable consensus on membership application. It is interesting to note that the people who display the most critical attitude towards this are the farmers, who are the ÖVP's most reliable supporters. The ÖVP is the party generally considered to be working hardest for EC membership; should the application succeed, they would reap the benefits. This could be one of the reasons for the conservatives' pressure for Austria's membership.

New thinking about neutrality

Most specialists in international law had for a long time regarded permanent neutrality as incompatible with EC membership. In 1978 the Austrian Professor Verdross stated this very clearly:

> Were the EEC Council of Ministers in an armed conflict of warlike character, with its members as participants or not, to issue unilateral export prohibitions, Austria would have to acquiesce therein if it were a full member. To do this would however infringe its neutrality obligations in that neutrality law . . . forbids unilateral export prohibitions in wartime. Were Austria to issue reciprocal export prohibitions, that would be an infraction of the EEC Treaty which envisages a homogeneous economic territory.[49]

These negative attitudes began to change in the 1970s, primarily because of the impact of EC integration and increased interdependence in international economic relations. One of the earliest restatements came from Theo Öhlinger, who thought that membership of a customs union, or even of an economic union, would not automatically undermine a neutral country's independence to such an extent that it would be unable to maintain permanent neutrality: independence must be regarded as relative. But since new members of the EC must subscribe to its political goals, a neutral member would lose credibility; and so, in the final analysis, neutrality cannot be reconciled with EC membership.[50] Other legal experts stated that EC membership, 'if hedged around with sufficient safeguards', is legally possible for permanently neutral countries.[51]

This line of thought was taken up by Hummer and Schweitzer in their influential book, *Austria and the EEC*, written for the Federation of Austrian Industrialists. The Luxembourg compromise and the escape clauses of Articles 223 and 224 of the EEC Treaty could be used by a neutral member to remain in conformity with the obligations of neutrality. Neutral status should be interpreted as an obligation Austria 'has accepted for the purpose of maintaining peace and international security' (Article 224 of the EEC Treaty). A neutrality clause included in the acts of accession might enhance the credibility of Austria's neutrality policy, but would not be necessary under a strict interpretation of neutrality law.[52]

Some specialists in international law took a fresh look at the three minimal reservations the neutrals had made in 1961 (see above). The first point, the treaty-making power, was no longer considered essential. It was only in times of war that the neutral would need to be free to treat the parties to an armed conflict even-handedly: a permanent autonomy with respect to external trade was not an essential prerequisite of neutrality. International interdependence had made autarky an impossible goal. Therefore points 2 and 3 would also have to be reconsidered.[53]

An important new aspect of this discussion was the idea, not only that neutrality should be interpreted more flexibly, but also that the EC treaties could be modified to fit neutrality more closely. Already in the 1960s the escape clauses in Articles 223 and 224 of the EEC Treaty were being regarded as a convenient way of making EEC law compatible with neutrality. But according to Article 225, the European Court of Justice may examine the actions of a member state to see whether it is making proper use of the powers provided in Articles 223 and 224; and this ultimate control by the Court of Justice has always been regarded as incompatible with permanent neutrality.

The new perspective on the subject is this: the problems with Article 225 could be overcome if the EC agreed not to use the controlling powers of the Court of Justice in those cases where Austria was seeking exemption from the EC treaties for reasons of neutrality law (for instance, in the case of embargoes favouring one party in an armed conflict). Such exemptions for neutrals would have to be instituted on the level of the Community's primary law; that is, by amending the EC treaties.[54]

Some politicians, legal experts and journalists have even started to talk about a reduction of Austria's permanent neutrality to a plain 'military neutrality', that is, one limited to military matters. Since the EC is not a military alliance, neutral countries could join it without difficulty.[55]

Others think that Austria should cooperate with the twelve democratic countries of the EC rather than with the countries of the N+N (neutral and non-aligned) group of the CSCE (Conference on Security and Cooperation in Europe): they favour, although not always explicitly, an abandonment of neutrality.[56] But the mainstream of Austrian opinion, both the elite and the general public, wants to adhere to neutrality, hoping that the EC will make the necessary concessions.

The economic implications of membership

The most important reason for Austria's application is the economic advantages that membership would bring. In a recent study, two Austrian economists tried to quantify these benefits. They took the economic model of the Cecchini Report on the projected outcome of 1992 and tried to apply it to Austria.[57] The main findings are shown in Fig. 10.3. The authors present two scenarios. One scenario (the 'integration scenario') shows the effects of Austrian participation in the internal market (that is, of accession to EC membership). The other calculates the effects of the status quo (that is, the EC completes the internal market while Austria remains an outsider).

Fig. 10.3 shows the quantitative effects of both scenarios in a 'magic polygon' (calculated for the sixth year after the completion of the internal market). The further away the data are from the centre, the better is the state of economic development. In the integration scenario, there is additional growth of 3.5% for the Austrian gross domestic product. Remaining outside the internal market, the Austrian economy would still gain 1.6% from developments in the EC. This means that through membership of the EC the Austrian economy would grow by an additional 0.3% a year. The inflation rate would decrease by 5.2% after six years and employment would increase by 1.5% instead of 0.7%. On the other

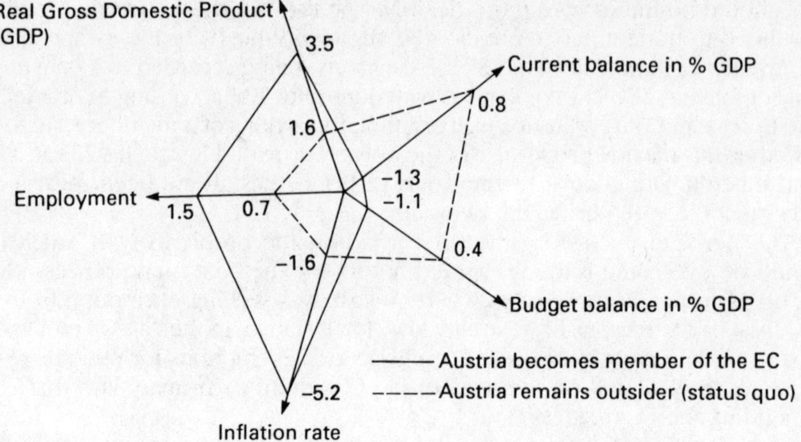

Source: Fritz Breuss and Fritz Schebeck, *Die Vollendung des EG-Binnenmarktes: Gesamtwirtschaftliche Auswirkungen auf Österreich* (Vienna, Österreichisches Institut fur Wirtschaftsforschung, 1989), p. 64.

Fig. 10.3 Economic consequences of the internal market for Austria

hand, the current account (trade in goods and services, transfers) would worsen (−1.3%). The budget deficit would also rise by 1.1% (because Austria would have to pay considerably more to the EC budget than it would get back). In the 'status quo scenario', the last two indicators should improve slightly in the first six years after the completion of the EC's internal market.

These data show that on the whole one can expect a positive development of the Austrian economy in the EC. But the economic advantages are perhaps not as great as some advocates of EC membership claim. One important point is that the alternative to membership could be something like a close association which would go beyond the status quo.

Conclusion

But will the EC accept Austria's application? It would have to be agreed to by the governments and parliaments of the twelve member states, as well as the European Parliament. In an early optimistic estimate of the situation, experts from the ÖVP believe that nine of the twelve member states have promised to vote for Austrian membership. Only Holland and Belgium are behaving 'ambivalently'. England is deemed not to have yet made a 'real statement' on this issue.[58]

In internal discussions, diplomats from the Twelve and officials of the Commission appear to be unenthusiastic about Austrian accession. Some of them warn that statesmen are being too hasty in saying, 'Austria, I love you': Vienna might try to play off one member state against another, so that no one would be able to say no to the country of Mozart, which undoubtedly belongs to Europe. In public debate, negative opinions on Austrian accession usually come from journalists, experts and retired statesmen, such as Helmut Schmidt and Edward Heath. Serving Belgian Foreign Ministers have been an exception. Leo Tindemans explicitly opposed Austrian membership on several occasions. His successor, Mark Eyskens, was at first very critical, but, after the upheavals in Eastern Europe, softened his criticism. As for the Commission, Jacques Delors' dislike of new neutral members is well known, though some other Commissioners, such as Leon Brittan, may be more favourable.[59]

The public statements of the governments of the Member States are also often unclear (does 'Austria belongs to Europe' mean that Austria is welcome to join the EC?) or contradictory. Chancellor Kohl explains on the one hand that 'another neutral member in the EC will be no problem' and on the other hand talks about creating a European army.[60] Margaret Thatcher talks about 'cooperation between independent sovereign states' in the EC, but London maintains reserve towards Vienna's EC ambitions.[61]

The critics point to the difficulties that Austrian membership would create for the 'political finality' of the Community. The decision-making processes would be complicated since there is no guarantee that Austria would not use the Luxembourg compromise for issues which are sensitive for its neutrality. That situation bears for the EC the risk of being neutralized on occasion. These points should not be ignored vis-à-vis the economic and other aspects. They may make the desirability of an Austrian membership doubtful.[62]

The decision on Austria's membership application will not be made until some time in the mid-1990s. The pertinent question now is: how will the EC and the world look then? Without aiming at prophecy, one can try to list some scenarios and show the possible consequences of Austria's efforts. Two factors have long been particularly relevant to a decision on Austrian membership: the internal development of EC integration and the external environment, especially East-West relations. Both factors are in a state of flux. The break-up of the Eastern bloc and the improved relations between the United States and the Soviet Union make neutrality a much less salient obstacle to participation in European Political Cooperation.

On the other hand, developments in Eastern Europe (German unification in particular) might lead the EC countries to hasten the establishment of an economic and monetary union. This would imply a more 'supranational' EC and could also lead to closer cooperation in foreign policy and even security policy. As long as there is no pan-European security arrangement, the Soviet Union could very well insist on the maintenance of Austrian neutrality. In this situation, Austrian accession to the EC would be difficult – except in the case of the creation of a two-tier community.

Austria should perhaps follow a dual strategy. It should use the membership application as a 'bargaining chip' to get, if not membership, then as close a relationship with the EC as possible. In the meantime Austria should do its utmost to modernize and internationalize its economy which is backward, compared to those of the other neutrals. It will be a difficult way – but Austria has little choice.

Notes

Some of the material in this chapter is drawn from my book *Neutrale in die EG? Die wirtschaftliche Integration in Westeuropa und die neutralen Staaten* (Vienna, Braumüller, 1988) and 'Austria's application for EC membership: historical background, reasons and possible results' in Finn Laursen (ed.), *EFTA and the EC: Implications of 1992* (Maastricht, European Institute of Public Administration, 1990). All translations from German are mine. The chapter should be read in conjunction with another contribution to this research project by Heinrich Schneider, *Austria and the EC* (RIIA Discussion Paper No. 24, London, Royal Institute of International Affairs, 1989).

1. Among them were Bruno Kreisky, then Foreign Minister, and Rudolf Kirchsläger, then specialist in international law in the Foreign Ministry.
2. The same conclusion is drawn by the conservative professor Heribert Franz Kock, *Ist ein EWG-Beitritt Österreichs zulässig*? (Vienna, Orac, 1987) and by the Marxist scholar Alfred-Johannes Noll, 'Rechtliche Aspekte einer weiteren Annäherung Österreichs an die EWG' in Margit Scherb and Inge Morawetz (eds.), *Der unheimliche Anschuss. Österreich und die EWG* (Vienna, Verlag für Gesellschaftskritik, 1988), pp. 165–92.
3. See the text of the Moscow (or Austro-Soviet) Memorandum in Alfred Verdross, *The Permanent Neutrality of Austria* (Vienna, Verlag für Geschichte und Politik, 1978), p. 26.
4. However, at one point during the negotiations about the EEC Treaty, when France was causing problems, Paul-Henri Spaak considered asking the Austrians to take the place of the French: Miriam Camps, *Britain and the European Community 1955–1963* (Princeton, Princeton University Press, 1964), p. 59, note 10.
5. Hans Mayrzedt and Waldemar Hummer, '20 Jahre Österreichische Neutralitäts – und Europapolitik (1955–1975)', *Dokumentation*, Teilband I (Vienna, 1976) pp. 336–68.
6. Jean-Victor Louis, 'L'adoption du premier mandat de négociation avec l'Autriche, 2 mars 1965', in *Les Missions permanentes auprès des organisations internationales*, tome 2 (Brussels, Emile Bruylant, 1973), pp. 359–426.
7. Paul Luif, 'Decision structures and decision-making processes in the European Communities' relations to the EFTA countries: a case study of Austria' in *Österreichische Zeitschrift für Aussenpolitik* vol. 33, nos 3–4 (1983), p. 142.
8. 'Gratz gegen neue EG-Diskussion: "Energien werden verzettelt"', *Die Presse*, 2 December 1985.
9. Andreas Khol, 'Im Dreisprung nach Europa: Kooperation – Assoziation – Union' in *Europäische Rundschau*, Vol. 13, No. 3 (1985), pp. 29–45.
10. Alois Mock, 'Aussenpolitische Erklärung' (unpublished manuscript) 11 May 1988.
11. This summarizes the 'Outline of the Austrian Integration Policy' approved by the government on 1 December 1987.
12. 'Kernelemente von Österreichs EG-Annäherung. Unzureichend geklärte Neutralitätsprobleme', *Neue Zürcher Zeitung*, Fernausgabe no. (FA) 173, 28 July 1988, p. 21.
13. Interview with Mayor Helmut Zilk in *Profil*, no. 13, 28 March 1989, p. 15.
14. 'Kein Beitrittsansuchen nach Brüssel', advertisement in *Profil*, n. 26, 26 June 1989, p. 53.
15. Elfriede Jelinek, 'Künstler gegen EG-Brief', *Volksstimme*, 25 April 1989, p. 3. This statement was called by a (leftist) commentator 'a culmination of political bad taste': see G. Pawlis, 'Euro-Manchestertum – eine unvermeidliche Notwendigkeit?', *Aufrisse*, no. 2 (1989), p. 35.
16. 'Europa – unsere Zukunft. Eine Stellungnahme der Vereinigung Österreichischer Industrieller zur Europäischen Integration', Vienna, Vereinigung Österreichischer Industrieller, May 1987, p. 46.

17. *Pressedienst der Bundeswirtschaftskammer*, 9 December 1987.
18. *Memorandum zur Vorbereitung Österreichs auf den Europäischen Binnenmarkt*, Bundeskammer der Gewerblichen Wirtschaft, December 1988, p. 2–3.
19. Hanna Kordik, 'Derfler fordert jetzt Antrag zum EG-Beitritt. Riegler: Brauchen mehr Budgetmittel', *Kurier*, 11 February 1988, p. 7.
20. Memorandum der Präsidentenkonferenz der Landwirtschaftskammern Österreichs für europäischen Integration, *Präsidentenkonferenz aktuell*, February 1989, p. 1–2.
21. Österreichischer Gewerkschaftsbund, Europa Memorandum, Vienna, December 1989, pp. 2–4.
22. This statement is an indirect critique of the agricultural interest groups. See 'Europa – Stellungnahme des Österreichisches Arbeiterkammertages', Vienna, January 1989, p. 6.
23. Jacques Delors, 'The broad lines of Commission policy', statement by the President of the Commission (manuscript), Strasbourg, 17 January 1989, p. 32.
24. Delors, *ibid.*, January 1989.
25. 'EG-Beitritt: Delors betont Skepsis', *Der Standard*, 25 January 1989, p. 1.
26. *Der Standard*, 25 January 1989.
27. '"Zielkonflikte vermeiden." Jankowitsch zu aktuellen Fragen', *Wiener Zeitung*, 25 January 1989, p. 4; and 'Jankowitsch-Reaktion: "Die EG wird nervös"', *Kurier*, 26 January 1989, p. 2.
28. 'Vranitzky für engere Kooperation EFTA-EG. Positive Reaktion auf das Angebot Delors', *Der Standard*, 30 January 1989, p. 2.
29. Heinrich Mathis, 'Graf: "Brief nach Brüssel" erst nach Afta-Ausprache mit Delors', *Der Standard*, 13 February 1989, p. 11.
30. Gerhard Friedrich, 'Gebremster EG-Fahrplan', *Der Standard*, 1 February 1989, p. 20.
31. Andreas Unterberger, 'Unruhe im europäischen Glasperlenspiel', *Die Presse*, 26 January 1989, p. 3. Among Austrian journalists, Unterberger is one of the strongest advocates of Austrian EC membership.
32. David Buchan, 'EC and EFTA ministers to hold formal talks on closer relations', *Financial Times*, 21 March 1989.
33. *Sozialpartnerstellungnahme "Österreich und die europäische Integration"*, Vienna, 1 March 1989, pp. 40–42.
34. *Österreich in Europa. Bericht des Parteivorsitzenden an das Parteipräsidium und den Bundesparteivorstand am 3.4.1989* (Sozialistische Partei Österreichs, Vienna, 1989), p. 10.
35. Liselotte Palme, 'Österreich/EG: Die Kunst des Möglichen', *Profil*, no. 15, 10 April 1989, p. 52.
36. *Bericht der Bundesregierung an den Nationalrat und den Bundesrat über die zukünftige Gestaltung der Beziehungen Österreichs zu den Europäischen Gemeinschaften*, Vienna, 17 April 1989, 111–13 der *Beilagen zum Stenographischen Protokoll des Nationalrats*, p. 1.
37. 'EG-Parteienvereinbarung vom 26.6.1989', *Wiener Zeitung*, 26 September 1989, p. 5.
38. *Parlamenskorrespondenz*, no. 109, 26 June 1989.
39. *Aussenpolitischer Bericht 1989*, p. 187.
40. Otmar Lahodynsky, '"Wir haben nichts gegen Österreich". Belgien Aussenminister Mark Eyskens hat aber Angst vor der Neutralität', *Die Presse*, 20 July 1989, p. 3; Herbert Lackner, 'Brüsseler Spitzen', *Profil*, no. 30, 24 July 1989, pp. 13–15; and Georg Posanner, 'Grünes Licht für Österreichs AG-Antrag', *Der Standard*, 29/30 July 1989, p. 2.
41. This statement was merely the most explicit in a long line of similar assertions in the Soviet press and by the Soviet ambassador in Vienna.
42. 'Erörterung von Österreichs EG-Plänen', *Neue Zürcher Zeitung*, FA 214, 15 September 1988, p. 1.

43. 'EG-Beitritt würde UdSSR alarmieren"', *Profil*, no. 41, 10 October 1988, pp. 38–39.
44. Franz Vranitzky, 'Njet auf 50 Prozent reduziert', interview with Josef Votzi, *Profil*, no. 42, 17 October 1988, pp. 16–17.
45. 'Sowjetische Erklärung zum EG-Brief', *Volksstimme*, 6 July 1989, p. 3.
46. Pierre Pescatore, 'EG-Beitritt Österreichs: Voraussetzungen Folgen, Alternativen', *Economy*, No. 2 April 1989, pp. 64–74.
47. Data from *Bericht über die Stellung der Schweiz im europäischen Integrationsprozess vom 24 August 1988* (Berne, Eidgenössische Drucksachen und Materialzentrale, 1988), p. 190; *Sverige och den västeuropeiska integrationen. Regeringens proposition 1987/88:66* (Stockholm, Allmänna Förlaget, 1987), information from Esko Antola; and Claudia Pichl, 'Internationale Investitionen. Verflechtung der Österreichischen Wirtschaft', *WIFO Monatsberichte*, no. 3 (1989), p. 169.
48. The opinion polls used were: April 1988: phone poll by OGM, published in *Wiener*, May 1987, pp. 130–31; sample of 498.
January 1988: poll by IMAS, published in Bernard Moser (ed.), *Unser Weg in die europäische Gemeinschaft* (Vienna, Politische Akademie, 1988) pp. 108–12: sample of 1550.
October 1988: poll by SWS; sample of 2046.
January 1989: poll by Gallup-Institut, published in *Der Standard*, 4 March 1989, p. 1; sample of 1000.
February/March 1989: poll by Fessel + GFK Institut, partly published in *Profil*, no. 14, 3 April 1989, p. 16; sample of 1500.
June 1989: poll by IMAS, sample of 1500.
February 1990: poll by IFES, sample of 1800.
49. Alfred Verdross, *The Permanent Neutrality of Austria*, p. 61.
50. Theo Öhlinger, 'Institutionelle (Grundlagen der Österreichischen Integrationspolitik aus rechtlicher Sicht. Eine Zwischenbilanz' in Theo Öhlinger, Hans Mayrzedt, Gustav Kucera, *Institutionelle Aspekte der Österreichischen Integrationspolitik* (Vienna, Österreichische Akademie der Wissenschaften, 1976).
51. Friedl Weiss, 'Austria's permanent neutrality in European integration', *Legal Issues of European Integration* no. 1 (1977), p. 126; and Michael Schweitzer, *Dauernde Neutralität und europäische Integration* (Vienna-New York, Springer-Verlag, 1977).
52. Waldemar Hummer and Michael Schweitzer, *Österreich und die EWG* (Vienna, Signum Verlag, 1987).
53. Waldemar Hummer, 'Österreichs Beitrittsoption zur EG-Wandel oder Aufgabe der Österreichischen Naturalitätskonzeption?' Österreichische Monatshefte, no. 6 (1988), pp. 25–28; and Josef Azizi, 'Verfassungrechtliche Aspekte eines österreichischen EG-Beitritts, in Hans Glatz and Hans Mozer (eds.), *Kopfüber in die EG? Herausforderung Binnenmarkt* (Vienna, Service Fachverlag, 1989), pp. 241–95.
54. This is the standpoint of the Austrian government. See *Bericht der Bundesregierung* (Note 36), pp. 39–41; Azizi, *op. cit.*, pp. 259–260; Karl Zemanek, 'Österreichs Neutralität und die EG. Rechtliche Vorausstzungen zur Wahrung der dauernden Neutralität Österreichs im Falle eines Beitritts zur EG', *Economy*, no. 4, June 1989, p. 63.
55. Gunter Bischof and Wolfgang Danspeckgruber, 'Ringen um den Staatsvertrag Vorbild für EG-Verhandlungen', *Die Furche*, no. 51–52, 23 December 1988, pp. 20–21.
56. Peter Michael Lingens, 'Die Sowjets als Vorbild nehmen. Wie sieht eine klare Linie in der EG-Frage aus?' *Profil*, no. 26, 27 June 1988, p. 12; and Andreas Unterberger, 'Österreich zwischen Perestrojka und Binnenmarkt. Die Suche einer neuen Balance', *Die Presse*, 8–9 April 1989, p. 111.
57. Fritz Breuss and Fritz Schebeck, *Die Vollendung des EG-Binnenmarktes. Gesamtwirtschaftliche Auswirkungen auf Österreich* (Vienna, Österreichisches Intitut für Wirtshaftsforschung, 1989).

58. Palme (Note 35), p. 52.
59. Leo Tindemans, 'Vollmitgliedschaft ist nich möglich', Interview von Lucian Meysels mit dem belgischen Aussenminister über die Erweiterung der EG, Neutralität und Militärpolitik, *Wochenpresse*, no. 32, 12 August 1988, pp. 14–15; and Otmar Lahodynsky, '"Ich sehe in Neutralität kein Hindernis". EG-Wettbewerbskommissar Leon Brittan ermutigt Österreich', *Die Presse*, 28 February 1990, p. 3.
60. Georg Possanner, 'SPD gegen "Fussnotenmitglied" in EG. Khol: Weiterer Neutraler kein Problem', *Die Presse*, 26 June 1988, p. 2; and Helmut Kohl, 'Deutsche Politik für Europa', Vortrag des Bundeskanzlers vor den Grandes Conferences Catholiques in Brüssel am 18 Oktober 1988, *Bulletin, Presse-und-Informationsamt der Bundesregierung*, Bonn, no. 137, 26 October 1988, pp. 1233–38.
61. 'Mrs Thatcher's speech at Bruges. Emphasis on sovereign identity of European state', *Financial Times*, 21 September 1988, p. 2; and Doris Kraus, 'London zurückhaltend zu Wiens EG-Ambitionen', *Die Presse*, 2 March 1989, p. 2.
62. Matthias Pechstein, 'Austria *ante portas*: Österreichs Neutralität als Hindernis für einen Eg-Beitritt?', *Europarecht*, 24, no. 1 (1989), pp. 54–74.

11 Finland
Esko Antola

A myth of non-political integration

The foreign policy context

An attempt to explain Finnish integration policy must take into consideration the peculiar combination of international and domestic constraints. This is no doubt a dilemma for all EFTA countries, but in the Finnish case it has a particular flavour. Harto Hakovirta calls Finland 'a deviant case among other neutrals' and defines Finnish integration policy as a 'wait-and-see policy'.[1] In the outspoken official version of Finnish integration philosophy, international imperatives determine the conditions of an adaptation process which has its sources in the domestic sphere.

In other words, international factors and foreign policy reflection have traditionally taken priority over immediate domestic interests. Finland has carefully sought to balance its international commitments and its domestic needs. A notorious case was the refusal to accept Marshall Aid in the late 1940s because it had associations with the Cold War. This was in spite of the obvious need for external funding during the years of reconstruction and the burden of war reparations to the Soviet Union to a value of US $300 million. At least a part of the potential Finnish share of the Marshall Aid was replaced by special loans from the United States for the recovery of the paper industries.[2] The years after World War II were marked by an actively passive foreign trade policy. An important change took place in 1955 when Finland joined the Nordic Council and at the same time took part in the ongoing negotiations on a Nordic customs union.[3]

The conventional starting-point for any description of Finnish integration policy in the postwar period is the characterization of Finland as a *status quo* country.[4] In one of the first scholarly assessments of this period, Klaus Törnudd accordingly used the concept of political imperative: 'Finland must not disturb her policy of neutrality.'[5] Törnudd points to the heart of the matter; any policy of economic integration cannot be in contradition with the policy of neutrality.

Finland's policy of neutrality has rested on perceptions of the bloc-based nature of the postwar European system. Europe, from the Finnish point of view, has had a predominantly bipolar system, whose central feature is a power hierarchy based on the hegemony of the superpowers. Finland has given an unwavering recognition to the prominence of the alliances, military and economic blocs, and their cohesion as an essential part of European stability. Finland has also acknowledged the essential rules of behaviour in the European order and has adapted itself with care to these constraints.

Notions of hierarchy also extend to the relationships between the various issues of European international relations. Finland has recognized the primacy of military-security issues and has assessed its options as regards other dimensions of international relations in this light, including its policy on economic integration. No matter how strong the domestic pressures for a new approach to integration have been, the established hierarchy of issues has dominated Finnish views. In reality this issue of hierarchy has been so largely accepted by Finnish opinion that economic interest groups, for instance, have never challenged it.

This position as a *status quo* country has been a deliberate choice and an aim in itself. It has kept alive a self-image of a bridge-building country for which neutrality and even absenteeism is a logical and confident option. The best example of this in practice arose from the question of the membership of the Council or Europe. Finland remained outside the Council until 1989 on the grounds that this body was part of the legacy of the Cold War, and therefore incompatible with Finnish neutrality.[6]

This *status quo* approach has not, however, prevented Finland from offering its good services in the interests of order and stability in Europe. The most outstanding expression of this was the role that Finland played in the CSCE process, a role that culminated in the signing of the Helsinki Final Act in 1975. The strong emphasis given to the hierarchical nature of the European postwar system, as well as the recognition of the hierarchy of issues, is what makes Finnish neutrality a unique position, a deviant case, as regards European integration.

Impact of neutrality

The definition of the 'political' scope of European integration thus poses a crucial dilemma for Finnish policy. Paradoxically, the political elements of integration are even analysed in contradictory ways: integration is either depoliticized or overpoliticized. On the one hand a Finnish decision to take part in some effort at integration may be defended on the grounds that Finland is taking part only in economic activities and that the particular settlement has no political strings attached. This policy thus encapsulates trade relations and separates them from political commitments: Finland looks for solutions whereby economic integration arrangements do at least appear non-political, and therefore acceptable vis-à-vis neutrality.

Similarly, some European ventures are viewed as being too political and are therefore excluded as inappropriate for Finnish participation. This technique overstates the danger of political commitments and is used when an opportunity to engage in integration is regarded as incompatible with the basic foreign policy line. Such arguments are used in particular to deny the feasibility of membership of the European Community (EC).

The definition of 'political' is primarily a function of the Finnish perception of neutrality. As far as European integration is concerned, neutrality appears in two ways: it demands respect for the *status quo*, and it rules out institutional obligations. The former rests on the power of *realpolitik*: Finland, according to its declared policy line, is neutral on matters which involve a superpower confrontation. Consequently, it chose not to join those international institutions or arrangements where there has been a confrontation between the superpowers. This approach did not create too many problems as long as the old European hierarchy prevailed, but it has obviously become much more problematic in the new architecture of Europe.

A parallel aim to this *realpolitik* has been to avoid supranational commitments. Finnish doctrine on integration regards as incompatible with a policy of neutrality membership of any international institution which exercises binding or supranational decision-making powers over its members. Neutrality is possible only subject to the precondition that a neutral country maintains its freedom of action in all possible situations.

The dimension of *realpolitik* has been interpreted more flexibly than the question of supranationality. Since the mid-1960s Finland has presented its policy on integration as a factor contributing to the stability in Europe. Neutrality was not viewed as incompatible with economic integration, but rather as a positive factor in enhancing *rapprochement*. An active integration policy by the neutral countries could, it was argued, actually benefit all partners concerned. Ahti Karjalainen, then Minister for Foreign Affairs, expressed it in 1967 as follows:[7]

> We are of the opinion that active participation by neutral countries in economic integration could benefit all parties concerned. It is obvious that a decrease in the trade barriers on the European continent will have to take place sooner or later. We also think that without loss of neutrality the participation of neutral states in the integration process at its various stages contributes towards a *rapprochement* among all European countries.

Until the mid-1980s, i.e. before the 1984 Luxembourg meeting between EFTA and the EC, the solution to the political dilemmas of European integration was solved by separately tailored arrangements. The first and purest case was the FINNEFTA solution: in 1961 Finland achieved a particular solution which provided it with the rights of an EFTA member, but also guaranteed its special interests. At the core of this was the relationship with the Soviet Union, vital both politically and economically. A special status as an associate was regarded as a guarantee that supranational commitments could be avoided, while the presence of other neutral states in EFTA indicated that EFTA was not engaged in East-West confrontation, in spite of the fact that it then had four NATO countries as members.

In addition, the association with EFTA responded to domestic needs. These comprised the market-oriented interests of exporters, wood and paper first and foremost, which were weighed down by the fragile base of industry geared to the home market. The interests of the latter were important since the Finnish economy was in the process of adjustment following a long period of postwar protectionism. Finland had abolished war-based restrictions and quotas in its trade with Western Europe only three years earlier. It therefore needed a longer period of adaptation than other EFTA countries.[8]

The 1973 Free Trade Agreement between Finland and the EC was essentially the same as those of other EFTA countries. There was, however, one politically important distinction: the Finnish treaty did not include Article 32, the so-called evolutionary clause.[9] The absence of such a provision reflected Finnish attitudes towards supranationalism. The Finnish government wanted thereby to stress that it was committed only to the free trade treaty and not to possible future developments. This particular Finnish approach to integration, with its key aim of avoiding all possible political commitments in the future as well, became even more evident at a time when the European Community had voiced more clearly than before its political goals and common foreign policy interests. The EC had taken steps in a direction which was, for Finland in the early 1970s, a most undesirable course.

The *realpolitik* dimension of the 1973 solution was secured by providing the Soviet Union with equal advantages in trade as those offered by free trade in Western Europe. The model of the FINNEFTA arrangement was followed. Finland also established a free trade system with the other European state-trading countries as well, through 'a comprehensive trade policy' which in theory gave Finland a unique position in the European trade system. In practice, however, the arrangement produced very few results and remained a dead letter, since the smaller state-trading countries actually provided only a low share of Finnish foreign trade.

This special status had already been eroded by 1977, when the Finnish government announced that, in spite of the lack of the evolutionary clause in its FTA, Finland was committed to developing its relations with the EC. Gradually Finland developed into a loyal and committed EFTA country, and by the end of the 1980s loyalty to EFTA had become a cornerstone of Finnish policy. Finland is now determined both to enlarge and to deepen the scope of integration, but within the limits of its policy of neutrality. By the mid-1980s it became evident that Finland had moved from a policy based on special arrangements to an EFTA-based approach. A natural turning-point was the Luxembourg High Level meeting.

Playing the EFTA Card

The Luxembourg meeting in 1984 encouraged Finland to take concrete steps towards a new integration policy. This reorientation was a result of gradual change rather than a sudden decision. An obvious and fundamental impulse was the EFTA members' desire to strengthen their position, given the prospect of the EC's single market. Finland, now stressing its loyalty to EFTA instead of reminding its partners of its special status, conformed to the EFTA pattern without reservations. As a first step, Finland joined the EUREKA programme in

1985, first facing a possible exclusion from it. The next step was the change in 1985 of its status in EFTA, from associate to full member. Finland also followed the pattern of other EFTA countries in seeking additional bilateral agreements with the EC to supplement the FTA.

This new Finnish doctrine rests on the so-called EFTA card: that EFTA should be the main tool in the integration policy of its members. The reason for this is the threat of marginalization, the risk of being left alone without any influence. For Finland the EFTA card is thus an insurance policy: if EFTA stays together, Finland is not alone.

The main idea of the EFTA card is to strengthen EFTA and to achieve a common view on as many issues as possible. It is difficult to judge from published sources what this means and what kind of an organization EFTA should be, since the arguments are not very precise. The idea of the Finnish government seems to be that EFTA should be stronger and thus become more attractive for its members – but as a tool, not as an institution for its own sake.

There is a certain incongruity in this philosophy. On the one hand Finland would like a common EFTA view on as many issues as possible in the area of the internal market, but, on the other, it has made no concrete proposals on how EFTA should be made stronger and more attractive. The EFTA card rests on a calculation of rationality: that EFTA countries have common interests to the extent that they prefer cooperation to going it alone. An important part of the cooperation argument is that EFTA, in its current form, is an adequate framework and that supranational commitments are not needed. This assumption is in line with the traditional Finnish view: neutral countries should not commit themselves to binding supranational institutions, not even to those consisting of predominantly neutral members.

An explanation for the great interest in the EFTA card is that Finland wants to avoid a situation of staying alone in a bilateral relationship with the European Community. A group of neutral states is a convenient framework in which Finland, in between the maximalists (Austria) and the minimalits (Switzerland), is in a rather safe position. It is unlikely that Finland would be the EFTA member state which deviated from the common interest. It is neither a likely defector nor a promoter of supranational EFTA.

Finland's strategy for the EES

A logical outcome of this EFTA policy is strong devotion to the creation of the European Economic Space. The EES is from the Finnish point of view an alternative to membership of the EC. A strong EFTA pillar in the EES is the Finnish ideal of what West European integration should look like. Finland supports the idea of an effective two-pillar EES which could prevent EFTA countries from applying for EC membership. Finnish interests thus coincide with the interests of the EC, but with different motives. The Finnish EES commitment incorporates the traditional estrangement from political commitments which EC membership involves. The Finnish policy has been repeated in many official statements and public speeches by the political and bureaucratic elite of the country. It has set this out in three reports, or White Papers, to the Parliament over a period of fifteen months. The general policy line has been accepted by the Parliament with large majorities.

Why the EES?

The motives of the Finnish government in advocating the creation of the EES are very close to the arguments presented by the various EC documents supporting the internal market programme. The third White Paper of March 1990 points repeatedly to the increase in the cost-effectiveness of the EES as a major asset. The logic of improving the effectiveness of the domestic economy through integration is stated on almost every page. Integration in Europe marches forward independently of what Finland does, and offers greater opportunities for the Finnish economy than the only alternative: to stay outside.[10] This statement is, no doubt, no more than a recognition of the inevitable. Since Finnish trade relations opened with the West European free trade system, the share of Finnish exports in the prospective EES area has grown from 56.3% in 1959 to 64.3% in 1989 (see Table 11.1). The figures are roughly the same for imports.

The 1990 White Paper lists five economic explanations of why the EES contributes in favourable ways to the Finnish national economy. These are the same as those presented in numerous Community documents as positive effects of the internal market. The Cecchini Report, in particular, seems to have influenced the Finnish government. The paper stresses as positive factors the simplification of administrative measures, opportunities for specialization that would allow the comparative advantages of the Finnish export industries to be realized, economies of scale, increased competition through the four freedoms and finally the possibility of larger markets promoting innovation and thereby economic growth.[11] In various sections of the White Paper particular emphasis is placed on the possible benefits for the domestic economy of intensified competition through the EES.

Participation in the EES is therefore the aim of the government's policy for two main economic reasons. First, to stay outside the EES would seriously harm economic and social development in the country and cause more severe problems of adaptation than taking part in it. The government stresses that so far the experiences of integration have generally been positive. The second positive

Table 11.1 Finnish exports to major trading partners

Year	*EFTA*	*EC-12*	*CMEA*	*Others*
1959	30.2*	26.1†	21.6	22.1
1972	24.7	46.2	15.2	16.9
1984	18.9	38.3	20.5	22.3
1989	20.3	44.0	16.2	19.6

* EFTA-7
† EC-6

outcome expected is the impact of increasing international competition in the home market. This assumption has its origin in the fact that the Finnish domestic market is still rather closed in many sectors, such as retailing, construction, services to a great extent, and naturally the whole agricultural sector, which is not covered by the FTA. The White Paper assumes that the opening of the home market for international competition will bring down the price level, thus benefiting both consumers and the export sector.[12]

Government policy is in line with the interests of industry. Finland is a deviant case among EFTA countries because its industrial lobby fully supports the government's policy of not aiming for EC membership. The aim of the Federation of Finnish Industries is to take a full part in the internal market of the EC via the EES. This solution should secure for Finnish companies the same scope as is available to EC companies to utilize the merits of the internal market. A particular emphasis is put on three issues: open access to the internal market, fairness in the conditions of competition, and the opportunity for equal utilization of different factors of production.[13]

In the view of Finnish industrialists the EES should include in principle the four freedoms to achieve open access to the internal market. In addition they wish to see most of the flanking policy issues developed: reduction of state aids, opening of public procurement, removal of anti-dumping rules, etc. Industry statements have also emphasized the need to be able to encompass access to technology and services. All in all, the declared view of Finnish industries is very favourable both to the EES in general and to the government's strategy, i.e. the use of the EFTA card.

How to achieve the EES

The Finnish strategy for achieving the EES was outlined in a first White Paper of November 1988. The paper categorically rejected the option of EC membership, which was regarded as incompatible with the policy of neutrality. The argument was presented in a way which did not allow any room for speculation concerning the future.[14] Although the two subsequent White Papers were less categorical as regards membership, they both pointed to the premises of the first White Paper, that is, implying membership would be ruled out in the early 1990s as well.

The first priority of the strategy is the EFTA card: i.e. cooperation with other EFTA countries and the reinforcement of EFTA and common EFTA views on as many issues as possible. The EFTA card is backed by an emphasis on Nordic cooperation and action together with other Nordic countries. Finland also has an interest in conserving the achievements of Nordic cooperation in changing conditions. Finally, the government has stressed the need for the provision of domestic measures in order to react and adapt to developments in West European integration. Such measures include the strengthening of the tripartite cooperation between the government, the unions and industry and the improvement of the government's information policies on integration issues.[15]

The second White Paper, of November 1989, outlined lines of action for the Finnish government during the formative negotiation process, which were to be based on ten principles.[16] The starting-point is that integration is a continuing process, independent of actions by Finland. In this framework Finland can secure its interests only by taking an active part in the process. Finland can do this by cooperating with other EFTA countries and aiming for arrangements between EFTA and the EC. The second White Paper repeated the views of the government concerning the positive impacts of the four freedoms and flanking policies. However, it stressed that participation in integration measures within the EES would make the domestic adaptation measures vital.

On this last point the Finnish government has declared its intention to negotiate special arrangements and national exemptions to protect vital national interests and to obviate any possible severe problems of economic adjustment. Integration policy is thus seen primarily as an adaptation policy, i.e. a process whereby the often conflicting interests of internationalized exporting sectors and insulated domestic sectors are resolved within an overall framework which is consistent with the *status quo ante*. Although the essence of the adaptation policy has shifted from a passive to a more active policy, the long-standing domestic constraints on integration policy have maintained their relevance.[17]

The question of national exemptions has been very much in the forefront of parliamentary discussions which have followed the publication of the White Papers. In reaction to the third White Paper, in particular, the Finnish Parliament held long plenum debates, accompanied by thorough assessment in parliamentary committees. This was historically important, since never before had the Parliament in Finland had a comparable opportunity to review the integration policy of the country in its formative stages. The Parliament adopted the paper with an overwhelming majority, but pointed to a number of issues which called for special treatment.

The Parliament pointed first to rather general principles to be followed in the negotiations: a broad and balanced approach to the issues which are important for Finland: the promotion of goals of sustainable development; and the pursuit of the interests of the EFTA countries in EES decision-making.[18] It also defined those issues on which the Finnish government should present national reservations. The list included four items:[19]

- national authorities must have powers to limit and control the extension of foreign ownership of Finnish companies and production facilities, as well as in the ownership of real estate;
- the level of the Finnish social security system must be kept at least at the present level and the scope for its further development must be maintained;
- Finland must secure the right to maintain and develop tougher standards of environment protection than those in the EC area; and
- the scope for a national regional policy should be maintained.

The Finnish government is thus tied by the Parliament to seek special arrangements and exemptions that reflect the concerns of the nation's political authorities and are vital to the necessary political consensus. In particular two of the reservations have special political importance. The concern over foreign ownership in the Finnish economy is widely shared throughout the political spectrum. Similarly, the apprehension about the maintenance of the welfare state is a key political issue. Maintaining the broadest possible consensus in policy on such issues has traditionally had a high priority for governments. The Finnish foreign policy tradition generally strongly emphasizes the importance of national harmony on major issues. In addition, a broad consensus is needed in the Parliament for a smooth passage of the legislation that would be needed as a consequence of acceptance of the *acquis communitaire*.

The institutional challenge

Because of the established *status quo* approach the problem of institutions and institutionalization of European cooperation poses a major challenge for Finland. Institutions contest the hierarchical power-oriented European system to which Finland has successfully adapted. Changes in Europe are shaking the foundations of Finland's European policy. Not only is the traditional East-West dimension losing its overall dominance, but also the hierarchy of issues is being changed. The inconvenience of the timing of the EES process from the Finnish point of view is that both the hierarchy of power and the hierarchy of issues are collapsing at the same time in parallel with the EES negotiations.

The two faces of 'political' are as relevant as ever in the EES discussions. In terms of *realpolitik* the EES is by its basic nature regarded as a safe solution. It is an encapsulated solution which does not disturb the role of an established *status quo* nation. Changes in the European security policy framework make the *realpolitik* dimension less pronounced in many ways. In fact the Finnish government stresses in its White Papers that the principle aim of Finland is to encourage economic cooperation in Europe on a broad pan-European basis. The second White Paper claims that the EES agreement increases the opportunities to intensify collaboration with other countries and groups of countries.[20] This argument is in line with the Finnish doctrine of the 1960s: neutrality and integration are not incompatible but neutrality and supranationality are.

An even more serious challenge to Finland is the anticipated decision-making system of the EES. Quite evidently the EES will necessitate new institutions with some kind of supranational enforcement and supervision capacity. The possible EES framework is a test of the traditional Finnish position that supranational commitments must be avoided in the name of neutrality.

The Finnish dilemma is rather obvious: EES institutions would add considerably to the weight of supranational elements and call for political commitments which go beyond the established Finnish limits of involvement. On the other hand, only participation in the process and the acceptance of common institutions would give access to decision-shaping, if not decision-making, in the framework of the EES. In addition, further institutionalization of integration is a possible step in the EC's development towards a political union.

The second White Paper addressed itself to this problem, emphasizing that any decision-making system should secure for Finland and other EFTA countries a real influence over the making of the rules of the EES. It was acknowledged that this should include effective instruments of supervision and implementation:[21] 'The government aims at a decision-making model which 'gives us an access to the shaping of decisions, which does not make decisions binding against our will and whereby the position of our own decision-making institutions can be secured.' The Finnish government thus aims at an EES decision-making system which would meet three rather different aims: access to a real influence; the possibility of some opting-out; and the retention by national institutions, first and foremost the Parliament, of a meaningful role.

The third White Paper addressed the problem of decision-making more thoroughly.[22] It outlined a decision-making model which would ensure Finland's participation in the preparations of EES decisions. This so-called 'comitology' was regarded as a suitable form of participation. At the end of the process, decisions, excluding those of a purely technical nature, should in the Finnish view be founded on consensus. In addition, the role of the Finnish Parliament and the President ought to be protected. The government also emphasized that the participation of social partners and the parliamentarians in decision-making should be secured.

A particular problem is posed by the enforcement and supervision of the decisions of the EES. The Finnish government does not see problems arising from reciprocity in the enforcement of EES decisions, provided that these are regarded as international treaties and agreements. Finland thus aims at solutions whereby the existing national enforcement procedures for international agreements could be maintained and the due role of the Parliament maintained. This aim was very explicitly stressed by the Constitutional Committee of the Parliament in its report.[23] This established policy line could, of course, be challenged by the possible evolution of the EES decisions.

The supervision of the decisions causes problems as well. In principle, Finland takes the view that EES decisions must have effective mechanisms for supervision. The Finnish government seems to be prepared also to accept the establishment of an EES Court of Justice and thus to recognize the power of a supranational legal order as a part of the solution. This is a relatively new element in Finnish policy and is a problem at least from the point of view of the traditional avoidance of supranationalism. But, as the third White Paper noted, by joining the Council of Europe Finland had already accepted the idea of a supranational level of legal supervision.[24]

The reports of the various parliamentary Committees have also pointed to the problem of decision-making. The Foreign Affairs Committee stressed the need to achieve EES decisions by unanimity. In its view unanimous decisions could be achieved only if EFTA countries had an adequate opportunity to voice their view at the preparatory phase of the decision-making, in a system based on the equality of the partners. The Foreign Affairs Committee also made a proposal for the establishment of a special institution of EES parliamentarians as a part of the package.[25]

Is there a membership option?

Finnish policy has gradually shifted towards a multilateral strategy. This is somewhat in contradiction with the traditional *status quo* policy. Multilateralism has, as its major tool, the EFTA card. It is preferred as the best alternative, since all of the currently neutral EFTA countries are essentially in the same boat. The basis of Finnish integration strategy is that all the EFTA countries are in a similar position and that therefore they have a common interest in acting together in order to improve their negotiating position. Recognition of high dependence on others' preferences and choices has been the reason for the move from a defensive to an offensive strategy.[26] It is very much in the interests of Finland to try to make common actions by 'like-minded' nations a viable alternative, not only in EFTA but in other forums as well.

Reservations and caution very much dominate the Finnish domestic debate on the future of integration policy. Government policy is widely accepted and a consensus prevails in the major dimensions of European policy. Parliamentary discussions following the second White Paper, however, brought up the first signs of a gradual emergence of a pro-membership constituency in the political system.

This has emerged gradually at the level of public opinion. Polls in the early 1990s indicate a shift in public opinion towards favouring EC membership. A poll published in May 1990 showed, for instance, that 60% of Finns favoured EC membership and only 13% were against. However, 22% of those interviewed believed that Finland already was a member of the EC.[27] These figures indicate two underlying facts about Finnish public opinion. First, it is probably not too familiar with the kind of arguments which the political and bureaucratic elites use in the domestic debate. Second, it is more open to the membership option and less attached to the traditional *status quo* than the official line. Dramatic changes in Europe, in Eastern Europe and in the situation in the Baltic Republics have made Finnish public opinion more flexible and adaptive.

Another factor shaping public opinion is the demonstration effect provoked by European integration. European trends and models gain support in all sectors of Finnish society. This has been most visible of course in the business sectors, but European influences are evident in many other segments of society, including public policy sectors. The prefix 'Euro' is seen almost everywhere in Finnish society. An example is the middle-class retail shop chain Anttila, a Finnish version of Marks & Spencer, which uses in its advertisements a slogan 'Europe in Anttila'. In this kind of 'Euro-atmosphere' a strong pro-membership current of public opinion is not a surprise.

The pro-membership claim is based on two major arguments. First, there is a considerable scepticism as to whether the EES option will be achieved and in that case the membership option would be the only viable alternative. Critical voices are mostly heard on the fragility of the government's reliance on a single card, namely its preparedness only for success of the EFTA card and the desired EES. The Finnish pro-EC membership constituency is a growing political factor in the country, though mainly as a fall-back, should the EES solution not materialize. A very broad national consensus prevails that the membership option should not be taken on to the agenda while the EES negotiations are under way. Until that point, all the eggs are put into the EES basket.

Consequently signs of a polarization of opinion are evident in the public debate. One line of argument criticizes Europeanist tendencies, claiming that more emphasis should be given to *status quo* factors, in particular to Finnish-Soviet relations. A counter-argument claims that the deepening of integration is a threat to the Finnish welfare state and, indeed, to the Finnish way of life and Finland's sovereignty.

The second argument, gradually emerging, which favours EC membership, results from the dramatic political changes in Europe. Public opinion is beginning to recognize that this may challenge the concept of neutrality. Any redefinition of neutrality would also lead to a new definition of Finnish attitudes towards supranationality. Membership of the EC is not viewed as conditioned by the structure of the European political order. On the contrary, neutrality, in the sense of the *status quo*, is seen as a potential burden in two ways: by preventing Finnish participation in the reconstruction of Europe; and by excluding Finland from decision-making in European integration. In particular this factor, the lack of influence which threatens to lead to marginalization, is becoming the critical element in the Finnish discussion of the 1990s.

Notes

1. Harto Hakovirta, 'Odota ja katso. Analyysi Suomen Läntisen integraatiopolitiikan perusmalleista', *Suomen ulkopolitiikka* (Jyväskylä, Gummerus: In Harto Hakovirta-Raimo Väyrynen, 1975).
2. Johan Nykopp, 'Jällenrakennusvuosien kauppapolitiikkaa', *Suomen ulkomaankauppapolitiikka* (Keuruu, WSOY: In Lauri Haataja, 1978), pp. 46–8.
3. On the history of Finnish integration policy, see Esko Antola and Ossi Tuusvuori, *Suomi ja Länsi-Eurgopan integraatio* (Turku: Finnish Institute for International Affairs, 1983), pp. 122–31.
4. I have elaborated this argument earlier in Esko Antola, 'Finnish Perspective on the EC-EFTA Relationship', in *EFTA and the EC: Implications of 1992*, by Finn Laursen (Maastricht: European Institute for Public Administration, 1990), p. 163.
5. Klaus Törnudd, 'Finland and Economic Integration in Europe', *Cooperation and Conflict*, vol. 4 (1969), p. 64.
6. See Maria Serenius, 'Euroopan Neuvosto ja Suomi', *Ulkopolitiikka*, vol. 4 (1976), pp. 38–40.
7. *Ulkopoliittisia lausuntoja ja asiakirioja* (Helsinki, 1969), p. 147.
8. Reino Rossi, 'Finland and the Economic Integration of Europe', *Annuaire européen*, vol. 7 (1969), p. 59.
9. See *The European Free Trade Association* (Geneva, 1980), p. 140.
10. 'Suomi je Euroopan talouslaue. Baltioneuvoston selonteka eduskunnalle Suomen suhtautumiseste Länsi-Euroopan yhdentymiskehitykseen', 13 March 1990 (Helsinki, 1990), pp. 8–9.
11. White Paper 1990, pp. 8–9.
12. ibid., p. 11.
13. 'Teollisuus ja Länsi-Euroopan integraatio', *Teoliisuuden keskusliitto* (Helsinki, 1989), p. 3.
14. *Suomi ja Länsi-Euroopan yhdentymiskehitys*. 'Valtioneuvoston selonteko eduskunnalle Suomen suhtautumisesta Länsi-Euroopan taloudellisaan yhdentymiskehitykseen', 1 Nov. 1988 (Helsinki, 1988), p. 7.
15. ibid., p. 7.
16. *Valtioneuvoston tiedonanto eduskunnalle Suomen suhtautumisesta Länsi-Euroopan yhdentymiskehitykseen* (Helsinki, 1989), pp. 31–2.
17. For a more detailed discussion, see Esko Antola, 'The Finnish Integration Strategy: Adaptation with Restrictions', in Kari Möttölä and Heikki Patomäki, eds, *Facing the Change in Europe: EFTA Countries' Integration Strategies* (Helsinki: Finnish Institute for International Affairs, 1989), pp. 55–60.
18. 'Eduskunnan ulkoasiainvaliokunnen mietinto Suomen suhtautumisesta Länsi-Euro-

opan yhdentymiskehityksaan koskevasta valtioneuvoston selonteosta', Helsinki, 1990.
19. ibid., pp. 28–9.
20. ibid., p. 31.
21. ibid., p. 32.
22. White Paper 1990, op. cit., pp. 118–23.
23. Report of the Constitutional Committee of the Parliament, in *Eduskunnan ulkoasiainvaliokunnan mietintö*, op. cit., p. 40.
24. ibid., p. 123.
25. *Eduskunnan ulkoasiainvaliokunnan mietintö*. op. cit., p. 26.
26. See Antola, 1989, op. cit., pp. 58–60.
27. *The Bulletin*, 31 May 1990.

12 Iceland

Gunnar Helgi Kristinsson

Introduction

Iceland shares with Western Europe – especially its northern parts – a common cultural heritage and close social and cultural relations. Its living standards and educational standards basically resemble those of other Northern European states. Survey research in Iceland indicates that Icelanders tend to identify strongly with these regions, and that there are to be found the political systems to which they look as models in many respects.[1] However, in two crucial areas of foreign policy, trade and security, Iceland has been, throughout most of the post-war period, only half European.

In the field of security and defence, Iceland has been highly dependent on its bilateral relations with the United States. As Iceland has no military forces of its own, the USA has taken the responsibility for its defence, with a military base in Keflavik designed to play an important role in NATO's surveillance and defence system. Within NATO – of which it is a member – Iceland has played an inactive role, depending to a great extent on the United States for guidance in security matters.[2]

As regards trade and foreign economic relations, Iceland has probably been less interwoven with the Western European fabric than any other Western European state. Thus, it has had extensive trade relations with both the United States and Eastern Europe in the post-war period, while it did not become a member of EFTA until 1970. A free trade agreement with the European Community (EC) was signed in 1972.

In recent years there have been some indications that in the fields of security and trade relations also, Iceland's foreign policy may be heading towards greater Europeanization. As regards security, there are clear indications that the Icelandic Government is becoming more willing to adopt a more active approach to security issues and participation in NATO, which in the long run is likely to pull in a European direction.[3] Nevertheless, in the short run there are obvious limits to this trend, because of Iceland's small capacity to take on important political security functions and also because of the value of the American military presence in Iceland to the other European members of NATO.

Iceland's dependence on trade with the EC has increased substantially in recent years, especially since the entry of Portugal and Spain in 1986. This, together with the increasing vitality of the Community, has belatedly sparked off a discussion in Iceland about the appropriate response to the new situation. It is premature to try to predict the outcome of this, but an analysis of the most significant factors seems in order.

A reserved European

Icelandic foreign policy goes back only 50 years, to the German occupation of Denmark in 1940. As an independent republic since the dissolution in 1944 of its union with Denmark, Iceland has been part of an international system which recognized the rights of weak states.[4] At the same time, it has drawn various benefits from the competition between East and West in the fields of economics, politics and security.

Nevertheless, ever since World War II, foreign relations have been the source of a fundamental division in Icelandic politics. Nationalism in Iceland – unlike its manifestation in many other European countries – came triumphant out of World War II, following a victorious struggle for independence. Subsequent pressures to bring Iceland into international cooperation were strongly resisted by nationalist forces, which feared that the achievements of the struggle for independence might be lost.

In the field of security and defence, Iceland had to take a stance early in the history of its foreign relations, with its entry into NATO in 1949 and the 1951 defence agreement with the USA which established US military bases in Iceland. In the field of trade relations, however, Iceland followed a separate path, keeping at a distance from the liberalization of trade going on around it, until the 1960s. Thus it did not join GATT until 1967 nor EFTA until 1970, and it has not sought to join the EC. Since the 1960s, Iceland's trade policy has generally favoured free trade for the products both of fisheries and of manufacturing industry, but there has been no desire to take part in further political and economic integration with Western Europe.[5]

Iceland's reasons for resisting integration differ from those of the EFTA neutrals, since Iceland, like Norway, is not a neutral state; they essentially concern sovereignty and economic interests.

A different pattern of trade

Iceland's substantial trade interests in other regions of the world, especially the USA and Eastern Europe, are based on a trade pattern in which political factors have played an important role. Conflicts with several West European states – particularly the United Kingdom – over the successive unilateral extensions of fisheries limits, as well as closer ties with the United States, have led to a considerable reduction in Iceland's trade with Western Europe.

Since World War II Iceland has had four major fisheries disputes with its Western European neighbours, in 1952–56, 1958–61, 1972–73 and 1975–76.

Considerable economic pressure was applied by the United Kingdom and the EC to prevent the extension of the fishing limits, using trade-distorting measures such as landing bans on Icelandic fishing vessels and tariff decisions unfavourable to Iceland.[6] Nevertheless, in each case Iceland more or less had its way, partly because international developments were favourable to its policy of exclusive rights to fishing resources; but also because alternative trading facilities were available in Eastern Europe and the USA.

Trade with the Soviet Union opened up in 1953, at a time when Iceland was first in conflict with its NATO allies over fishing limits. Undoubtedly, the Soviet Union was primarily motivated by political considerations in developing this trade,[7] which reached a peak during the late 1950s, when one-third of Iceland's exports went to Eastern Europe, but continued to provide an important market for Icelandic exports also during the 1960s and 1970s.

The USA had an even greater economic weight than Eastern Europe vis-à-vis Iceland. Its importance arose partly from direct economic assistance in the early post-war period; partly from incomes from servicing the US military bases; and partly from the development of the USA as a major market for Icelandic goods and services, which was in turn stimulated by political goodwill. In 1971, when exports to the US were at their peak, they amounted to 37% of the value of total goods exported, while imports from the US were generally much lower. Fig. 12.1 shows how Iceland's exports were divided between different regions from 1948 to 1988.

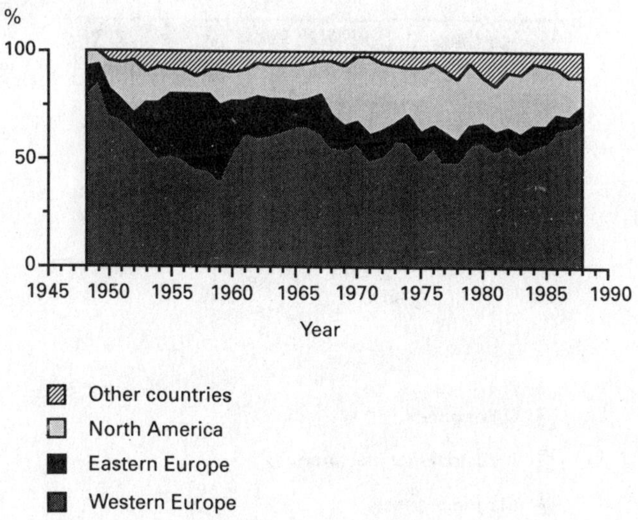

Fig. 12.1 Icelandic exports divided by region, 1948–88

The reasons for Iceland's reluctance

While Western Europe is to a certain extent the 'natural' market for Icelandic exports, on account of relatively shorter distances and a culture that is shared in many respects, two factors, above all, appear to have diverted Iceland's trade away from Western Europe. First of all, conflicts with a number of Western European states on the issue of fishing rights in the 1950s and 1970s encouraged Iceland to seek markets elsewhere. The bipolarity in Iceland's international environment created openings for such trade, not only because of Iceland's conflicts with its Western European neighbours, but also because of the strong pull of the favourable US market (especially after Iceland's accession to GATT in 1967). Consequently Iceland lacked strong incentives to become involved in Western European economic integration.

The second reason for Iceland's avoidance of close integration with its Western European neighbours has been the way in which Icelandic governments have perceived and reacted to the country's vulnerability in relation to its international environment. The Icelandic population is very small (a quarter of a million), located on the periphery of Europe, with rather one-sided natural resources and quite far from the major European trading centres. Fig. 12.2 shows the different sectors into which Icelandic exports fell in 1960–88.

Iceland's main exports are fish and marine products: in the post-war period they have usually constituted between 70 and 90% of the value of exported

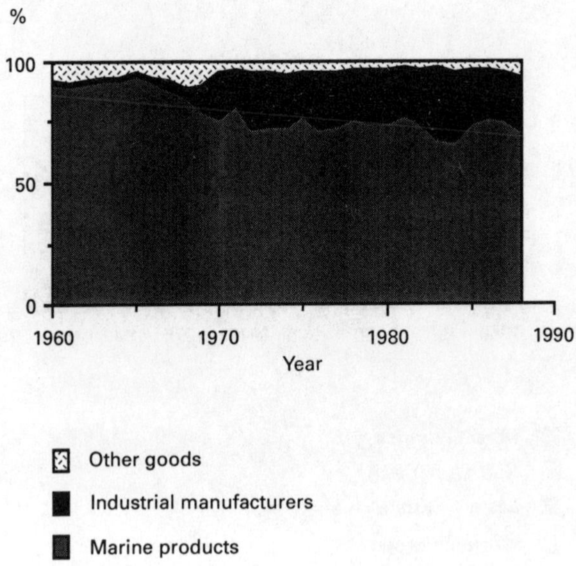

Fig. 12.2 Icelandic exports classified by economic sector, 1960–88

goods, and comprise much the most important sector of the economy. The share represented by the manufacturing industry has, however, increased significantly since the late 1960s, on the basis of energy intensive industry which utilizes the country's hydroelectric power resources.

Fishing and fish processing are mostly carried on by very small firms, scattered around the coast, which regularly experience considerable fluctuations in their incomes. Economic policies have generally aimed at safeguarding the position of these firms, as well as maintaining a regional balance and preventing local unemployment. Thus the state has had to play a fairly active role in the economy; it has affected the distribution of incomes through devaluations or various currency restrictions and through enforced wage and price freezes, low interest rates and various other means. Such economic policies have ensured full employment and flexibility in the economy, but at the cost of a high degree of instability, high inflation and a record number of strikes, all of which makes life very difficult for firms and institutions outside the fisheries sector.[8] The distinctive style of Icelandic economic management is not easily compatible with close economic cooperation with other states or openess towards the external world.

The barriers to foreign influence which Iceland has raised have been of various kinds. Until the 1960s there were substantial restrictions on imports, both to protect domestic industry and to avoid an unfavourable balance of trade. Restrictive practices in the granting of export permits have also been used to strengthen the large export organizations connected with fish processing. In general, rules on foreign capital and foreign investment in Iceland are fairly restrictive, in accordance with the view that the Icelandic economy and its resources need protection against foreign influence and ownership. These restrictions vary according to sector and in some cases are open to a flexible interpretation by the authorities.[9]

In general, the restrictions are greatest in the fisheries sector, prohibiting foreign ownership and even the landing by foreign vessels in Icelandic harbours. With only very minor exceptions, Iceland prohibits all fishing by foreign nationals within its fishing limits: having never depended to any significant extent on distant water fishing, and suffering from overcapacity in its own fleet, it has not been inclined to grant fishing rights to others.[10] As a matter of principle, Iceland does not exchange access to resources for access to markets.

On account of an extremely small population, the free flow of people, as in a common labour market, has always been considered a potential threat to the national identity and the national culture. Though experience has shown that Iceland in fact needs foreign labourers in considerable numbers, the restrictions have remained, and Iceland did not join the common Nordic labour market when it was established in the early 1950s.

Asymmetry of interests

A third reason for Iceland's reservations about economic cooperation has to do with the nature of its main product. Fishing generally tends to be grouped with agriculture (however strange this may seem to most Icelanders); in terms of international trade it is treated more like a kind of agriculture than a type of industry. To most industrialized nations, free trade in manufactured goods is of considerable economic importance, whereas many of them have reservations about free trade in agricultural and fishery products. International economic cooperation has tended to reflect this order of priorities.

For Iceland the reverse holds true; it has a paramount interest in free trade in marine products, while most branches of its manufacturing industry have been engaged in an uphill struggle against foreign competition ever since Iceland joined EFTA.[11] This asymmetry of interests is among the major reasons why Iceland has been slow in relating to international cooperation.

Nevertheless, in the late 1960s and early 1970s Iceland joined the free trading nations through accession to GATT, membership of EFTA and a free trade agreement with the EC. What made this possible was that Iceland's fishing interests were better served by joining than by abstaining. Iceland's accession to GATT followed the important tariff concessions which were obtained in the Kennedy Round in the 1960s and had a favourable effect on its exports to the USA. Membership of EFTA was negotiated at a time of considerable economic difficulties, in order to obtain the limited tariff concessions available for marine products within EFTA and to secure the future position of Icelandic exports in Western Europe. The free trade agreement with the EC was fairly favourable to Iceland, as it secured tariff concessions for 70% of Iceland's exports to the Community, an additional 20% being tariff free.[12] In fact, the free trade agreement secured far better access to the EC markets for the Icelandic fisheries than they enjoyed within EFTA.

The question of Icelandic membership of the EC was not, however, raised at the time of the enlargement of the EC in the early 1970s. Preliminary investigations by the Icelandic government during the early 1960s of what membership might involve had led to negative conclusions; from then on the government became chiefly interested in some kind of a mutual arrangement, excluding membership, which would maintain Iceland's economic and other links with Western Europe. The formation of the Common Fisheries Policy (CFP) by the EC may be said to have put the lid on the membership question in Iceland for the time being.

The CFP initially established the principle of equal access for the fishermen of the member states to each others' fishing zones. An important stimulus for its creation was the hope then enjoyed by the six original member states of gaining access to the much larger fisheries of the nations applying for membership in the early 1970s.[13] To a nation such as Iceland, dependent on the fishing resources around its coasts, the policy of equal access was clearly unacceptable. Negative evaluation of the CFP closed the issue not only in Iceland; it played a role in Norway's rejection of EC membership in 1972 and had an important impact on the decision by the Faeroe Islands not to follow Denmark into the EC. It also influenced the considerable opposition to membership which was manifest in votes on the issue in Greenland, Shetland and the Hebrides.[14] Indeed, once it had been granted home rule, Greenland decided to leave the Community. Thus Iceland, along with those of its neighbours most dependent on fishing, had a clear economic interest in not joining the European Community at the time.

Re-evaluation in the 1980s?

With Iceland joining EFTA around 1970, the preconditions for consensus on the issue of foreign economic policy were created. Iceland gained relatively easy access to foreign markets for its fishery and other products, while managing at the same time to avoid moving towards the coordination of policies or free flow of capital, labour or services. This consensus has more or less endured in the 1980s, but its economic foundations are increasingly being called into question.

The changing circumstances of the 1980s reflected partly new developments in the global political economy and partly economic developments in Iceland, as well as developments within the EC. A major factor has been the fundamental change in Iceland's trade pattern which has come about since the mid-1970s. While the share of the USA and Eastern Europe in Iceland's foreign trade has declined, the EC has become Iceland's main trading partner, providing more than half of its imports and taking close to 60% of its exports (Fig. 12.3).

A number of long-term factors seem to be working to increase the importance of Iceland's trade with the EC. The USA market has become less secure, through increasing competition from Canadian fish exporters, although the main reason for its reduced share since the mid-1970s is increasing demand from the EC countries. At the same time, trade with Eastern Europe has continued to decline; and increasing concern at the lack of efficiency in the Soviet Union, as well as the enormous economic difficulties faced by Eastern Europe, may make this trade more difficult.[15] The present EFTA countries have never

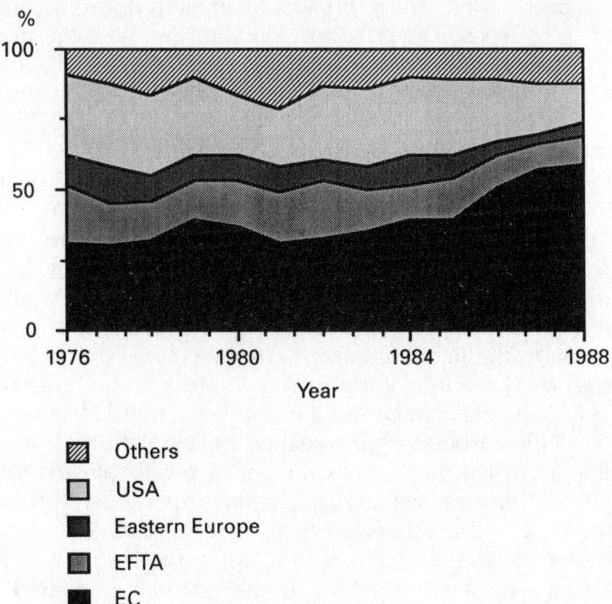

Fig. 12.3 Icelandic exports divided by markets, 1976–88

been among Iceland's main export markets, and there are a number of limitations on Iceland's ability to increase substantially its trade with countries outside Europe and North America.[16] The increasing weight of the EC in Icelandic foreign trade is accounted for, above all, by its enlargement, by the normalization of political relations after the 'cod wars', and by the increasing profitability of EC markets for many fish exporters.

The importance to Iceland of the West European market has created a pressure to adapt the Icelandic economy and society to this development. Long-term trends in Icelandic society seem to be towards greater similarity to its European neighbours; the pressures from Western Europe are likely to accelerate this, both because of the important economic interests at stake and because of Iceland's participation in EFTA. Although the cost of full adaptation to the EC's internal market would still be substantial, the 1980s have seen liberalization in a number of fields in Iceland, as well as growing pressures for structural rationalization and economic openness.

Regulations concerning capital and services remain strict in many areas, not least as regards foreign ownership and capital. The small size of many Icelandic companies would probably put them at a disadvantage in a more liberal system. Nevertheless, considerable deregulation in the financial system has taken place in recent years, making it more like that of neighbouring countries. Government policy in the 1980s has also tended to favour greater cooperation with foreign firms and foreign investments in Iceland, although progress has been slow.[17]

In the field of taxation, full adaptation to the internal market might require important changes in Iceland. The present system of taxation is based above all on indirect taxation. Thus, when VAT was finally introduced in January 1990 – primarily for the purpose of harmonization with Europe – the rate was set at 24.5%, which is much higher than the EC average.[18] If it is not brought closer to the European norm, it may have various unfortunate consequences for Icelandic business.

The adaptation of various health and safety standards is not likely to be a major problem. Fishing and fish processing are most likely to be affected: but here Icelandic standards tend to be similar to or higher than the standards applying in the EC. As for other types of trade, the rules vary, but Icelandic standards are often lower than those of the EC; and so the change to Community standards would not be detrimental to Icelandic consumers.[19]

Free movement of people would be among the most sensitive areas in Iceland's adaptation to the internal market, given the small size of its population. Although there are powerful natural barriers to the naturalization of foreigners in Iceland (especially the climate and the language), there are widespread fears that openness in this respect might create problems. Nevertheless, it is increasingly being realized that the free movement of people also includes for Icelanders the possibility of seeking education, experience and employment abroad. In particular, there is concern over the possibility that educational opportunities for Icelanders might be limited, in the EC, as they have always relied on West European universities for higher education. In 1983 Iceland joined the Nordic labour market, but retained the option of controlling immigration; a recent parliamentary report suggests that a similar formula might be employed in the West European context: 'the basic policy might be developed towards greater openness, while safeguards could be maintained to make governmental action possible in case of undesirable effects'.[20]

However, Iceland's economic policies remain the aspect that presents the greatest difficulty. Iceland has still a long way to go before being able to link its economic policies to a larger West European entity. At the very least this would demand structural rationalization of the economy – including such sectors as fishing, fish processing and agriculture – and greater economic stability, with less frequent strikes, lower inflation and a stabler currency. It is widely recognised that all of these goals must be achieved in any case, but so far they have proved elusive. It is in this context that the idea of Iceland joining the EMS must be understood: it has been put forward as a means of making it impossible for governments to keep on devaluing the króna in order to save the small firms in the export sector, and hence of imposing greater discipline on economic agents in Iceland. The counter-argument is that without prior stabilization of the economy, a fixed currency might lead to loss of competitiveness and an unfavourable balance of trade.

Agriculture enjoys a high degree of protection in Iceland, including an almost complete ban on all imports of products in which Iceland is self-sufficient.[21] Until about 1980, rationalization played a small role in Icelandic agriculture and despite greater efforts in the 1980s, the system remains wasteful in economic terms. For the 5% of the Icelandic population which subsists on agriculture, the liberalization of agricultural trade or participation in the Common Agricultural Policy (CAP) would create considerable difficulties.

The structure of Icelandic fishing and fish processing has likewise been highly affected by regional concerns. On the whole, this sector seems to be characterized by over-investment: too many firms with too little productivity, which have difficulties in dealing with fluctuations. This is a major cause of the instability in the economy; in recent years there have been increasing pressures for structural rationalization in the sector, and government policies seem to be turning in that direction.[22] However, such policies clearly require time to bring about substantial changes.

In the 1980s, Icelandic fisheries and fish processing faced also a new situation in the West European market. The new CFP of 1983 and the accession of Portugal and Spain in 1986 have radically affected the balance of costs and benefits of membership (or non-membership).

A fishing nation outside the community faces an increasing danger of protectionism within the EC, as well as increasing pressures for access to its resources, in exchange for concessions with regard to trade. The CFP of 1983 represented a compromise between the members of the Community on the division between the member states of the much reduced catches (following the introduction of the 200-mile limits) available to Community fishermen. The entry of Spain – with its enormous fishing capacity – was not allowed seriously to upset this compromise, but it dramatically increased the drive to obtain fishing rights in third-country waters for Community fishermen. Nations outside the EC may thus either find themselves coerced to grant access to resources, or lose markets to other third countries which have shown more willingness to negotiate.[23]

Iceland has been unwilling to discuss the question of exchanging access to markets for access to resources, insisting that these are two entirely separate issues. The main problem with a mutually beneficial exchange of quotas is that Iceland does very little distant water fishing, and it is doubtful whether the Community has much to offer in exchange for fishing rights in the Icelandic zone. Nevertheless, discussions on the issue were opened early in 1989, primarily in order to establish Iceland's good faith.[24]

At the same time, Iceland increasingly needs a renegotiation of its free trade agreement with the EC, as the terms agreed in 1972 have in some respects become obsolete. All attempts to gain new long-term concessions on tariffs have, however, been refused by the Community, so long as access to resources is not granted.

The chief problem at present facing Iceland is that of salted fish, which in 1988 constituted 18% of the value of Iceland's exports. When Iceland negotiated its free trade agreement, salted fish was not included, as imports were free of tariffs and Iceland's most important markets for these products were outside the EC. In the 1980s, however, with the enlargement of the Community – especially the entry of Portugal – most of Iceland's exports of salted fish go to the EC, while a change of policy in the EC requires Iceland to pay tariffs on an increasing share of its exports of salted fish. This has created considerable difficulties for the producers of salted fish, and a few have in fact transferred their production to the United Kingdom, to escape discrimination.

More generally, Iceland's inability to have the free trade agreement renegotiated constitutes a dangerous threat to the long-term development of the Icelandic fishing industry. New transport techniques are making it easier to export whole fresh fish, which means that Icelandic fish processing faces even tougher competition for its raw material. At the same time, the 1972 free trade agreement does not cover such products of fish-processing as fresh fish fillets, herring or ready prepared seafoods.[25] A basically new sector in the Icelandic economy is fish farming, which is consequently not provided for in the agreement. Therefore this agreement, if unchanged, may delay the development of new products or else mean that their processing will have to be moved to EC countries, such as the United Kingdom.

The same events which raised the economic cost of doing business with the EC from the outside, have actually lowered the probable costs of membership for a fishing nation such as Iceland. This is chiefly because the CFP package of 1983 substantially modified the principle of equal access. In the new CFP, the total allowable catches were divided into quotas which were allocated on a member-state basis, according to three criteria: traditional fishing patterns; the needs of regions especially dependent on fishing; and losses in third-country waters after the introduction of 200-miles zones. Furthermore, the distribution of quotas was to aim at stability of fishing activities, with priority given to regions especially dependent on fishing.[26]

Thus in the event of application by Iceland for EC membership, the all-important question is: what kind of deal could it get under the CFP? This would be the crucial issue in any membership negotiations, and the one which in all likelihood would decide whether membership was a feasible option for Iceland. Most probably, if there was willingness on both sides to reach an agreement, the question of quotas would not necessarily exclude Iceland's membership of the EC.

Traditional fishing patterns and dependence on fishing should work in Iceland's favour against the possibility of losing access to resources. Other states can no longer claim traditional rights in the Icelandic zone, and Iceland's dependence on fishing can hardly be called into question. On the other hand, Iceland was among the major beneficiaries of the 200-mile zone, while the EC as a whole, as well as every member state, lost access to fishing resources. Hence, any reallocation based on compensation for losses in third-country waters would tend to work against Iceland's interests.

How the allocation rules would be interpreted with regard to new entrants into the EC may be seen from the entry of Portugal and Spain. Spain in particular, demanded access to the zones of other member states, to be based on its catches before the creation of the 200-mile zone. This was rejected by the Community: in fact, the compensation criterion appears to have been used only to formulate the initial allocation of quotas in the CFP, but is no longer of practical significance.[27] There is thus every reason to believe that in Iceland's case a satisfactory solution could be negotiated for the fisheries sector.

The strong economic reasons for not joining the EC that existed in the early 1970s are now clearly far less significant. While the outcomes of the economic calculations depend, among other things, on how strong the protectionistic tendencies within the EC may become, there are already strong economic pressures for reviewing Iceland's present relationship with the Community. The argument against joining the EC that carries most weight concerns the fear of supranationality, although the prospect of an increasing mobility of capital, people and services also continues to be regarded with scepticism by some.[28]

The emerging debate

The question of Iceland's adaptation to the processes of change in Europe is highly sensitive politically. In particular, if economic motivations should seriously begin pulling in another direction than concern with national sovereignty, this could result in major domestic political divisions. The sensitivity of the issue has, in fact, probably acted as a brake on the debate: thus discussions of it started later than in most of the other EFTA countries, and the policy positions of the major political actors remain vague.

Government strategy has partly reflected the issue's sensitivity. Governments have basically adopted an incrementalist approach, without stating any clear long-term objectives, in the hope, it seems, of above all avoiding a political crisis. In effect, this has meant efforts to minimize the amount of change which must take place in Iceland in the course of integration into Western Europe.

While no government has produced any general policy papers on this subject, successive governments have made it clear that membership of the EC is not on the agenda.[29] Instead, the short-to-medium term government strategy to deal with the immediate challenges raised by the developments in Europe has had two major components.

In the first place, it has relied on EFTA to prevent Iceland from becoming isolated within Western Europe and thus to solve most of those general problems of adaptation which Iceland shares with the other EFTA countries. But EFTA's limitation in this respect is that Iceland's major interest, free trade in fishery products, is not shared by the other EFTA countries. It was only after almost twenty years of struggle that Iceland managed to get EFTA to accept the principle of free trade in fishery products – by threatening, at a moment psychologically crucial for some of the others, not to sign the declaration of the Oslo meeting in 1989.[30] Despite EFTA's acceptance of the principle, it seems unlikely that this issue will be given a high priority in its dialogue with the EC.

Hence the second component of Iceland's strategy is the renegotiation of its free trade agreement with the EC, so as to secure the competitiveness of its marine products. In fact, the emphasis on free trade in relations with EFTA may be chiefly regarded as an attempt to strengthen Iceland's case in negotiations with the EC.[31] Icelandic political leaders have been preparing the ground for such negotiations in a series of meetings with colleagues in the EC member states and the Commission itself.[32] Iceland may even be prepared to discuss cooperation on fisheries issues, although it is not likely to give ground on its insistence on discussing access to resources and access to markets as two separate issues.

The attitudes of the parties

The long-term objectives of the political parties with regard to the EC tend to be rather vague. This is not an unusual situation in Icelandic politics: the policy-making functions of the parties tend to be limited, since they are, in various degrees, non-programmatic cadre organizations. Hence, in most cases, decision making is exercised by the party parliamentarians or ministers, on an *ad hoc* basis. In the case of the EC, the parliamentary parties have established a special parliamentary committee, the Europe Committee, to consider the impact on Iceland's economy of the changes in Western Europe, and means of adapting to those changes. The work of this committee, though necessarily limited in depth, appears to be the main attempt by a policy-making body to investigate the issue systematically.[33] So far, disagreements within the committee have mostly been concerned with foreign capital and investment.[34]

In the second half of 1989, however, the positions of some of the parties have increasingly become clearer. This is particularly true of the parties with a pessimistic and defensive attitude to the developments in Europe: the Women's Alliance, the People's Alliance and, to some extent, the Progressive Party. Individuals from these three parties have, in fact, formed an Information Organization on Iceland and the EC, with the clear aim of warning the public of the dangers involved.[35]

The People's Alliance has its roots in left-wing splinter groups from the Social Democratic Party and the Communist Party. Its share of votes in the post-war period has normally been around 15–20%. The People's Alliance has been the backbone of the opposition to the US military bases and Iceland's membership of NATO, primarily on nationalistic grounds. It opposed Iceland's membership of EFTA in 1970, and while it has since accepted EFTA membership, it supports the EFTA-EC process only with considerable reservations concerning supranationality and the mobility of capital, people and services.

The Women's Alliance, established in the early 1980s, in some respects resembles the People's Alliance in its ideological profile, although it tends to place a greater emphasis on the interests of women and various 'green' issues. In fact, a large proportion of its 5.5% of votes in 1983 and 10.1% in 1987 came from dissatisfied People's Alliance voters.[36] The Women's Alliance is even more critical of European integration than the People's Alliance; it does not support Iceland's participation in the proposed European Economic Space, but favours bilateral negotiations with the EC on new free trade agreements.

The Progressive Party, originally established as a farmers' party, represents regional development in Icelandic politics, mixed with a certain amount of nationalism. Its share of the vote has usually been around 25% in the post-war period, but in recent years it has been facing increasing electoral difficulties. In the late 1960s the party abstained in the final parliamentary vote on EFTA membership, thinking it premature; its present positive attitude towards EFTA is matched by a reluctance to be drawn too closely into the fabric of West European cooperation.

A more positive attitude to the new developments in Western Europe is to be found in the Independence Party and the Social Democratic Party. These two parties in a coalition government lasting from 1959 to 1971 were the driving force behind the introduction of free trade as the major principle of foreign economic policy. They remain the parties most favourably disposed to Iceland's participation in economic cooperation in Western Europe, and more generally in the Western Alliance.

The Independence Party is a centre-right party and the largest in Iceland, usually getting about 40% of votes. It split before the 1987 election but seems well on the way to recovery, according to the opinion polls, while the splinter group has all but disappeared. The Independence Party has expressed an interest in negotiations with the EC; this does not mean that the party wants Iceland to apply for membership of the EC, but rather that it belives that the possibility of closer cooperation should be explored in general bilateral negotiations. There would undoubtedly be some resistance in the party to an application for membership. To the Independence Party the need for adaptation to the unification process is Western Europe is an important argument in favour of its demands for liberalization of the Icelandic economy, while at the same time it is not attracted by what it sees as a tendency towards excessive centralization in Western Europe.

The Social Democratic Party in Iceland is much smaller than most of its Northern European counterparts, usually with around 10–15% of votes. It is arguably the party most positively disposed towards West European integration. Although the party has at present no plans for applying for membership, it has warned against the dangers of economic and political isolation in Europe and advocated seeking new ways of linking Iceland to Western Europe.[37]

The business community and integration

In the issue of Iceland's relations with the EC the initiative rests at present chiefly with the business community; business organizations and individual business leaders.[38] The discussion has been led by the major business organizations, such as the Chamber of Commerce and the Employers' Federation, which possess a large proportion of the country's expert knowledge of the issue, and have been active in informing their members and the general public.

It appears that employers in different branches of trade are showing varying amounts of enthusiasm towards integration. The wholesalers' organization has publicly stated that it regards membership of the EC unfavourably, while the chairman of the organization of industrial manufacturers is among those most clearly in favour of a membership application.[39] It is however the fishing and fish processing sectors, which carry a great deal of weight in Icelandic politics, that are likely to have most influence on the country's European strategy.

Fishing and fish processing cooperate in the Chambers of Fisheries on issues of fisheries policy. They have also established a special committee of employers to coordinate their policies, not least with respect to the EC.[40] Nevertheless, there has evidently been a certain difference of emphasis between the leaders of the two branches of the fisheries sector. Thus the leader of fishing vessel owners has repeatedly stated that although Iceland must find a solution to its export problems, it cannot, in the foreseeable future at least, join the EC.[41] On the other hand, leaders in fish processing have hinted at a much more far-reaching revision of Iceland's present relations with the EC. Thus, even if full membership should not be a realistic possibility at present, the adaptation to Western Europe, with regard both to domestic structural change and to the bilateral relations with the EC, should be of primary importance in Icelandic foreign policy.[42]

Thus the greatest pressures on the government to act have come from sections of the business community: the political parties have not, so far, been particularly active on the issue.

The government's European policy

The government's strategy has been aiming at satisfying the short-term needs of the business community without threatening the political consensus. How far this consensus can be maintained depends above all on whether adaptation through EFTA, combined with a renegotiation of the free trade agreement, will lead to a satisfactory solution for Iceland's economy.

The government's main problem is Iceland's economic insignificance in a European context, which limits its ability to apply pressure or offer rewards to the EC. Although Iceland is like most EC member states, a member of NATO, it remains essentially dependent on the goodwill of its West European neighbours if it wishes to stay outside the European Community.[43] Making an issue of the US military bases and NATO membership in relation to trade negotiations may strengthen Iceland's position marginally, but essentially these are factors which under normal circumstances are not sufficiently concrete and credible to be used as a pressure on the EC member states.

Apart from the question of whether the EC is likely to take a benevolent attitude towards Iceland, there are two factors which could undermine the present government strategy. One is the development of EFTA and Iceland's role in it; the other is the possibility of Norway joining the EC.

For Iceland, EFTA plays the role of a substitute for EC membership. Consequently, Iceland has an interest in EFTA's becoming an active partner in the EC, which would largely solve the problems of adaptation for its member states. Iceland's position is paradoxical, however, in that it does not really wish to see EFTA transformed: since the more EFTA comes to resemble the EC, the smaller its value to Iceland compared to EC membership. On the one hand, with regard to opposition to supranationality, Iceland has stated reservations about the strengthening of EFTA as an organization or the introduction of supranationality into the proposed EES. It would be quite illogical for Iceland to grant EFTA the scope and powers which have blocked Iceland's membership of the EC. In this, Iceland's interests may differ significantly from those of some of the EFTA neutrals.[44] On the other hand, for those in Iceland who have strong reservations concerning the free movement of people, capital and services, the EFTA strategy could become less and less satisfactory, if it leads to a fairly open EES.

The possibility of a Norwegian application for EC membership is another factor which might affect the present government strategy. Norway is not only a valued neighbour, with close historical and cultural ties to Iceland; it is also among Iceland's main competitors in the European fish markets. Norway's access to the EC fish market is not at present as favourable as that provided by Iceland's 1972 free trade agreement. Norway's membership of the EC would undoubtedly give it a competitive advantage over Iceland; it might also increase the EC's ability to put pressure on Iceland, by making it much more self-sufficient in the provision of fishery products and less dependent on imports. And though Norway might have no wish to harm the interests of its North Atlantic neighbours, it might none the less be forced to do so, given a tendency within the Community to try to resolve internal conflicts at the expense of third countries. The result, as a Norwegian specialist has put it, might be 'catastrophic for countries such as Iceland and the Faroe Islands'.[45]

Thus several factors, including the attitude of the EC, the development of EFTA and the position taken by Norway, bear on the government strategy of maintaining consensus. A debate on membership may be inevitable. In fact, even if government strategy were successful in securing an improved free trade agreement and satisfactory EFTA-EC relations, the issue of membership might only be temporarily delayed, since a new free trade agreement might easily become outdated in a decade or two, just like the previous one.

Options for the future

If the issue of membership should be raised in Icelandic politics, it may well be decided within a short time, given Iceland's reactive style of decision making. In the event of a serious failure of the present government strategy, Iceland faces two broad alternatives. On the one hand, it might consider applying for membership of the EC, or at least start negotiations on far-reaching cooperation which might include the possibility of membership. Such a move need not lead to immediate or full membership for Iceland, but it would put to the test different options for cooperation. The possible outcomes of such negotiations include membership, with Iceland being given considerable time to adapt to the different EC policies; association, aiming at membership at some future time; and some combination of bilateral and EFTA approaches, which might safeguard Iceland's economic interests in Western Europe.

On the other hand, there exists the possibility of resisting further economic or political integration with Western Europe. The consequence might well be a reduction in trade with Western Europe. Many in Iceland argue that the present dependence on trade with the EC is unhealthy and advocate a policy of diversification by increasing trade with alternative markets, such as the USA, Japan or Eastern Europe: in place of closer political ties with Western Europe, Iceland could seek to increase its economic relations with other parts of the world.[46]

Each option raises difficult questions. The EC option depends not only on the EC's willingness to look with favour on Iceland's application, but also on whether a government willing to pursue this policy can be formed. This would probably have to be a coalition government of the Independence Party and the Social Democratic Party; but such a combination has not been tried since 1971, because of either insufficient parliamentary strength or disagreements among the party leaders. A strategy of trade diversification, on the other hand, would probably be very costly in economic terms; and if it were to be anything other than a disorganized retreat from Western Europe, it would require the kind of careful long-term policy making which is most uncharacteristic of the Icelandic political system.

In the end, public opinion will have a great impact on Iceland's response to the challenges it is facing. A number of surveys have revealed a very positive public attitude towards European integration; a far more positive one, in fact, than prevails in the organized world of political parties and interest organizations. On four occasions between May 1989 and March 1990 the public has been asked whether it supports the idea of applying for EC membership: the response is shown in Table 12.1.

On each occasion a majority of the electorate was in favour of an application, and this majority has been increasing with time. By March 1990, those in favour outnumbered those against by two to one, although many remained undecided. A more thorough survey carried out in October 1989 revealed that a substantial majority not only wishes to take a great part in the integration process (thus rejecting the option of reduced ties), but also supports the things it would lead to, such as greater mobility of capital, people, goods and services between Iceland and Western Europe.

Table 12.1 Icelandic attitudes to application for EC membership, May 1989–March 1990 (%)

	May 1989	*June 1989*	*Oct. 1989*	*Mar. 1990*
In favour	35.2	33.6	35.6	44.3
No opinion	35.5	42.2	43.8	33.3
Against	29.3	24.2	20.6	22.4
Total	100	100	100	100

Source: The Social Science Research Institute at the Faculty of Social Sciences, University of Iceland.

On the whole, the attitudes bear some relation to party sympathies: thus Independence Party and SDP voters are the ones most positively inclined towards Western Europe, while the voters of the Women's Alliance, the People's Alliance and the Progressive Party are more critical. But the variable most strongly related to attitudes towards Western Europe is the age of the respondents. The younger voters are by far the more positive towards integration, while the older ones appear much more reluctant. This pattern emerges in all the different issues concerning Iceland's relationship with Western Europe, indicating that with time, the current of opinion for a membership application may grow in strength.

Conclusion

The strategy followed so far by the Icelandic government aims primarily at maintaining consensus on the issue of Iceland's adaptation to developments in Western Europe. It consists of a double emphasis on adaptation through EFTA, to take care of the interests Iceland shares with its EFTA partners, to be complemented eventually by a bilateral approach to secure the access for Icelandic fishery products to EC fish markets.

This strategy has, in the long run, only a modest chance of succeeding: how much of a chance depends on the benevolence of the EC towards Iceland and EFTA. Iceland is not particularly well integrated into EFTA; its interests and problems are in many respects different from those of the other members; and on its own, the EFTA strategy is very unlikely to solve Iceland's main problem, which is that of market access for fish. What would be likely to persuade Iceland to abandon the EFTA strategy as the dominant response to European integration would be either the failure to secure a satisfactory free trade arrangement for its fishery products with the EC, or the abandonment of EFTA by one or more of its Nordic members.

The reason why a fairly broad consensus on the EFTA strategy prevails in Icelandic politics is that it delays conflicts over sensitive issues, while offering some hope – however small – of avoiding them altogether. Those averse to much more integration with Western Europe believe that the EFTA strategy should be pursued as a lesser evil than partial or full EC membership. For those, on the other hand, who want a far-reaching integration, the EFTA strategy is at least a start for Iceland on the road to integration, without the necessity of first making important and painful decisions, yet step by step drawing closer to fully integrated membership of the community of nations in Western Europe. If a decision has to be made on membership of the EC, it will be much easier if Iceland is already half-way there.

Notes

1. Ó. Th. Hardarson, *Vidhorf Íslendinga til öryggis- og utanrí kismála* (Reykjavik, Öryggismálanefnd, 1984), *Thjódlí f*, June 1989.
2. A. Jónsson, *Ísland, Atlantshafsbandalagid og Keflavikurstödin* (Reykjavik, Öryggismálanefnd, 1989).

3. G. Gunnarson, *Icelandic Security Policy* (Reykjavik, Öryggismálanefnd, 1986).
4. M. Handel, *Weak States in the International System*, (London, Frank Cass, 1981) pp. 265–74.
5. G.Th. Gislalson, 'Ísíensk efnahagsthróun og althjódleg samvinna', *Fjármálatí dindi*, 1980, no. 3; G.H. Kristinsson: *Ísland og Evrópubandalagid* (Reykjavik, Öryggismálanefnd, 1987).
6. B. Thorsteinsson, *Tíu thorskastríd 1415–1976* (Reykjavik, Sögufelagid, 1976).
7. B. Bjarnason, 'Iceland between East and West: trade and security' (unpublished paper, 1983).
8. G.H. Kristinsson, 'Iceland: vulnerability in a fish-based economy', *Cooperation and Conflict*, XXII, 1987.
9. Based on a report from the Ministry of Trade, Alth.t d. 1986–87, vol. 19, thskj. 700.
10. The main exceptions concern cooperation with the neighbouring countries of Norway, Greenland and the Faeroe Islands on the utilization of resources, as well as a very small (and declining) amount which Belgian vessels are allowed since the settlement of fisheries disputes in the 1970s.
11. As regards the limited range of agricultural products produced in Iceland, farmers are still shielded from foreign competition.
12. Th. Ásgeirsson, 'Iceland and the European Economic Community', Ministry of Trade, 1982.
13. M. Leigh, *European Integration and the Common Fisheries Policy* (London, Croom Helm, 1983); M. Wise, *The Common Fisheries Policy of the European Community* (London, Methuen, 1984).
14. Á. Olafsson, 'Færøerne og EF', paper presented at a conference on Norway, the EC and the fisheries, Norges fiskerihøgskole, March 1989.
15. The Soviet Union has, probably as a consequence of the 'perestrojka', recently indicated its wish for access to Icelandic fishing resources, in relation to the trade with Iceland. It is unlikely to obtain this. There may, however, be possibilities of increasing exports to the Soviet Union of techniques and expertise for the production of marine products.
16. An important problem is the cost of transportation and lack of knowledge of the needs of the markets which are limiting factors, although the Japanese market has shown some promising signs in recent years. In the less developed countries, the main problems are insufficient purchasing power and/or the extreme volatility of such markets.
17. Evrópubandalagid ogí slenskur idnadur, (Reykjavik, Idnadarráduneytid, 1988); Foreign Minister's report 1987, p. 42.
18. 'Ísland og Evrópubandalagid', Verslunnarrád Islands, Vidskiptathing 89.
19. 'Ísland og Evrópubandalagid'; see also 'Nefnd um stefnu Islendinga gagnvart Evrópubandalaginu', *Island og Evrópa*, vol. 3 (Reykjavik, 1989). It may be noted that most slaughterhouses in Iceland have had to cease exports to the EC as they could not satisfy EC regulations.
20. 'Nefnd um stefnu Íslendinga gagnvart Evrópubandalaginu', *Ísland og Evrópa*, (Reykjavik, 1989) vol. 3, p. 27.
21. The range of agricultural products which can be produced in Iceland is rather limited.
22. B. Valsson, 'Fjárfesting sjávarútvegi: meira af kappi en forsjá', *Sjávarfréttir*, vol. 17:1, 1989.
23. J. Farnell and J. Elles, *In Search of a Common Fisheries Policy*, (Hants, Gower, 1984) ch 7; P. Holm: *Handelshindringer pa norske fiskeprodukter i EF*, (Oslo, FAFO utrdening, 1985).
24. It may be noted that this step created some stir at the time, despite its cautious nature.
25. M. Gunnarsson, 'Ísland og sameiginleg sjávarútvegsstefna Evrópubandalagsins',

Sjávarfréttir vol. 16:3, 1988; samningur Islands og Efnahagsbandalags Evrópu. . . .

26. Wise, *The Common Fisheries Policy*; Farnell and Elles, In *Search of a Common Fisheries Policy*; *The European Community's Fishery Policy* (European Documentation, 1985).
27. R. Churchill 'The EEC's fisheries management system and its implications for Norway in the event of Norwegian membership of the EEC', Paper presented at a conference on 'Norway, the EC and the Fisheries', Norwegian College of Fishery Science, Tromso 16–17 March 1989, pp. 11–12.
28. Even if the fears of supranationality should be somewhat exaggerated at present, it must be noted that because of the CFP, it would affect Iceland more than the present member states.
29. The left-wing government formed in the autumn of 1988 went so far in its policy declaration as to state its aim of 'adapting the economy to the new circumstances and securing the competitiveness of Icelandic businesses without membership of the European Community'.
30. See *Morgunbladid*, 23 March 1989.
31. Thus Iceland had previously had some difficulty in explaining to EC representatives why it expected the EC to accept something which even its EFTA allies had rejected, namely, removing the barriers to Iceland's exports of fish.
32. Iceland's Foreign Minister Mr. Hannibalsson has however stated that formal negotiations should not start until a favourable outcome for Iceland seems secure.
33. In addition, an administrative committee has been set up to follow the EFTA-EC cooperation, and several interest organizations have also been making an effort to scrutinize the impact on their constituents of the developments in Europe.
34. *Thjódviljinn*, 21 February 1989.
35. *Thjódviljinn*, 6 June 1989.
36. Ó. Th. Hardarson and G.H. Kristinsson, 'The Icelandic Parliamentary Election of 1987' in *Electoral Studies*, vol. 6, no. 3, 1987.
37. A proposal was put to the Social Democratic party conference in 1988 to adopt the policy of applying for membership and to have a referendum on the issue, but the proposal was withdrawn without being put to a vote.
38. The wage earners' organizations, on the other hand, have devoted only marginal attention to the issue.
39. *Morgunbladid*, 28 October 1987, 23 November, 1988, 9 February 1989.
40. *Morgunbladid*, 2 March 1989.
41. *Morgunbladid*, 18 November 1988, 11 March 1989; 'Stækkun EB og Utanrí kisvidskipti Íslands 1961–1985', *Landsnefnd althjóda verslunarrádsins*, 1986.
42. 'Stækkun EB og Utanrí kisvidskipti Islands 1961–1985', *Landsnefnd althjóda verslunarrádsins*, 1986.
43. The argument that the EC is dependent on Icelandic fish greatly overestimates its replacement costs for the EC consumers. Those who most depend on Icelandic fish are probably some fish processors in the United Kingdom and the Federal republic of Germany, but these hardly carry enough political weight in the Community to be able to secure Iceland's economic position.
44. At the Oslo meeting of the EFTA leaders in March 1989, Iceland's Prime Minister Steingrí mur Hermannsson, although he signed its declaration, stressed that Iceland could not become party to a supranational institution.
45. P. Holm, 'EFs fiskerier og fiskeripolitikk fra 1972 til i dag', paper presented at a conference on Norway, the EC and the Fisheries, Norwegian College of Fishery Science, 16–17 March 1989.
46. An idea sometimes connected with the idea of trade diversification is the possibility of negotiating a free trade agreement with the US. An investigation into the matter by the Iceland National Committee of the ICC in 1986 indicated, however, that for the

fishery products presently exported to the US such an agreement would be of marginal importance, since the tariffs paid constitute only 1% of their total value. The rationale of the idea of a free trade agreement lies more in the possibility of gaining access to the US market for industrial manufacturing and attracting foreign firms to Iceland, to enjoy free trade with both the US and Western Europe.

13 Norway

Martin Saeter and Olav F. Knudsen

As a small country on the periphery of Europe, Norway has never been in a position to influence the agenda-setting of European integration policy to any noticeable extent. Its role has been rather that of reacting or adjusting to changes in the international environment brought about by others. From the time when Norway, as a result of World War II and the ensuing East-West conflict, left the policy of neutrality in favour of membership in the Western alliance, it has followed the leadership of Great Britain and the United States in its foreign and security policy. This 'Atlantic' orientation was reflected in its restrictive attitude towards extending Nordic cooperation into the political sphere in a way that might weaken its NATO attachment; in its EFTA policy of supporting the British 'free trade area' approach as opposed to the 'union' approach of France and other EC members; and in the consequent subordination of its European integration policy steps to the aim of maintaining the existing wider Atlantic security arrangement built on NATO and US leadership.

Since 1972, when the Norwegian referendum resulted in a 'no' to membership in the EC, there has been an increasing uneasiness in government and other elite circles about the possible consequences of non-membership for Norwegian security and foreign policy, a concern that has been strengthened by the development of a more 'independent' EC position within the Atlantic framework. With Great Britain inside the EC, Norway as a non-member could no longer follow British policy as it used to. The recognition of this new reality was part of the shock experienced by the government in connection with the 'no' vote. The desire to prevent misinterpretations abroad and to demonstrate the continuity of Norway's foreign policy orientation to a great extent explains why the government in the following years sought to 'compensate for' non-membership through a stronger emphasis on NATO and the United States in security and alliance matters.

Given the dynamic character of the EC development, however, this could only be a short-term strategy, because the general patterns of European security policies proved to be increasingly influenced by the changes in Europe that were linked to the integration process in the EC.

For many years after the 1972 referendum, however, the domestic political situation in Norway did not allow for a new debate on the EC issue. Even today, the Norwegian policy towards the EC cannot be understood without taking into consideration the traumatic experience of the 1972 debate. Foreigners who are not familiar with the severe strain inflicted on the whole Norwegian political system by that debate may find it difficult to understand Norway's present non-member status.

Norway is the only West European NATO country remaining outside the EC (except for Turkey and the special case of Iceland). It is, furthermore, dependent on the EC market for more than 70% of its exports. In the 1980s its economy became internationalized within the OECD framework to about the same degree as the economies of most EC countries. And the Norwegian government has demonstrated its intention of cooperating with the EC as closely as possible. Why then should Norway abstain from seeking membership of the EC? Why has the government given priority to the multilateral EFTA approach of adaptation, and what is the longer-term aim of such an approach? Is the strategy of adaptation aimed in reality at full membership? How far is Norway's position similar or parallel to the position of the other EFTA members? Taking into consideration the fact that the Community process is also increasingly a political one, is NATO membership something which in crucial respects gives Norway a position quite different from that of the four neutral EFTA countries?

In discussing these questions, we shall try to look into two main aspects affecting most of them: domestic politics (the internal dimension), and foreign policy (the external dimension).

The internal dimension: the 1972 referendum

We shall begin by sketching out those events of the early 1970s which still have such traumatic impact on Norwegian politics. Before the referendum in which the Norwegian electorate narrowly rejected EC membership, there was a clear majority in the Storting (parliament) in favour of membership. During 1971–2, this majority oscillated around the three-quarters of the membership which would be required for approval of the agreement. The voters, however, disagreed with their political leaders. A red-green 'anti-EEC' alignment, originally formed in the 1961 round of the EC debate, was restored in the autumn of 1970, uniting city radicals, environmentalists and rural voters in general. This coalition of 'no' groups was later opposed by a 'yes' movement. Both were *ad hoc* popular movements cutting across party loyalties.

For that reason, political parties suffered severely: the shaping of opinion on the EC issue gradually restructured the political landscape and the effects lasted for years. During the winter of 1971–72, the anti-membership side lined up the national party leaderships of the Socialist Left Party, the Centre Party and the Christian People's Party. In the process, the (smallish) Liberal Party was splintered; fundamental disagreements were exposed in the two medium-sized parties of the centre, (the Centre Party and the Christian People's Party), and the (leading) Labour Party was severely troubled. Of the established parties, only the Socialist Left and the Conservatives remained fairly intact.

The parliamentary combination which promoted membership in 1972 was a minority Labour government, tacitly supported by the Conservatives. But the decision to hold a referendum, and the Labour Prime Minister's threat to resign if it should go the wrong way, effectively undermined the national political leadership. For a brief moment, all national politics were focused on the September referendum.

The no's won by 53%: as it turned out later, a large segment of Labour voters had split off in that direction. The no's were also strong among all voters in the rural areas, in peripheral areas generally, and among lower income groups everywhere.

Although in 1972 industry was by and large in favour of EC membership, important segments were opposed to it, and these contributed substantially to the financing of the anti-membership campaign; in particular the agricultural food industry such as dairy produce and meat and fish preparation. Hence, on the No side as well as the Yes side, industry and labour joined hands.

The external dimension: the new challenge of the 1980s

The 1973 EC-EFTA rearrangements did not bring about any major immediate change in the pattern of economic relations between Norway and the Community, thanks to the free trade agreement. Taken as a whole, the EC was now by far Norway's most important economic partner; its relative weight increased throughout the 1970s and the 1980s, perhaps most significantly because of Norway's new role as a petroleum exporting country, but also because of the second and third enlargements of the Community to include first Greece and then Spain and Portugal. The free trade agreement was generally regarded in Norway as functioning well. After some rounds of difficult negotiations, an agreement on fishery regulations and quotas was reached in 1978 and has been renegotiated annually since then. The special zone of preservation around Spitsbergen, established unilaterally by Norway in the early 1980s, raised some controversial issues concerning both the status in international law of this group of islands and, more specifically, fishing rights for EC countries; this did not, however, lead to serious conflict. In the field of monetary policy, Norway participated in the socalled 'snake', but in 1979 chose, together with Sweden and Great Britain, not to join the EMS, a decision about which there has since been some domestic disagreement. Closer economic cooperation with the EC seemed to be non-controversial, but only so long as it did not escalate into any kind of formalized 'supranational' structure.

By the middle of the 1980s, however, neither Norway nor the other EFTA countries could escape any longer from considering again the true significance of participation in a European integration process centred on the EC. In their Luxembourg Declaration of 9 April 1984 the EC and the EFTA countries agreed on a new conception of cooperation, with the end in view of developing a 'dynamic' common European Economic Space (EES), thus linking the integration policies of EFTA countries to the dynamics of EC developments. The common free trade area was already completed. The establishment of the EES could mean that the EFTA countries were adapting to the more extensive integration aims of the EC. The Luxembourg Declaration was a means by which they defined themselves as partners in an integration process led by the EC. As confirmed by the Single European Act of 1986, this process to an increasing extent covers both economic and political aspects of the policies of the member states: the single market, including free movement of goods, people capital and services; economic and social matters; technology and research; monetary policy; environment; and, not least, the development of a harmonized and eventually common external policy.

The official Norwegian response

The Luxembourg Declaration did not attract immediate attention in the Norwegian public debate. It was only after the EC had decided on the internal market and adopted the Single European Act that the Norwegian government again began to concentrate on questions of European integration. In May 1987 a Parliamentary Report on these questions was presented by the Foreign Ministry of the Labour government under the title 'Norway, the EC and European cooperation'. It was supplemented by another report from the Ministry of Commerce and Shipping, which dealt in greater detail with the questions of trade and the role of EFTA. These two documents, particularly the first one, called the 'European Report' for short, constitute the foundation on which the Norwegian Labour government subsequently built its policy towards questions of European integration and cooperation.[1]

Contrary to expectations in some circles, the government did not deal with the question of EC membership, confining itself to attempting 'to identify the tasks and challenges facing Norway in relation to the EC on the basis of the present form of association'. The report also sought to provide 'the basis for a more comprehensive debate on Norway's position in Europe and the country's role in European politics'.[2] The European Report contains a broad analysis of the different dimensions of European integration politics, and a broad and informative discussion of the aims and methods of what the government had chosen as its strategy, the policy of adaptation. The long-term goal of this strategy was not, however, spelled out very clearly. The foundation laid down by the report was also adopted by the Conservative coalition government which took over after the 1989 general election.

The internal market, cooperation on technology and research, and political cooperation (EPC) are underlined in the report as areas of central interest to Norway. In what follows technology and research will not be dealt with, not because this area is unimportant, but because the government's generally positive stand is non-controversial. If anything, the government is criticized for not going far enough in participating in the EC programmes.

As regards the internal market, it is the government's view that Norway 'must adapt to these changes as far as possible in order to avoid new trade barriers'.[3] The significance of the Luxembourg Declaration is strongly emphasized: through this common declaration Norway has given its consent to the development of the EES as a framework for multilateral EFTA adaptation to the EC process. According to the report, the EFTA-EC cooperation has 'entered a new phase'. Its new features consist in

> ... the character of the proposed areas of cooperation and in that they are all taken from the EC White Book. Thus the cooperation between EFTA and the EC has become linked to a pre-decided and pre-scheduled EC agenda. This means that the schedule of the EC Commission now acts as a strong driving force in the cooperation between the EC and EFTA.[4]

It is the government's view that the establishment of a single large Western European market will bring advantages for the Norwegian economy as a whole. 'The government therefore regards it as important that the cooperation with the EC on this, both bilaterally and through EFTA, should develop in parallel with the EC schedule for the internal market'.[5]

This short extract from the European Report is sufficient to show that the Norwegian government, without any explicit reservations, intends to adapt to the development of the internal market 'as far as possible'. The term is undefined but can hardly be interpreted otherwise than as an intention to adapt as far as the domestic political situation allows.

The membership question

The Norwegian government's main argument for not raising the question of membership at present is that this could reopen the kind of disastrous debate that took place in 1972. Speaking in the European Parliament on 26 October 1988, Prime Minister Gro Harlem Brundtland thus developed the argument:

> The 1972 debate left us with a trauma which has still not been overcome. Community policies represent challenges for Norway, regardless of the form of our relations. It is important that Norwegian society should be ready and able to discuss these challenges without being eclipsed by a new and premature debate on Norwegian membership of the Community. ... Our policy approach to the challenges of European integration is to lay the foundation for a new domestic awareness of the European dimensions of our national interests.[6]

The seriousness of these statements should not be doubted. They do not reflect a negative attitude towards the idea of Norwegian membership, but rather a concern that a 'premature' debate should not be allowed to destroy the prospects of a harmonious development in that direction.

The exclusion from the long-awaited European Report of what most people thought was the main question serves to explain why it did not cause very much discussion. Because of the government's statement that membership was not currently of interest and that relations with the EC would continue to build on the existing trade treaty, the press as well as the public lost interest in the issue: in this way even the internal market debate was delayed further.

The failure to tackle the membership question in the European Report might also to some extent be tactical, a way of coping with a serious lack of public support – the aspect to which we shall turn next.

Public debate and domestic opinion

A comprehensive picture of politically relevant attitudes on the membership issue would require an account not merely of mass opinion, but also of party (or party leadership) and business (or business leader) opinion. What follows is only a very rough sketch.

By the late 1980s it could be asked whether anything essential has changed since 1972. The distribution of electoral support for Norwegian political parties was largely as it had been in 1972, although the conservative side was somewhat stronger but also less homogeneous: the neo-conservative Progress Party had not existed in 1972. It has recently stolen large numbers of supporters from other parties – not least the Conservatives – and gained substantially in the 1989 elections.

Table 13.1 compares party attitudes to EC membership in 1972 and 1989. The general pattern it reveals is that the voters of the larger parties are even less likely to favour membership in 1989 than they were in 1972. The outcome of the referendum probably partly explains this change, together with a subsequent adjustment of pro-EC attitudes to fit the realities of Norwegian political life. An interesting deviation from this pattern is the Socialist Left party, whose younger parliamentarians in particular have recently voiced pro-membership views.

It is notable that while the Labour Party's voters were clearly in favour in 1972, they are now just as clearly opposed. Only the two parties on the right have a majority in favour of membership. The other parties are nowhere near the 50% mark, including the three non-socialist parties at the middle of the spectrum.

How the 1989 situation developed during the preceding couple of years can be seen in Table 13.2. This shows the results of a series of surveys, all using identical questions, and three of them conducted by the same research unit. Unlike Table 13.1, the figures include all responses given, not just those in favour. They reflect a persistently low level of support for Norwegian membership. The opposition shows no sign of weakness in late September 1989, but the 'don't knows' continue to provide a substantial factor of uncertainty.

Table 13.1 Party affiliation and attitude to EC membership in Norway (The figures indicate percentages of those in favour: those undecided are excluded)

	Soc. Left	*Lab.*	*Lib.*	*Chr. Dem.*	*Centre*	*Cons.*	*Prog.*	*Total*
1972	3	65	42	18	5	90	—*	47
1989	18	37	39	19	1	75	53	40
Party size:								
Vote '89	10	34	3	9	7	22	13	%

* The Progress Party did not exist in 1972.

Source: Henry Valen, 'EF-saken i norsk opinion', figure 1, mimeo, Institute for Social Research, Oslo 1990.

Table 13.2 Public opinion on the issue of Norwegian membership in the EC, 1987–9 (%)

	*June 1987**	*Jan. 1988**	*June 1988**	*Oct. 1988†*	*Sept. 1989‡*
Yes	28	34	38	27	32
No	39	45	38	37	47
Don't know	33	21	24	31	21
N	1000	1000	1000	1067	2200

* Norsk Gallup for *Aftenposten*, published 11 June 1988. The wording of the question is virtually identical with the October 1988 question quoted below. Personal interviews in June 1987 and January 1988. Telephone survey in June 1988. Identical sampling methods (quota sampling).

† MMI for Henry Valen. Question, translated: 'Let us suppose that a referendum were to be held tomorrow on the issue of Norwegian membership in the EC. Would you vote yes or no?' ('Don't know' was not offered by the interviewer as an alternative response. Quota sampling.)

‡ Institute for Social Research and the Norwegian Bureau of Statistics. Question identical to that posed in October 1988.

Source: Henry Valen, 'EF-saken i norsk opinion', mimeo, Institute for Social Research, Oslo, 1990.

Judging by these polls, even by the end of 1989 the Norwegian electorate was nowhere near giving its blessing to a pro-membership policy.

Significant features of the voting pattern

The September 1989 survey brings out other significant characteristics of the pattern of voters' attitudes. Age does not differentiate strongly between supporters and opponents: younger people are not significantly more in favour of membership than other groups.

Men would vote differently from women who in all age groups appeared significantly more opposed to membership than men. Geographically, the 'yes' side remains strongest in the Oslo area, while the 'no' side has the upper hand in the rest of the country.

In another poll, conducted by MMI for *Dagbladet* in April 1988, voters were asked how well informed they considered themselves to be on the European Community plans to complete the internal market by 1992. Fully 68% considered themselves to be 'rather poorly informed' or worse; only 23% said they were 'fairly well informed' or better.[7] Other surveys have consistently shown support for membership rising with the level of education.

The *Dagbladet* survey in April 1988 asked about people's expectations of the effects of '1992' on the Norwegian economy. While 26% had positive expectations and 32% negative expectations, 41% replied, 'don't know'.

The attitudes of business élites are undoubtedly favourable to membership. The umbrella organization NHO, which unites the employers' federation and the association of industries, took in 1989 a formal stand in favour of EC membership. Nevertheless, some of the food processing industries continue to convey tacitly a basic scepticism. An anti-EC information service, backed by the agricultural associations, was established in the autumn of 1988. The trade unions have avoided taking a common stand. Opinion within is clearly divided, to judge from public statements.

The parliamentary basis

As mentioned earlier, the governing coalition of the Conservative, Centre and Christian People's Parties is split over the membership question, as is the Labour Party. Moreover, the government is in a minority. To be able to continue in power, the coalition needs *ad hoc* support from either the Progress Party or the Labour Party. The carefully formulated agreement (the Lysebu Declaration) on which the coalition is based makes it clear that the collaboration will come to an end as soon as the membership issue is raised in earnest.

All the aspirations of the coalition government are staked on the EC-EFTA process. The key to a possible policy change in the future is the Labour Party and the outcome of that process. For the foreseeable future, at least, it is almost unthinkable that the Labour Party should take a stand against membership, whether it is in government or not. A move in the other direction would, however, depend on the polls, as well as possible coalition partners.

In the parliament as a whole there is probably a majority in favour of Norwegian membership – as there was in 1972. Judging from the parliamentary debates, as well as from public discussions in the press and elsewhere, the political atmosphere surrounding the membership question is now much more relaxed than it was in the early 1970s. There is general agreement among the parties that a new referendum will be necessary. However, neither of the major parties wants a referendum to be held unless there is considerable certainty that a very substantial majority of the population will be voting for membership.

The Norwegian EFTA strategy

In economic terms and in the requirements of adaptation to the EC's internal market, Norway closely resembles the other EFTA countries. Their economic and organizational platform in EFTA is the same; and, except for the severe political constraints placed on Norway as a result of the referendum, they are facing much the same problems at the domestic economic level in connection with the adaptation process. The EC has stated its preference for dealing with all the EFTA countries in parallel.

This is where the concept of the 'dynamic' European Economic Space comes in, as a multilateral legitimation of such steps. It has made it easier for Norway to put off the question of membership and for the neutrals to participate in the process without broaching the controversial issue of neutrality.

The process of developing the EES is regarded by the present Norwegian government (as it was by the previous one) as consisting of three main elements: the renewed EC dynamics, the bilateral relations between the EFTA countries and the EC, and the multilateral cooperation between the EFTA countries and the EC. Norway is interested in developing EFTA as a multilateral instrument: 'In order to avoid new trade barriers between the EFTA countries, this is the only practicable way of cooperation.'[8]

Norwegian participation in EFTA has traditionally been very non-controversial in domestic politics. Therefore the government's underlining of the role of EFTA in the process of adapting to the EC seems to be prudent from a tactical point of view also: everything that comes through the multilateral EFTA framework – especially where there is Nordic agreement – can be expected to be politically acceptable at the domestic Norwegian level.

Nevertheless, the government has to balance carefully between those on the one side who are afraid that the adaptation strategy means bringing about Norwegian EC membership *de facto* and those on the other side who are opposed to any kind of policy orientation that might hinder or exclude Norwegian membership in the long term. It also, of course, has to take into consideration the interests of the other EFTA states.

EFTA is seen as important in a Nordic context also, as the foundation for free trade among the Nordic non-EC members. Sweden is Norway's most important trade partner, ahead of both Great Britain and West Germany if petroleum is excluded. The attitude of Sweden to the market questions in Western Europe will therefore be of great significance to Norway.[9]

As regards the longer-term goals of the process of adaptation, the European Report states:

> In our view the possible establishment of the EES will be a long-term process that has to be able to include new elements when this appears natural and necessary. In the first phase, the content of the EES could consist of free market access for industrial goods, fish, processed agricultural products and certain services, as well as the implementation of equal terms of competition. This would imply that questions related to technical barriers of trade, public procurement, research and development, policy of education, environmental safeguards, consumer policy, and economic policy must also be discussed.[10]

At the EFTA summit meeting in Oslo in March 1989, Norway, as chairman, played an active part in securing a common positive answer to the suggestions, made in January 1989 by the President of the Commission, Jacques Delors, of strengthening the institutional links between EC and EFTA. As demonstrated both at the EC-EFTA ministerial meeting on 20 March 1990 and at the Kristiansand EFTA meeting on 15 June 1989, as long as it was in office, the Labour government continued to give priority to the EFTA strategy of far-reaching adaptation.

The replacement of the Labour government by the coalition government was marked by a striking degree of continuity in the Norwegian position on the most vital questions considered in the EFTA-EC dialogue. In the so-called Lysebu Declaration, the three parties to the coalition stated their intention of following the guidelines drawn up in the government's 1987 European Report and by the EFTA meeting in March 1989. The 'fullest possible' implementation of the free movement of goods, services, people and capital is accepted as an aim. In accord with the Labour government's policy, the coalition document stresses certain conditions:

- An EES treaty must be given the status of international law, binding upon states, but not upon companies or persons.
- As a separate step, the EES rules must be incorporated into national law.
- A common EES court must include members from the EFTA countries also.
- Formal EES declarations must be unanimous.
- All the EFTA countries must be equal parties to the treaty and have the right of initiative and 'real' influence, as regards both formal decisions and the law-making process.

Furthermore, a number of reservations are made concerning specific areas:

- Border control must be maintained.
- A common agricultural policy is not to be considered.
- Each country must be granted the right to maintain higher standards of health, labour security and environment.
- National control over the management of resources and the environment must be maintained on a reciprocal basis.
- Some kind of labour migration control must be continued.
- The use of fiscal duties for social, environmental and health purposes must be permitted.

These conditions and reservations, which have been incorporated into the common EFTA approach towards the EC, serve the function, at any rate in the Norwegian domestic political setting, of securing a viable national consensus, as well as of keeping the coalition government together. However, they seem rather unrealistic with respect to reaching agreement with the EC. Concessions of the kind demanded would in practice mean a change of the actual EC system, which would probably be unacceptable to most of the EC countries. An EC refusal would, however, inevitably create additional domestic strains in these countries. In Norway, the coalition would be unlikely to survive such a development.

While the Centre Party is supporting the EFTA-EC dialogue as a means of reaching an alternative solution to Norway's membership, the Conservatives accept it as a possible means of eventually bringing about membership. The Centre Party wants the conditions and reservations to be as rigid as possible, to underline the difference from membership. Paradoxically, the Conservatives are agreeing to this intransigent approach in the tacit expectation that it will fail, thus making membership the only remaining realistic possibility. The longer the process of adaptation is carried on, the less dramatic will be the switch to a membership strategy.

The slow process of economic adaptation

The legislative adaptation to the EC internal market directives appears to be proceeding on a wide scale in the various ministries, in close consultation with export industries and labour and employers' organizations, as well as other interest groups. Astonishingly, there is as yet very little public debate about this aspect of adaptation. Politically, silence may be convenient in the short term, but its contribution is rather dubious with regard to the obvious need for a thorough discussion of the different aspects of restructuring Norwegian economic life. Above all, it creates uncertainty among industrialists and investors about whether or to what degree Norway will be inside or outside the internal market, and what the difference might mean in practice.

High petroleum incomes during the 1970s made it all too tempting for successive Norwegian governments to use oil money in pursuing a 'counter-cyclical policy', thus postponing economic reforms of the kind undertaken in other West European countries. High employment was maintained, but at the cost of rising inflation and reduced competitiveness. Industrial growth, apart from the oil and gas sector, stagnated in the period 1974–83. Other countries, which had been forced to restructure their industries earlier, showed an increased growth. Even more than in the past, Norway's export profile became based on raw materials.

As the oil and gas surpluses disappeared in the early 1980s, the weaknesses in the Norwegian economy were brutally disclosed. Since then the government has deliberately, and to an increasing extent, allowed the Norwegian economy as a whole to be more directly exposed to the factors of internationalization. Capital, finance and banking transactions were liberalized, resulting in high rates of interest, speculation on the stock exchange and so on. State subsidies were reduced at the cost of rising unemployment. State spending on welfare stagnated, causing social unrest.

All this happened without any explicit reference to or connection with the EC-EFTA development. However, it no doubt helped to prepare the Norwegian people for the kind of restructuring required by the policy of EC adaptation. The latest example is the GATT decision to reduce state subsidies for agricultural production, which will probably mean that Norwegian state subsidies in this sector will be reduced irrespective of EC membership. As for the fisheries sector, a large part of it now seems to consider market access in the EC for Norwegian products to be more important than national Norwegian control over resources.

On the other hand, there is always the possibility that the economic sacrifices and other unpopular measures connected with the general internationalization of the Norwegian economy will be increasingly identified in public opinion with the policy of EC adaptation. This might result in the general strengthening of anti-EC attitudes.

Norway, Nato and EPC

In about 1980 the Norwegian government began to attach greater importance to the development of European Political Cooperation (EPC). This took place against the background of the increasing divergences between the United States and Western Europe on questions of foreign policy and security. The support for NATO membership among the Norwegian people was as strong as ever, but there was a growing fear that Norway, by standing outside the EC, risked being left out in the cold in a situation of increasing tension between the two superpowers.

During his official visit to Brussels in November 1980, Prime Minister Nordli advocated extending and strengthening the bilateral political relations, stressing Norway's interest in taking constructive part in the EPC process, and underlining the need for West European foreign policy coordination at a time when the policy of detente was at stake.[11] This initiative met with positive response from all political quarters in Norway. The contacts with the EPC were formally confirmed by the succeeding Conservative government.

However, it should be noted that neither at government level nor among the Norwegian public was there any inclination to think of the EPC as an alternative to NATO as the main forum for security policy coordination. There was never any support in Norway for the idea of Western Europe as an exclusive entity, especially where security was concerned. If there were to be any fundamental change in alliance structures, it would have to take the shape of a broader European security arrangement and be brought about by a concerted policy of detente. This explains the earlier Norwegian interest in participation in the EPC process without becoming a member of the EC.

Since it was soon realized, however, that the only way to Norwegian participation in the EPC lay through EC membership, the EPC discussion in Norway lost ground, because membership was out of the question. When the government was confronted in the 1980s with the challenges of the internal market, there took place an apparently paradoxical reversal of its arguments: now the emphasis was once again on the economy and not on security. Membership being still anathema, the government had to find some way of separating the discussion on the internal market from the political aspects of membership. The policy of adaptation, which was explicitly defined as not being about membership, simply had to leave EPC out of the discussion, because it proved too much to ask that people should readily distinguish between EPC and other political aspects of the EC process.

A further consequence of separating discussion of the internal market from politics was that Norway's NATO membership was also excluded from the discussion about adaptation strategy. The choice of the multilateral EFTA strategy naturally made it inopportune for the government to speak about NATO linkages: by focusing on the political aspects, it risked setting off a more general discussion about these questions in the neutral EFTA countries. These countries obviously face a more problematic situation than Norway, in this respect. On the other hand, to tie Norway's EC policy to the situation of the neutrals (by letting constraints of neutrality become constraints on Norwegian policy also), would certainly be an unacceptable policy, given Norway's strong support for NATO.

However, in its European Report the government in no way tries to play down the importance of EPC. Indeed, it regards EPC as of paramount interest for Norway, in that it is likely to 'have an increasing impact on all the main areas of Norwegian foreign policy ... without any direct Norwegian influence on the process'. Staying outside represents 'a growing challenge', especially in areas such as Atlantic cooperation, East-West relations, arms control and disarmament, and North-South relations: 'Insofar as West European and Western discussions of such matters become centred on EPC and on an EPC-United States dialogue, this will clearly restrict our scope for promoting our interests and making our views known'.[12]

The European Report reveals much uncertainty on the part of the Norwegian government about future EPC development. On the one hand, it concludes that 'there is reason to expect EPC to continue developing as the most important forum for the formulation of the attitude of EC countries to their relations with the rest of the world, and accordingly for Western European action in important international matters.[13] Pointing in this direction are factors such as 'a more pronounced West European profile also where security policy is concerned', 'differences of views and emphasis between the United States and Western Europe concerning policy towards the Warsaw Pact countries', etc. On the other hand, the report also makes the strong statement that, in spite of greater European independence and growing divergences of view and behaviour between the EC and the United States,

> such a development . . . could not alter the fundamental community of interests and values or the interdependence on which cooperation between North America and Western Europe rests . . . There is the same broad agreement as before among the EC countries that the necessary political and military balance in relation to the Soviet Union would be impossible to maintain without the USA's strategic security guarantee for Western Europe, or the general mutual solidarity and close cooperation with the United States.[14]

Thus at the level of security policy, the report reflects a strong inclination to think in status-quo terms as regards security. The main emphasis is on the role of the superpower relationship, the reduction of tension, arms control, increased contacts between the two parts of Europe, etc., and not on an asymmetrical kind of 'Europeanization' directed towards replacing the existing bloc system by an all-European system of cooperation and common security.

The question is, of course, whether this bloc-to-bloc orientation is adequate in adapting Norwegian security and foreign policy to the dynamic change in European politics that has been brought about by EC developments and by the process of reform in Eastern Europe; the answer is, probably not. It restricts the government's scope for discussion and action to mere adaptation to EC initiatives. It fails to establish a vision of the longer-term goals of its European policy. It makes official coordination with the EC countries difficult in matters implying potential change in security approach. And above all, it prevents Norway from adjusting officially and actively to such security changes in its own geographical surroundings as follow logically from the process of Europeanization: whether confidence-building and disarmament measures in the follow-up to the Stockholm Conference on Disarmament in Europe (CDE); bilateral cooperation with the Soviet Union as part of the all-European approach; or coordination of the policies of the Nordic countries towards asymmetrical changes in the East-West context (EPC, EC-Comecon, arms control measures in the Nordic area, etc.).

Conclusion

The present parliamentary situation in Norway seems to limit the government's choice to pursuing the EFTA strategy as far as possible. The coalition's platform does not offer much scope for compromises on basic questions such as those about institutional arrangements and common decision-making. Because of the seemingly impossible task of reconciling EFTA demands with EC structures, the EC-EFTA dialogue in its present form is likely to fail. The EFTA approach, however, might be redefined, depending on what role the EC will attribute to it in the larger context of European integration. In any case, the basis of the coalition government is likely to become weaker, both because the unreality of the present strategy will become more apparent, and because a redefinition of EFTA into the all-European context will most probably have the effect of altogether reducing the coalition partners' interests in EFTA.

In such a situation the membership question would inevitably again become more acute in the EFTA countries, especially Norway. This time security considerations would undoubtedly become more dominant. In a Europe where the EC is opening up to the East European countries, and where NATO is no longer the main forum for policy coordination in Western Europe, the tendency in Norway would probably be towards strengthening the ties with the EC. Resistance from the left against EC membership would be likely to diminish in parallel with increased East-West cooperation, especially if the neutral Nordic countries were also able to join.

However, the trend of public opinion is not necessarily amenable to overall reasoning of this kind. The enduring fact of Norwegian political life since 1972 will continue to be that a government must heed not only its parliamentary base and its international negotiating engagements, but equally the *vox populi* of opinion polls, whenever issues concerning independence and sovereignty are at stake.

Several quick polls taken in the spring of 1990 seem to indicate a substantial shift of Norwegian opinion in favour of membership. If confirmed by more reliable surveys, this may turn out to be a consequence of the substantial changes in Eastern Europe late in 1989. It nevertheless remains an open question whether a swing in this direction is likely to be enduring, or just a passing 'shock effect' of the surrounding European transitions.

Notes

1. *St. meld. nr. 61, 1986–87*, 'Norge, EF og europeisk samarbeid', by the Ministry of Foreign Affairs, and *St. meld. nr. 63*, 'Om enkelte handelspolitiske spørsmal', by the Ministry of Commerce and Shipping. A non-official and incomplete translation of the former report is used in most of the quotations in this chapter.
2. *St. meld nr. 61*, p. 3.
3. *St. meld nr. 61*, p. 4.
4. *St. meld nr. 61*, p. 33.
5. *St. meld. nr. 61*, p. 33.
6. 'Norway, the European Community and European cooperation', speech, text available from the Office of the Prime Minister, Oslo.
7. *Dagbladet*, 2 June 1988.
8. *St. meld. nr. 63*, p. 30.
9. *St. meld nr. 61*, p. 33.
10. *St. meld. nr. 63*, p. 30.

11. *Arbeiderbladet*, Oslo, 22 November 1980.
12. *St. meld. nr. 61*, p. 53.
13. *St. meld. nr. 61*, p. 52.
14. *St. meld nr. 61*, p. 51.

14 Sweden

Carl-Einar Stålvant and Carl Hamilton

The relaunch of economic Europeanism

Whenever the issue of European integration has been discussed in the Nordic countries the impulse has come from abroad. For a long time new departures in British policies were the most important factor. Since Britain joined the European Community, influences have stemmed from EC decisions to push ahead with economic and political cooperation. The decisive developments in the EC in 1985 prompted a vigorous reaction in Sweden.

Overall relations between Sweden and the Community have undergone interesting developments during the lifetime of the Free Trade Agreement. The changes have been concentrated in areas beyond and with marginal connection to trade issues. These so-called second-generation agreements have institutionalized broad networks for regular exchanges of views in fields such as foreign development aid, the environment, consumer protection, labour market policy and medium-term economic policy. Research and development cooperation is managed by a separate bilateral committee, under a general agreement designed to facilitate Swedish participation in EC research programmes on the basis of proportional co-financing. But of these seventy or so agreements, none gives Sweden any rights to participate in Community decision-making. It is against this background that Sweden's relationship with the EC is analysed, and possible conflicts in the Swedish debate about integration are discussed. The conclusions set out the motives, real and perceived, for the Swedish Parliament's statement 'that Swedish membership of the Community is not an objective for the negotiations which are now starting'.[1]

Sweden's economic relations with the Community

Sweden's economic relations with the Community are extremely close. This does not mean, however, that the Community is particularly dependent on Sweden. In considering the country's economic importance, several measures of interdependence can be applied, such as trade in goods, trade in services,

Table 14.1 Shares of home market for manufactures and agriculture: Sweden, EC and EFTA, 1985

	Manufactures (%)	*Agriculture (%)*
EFTA's share of the EC home market	3.5	0.7
Sweden's share of EC home market	1.0	0.1
EC's share of Swedish home market	24.6	6.0

Source: Calculated from OECD data

foreign investment, migration, exchange rate arrangements and so on. It should be noted that the Community's external trade is fairly small in relation to its home market. This is a reflection of the simple fact that today's Community is an economic superpower with twelve member states, some 320 million inhabitants and a GNP which is only 15% less than that of the United States.

Our analysis starts with an unusual but accurate measure of interdependence through trade, that is a comparison of trade with total home demand (apparent consumption: i.e. domestic production plus imports minus exports). EFTA's exports as a share of the Community's home market for manufactures are presented in Table 14.1. EFTA's share was 3.5% in 1985, with Sweden supplying approximately 1%. Turning this round to assess the Community's share of home demand in Sweden reveals a glaring asymmetry: in 1985 the Community supplied approximately 25% of the Swedish market for manufactures.

Assuming that the most essential internal market proposals are implemented, what would be the consequences if Sweden adjusted fully to the internal market and followed the Community's decisions in line with the objectives stated by the Swedish Parliament? The next section points out the most important economic consequences likely to follow from the coordination of Swedish policies with those of the EC. This is not an academic exercise, since a professed aim of Swedish integration policy is to remove border controls between itself and the EC and to avoid discrimination against Swedish firms and consumers. The option of a customs union was also mentioned in EC Commission President Jacques Delors's speech of January 1989 suggesting a 'structured relationship and common decision-making' between EFTA countries and the EC.

Coordination of policies

Coordinated external trade policy

Prior to abolishing joint border controls, the Community would require Sweden to impose the same external trade barrier as it does itself, that is to establish a customs union. A common external trade policy is necessary since with customs posts abolished, prices on the two sides of the removed border would tend to equalize. If Sweden's external trade policy were different, a product which faced a high trade barrier in the Community and a low trade barrier in Sweden could be exported to the Community via Sweden to avoid the higher Community barrier. This would be unacceptable to the Community, of course, and correspondingly for Sweden in contrary examples.

An adjustment of Sweden's average tariff to the Community's common external tariff for manufactures would mean accepting a level of approximately 4% compared to the present 3%. However, Sweden would also have to apply the Community's non-tariff measures. Leaving aside agriculture and fishing, probably the most important restrictions today are on imports from Japan of household appliances, videos and similar goods as well as automobiles and motorcycles. Some imports from developing countries such as textiles and clothing are subject to export restrictions (voluntary export restraints). If non-tariff measures like these were not harmonized with those of the Community, a product subject to an import quota in the Community could enter through the Swedish 'back door'.

The Community now has three associated members, Turkey, Malta and Cyprus, and preferential agreements with Yugoslavia, Israel and a number of Arab countries bordering on the Mediterranean. In order to achieve a common external trade barrier, a would-be participant in the EC's customs union would have to observe these trade agreements as well. If such adjustments were made in Sweden today, consumers would have to pay more for several products from Japan, and perhaps less for some products from developing countries, like fruit and vegetables from certain Mediterranean countries.

Coordinated agricultural policy

An approximate harmonization of prices for agricultural products in Sweden and the Community would probably be feasible, given time for adjustment. (If undertaken today, Swedish milk producers would have to accept significantly lower government purchase prices.) Possibly more important for Swedish consumers and society as a whole, abolition of border controls vis-à-vis the EC would hold back the agreed reform of Swedish agricultural policy which tends towards lower production and reduced consumer prices. It is not that the principles of agricultural policy diverge very much at present, and the Swedish government had few reservations about including agriculture in the 1970–2 negotiations with the EC. Current attitudes are more reserved, partly because of the changes expected in EC policy. Although the Community's struggle to reform the CAP envisages similar measures, the complexities involved are of a quite different magnitude.

Coordinated indirect taxation

Adjusting indirect taxes would mean two things for Sweden: first, harmonization of the tax base to that of the EC (i.e. accepting EC decisions on which goods and services should bear indirect taxes); and second, harmonization of the rates of indirect tax. In 1987 the EC Commission suggested that member states should impose a VAT rate for two-thirds of all goods and services in the range of 14 to 20%, with a lower rate for food – between 4 and 9%. The suggestion regarding the standard rate has since been modified, to a minimum of 17% with no upper limit.[2] Compared to most Community countries, Sweden's indirect tax rate is high at 23.5%. Recent fiscal decisions mean that Sweden has broadened the tax base – allegedly to conform with the profile suggested by the EC Commission. Sweden would also have to reduce the VAT rate on food and some other products to less than half the current rate, and, at the same time, reduce the VAT rate on remaining goods and services to some 20%. Clearly, total revenue from indirect taxation would be significantly reduced, which of course worries the Minister of Finance.[3] One might well ask why anyone outside Sweden, or any other high-tax country for that matter, should mind about Swedish tax rates, so long as they remain above those of neighbouring countries. The Swedish tax collector would be the only sufferer if Swedes travelled abroad to buy their goods and services.

To avoid excessively resource-consuming cross-border trade, prices of goods such as petrol, tobacco, wine and spirits would have to be approximately the same as in neighbouring countries. In Table 14.2 the change in retail prices in Sweden is calculated, assuming the Commission's proposal for 1992 were implemented in 1987. Apart from the steeply reduced tax on alcohol, the present duties on Swedish charter flights are worth noting. (This tax can be regarded as an import tariff on tourist services.) The abolition of the charter flight tax would be an obvious objective for the Community's negotiators, since it hits employees and capital owners in the Community's service sector, as well as Swedes looking for sun and a change of culture.

It is important to note, however, that the EC still has some way to go on the issue of indirect taxes. Probably not until some time in the mid-1990s will we know the final outcome of the internal bargaining process. One possibility is that there will be a harmonization of the tax base and limited harmonization of

Table 14.2 Taxation of certain items: the Commission's proposal for 1992 applied to Sweden in 1987

	Difference in selling prices (%)
Petrol	+2 to 3
Oil for heating	−15
Heavy oil	−25
Excise on charter flights (SEK 300)	disappears
Cigarettes (average)	+17
Alcoholic beverages:	
Absolut, Swedish vodka	−67
Johnny Walker whisky	−40
French table wine	−68

tax rates, then a trial and error period of several years during which governments observe how intra-Community cross-border trade develops. Countries which lose their tax base to their neighbours will reduce the gap by reducing taxes. This would imply a form of 'competition among rules' for indirect taxation. Sweden would have to see how high it could keep its taxes without losing too much of the domestic tax base to neighbouring countries.

The EC proposals for reduced barriers to trade and freer movement of factors of production raise a general problem for high-tax countries like the Nordic ones in that the tax base will more easily be able to move to a low-tax country. So far, however, the experience is that individuals at least have proved fairly unwilling to move within Western Europe, in spite of the fact that many – like car workers – could increase their after-tax income two to four times by moving to another country.

The effect of high-tax countries reducing their indirect taxes will, of course, depend on what other measures the governments take at the same time. If the alternative is higher personal income taxes, economic efficiency could be reduced because of larger tax wedges (i.e. a greater difference between the individual's return on extra work and society's return). A decision on increased personal income taxes would, however, go against the present international trend and also against decisions taken by the Riksdag (the Swedish Parliament) in 1989 and 1990. If the alternative is reduced public expenditure, the effects on economic growth of the economy would depend on which expenditures are reduced.

The important conclusion from these very brief remarks on Swedish taxes and 1992 is that a Swedish adjustment to the internal market is likely to imply significant constraints on both the formulation of tax policy and the rates to be paid.

Coordinated migration policy

Dismantling border controls implies a need for a common policy regarding migration from outside Western Europe. However, national requirements for work permits and residence permits for individuals from countries outside a common passport union and labour market will remain in force.

The Swedish government has stated that it is prepared to participate fully in a common labour market, arguing that this would just be an extension to the rest of Europe of the Nordic passport union. Membership of a common passport union implies that a Swedish citizen would not need a residence or work permit in any Community country. In the name of reciprocity, the same would hold for EC citizens who wish to work and live in Sweden. Swedish degrees and diplomas would give Swedes the right to exercise their profession freely in the Community on the same liberal terms as Community citizens, and vice versa in Sweden. Today's discrimination against Swedish students would disappear, for example with regard to fees in the United Kingdom, and participation in educational programmes such as Erasmus, which facilitates students exchanges.

Long-term costs and benefits

Adjustments to external trade policy, agricultural policy, indirect taxation, trade in services and migration policy imply adjustments to regulations and laws, and some changes in conditions for economic activity. Would these adjustments produce generally higher living standards and economic growth for a non-member country like Sweden, which has embarked on a course of developing as close links with the EC as possible?

Some of the evidence suggests that the result might be lower growth rates. Sweden has a small and very open economy. For this reason Sweden has in the past been forced to accept structural change more quickly than it would probably have had to if it had been closely integrated with the EC's common institutions. In the past, after initial heavy subsidies, declining sectors such as shipbuilding, steel, textiles and clothing have been dismantled more rapidly in Sweden than in the Community, where government support was more prolonged, e.g. through protection against competition from Japan, steel production quotas, subsidies, etc. If there were a severe slump in the Swedish car industry, for example, that sector would be too big, relatively speaking, for the government to support it for any extended period.

On the other hand, two obvious factors might favour higher growth rates following the abolition of border controls and integration with the Community. First, the deregulation of sectors such as international transport or financial services, and increased opportunities for training and employment in other countries obviously cannot be enacted by one country in isolation, but only simultaneously by all those concerned. Integration with the Community is thus a precondition for increased competition in these areas in Sweden; this should enhance efficiency and thus lead to a decisively increased growth rate. Second, through full integration with the EC, Swedish firms will have the opportunity to compete on equal terms with their Community competitors in the Community market. For Sweden equal treatment in public procurement is particularly vital, since several of its firms, including Volvo, Ericsson, Skanska, Saab-Scania and ASEA Brown Boveri, sell a considerable proportion of their output to the public sector in foreign countries.

However, more important than the reduction of existing barriers is the fact that a decision to abolish border controls against Sweden completely would mean a decision by the Community to withdraw all its instruments of protection against trade with Sweden. It would mean that firms located on Swedish soil are guaranteed full and equal access to the Community markets.

This total abolition of trade barriers is likely to affect the choice of location of future investments. Firms' propensity to invest at home should increase, whether they are involved in trade in goods or in services such as banking and insurance. Further, this guaranteed freedom from trade barriers will influence investors from countries outside the Community, e.g. North American or Japanese, when they are looking for possible locations in Europe for production for the Community and EFTA markets. In the absence of this freedom, non-EC Nordic, American and Japanese firms will require a risk premium – i.e. a higher rate of return – when investing in Sweden. Since the value of capital in the longer run is set internationally, the risk premium for investors would have to be secured by returns on other factors, i.e. lower wages, salaries and return to land than otherwise would be the case. A possible indication of the magnitude of the problem is apparent in 1988–9 investment figures. Swedish companies invested eight times more in EC countries than EC firms invested in Sweden.

Free capital movements

Free capital movements are not an essential part of an institutional agreement with the Community, but it would be illogical not to accept them if certain other parts of the integration package are accepted, especially reciprocity in rights of establishment of banks and insurance companies.

For Sweden free capital movements would mean a new situation for – on the one hand – commerical banks and insurance companies, and – on the other – for those responsible for monetary and fiscal policy. For the commercial banks free capital movements mean increased competition. This would benefit consumers of bank services, and could typically be expected to be opposed by the producers. The same conflict of interests applies to consumers and producers of insurance services. According to most observers, an international comparison shows Swedish banks to be quite competitive. If this is correct, the internal market would give them an opportunity to expand in the Community and still keep their base in Sweden.[4]

With free capital movements the influence of the central bank on short-term interest rates will disappear. Sweden can, with or without membership of the EC, join the European Monetary System (EMS). If it does so, changes in the exchange rate would be possible only if agreed with the other governments and central banks of the EMS. In a Swedish context, membership of the EMS could make the government's stated anti-inflationary policy more credible, and also enhance the credibility of its undertaking in 1982 never to devalue again. In this perspective, inflationary wage settlements would be held back since both employers and trade unions would know in advance that they would be opposed not only by their own government – often a minority one – and their own central bank, but also by the governments and central banks of the EMS countries. If the foreseeable alternative were low profits and higher unemployment, employers and unions would avoid inflationary wage settlements.

Coping with the internal market

The government's policy paper

The Swedish government submitted a major policy paper to the Riksdag in December 1987, summarizing national policies and regulations within all the fields covered by the internal market programme. In effect, it went beyond this somewhat narrow preoccupation and conveyed a statement of Sweden's

European identity: 'Sweden is a part of Europe. That is where we are situated geographically. That is where we have our historical and cultural roots. Developments in Europe are of great importance when we draw up today's and tomorrow's policies.'[5]

It continued to deny that Sweden's interest in the EC was solely based on economic concerns: 'these commitments also reflect a feeling of affinity that has several dimensions other than purely economic ones. There is a community of values that includes concepts such as democracy and defence of human rights.'

The policy paper also touched on issues such as the environment and research and technology. Indeed it aimed to establish certain guidelines for Sweden's participation in 'broad West European cooperation'. These themes were followed up by the Prime Minister, Ingvar Carlsson, during his tour of Madrid, Brussels, Bonn and London in the spring of 1988 and in subsequent visits to most EC capitals.

Pressures for injecting political zeal into Swedish integration policy had been mounting for some time as the internal market programme gained momentum. The government justified the timing of the policy paper by mentioning 'intensification of work in both the EC and EFTA' and pointing out 'that the Riksdag and the general public have shown an increased interest in related questions'.[6] This was something of an understatement, since European integration had figured more frequently in Riksdag debates during the preceding two years than it had during the twelve years that the Free Trade Agreement was in force. Motions signed by leading representatives of the bourgeois opposition parties introduced in the 1986–7 session had pre-empted the most intriguing question, by showing that a substantial majority supported the government's view that there was no reason for reconsidering attitudes towards membership of the EC.[7]

In the subsequent Riksdag deliberations the government's policy paper resulted in four motions tabled by parties and nine private member's bills. In the protracted discussions – the plenary debate did not occur until 5 May 1988 – all specialized committees other than defence were involved. Overall responsibility and coordination resided in the Foreign Affairs Committee, which broke ranks on some issues with opinions put forward by other specialized committees as it wished to avoid obstacles to flexibility. Despite the fact that Community relations impinge on practically all walks of life, the committee upheld its prerogative to define the issues in ways that leave much discretion to the government.

The outcome was determined by a compromise between the four major parties (the Social Democrats, Liberals, Centre Party and Moderate Party (conservatives)); the Communist Party was thus alone in its opposition to closer relations with the EC. Not that consensus was reached on each and every item. The Moderate Party sustained its image as the most EC-minded. It even proposed a customs union as the desirable goal for negotiations but the motion was turned down. Neither did its proposal for joining the EMS gain acceptance. But despite these and other defeats, some of the bourgeois parties' specifications and ideas left their imprint on the ensuing policy platform. It was carried with 288 votes in favour and 17 against.

This truce between parties was due mainly to a more cautious stance on the part of the Moderate Party, the traditional champion of membership. Its leader, Mr Carl Bildt, maintained the view 'that neutrality politics requires us to abstain from making a commitment to binding foreign policy cooperation'.[8] This conclusion converges with the incompatibility doctrine first enunciated by Mr Olof Palme in 1971.

Hence, no motion committing Sweden to apply for membership was put forward. Neither was there any clear alternative to the government's flexible view on institutional solutions. In these circumstances, a majority of the Foreign Affairs Committee endorsed the conclusion reached, 'that membership of the Community is not an objective for the negotiations which are now starting'.[9] By common consent the compromise seems likely to last at least until 1992. Having secured the operational goal, the political parties have become less guarded in their attitudes towards the EC. The Social Democrats follow the most cautious line, avoiding open splits. One faction deplores the insertion of the temporal adverb. The Centre Party has swung towards increased hostility to the EC.

The government's general orientation and effort to adopt a broader, multidimensional European concept across a wide range of concerns received general support. But the 'historic compromise' meant that some of the proposed guidelines were sharpened. In effect, it is stated that Sweden is prepared to become a member of the Community in all respects except for such foreign policy requirements as could diminish the credibility of the policy of neutrality. The original formulation by the government asserted that: 'we shall participate in EC and EFTA work to create a freer movement of goods, services, persons and capital in Western Europe.'

This was transformed into an operational guideline that Sweden would be 'working for the establishment of a common market encompassing all eighteen EC and EFTA countries'. The opposition felt this wording tended to blur the significant distinction between the former 'common' and proposed 'internal' market. Another formulation by the Riksdag majority reinstated the Community's White Paper as the referent for Sweden's central integration objectives: 'With regard to the proposals in the [Community's White Paper], Swedish consumers and Swedish firms should have all the same rights and the same obligations as have consumers and firms of the Community's member countries, and Swedes and Swedish firms should in no way whatsoever suffer discrimination.'[10]

The position is somewhat less explicit concerning a Europe without frontiers: i.e. as to whether administrative barriers could be dismantled entirely. The government claims that 'efforts should be directed towards practical measures with the aim of abolishing existing frontier barriers as far as possible and in order to achieve non-discriminatory treatment on the entire West European market'. A consensus seems to reign concerning the desirability of developing policies in parallel with the EC's work on the internal market. To that end, the government has started to investigate the justifications for Swedish border controls in order to find out whether they could be abolished, simplified or replaced by checks at the source. Further, 'Sweden has a clear interest in coordinating the free Nordic labour market and passport union with the (equivalent future) system of rules of the Community.'

To sum up, the objectives of Sweden's discussions with the EC imply that the country's border with the Community should, if possible, be as easy to cross in both directions as the borders between EC member states will be in 1993.

The execution of policy on the EC

Several features stand out in the execution and continuous reformulation of Swedish policy on the EC. A number of administrative and political changes are both preconditions for, and consequences of, the course adopted.

The basic dilemma is the need to find a course between the Scylla of membership, an option by common agreement 'now' foreclosed, and Charybdis, that is marginalization. The basic parameters were fixed by the Riksdag majority. The policy of 'taking part in the internal market as far as possible' and the political judgment that 'neutrality is incompatible with membership' provide the government with a broad platform for conducting negotiations, despite the more specific guidelines on ensuring access without discrimination.

The middle road is an effort to combine the inducements of a multilayered partnership with acquiescent and unilateral adaptation. The rationale is that adaptation avoids discriminatory treatment and creates conditions for mutual advantage. The idea of adopting positions substantially close to or equal with those enacted by the EC is not new; similar proposals were advanced during the 1971–2 negotiations. The internal market programme makes such parallel action a more demanding enterprise because the interests affected are crucial.

Another approach builds on the Community's presumed interest in taking advantage of Swedish achievements. A series of suggestions have been made backed by the image of Sweden as a prosperous purchaser and a technologically and industrially advanced partner.[11] The partnership idea pervades both bilateral and multilateral overtures. Adoption of a multidimensional integration concept facilitates contacts with EC member states as well as with the common institutions across a range of matters. Europeanism has begun to pervade almost every aspect of public activity.

Political and administrative structures are already in place. The government has streamlined a cross-departmental organizational network, an ambitious set-up unique in Swedish constitutional history. A subcommittee has been formed within the government, chaired by the Prime Minister. It is responsible for framing integration policy. Its members, reflecting the thrust of EC relations, include the ministers of foreign affairs, foreign trade, finance and industry. A small group of high-level officials from the core ministries assist in policy formulation, backed by twenty-five different issue-specific working groups. The chief negotiator for EC-EFTA relations, at present Ambassador Ulf Dinkelspiel, chairs the policy preparatory group which comprises all the chairpersons of the working groups. A secretariat for integration questions has been established, responsible for internal adjustments and the implementation of domestic integration policy. Responsibility for external contacts remains with Division 1 of the Department of Foreign Trade within the Foreign Ministry. Questions of public information are dealt with by a special working group. The government has also created an Advisory Council based on a representative sample of the Swedish industrial/corporate power structure.

The review of the policy implications under way demonstrates just how demanding a task it is to harmonize substantial parts of Swedish legislation and regulations. Two major problems are involved. The first is to cope with new directives and decisions taken by the EC on the internal market. The second is the need to catch up with all derived community legislation, the *acquis communautaire*. The government has accepted that it will have to take this on board, – an unprecedented step necessitating a thorough review of prevailing EC legislation. It is estimated that this means about 1,400 legal acts. A significant number are already practically identical with Swedish regulations or rules. Others require either common agreement or Swedish unilateral measures. A certain number have been identified as likely bones of contention where Swedish laws are perceived as more strict and giving a higher level of protection than corresponding EC directives. This applies to areas such as consumer protection, work-safety environment and social security.

In order to secure adequate parallelism, an extraordinary decree was adopted by the government in June 1988.[12] Every expert inquiry or Royal Commission must, if proposing a policy in fields related to the internal market or European integration, evaluate its compatibility with corresponding EC legislation and Commission proposals. The burden of proof of compatibility rests on the proposer and any proposals to diverge from EC legislation must be justified. 'EC compatibility' also has to be considered in the judicial review of government bills.

The domestic scene

A number of issues still divide the major parties. An important example is a disagreement between the Social Democrats and the bourgeois parties as to what restrictions should be maintained on foreign ownership of Swedish companies. The government has defended controls over foreign ownership whereas the opposition has maintained that unilateral alignment to the controls prevalent among other European OECD countries would make Swedish efforts to harmonize more credible. A second issue is the timetable for deregulating exchange controls. In the 1989 finance bill, the Minister of Finance signalled his intention gradually to dismantle most remaining exchange controls.

Experience from Sweden's previous debates on the EC and the political upheavals in countries which have applied for membership have undoubtedly influenced current policies. Representatives of the government have not only taken the lead in suggesting that 'Sweden must embark on the road followed by the EC', but have also worked hard to create an improved Community image. The issue has not been regarded as attractive in electoral politics. Parties which have tried to win votes on 'Europe' risk being accused of abandoning the policy of neutrality. But avoiding the issue entirely could also lead to set-backs. One unexpected result of the 1988 elections was the strengthening of the anti-EC opposition, although the EC issue was not at the forefront of the election campaign. The Greens, the first new party to enter national political life for seventy years, advocate fierce resistance to integration, as does the Communist Party. In fact, during their first term in the Riksdag, they introduced no fewer than 36 motions critically examining individual issues and urging the government to 'stop EC harmonization'. There have also been many questions and interpellations.

The consensus reached among the main parties has two effects on government policy. First, it means ministers can rely on a broad internal base, a position traditionally heralded as ideal in foreign affairs. Second, it means the longer-term dilemma can be overlooked as the importance of current work is enhanced. What matters 'now' is not the final state in 1992; the preconditions for reaping later benefits are to be sought by a continuous process of adjustment. This consensus pervades large parts of Swedish opinion and society.

Corporate Sweden, that is labour unions and the spectrum of interest organizations, are conditionally in favour of the broad thrust of policy. The two main organizations representing capital and industry in Sweden – the Employers' Confederation (SAF) and the Federation of Swedish industries – have avoided advocating membership, warning the government against lowering its ambitions and pointing out the potential shortcomings of the current policy. The unions' support is dependent on their retaining their influence on the formulation of public policy and the implementation of EC-derived norms and regulations in working life. Anxieties have been expressed that negotiated agreements with Brussels could gradually erode 'the Swedish model'. In general, industry-dependent unions have become more favourable to European integration. A substantial workload will fall on the employees of the public sector, because in the last instance internal market harmonization implies changes in rules, norms, standards and rigid controls. Indicative of the reorientation is the active participation of the Swedish Trade Union Confederation (LO) and the Central Organization of Salaried Employees (TCO) within the ETUC. Recently the two organizations also decided to establish a liaison office in Brussels. Somewhat more surprisingly, the Association of Swedish Farmers (RLF) though closely affilated with the Centre Party, has come out in favour of membership. It regards the 'EES concept' as too narrow, disproportionately favouring industry and the tertiary sector.

Positions are more polarized in the public debate. Many journalists, academics and individual company directors argue that the government's stated objectives are irreconcilable with its strategy, and that only membership can ensure the benefits sought. Yet hardly anyone has suggested that the policy of neutrality should be abandoned, or that neutrality reservations should not be made in a potential application for membership. However, so far, opposition to the current West European integration policy is muted and has not mobilized wider opinion. The rather technical substance of market integration has not aroused public demonstrations or political activism. The contrast with the situation in the Nordic countries in 1971–2 is striking. Divisions are likely to appear only at moments of hard choice; and only then if the government does not succeed in its 'middle way' between membership and non-participation.

One or many roads to Brussels?

A complex strategy

'We shall further develop the Nordic cooperation, we shall strengthen EFTA at the same time as we extend and deepen cooperation with the EC as far as this is compatible with our policy of neutrality.'[13]

The government is pursuing an exploratory course and maintains that the different elements are mutually supportive, with a blend of bilateral and multilateral instruments. The government's criteria for judging results hinge on substantive interests pursued case by case. It is recognized, however, that in the end individual issues and considerations will have to be evaluated in relation to a comprehensive whole. Some elements depend on bilateral negotiations. Others depend on parallel or joint action by the EFTA countries. Yet other dimensions, such as the social dimension and the free movement of people, touch on collective Nordic interests. Finally, for a significant number of the 286 proposals in the EC White Paper, unilateral adaptation is deemed appropriate.[14]

About half the White Paper's individual proposals could be accepted in Sweden without formal consultations with the EC. Some Swedish and EC approaches are already compatible: this is the case with many technical rules and with the removal of obstacles to the free circulation of goods. In principle, the coordination of indirect taxation (VAT and selective excise duties) and liberalization of capital movements could be treated in the same manner.

Freedom of trade in services (both transport and financial) would require a legal, institutional arrangement with the EC. Research and development questions and Swedish participation in research programmes are already covered by a general agreement. More recent EC programmes, such as Comett and Erasmus, are under discussion. Open tendering in public procurement, and environmental protection are vital preoccupations for the Swedish government; these and intellectual property rights are old issues and already partly covered by limited arrangements. The EES concept would elevate them into a more comprehensive framework and give them a new significance.

EFTA work overlaps with many bilateral and unilateral issues, as well as serving as a common sounding-board and information exchange, despite the fact that most formal agreements are bilateral. EFTA's role has become increasingly multilateral, not least because the Commission has preferred to treat the EFTA countries as a group. The fields of cooperation encompass both the classical ground of the Free Trade Agreements (such as technical barriers to trade, simplification of rules of origin, elimination of state aids that distort trade, etc.) and new issues. Following President Delors's speech and the EFTA countries' subsequent endorsement of his approach, the EFTA pillar has been strengthened to permit EFTA members to negotiate as a team.

The Nordic dimension also has wide relevance. Although traditional trade problems have been overtaken by larger issues, some aspects of the internal market programme impinge directly on Nordic cooperation. Road transport is one example. In the Swedish debate great importance is attached to the need to make new EC rules compatible with what are commonly regarded as the main achievements of Nordic cooperation, i.e. the labour market, the passport union and the social convention. The government would like to see an EC system that incorporates Nordic solutions and does not create new barriers to free movement.

Contrasting attitudes

The agenda is overwhelmingly complex. Is it possible to achieve the single strategic objective of avoiding economic marginalization, without a conceptually simple formula? Sweden's objective is as ambitious as the legal commitments entered into by members of the Single European Act (SEA). Could a non-member state achieve them in unorthodox ways?

At the level of doctrine, the answer is no; the Community forms a balanced package of rights and obligations. Even the leading foreign policy specialists in the Social Democratic Party admit that of all the possible formulas. Europe *à la carte* is the most difficult.[15] The repeated complaint from Spain, for example, that non-members should not be allowed to pick out 'the raisins from the cake' without making costly undertakings, underscores the serious obstacles ahead. On this point, two different attitudes are evident: for the short term, current policies could be pursued until 1992; but in the long term pragmatism cannot provide an answer, while advocates of membership are more explicit in signalling the dangers of making Sweden's current status permanent.

An important advantage of the current policy is that 'muddling through' seems to be the Commission's preferred solution as well. In essence, this means that the Community gives priority to the completion of the internal market, that the Community does not recognize any formal right of non-members to take part in EC decision-making, and that EC-EFTA cooperation should be guided by the principle of 'reciprocity'.[16] On the other hand, the Community has already committed itself to developing a form of Europe-wide partnership, first with the adoption of the joint EC-EFTA declaration on a 'dynamic European economic space' in 1984, then with the new negotiations agreed jointly in December 1989. The strength of the concept – although no consensus exists as to its political meaning – is derived from the allusion to two complementary strategies for inducing economic growth: market-building and technological innovation.[17] The drawback of the Luxembourg declaration from the Swedish point of view was its timing. It was issued well before the internal market had gained momentum and the target of 1992 had been set. President Delors outlined two options for the EFTA countries in his speech to the European Parliament in mid-January 1989. He observed that the need for a conceptual alternative to the Luxembourg process was overwhelming. His suggestion that progress could only be secured if EFTA were strengthened received a warm welcome from the Swedish government. The government's advisory council acquiesced in this view, concluding that strengthening EFTA would be a top priority. The prospects for realizing Delors's 'two-pillar' multilateral partnership would be tested under the Swedish presidency of EFTA in 1990. The institutional issues are tricky.

The long-term costs for countries of adapting themselves unilaterally to decisions taken by others are unknown. There are probably psychological as well as economic breaking-points. Sovereignty not matched by autonomy could easily become illusory. However, the steady incremental decision-making mode of European integration makes drastic upheavals and reversals in policy less likely. Given that so much else is in flux at the same time and thus that the perils are offset by countervailing influences, is Sweden marching along with the EC towards the realization of the goal condition?

The chief negotiator, Ambassador Ulf Dinkelspiel, has characterized the problem of adequate parallelism as 'a 64,000 dollar question'. It is premature to say whether the process of parallelism has begun, and whether EFTA countries are comfortable co-travellers. The prevailing official mood has nevertheless been one of optimism and steadfastness. The recognition in Sweden of the West European trading system as a mutually beneficial and stabilizing element in the world economy is regarded as a solid foundation. It is strengthened by the shared view that cooperation is a prerequisite for facing increased competition from the United States and Japan. The contours of a wider West European preferential zone could slowly emerge as a negotiated reality and a new factor since it would go beyond the exceptions allowed by GATT.

One alternative to the uncertainties of muddling through is known: membership. Given the key elements of Community doctrine, it is highly questionable whether Sweden could achieve the objective of non-discriminatory treatment without membership. A fundamental component of the Community's decision-taking is that it does not allow third countries an explicit influence or accept constraints on its internal processes. The Community has stated this as one of the preconditions for its talks with the EFTA countries. In addition, it has asserted that its own integration process always takes top priority.

However, the EC may want firm commitments from the Swedes. Can the Community be convinced that Sweden will follow its common external trade policy, including all future changes in that policy? In our judgment it would not be enough for the Community to be given a written assurance by the Swedes – even by treaty – that they would slavishly implement its external trade policy. The Community would also have to assess whether future Swedish governments would always be able or willing to honour so far-reaching an undertaking. After all, a government operates in a democratic setting, with parties and special-interest groups constantly competing for power and influence. The Community must feel it would be unwise to assume that all future Swedish governments would be able to honour such external agreements unless they also had some influence over the formulation of the relevant policies. The Community's line in similar situations has been that governments which are not integrated into the Community's common institutions and decision-making processes through membership cannot be expected to implement policies at home that are decided for them abroad, in this case by the Community.

Only if Sweden allows itself to participate as a Community member in the formulation and adoption of decisions will the EC be sure that at home a Swedish government will always be able to defend and implement decisions taken in Brussels. Only given a strong institutional link between them could the Community for its part accept the abolition of its border controls against Sweden. In other words, the economic objective of non-discrimination sought by the Swedish government and Parliament is unrealistic, unless Sweden also becomes fully integrated into the Community's common institutions in the relevant areas; i.e. as if a full member of the Community, presumably in all spheres except foreign policy. Thus the possibility of achieving the economic objectives is closely related to the issue of how Sweden should be linked institutionally to the Community.

This conclusion cannot be disproved. However, it is conditioned by the logic of Community integration and the assumptions that the internal market programme will entail the predicted consequences, and that changes in Swedish and other EFTA countries do not create viable alternative solutions. With this in mind we would like briefly to outline a few issues that very well could impinge on the current dynamism, and change the calculation and the objectives.

Achieving a wider Western Europe?

In the economic field, a distinguishing feature of the internal market programme has been its neglect of the external dimension. Neither the implications for the Community's own trade policy and foreign economic positions, nor the consequences for the outside world were given any consideration at the outset. On the fringe of the 'costs of non-Europe' research project, some calculations have been made of the magnitude of the effects on expected extra-EC imports.[18] No quantitatively supported studies have been carried out in Sweden on the effects of the internal market, using different assumptions as to the removal of barriers. The political conditions are as hard to estimate in a precise way, though some features stand out. We would like to argue that the final outcome will be determined as much by the interaction of political forces as by the intensification of cross-border transactions and shifts in relative competitiveness.

Some of the issues – trade in services, public procurement, etc. – are not yet regulated in GATT, though they are under discussion in the Uruguay Round, The EC and the USA are at loggerheads, the former advocating selective reciprocity and the latter general reciprocity (MFN treatment). Assuming that some sort of agreement is reached between the EC and the EFTA countries, the concept of a 'European economic space' will be met with suspicion by the USA, since such market integration goes beyond the MFN concepts enshrined in the GATT regime.

The internal West European debate is likely to continue to reflect the tensions in the case for the Community's geographical extension, the material competence of its institutions and economic realities. Such tensions could be expected to increase rather than diminish as the internal market reaches completion. The rationale for this expectation is the contradictory pattern of political alignments that are evolving, creating cross-cutting alliances of interests. Reforms in the East are likely to have repercussions on the priorities of all governments according to their situation and experience. They could divert attention from the EC-EFTA dialogue but do not invalidate the realities of this 'economic and monetary zone of stability'.

Within the Community, two points of conflict are currently in evidence, and both are of great relevance to the Swedish debate. First is the argument for cohesion measures to offset market effects: to some extent this has been resolved, since the Community agreed to transfers of resources in the text of the SEA and the agreement to double the structural funds by 1993.[19] The same approach is found in the Commission's support for improved access for the Spanish to EFTA markets.

Second, on the issue of confederation versus union, Jacques Delors stated his challenge in his speech to the European Parliament on 6 July 1988 when he forecast moves towards a common European government and the transfer of 80% of economic, and perhaps fiscal and social, decisions to Brussels. Mrs

Thatcher's sharp reaction in her Bruges speech and at the Tory conference reopened a dossier that had found a compromise solution in the SEA. This controversy, long familiar within the Community, pervades to the EC-EFTA debate.

One of its elements is the debate for and against a supranational law on the 'social dimension'. The internal EC debate on the social dimension has led to a rapid realignment of forces. Mr Delors's appearance at the EFTA-EC gathering of Socialist and Social Democratic parties, and the institutionalization of this forum, added new complexities to the European fabric. With EFTA taking up the issue collectively, we could very well witness the astonishing spectacle of non-members of the EC becoming ardent supporters of strong *communautaire* institutions and the kind of technical, law-based and rational problem-solving in social policy that is the Community's hallmark in economic areas. After all, a Community without state-type institutions might support only a diluted version of market integration.

Neutrality and European political cooperation

Swedish neutrality

There are well-known differences between the European neutrals. The character of Swedish neutrality is coloured by its long internal legacy – it can be traced back to 1834 – and the fact that it is devoid of legal codifications. Bills to that end have been rejected by the Riksdag since 1883. Moreover, being self-declared, the policy has no need of formal recognition by other powers that might constitute some kind of *droit de regard* over autonomous decision-making on a vital issue.

Given such a solid foundation as a political fact of life, Swedish fears about joining the EC have sometimes provoked sour comments in relation to other political situations, such as the problem of joining the International Energy Agency or the drive to sell Swedish Viggen combat aircraft to smaller NATO members.[20] Former President of the Commission Roy Jenkins scored a point in contrasting Swedish 'political neutrality' to the international legal recognition of Swiss 'professional neutrality'.[21]

Such polemics notwithstanding, what are the core arguments that made Sweden opt for an association in 1962, explore all possible forms of 'enduring, close and comprehensive' relations in 1967–71 (including that of possible membership), and now reject membership as an objective of talks about the internal market? A possible answer could be found in earlier experiences of reconciling neutrality and European integration, and in the logic of official thinking on neutrality requirements. In all probability, the strictness of such reasoning is influenced by the overall political and strategic atmosphere between East and West in Europe. Lastly, the Community's own upgrading of foreign political cooperation to a legal commitment in the Single Act is significant. Later pronouncements on the 'European vocation' of the Community, in view of a post-1992 political union, including security commitments, do not diminish Swedish 'Behrürungsangst' (anxieties).

Earlier experiences

Swedish views on EC relations have been enunciated on two occasions as preludes to negotiations, following two different approaches. The first attempt in 1961 was clearly legalistic. Situations were defined where neutrality reservations and particular clauses in the Treaty of Rome were irreconcilable. The overture a decade later could be characterized as political. Two sets of premises underpinned the effort. On the one hand, similarities in substantive rules and in the level and structure of the Swedish economy, implied that Sweden needed to make only a few, moderate reservations to adapt to Community rules. On the other hand, the Swedish negotiators put their main effort into emphasizing the value of neutrality, in an attempt to gain recognition for its contribution to European stability. If EC members could be convinced that an unchanged Swedish orientation was in their own interests, a door might be opened to a reservation on neutrality couched in general terms. Such a reservation would anticipate situations where interests might diverge and might ensure that the objectives of other EC members were not impeded.

However, no collective agreement resulted. EC members were reluctant to explore a formula that departed from Community assumptions, though it could have reached an accommodation with a country anxious to establish more intimate relations than free trade. When, in the early 1970s, France's encouraging attitude was combined with a negative British and Dutch position, it looked as if Sweden might become a source of friction, particularly in view of the Community decision to deepen integration into foreign policy cooperation. Thus, the EC's adoption of the Davignon Report was publicly cited by the Swedish government as the main reason for abandoning the idea of membership. However, the minor set-back for the Social Democrats in the 1970 Swedish elections and the increasingly anti-Community trend in public opinion were probably equally decisive.

The Single European Act

The SEA has not made Swedish membership any easier, since it formally recognizes the link between inter-governmental political cooperation and treaty-based integration. The old question of how to predict the political implications of an open-ended commitment to the Treaty of Rome is thus transformed into a choice over an open-ended political undertaking in the field of foreign policy. The Swedish would rather build firm barriers between economic integration and cooperation on foreign and security policies.

Official thinking is probably based on then opposition leader Olof Palme's statement, 'Sweden at the side of the EC', in 1981.[22] On the one hand, he acknowledged the Community's success in foreign policy cooperation. On the other hand, he set out the reasons why Sweden could allow little leeway for ambiguity:

> During the EEC negotiations we were jokingly reminded in one of the capitals of Europe that the Rome Treaty was a 'catholic' creation. When converting to Catholicism

> you cannot make reservations against one or the other of the dogmas determined by the Vatican. In a similar way one cannot make reservations and ask to remain outside one or another aspect of cooperation when one becomes a member of the EEC. But in the same way that a person, once converted, can receive absolution if he breaks his obligations as a good Catholic, a member of the EEC can similarly abuse his privileges, pay lip-service, but in practice withdraw from unpleasant obligations. A neutral country such as Sweden could never handle foreign policy in such a way. We have to act with frankness, firmness and consistency.... The Rome Treaty certainly contained no major stumbling-blocks.

Under-Secretary of State for Foreign Affairs Pierre Schori adhered to these principles when he stated that fear of loss of economic sovereignty is now groundless. Majority voting and community legislation would be acceptable. Neutrality is now the main problem. The current Swedish position of course implies that the Community should abandon its insistence that participation in European Political Cooperation (EPC) must be a consequence of membership.

At the insistence of Ireland, together with Denmark and Greece, political cooperation is limited to no more than the 'economic and political aspects of security'. Given a wide range of opinions on the exact meaning of such terms, the explicit absence of a reference to military security opens up the question of how to distinguish civilian power alliances from their military counterparts. For the EC general concertation on foreign policy is an important means of developing a 'European identity'.

The Swedish government has made it clear that no solution can be built on the Irish analogy. It has dissociated itself from Austria by underscoring the point that geo-strategic circumstances vary and give Swedish neutrality a different European role. Moreover, the symbolic value of not being seen to take part in EC foreign policy cooperation makes all the difference. The underlying tension between form and substance is, however, evident as the Swedish government recognizes 'that our positions on many foreign policy issues are close to those of the EC and even coincide with them'.[23]

Three arguments have been put forward as paramount obstacles to 'cooperating with Community institutions in foreign policy'. The first is the obligation to coordinate and elaborate common positions. Second is the obligation to undertake such consultations 'with a certain group of countries', undermining the universalism of neutrality. Third, the fact that 11 out of 12 members belong to the same military alliance makes participation in EPC impossible.

Neutrality and developments in the East

Reforms within East European countries and the subsequent disintegration of the Eastern bloc were initially viewed with some scepticism in the Swedish foreign policy establishment. The unpredictability and reversals in the Eastern bloc strengthened support for the traditional policy of neutrality. The swift pace of change served to fend off criticism of the government's commitment to the inviolability of neutrality in relation to Western Europe and the EC. Events seemed to prove that an unchanged Swedish policy facilitated reforms and the development of new aspirations in Eastern Europe.

In northern Europe, there is the added dimension that the Baltic republics' struggle for independence challenges the nature of the Soviet state. Having formally recognized the incorporation of these countries into the Soviet Union in 1940, Sweden's position differs from that of many other Western countries. On the other hand, the Baltic states are trying to redefine their identity by focusing on their affinities with their Nordic neighbours. The national fronts now in power have signed a statement proposing sovereignty in a 'democratic and atomic weapon-free Baltic-Scandinavia'. Thus a completely new matrix of trade-offs between security considerations, new territorial systems and changing patterns of interaction is becoming apparent.

The credibility threshold

A debate on neutrality in the context of the SEA and EPC is taking shape, although confined to a few foreign policy specialists. The leader of the Moderate Party has suggested a broad public examination of the issues involved.

Maximalists on neutrality argue that EPC would compromise the credibility of Swedish non-alignment. Irreparable harm could be inflicted upon the foreign policy stance, because to a large extent neutrality is simply a code word for independence. The more interdependent the European economies become, the more important are the expressions of formal sovereignty. 'Neutrality is no trading commodity', claims Pierre Schori. A Swedish EC presidency, which would represent France and Britain as well as other EC members in political talks with the Russians, will only be possible, claims former Swedish chief negotiator with the EC and senior diplomatic expert on Swedish neutrality Sverker Åström when the lambs and the lions lie down together. The implication is that a neutral country would be the last to join.

The minimalist position raises the question of the height of the credibility threshold. Factors such as the actual degree of economic integration already achieved within Western Eurpe create economic vulnerability, the implications of which are easily understood by the shrinking number of observers wearing marxist spectacles. Another argument is that although Sweden's will to remain neutral is beyond question, the ability to remain neutral may already have been overtaken by military technology. Hence security is no longer that paramount. One suggestion is that Sweden must be allowed to make it clear that the Community does not actually have the potential to become a military alliance. If a neutral country joined EPC, this would in itself alter the political constellation by giving it equal rights to interpret Europe's identity. The neutral EC member would be obliged to defend its interests by political means in EPC consultations.

Yet there are obstacles ahead that would demand certain reservations vis-à-vis the EC. Carl Bildt argues that Sweden would not be able to join politically motivated trade sanctions within the East-West conflict should times get rough. Second, the crisis management procedures of EPC could convey false messages. One could conceive of situations where Sweden could not join in such procedures – situations precisely in which other EC partners would find the procedures most useful.

Hence, the fact remains that irrespective of how far Sweden could stretch its position, it might not be far enough for the EC. EC members also seem to have the same understanding of the problem. It would be premature to argue that serious efforts have been made to accommodate the different positions.

Lasting detente and a new calculation on the balance of forces within the EC in connection with new applicants could alter current attitudes. Meanwhile, both parties seem more comfortable marching along parallel tracks – at least until 1993. With a diminished likelihood of war and the development of a European system for collective security, members of all major parties have begun to advocate membership.

Notes

1. 'Utskottet konstaterar att svenskt medlemskap inte är ett mål för de diskussioner med EG som nu förestår'.
2. *The Economist*, 31 October 1988.
3. A compensation scheme has also been suggested by the Commission, the aim of which is to restore the principle of VAT collection in the country of final consumption.
4. Swedish insurance companies, however, do not seem to have a similiar reputation for competitiveness. The internal market would then inject increased competition into the Swedish insurance market, possibly leading to a considerable shake-up among insurance companies.
5. *Sverige och den västeuropeiska integrationen*, Proposition 1987/88: 66, Stockholm, December 1987, p. 1.
6. Ibid., p. 3.
7. See Subcommittee of Foreign Affairs, 1986/87: 18.
8. Speech at the Swedish Institute of Foreign Affairs, 13 May 1987.
9. Foreign Affairs Committee 1987/88: 24, p. 19.
10. Ibid., p. 21–2.
11. See speeches by Prime Minister Ingvar Carlsson in Madrid, Bonn, Brussels and London, May 1988.
12. *Kommittedirektiv* 1988: 43, 1988-06-20.
13. Prop. 1987/88: 66, p. 4.
14. Speech, Exportforum, Gothenburg, 27 October 1988.
15. Under-Secretary of Foreign Affairs Pierre Schori in *Sverige och den Västeuropeiska Integrationen*, AIC Seminar Report, 29–30 January 1988.
16. The term has slowly become a key word repeated by Commission representatives in a number of speeches since 1987.
17. 'Europe 1992: World Trade Partner', declaration by William de Clercq and Lord Cockfield, European Commission, 19 October 1988.
18. *Rapport sur la position de la Suisse dans le processus d'intégration européenne*, Conseil Fédéral Suisse, August 1988, p. 33.
19. Declaration of the leaders of the Socialist and Social Democratic Parties of the member states of the European Community and of EFTA, adopted at the conference 'EC-EFTA Common Future 1992', Berlin, 6–7 November 1988.
20. *Dagens Nhyter*, 24 October 1987.
21. 'Sweden at the side of the EC', speech by Olof Palme, 9 November 1981, Swedish Social Democratic Party.
22. Proposition 1987/88: 66.
23. Article in *Svenska Dagbladet*, October 1988.

15 Switzerland

Richard Senti

In its integration report of 24 August 1988, the Swiss federal government states that 'the credibility of the traditional Swiss policy of neutrality, pursued autonomously and at its own discretion, could be placed at risk if Switzerland adopted the EC's political objectives as they appear today. At the same time, the federal government believes that Switzerland's political stability and neutrality together with a credible security and defence policy are not only in the interests of Switzerland itself, but of Europe as a whole, because this continuity makes a major contribution to detente and stability throughout Europe. Under these conditions, accession to the EC cannot – on present evidence – be an objective of Swiss integration policy.'[1]

This paper describes the integration policy pursued by Switzerland since World War II; Switzerland's links with its European neighbours in terms of trade, labour and capital; alternative integration policies currently being discussed; and the main issues today.

The historical perspective

In July 1947 Switzerland accepted the invitation extended by France and Great Britain to participate in the Paris Conference on the reconstruction of Europe. This reflected its standpoint that an interest in strengthening the economic unity of Europe was compatible with Switzerland's neutral status. On the eve of the conference, in order to anticipate any misunderstandings, the Swiss government addressed a note to the French and Swiss legations in Switzerland stating that it would enter into no commitment which could affect its traditional neutrality. Moreover, any decisions taken at the conference concerning the Swiss economy would only be binding after it had received official approval. Finally, Switzerland claimed its right to continue or negotiate trade agreements with third countries at its own discretion.[2]

These three conditions, established in the immediate post-war period, have come to be a national and economic creed to which Switzerland still adheres in its approach to international agreements and organizations. They were expressly repeated in negotiations or statements of position, for example when the

Organization for European Economic Cooperation (OEEC) was reorganized as the Organization for European Cooperation and Development (OECD) in 1960;[3] when Switzerland refrained from joining the EEC in the 1950s;[4] when it signed the General Agreement on Tariffs and Trade (GATT) in 1966;[5] when it concluded the free trade agreements with the European Economic Community (EEC) and the European Coal and Steel Community (ECSC) at the beginning of the 1970s;[6] and in the Federal Council's report in 1988 on completing the internal market.[7]

An analysis of the reservations made during the various integration phases shows that there has been a shift of emphasis over the years. In the 1950s, the Federal Council argued that it was impossible to join the EEC because the overall aims of the EEC were incompatible with the principles laid down in Switzerland's constitution and thus constituted an insuperable obstacle for Swiss membership.[8] The 1988 integration report is less absolute in its wording and admits that it would be 'legitimate and credible' today to pay the political price for the political objective of helping to shape Europe, provided that there were signs among the population of 'a credible basic desire for accession.'[9] This new approach is apparent not only in political matters but also in economic policy. In the 1950s the main focus was on the disadvantages of joining the EEC, such as the high EEC customs tariffs which would make Switzerland less competitive.[10] Contrariwise, the most recent integration report suggests that possible risks for the Swiss economy lie not in joining the EC, but much more in remaining outside the European Community. The completion of the EC internal market would lead to fiercer competition both within the single market and in non-EC markets.[11]

Political activities in Switzerland, as in any other country, are shaped by three considerations which are partly complementary and partly contradictory: retaining political independence and strengthening national identity at home; recognizing the necessity for economic links with foreign countries; and the fact that it is to the advantage of every country to contribute to political and economic stability worldwide.

It is against this background that Switzerland, in its international negotiations, has always balanced the advantages and disadvantages of what was desirable in terms of domestic policy against what was necessary in terms of foreign policy, and has often refrained from signing a treaty or joining an organization.

In the immediate postwar period, Switzerland became a member of the OEEC, and subsequently of the OECD. It signed the EFTA Convention 1960 and GATT in 1966. The free trade agreements between Switzerland and the EEC and ECSC date back to 1972, followed by more than a hundred bilateral agreements between Switzerland and the EC. At the same time Switzerland was active in numerous special United Nations (UN) agencies, such as the International Labour Organization (ILO) and the Food and Agriculture Organization (FAO), and it has participated in most of the international agreements on raw materials.

Switzerland has refrained from becoming a member of the UN, the International Monetary Fund (IMF) and the World Bank (IBRD), though it has always made its capital market available for World Bank issues and is a member of the Club of Ten. Currently, membership of the Bretton Woods institutions is being considered.[12]

Economic links between Switzerland and the EC

Being a small country with few natural resources, Switzerland has always maintained strong links with other countries. On the one hand, Swiss industry needs foreign raw materials, while on the other hand, the domestic market is too small for rationalized production. As the following data show, there are particularly close links between Switzerland and its European neighbours.

Table 15.1 shows the share of the world market of North America, Japan, the EC (12), EFTA (6) and Switzerland. Some 15 years ago Switzerland's share was 1.7% and has in the meantime risen to 1.8%. The EFTA and EC share of the world market has also changed relatively little. Japan's share, however, has increased, at North America's expense.

Table 15.2 shows that the EC and EFTA countries account for more than 80% of Switzerland's imports and almost 70% of its exports. The EC is by far Switzerland's most important trading partner: 79.3% of Switzerland's total imports are from the EC. The EC share of exports is 60.4%. West Germany accounts for

Table 15.1 Share of World trade: North America, Japan, EC, EFTA and Switzerland, 1973 and 1988 (in US$ million and as percentage of world trade)

	1973		*1988*	
	$	%	*$*	%
North America	98,890	17.0	437,450	15.2
Japan	36,930	6.3	264,915	9.2
EC (12)	219,200	37.7	1,065,150	37.0
EFTA (6)	35,900	6.2	177,250	6.1
Switzerland	10,000	1.7	51,000	1.8
Other countries	181,095	31.1	886,555	30.7
Total (world)	582,015	100.0	2,882,320	100.0

Source: GATT, International Trade 1988–9; *Eidg. Oberzolldirektion*, Foreign trade statistics (various years); *Bundesamt für Statistik*, Statistical yearbook for Switzerland (various years).

Table 15.2 Total Swiss foreign trade, 1989

	Imports		*Exports*	
	SFr million	%	*SFr million*	%
EC	5461.9	79.3	4046.9	60.4
of which FRG	2652.3	33.5	1430.7	21.4
EFTA	555.7	7.0	438.3	6.5
OECD	6994.8	88.3	5407.0	67.0
Total	7925.4	100.0	6697.3	100.0

Source: Eidg. Volkswirtschaftsdepartement 63(1990)3, Table B8, p. 21.

almost half the trade with the EC. Foreign trade with EFTA states shows an import and export share of just above 7%.

The main imports from the EC in order of importance are: (1) machines; (2) chemicals; (3) vehicles; (4) metals and metal goods; (5) textiles. West Germany heads all these product groups, followed by France and Italy with roughly the same share each.

Metals, machines and equipment rank first in the list of exports, followed by chemicals. Exports to the EC of watches, the traditional Swiss product, is at a somewhat modest 20 to 25% of total watch exports. Of the approximately 100 million watches sold in the EC, only some 10% are of Swiss origin.[13] Cheese and chocolate, those typically Swiss exports, are of minor importance. With almost 40%, West Germany has by far the highest share of exports to the EC. France and Italy rank second and third with a share of 16.4% and 14.8% respectively (calculated on the basis of the documentation for Table 1).

The Swiss National Bank estimates current Swiss foreign investments at SFr. 55 billion. A steadily growing share is invested in the EC, at present approaching 50% or SFr. 27.3 billion. The Swiss National Bank estimates that Swiss investments have created some 370,000 jobs in the EC. The main target countries for Swiss investments in order of importance are: USA, West Germany, Netherlands, France, Great Britain and Italy.

Switzerland has a population of some 6.4 million, 16% (about 1 million) of whom are foreigners. Of the 3.2 million people gainfully employed, 834,000 or 26% are of foreign origin. The proportion of foreigners is much higher in Switzerland than in all the other neighbouring European countries. (See Table 15.3)

There are very close transport links between the EC and Switzerland. As Table 15.4A shows, almost 25% of the overall north-south heavy traffic passes through

Table 15.3 EC nationals working in Switzerland, 1988*

	Total	*Per cent*
Italy	285,988	45.0
France	95,500	15.0
Spain	88,470	13.9
West Germany	79,460	12.5
Portugal	61,895	9.7
Great Britain	8,667	1.4
Netherlands	6,592	1.0
Greece	4,662	0.7
Belgium	2,880	0.5
Denmark	1,022	0.2
Ireland	555	0.1
Luxembourg	370	0.1

* Annual permits, residence permits, seasonal permits, frontier commuters.

Source: Calculated according to the *Bundesamt für Ausländerfragen*, Foreign population in Switzerland, August 1988.

Table 15.4A Transalpine flow of goods in 1,000 tonnes

	Switzerland 1984	*France 1984*	*Austria 1984*	*Total 1984*
Rail	9,151.0	7,192.0	2,727.0	19,070.0
% of traffic carried	48.0	37.7	14.3	100.0
Piggy-back	1,251.0	695.0	473.0	2,419.0
% of traffic carried	51.7	28.7	19.6	100.0
Road	750.0	10,501.0	15,168.0	26,419.0
% of traffic carried	2.8	39.7	57.4	100.0
Total per country	11,152.0	18,388.0	18,368.0	47,908.0
% of total volume	23.3	38.4	38.3	100.0

Table 15.4B Transalpine flow of goods, according to country and transport carrier, in per cent

	Switzerland	*France*	*Austria*	*Total*
Rail	82.1	39.1	14.8	39.8
Piggy-back	11.2	3.8	2.6	5.1
Road	6.7	57.1	82.6	55.1
Total	100.0	100.0	100.0	100.0

Source: Calculated according to the EVED (Swiss Ministry of Transport and Energy), *Transalpine Goods Traffic*, Volume V (Berne, 1986), p. 121.

Switzerland. The remaining traffic is spread more or less equally between France and Austria. In Switzerland 48% of total traffic is by rail, as opposed to 37.7% and 14.3% for France and Austria respectively. The Swiss share of piggy-back transport is even higher. Conversely, France and Austria, with a total of 97%, rank first in road traffic. Austria alone accommodates almost 60% of the total north-south heavy road traffic.

Table 15.4B is a domestic traffic breakdown showing that piggy-back traffic, totalling 5.1%, is of minor importance overall. 39.8% of total traffic is by rail and 55.1% by road. There are considerable differences between countries: in Switzerland rail and piggy-back have priority, while in France and particularly in Austria it is the road.

Strategies for closer links with the EC

Integration discussions faded out in Switzerland after the conclusion in 1972 of the free trade agreements with the EEC and the ECSC. It was not until the EC began expanding southwards at the beginning of the 1980s that it became apparent that European integration had not yet been completed; but this was insufficient to revive the discussion on integration. The events between 1984 and 1987 had, however, a different effect. Publication of the proposal for completing the internal market and the approval and ratification of the Single European Act by the twelve member states created a certain insecurity both in Switzerland and in the other EFTA states, and triggered the question of whether they were on the right path.[14] In addition, the EFTA states interpreted the 1984 Luxembourg conference as signalling that the EC was ready to intensify cooperation between the two groups of countries.

What follows gives an overview of possible approaches to closer links with the EC which are currently being debated in Switzerland.

Parallel legal development

The idea behind parallel legal development is that EC regulations should be autonomously enacted within the EFTA states and that national legislation should be adjusted to EC regulations, in order to create the conditions necessary for a cross-border single market. Three possibilities have been discussed. One involves taking over EC regulations direct: for example, Switzerland would take over the EC safety regulations for transporting highly toxic materials (Seveso II); Austria would take over the EC index of used materials and the European guidelines for product liability. A second possibility is that of using the regulations laid down by a major EC trading partner: for example, Austrian legislation on detergents would be adjusted to that of West Germany. The third possibility involves adopting EC regulations through harmonization conventions under international law, so that international organizations would indirectly take over EC regulations. In this way EC law would flow into the legal systems of the individual European non-EC states via an 'incorporated international law of contract'.[15]

There is full awareness in Switzerland of the need for unified European legislation. Accordingly, in May 1988, the Federal Council decided to study all reports and proposals submitted to parliament, and draft directives to determine whether they were compatible with European usage and in order to see how far the proposed Swiss laws were compatible with European law.[16] It was to be a question, not of automatically taking over European law, but of avoiding unwanted or unnecessary differences.

According to the Swiss Association for Trade and Industry (Vorort), compatibility of legal standards means that Switzerland must curb its occasional tendency to introduce special legal or technical regulations and must take care not to create differences between Swiss law and the corresponding Community requirements, except for urgent reasons.[17] Secretary of State Franz Blankart, director of the Federal Office for Foreign Trade, also warned against creating avoidable legal disparities: 'Celebrating the special case in law is not proof of sovereignty.'[18]

So far discussion on parallel legal development has invariably been based on the assumption that adopting EC legislation or creating equivalent standards is enough to guarantee free traffic between the EC and EFTA. This assumption is incorrect. A single market can only be created if a bridge is built between the EC rules and those of the non-EC state: in other words, if an agreement is reached which will lead to mutual recognition of the two regulations (mirror legislation and bridging arrangements). Without mutual agreements there can be no mutual rights and duties.[19]

Bilateral agreements

In the preamble to the 1972 free trade agreement, the contracting partners, Switzerland and the EEC, declared that they were prepared to '... study possibilities for expanding and strengthening their relations if expansion to areas not included in the agreement should appear to be in the interests of their economies'. Article 32 of the agreement again takes up this statement of intent and lays down that the contracting partners may request expansion of the relations created in the agreement. Negotiated agreements deriving from such requests require 'ratification by the contracting partners according to their own procedures'.

Currently, there are some 180 bilateral agreements between Switzerland and the EC. According to photocopied documents issued by the Swiss integration office, two-thirds of these relate to the free trade agreements between Switzerland and the EEC and Switzerland and the ECSC, thus continuing and in many sectors completing the agreements.

The objective of integration by means of continuing the free trade agreements is to regulate the bulk of the economic sector through bilateral agreements between Switzerland and the EC. The Swiss Association for Trade and Industry has reached the conclusion that closer cooperation on the basis of existing agreements is, at present, the 'most realistic option and the one that serves our (Swiss) interests best'. It is the road that Switzerland has been travelling and that has proved worthwhile on the whole: but it is important to be aware of the limits. Since Switzerland has remained outside the EC, its possibilities for influencing the integration process are also limited: this means that the danger of discrimination can be confined but not entirely eliminated.[20]

Franz Blankart is convinced that Switzerland will be able to survive with regard to the EC if it continues to 'eliminate discrimination through balanced agreements'.[21] Jakob Kellenberger, head of the Swiss integration office, considers the 'dense network of contractual agreements' and the 'closely-woven web of mixed committees, consultation and information mechanisms' as the bricks and mortar of 'what EFTA states and the EC have jointly aimed for since Luxembourg 1984, namely, the creation of a dynamic European economic area'.[22]

The supporters of this strategy advocate the incorporation of problem-specific solutions into the bilateral agreements, in such a way that every country would retain full treaty-making power; neutrality and sovereignty are not to be affected; and individual agreements could be terminated without jeopardizing European integration as a whole.

The disparity between the market participants is an argument against integration via bilateral individual agreements; on the one side there is the EC, with a total of some 320 million consumers, and on the other Switzerland, with a population of just over 6 million. Moreover, integration via bilateral agreements tends to multiply the number of individual regulations and, in terms of law and economics, to become so complex, vast and unwieldy that it constitutes a real impediment to trade, particularly for small and medium-sized companies. Such fears have led to the proposal of multilateral agreements.

Multilateral agreements

The EEC-EFTA agreements on the standardization of goods documentation and on transit procedures are examples of multilateral agreements. They were signed in May 1987 by the ministers of the EFTA states and the EEC Commission and came into force on 1 January 1988.

Through the standardization of goods documentation, one standard document has replaced the various national import and export declarations, transport papers, and many other official documents. It reforms the standard document by harmonizing European customs documentation. As it is necessary to conform to the requirements in the various countries concerned, standardization has not led to simplification. On the contrary, the standard document is so complex in structure that for many companies it is proving to be an additional obstacle to trade.

The transit agreement is an expansion of the former dispatch agreement between the EEC, Austria and Switzerland with regard to the Scandinavian EFTA states. This agreement means that in 18 European states today there are standard transport and administrative regulations for goods being transported via a third country, reloaded in a third country or stored there.

At present neither EFTA nor the EC appears to be making any effort to draw up and enact new multilateral agreements. The various states are obviously giving preference to bilateral agreements tailored to individual requirements.

General agreements

Unlike bilateral agreements, which refer to trade in certain products, specific procedures and so on, general agreements can be defined as basic framework agreements or process regulations providing a basis for opinion moulding, decision taking and legal action, as well as helping to solve individual problems.

During the past year the debate in Switzerland has focused mainly on a consultative document proposed by Willy Zeller, editor of the *Neue Zürcher Zeitung* (NZZ).[23] In his proposal, Zeller asks whether selective pragmatic starting points (that is, the existing bilateral agreements) are enough to enforce the participation of the EFTA states. Should the answer be in the negative, Zeller concludes that 'a new type of agreement beyond the free trade agreement must be envisaged. It could take the form of a general agreement containing institutional and procedural elements rather than material ones. Its purpose would not primarily be to form an umbrella over the dozens of existing agreements with the EC, but rather to generalize and institutionalize consultation rights and, wherever possible, to make them automatic'.

This proposal was in no way intended to devalue the existing free trade agreements: the development clause they contained would continue to be applied for those purposes for which it was intended, to regulate trade in various products and product groups. However, the need for 'comparatively permanent information and consultation on EC procedures connected with integration affecting the overall west European free trade order' could be met through a new general agreement, a so-called consultative agreement.[24]

The proposal to negotiate a consultative agreement highlights the desire to exert greater influence in opinion forming and decision taking in the EC. It is still unclear whether and to what extent the EC bodies are willing and able to acquiesce to such desires and demands from the EFTA states. The decision of the EC Council of 13 July 1987 on establishing mechanisms for implementing the Commission's executive tasks gives rise to the assumption that Brussels is trying to render the decision-making process more efficient by short-circuiting some procedures.[25] Participation by non-EC states in the decision-making process could make the EC internal procedures more difficult, which would hardly be in line with the Council's present policy.

The statements made by the EC Commissioner Willy de Clercq during his meeting with EFTA ministers in Interlaken on 20 May 1987 showed clearly that Brussels was not interested in joint decision taking implementing the internal market took priority. At that point in time, the EC needed to retain autonomy in decision taking. For the time being the EFTA states could not participate in the EC's decision-making procedures.[26]

Customs union

A further means of structuring future EFTA-EC relations has been proposed in the form of a customs and economic union within EFTA on the one hand and/or between the EFTA states and the EEC on the other.[27] This proposal aims at creating an overall West European internal market levying a standard customs tariff for third countries and having within it no frontier controls or formalities. Through bilateral alignment of tariffs for external trade, it would no longer be necessary to provide documentary evidence of origin, nor to levy duties on imports not originating in the exporting country and not adequately treated or processed.

These are the particular reasons for the creation of such a union:

- Closer links within EFTA would strengthen its position in negotiations with third countries.
- The individual customs tariffs for external trade levied by the EFTA states are very low, averaging 3 to 4% and are also very similar in structure.
- The same applies in comparison with the EC. With an average of 4%, the EC tariff rates are somewhat higher than those of the EFTA states. Tariff structures of the EFTA states and the EC are similar. Unified customs duties for external trade between the EFTA states and the EC would also have no noticeable effects with regard to customs duties.[28]
- As mentioned earlier, frontier controls have become one of the main barriers

to trade, particularly for small and medium-sized companies which cannot afford to employ export specialists because of their relatively low volume of exports. The abolition of customs formalities would not only lead to overall savings (both for the EFTA states and for the EC), but would also make the small and medium-sized companies more competitive. The present documentary evidence of origin alone generates costs of roughly 1% of the trading value;[29] an EC study arrives at a cost saving of 1.7%.[30]

- In Switzerland a proposal which confines itself to economic matters will receive priority, because the Swiss wish to retain their neutrality and sovereignty.
- It is particularly important at present to work towards a customs and economic union because, with complete or partial implementation of the EC internal market by 1992, EC discrimination towards third countries is likely to increase.[31]

A long-term strategy to achieve an overall European economic union does not mean that a customs union should not be established first, albeit perhaps not applying to some sensitive goods. But even with only partial solutions, the global objective of an internal market free of frontier controls must always be kept in view. This seems to offer a viable alternative particularly for countries such as Switzerland, Sweden and Finland, which are not prepared to integrate politically.

The various reactions to the proposal to establish a customs and economic union (within EFTA, between EFTA and the EC or between Switzerland and the EC) demonstrate that there are risks involved. The Swiss Association of Trade and Industry has pointed out that Switzerland might lose its trade autonomy if it entered into a customs union with the EC. The credibility of Swiss neutrality depended on autonomy in its trade policies.[32] In political circles it is generally believed that Switzerland's development in a large economic bloc would irreparably damage Swiss customs autonomy.[33]

Problems and prospects

In the following section attention will be drawn to some problems which are of particular importance for Switzerland in today's European integration process. They are connected with the country's political independence, the high concentration of foreign nationals, agriculture and transport.

Political independence

As already emphasised, the Swiss set great store by their neutrality and sovereignty.

In its essence, Swiss neutrality is an armed one and means non-involvement in any armed dispute. It also means, the right to territorial inviolability, which entails three duties: the duty of *abstention*, which means renouncing the active preference and support of warring parties; the duty of *prevention*, so that actions violating neutrality on Switzerland's territory cannot be tolerated; and the duty of *toleration*, so that controls on Swiss vehicles or goods sent abroad must be countenanced. At the same time, neutrality has an economic aspect: in times of war private entrepreneurs have full freedom of trade; however, in its economic policies the state may not favour any warring party.[34]

So far, the EC is not a military alliance. 'Thus, under the present circumstances, accession would not restrict neutrality.'[35] However, the declaration of intent in the Single European Act (Article 30) to cooperate in the long-term on questions pertaining to European security poses certain problems, since it is incompatible with Switzerland's perpetual and armed neutrality. The same applies to the economic sector: Swiss membership of the EC, for example, would mean that Switzerland would lose its autonomy in shaping its foreign trade policy.

In its most recent integration report, the Federal Council expresses the view that the political objectives of the EC threaten Swiss neutrality.[36] Even a purely economic link, for example via a customs union, would be tantamount to renouncing Switzerland's 'autonomous foreign trade policy based on neutrality'. For this reason, such links with the EC must also be rejected.[37]

At the end of the 1960s there was some discussion – though without tangible results – of Switzerland's accession to the EEC, subject to reserving its neutrality; comparable to Austria's request to the EC that the 'perpetually neutral' state of Austria should be admitted to membership.[38]

So far there has been no support in Switzerland for the opinion that Switzerland as a member of the EC could retain its neutrality without reservation.[39] According to Jürg Martin Gabriel, 'the Swiss identify so strongly with their neutrality that they demand an acceptable legal and political solution'.[40]

Sovereignty, in the form of Swiss federalism and direct democracy, constitutes a further important problem in Swiss integration policy. Through federalism the various regions of Switzerland, which differ greatly in terms of economy and culture, are guaranteed a certain autonomy and independence which – as opinion polls invariably confirm – they are not ready to cede. The same can be said for direct democracy at national level. The new direction, proposed in the EC's White Paper and Single European Act, of pursuing a strategy of mutual recognition of law instead of harmonization, while keeping many nationally sensitive sectors subject to the veto of individual states (unanimous decisions), may contribute towards eliminating these obstacles.

Foreigners in Switzerland

The increasing proportion of foreigners living and working in Switzerland has become a major political issue in the past few decades. As early as 1965 – as a reaction to the rapid increase in the numbers of foreigners in Switzerland from 7% in 1955 to some 14% in the mid-1960s, there was a first popular initiative 'against the infiltration of foreigners' which, however, was withdrawn after debate in parliament. This was followed in 1969 by a second such initiative, which was rejected in 1970. The third initiative 'against the infiltration of foreigners and over-population of Switzerland' followed two years later and was rejected in 1974. In the same year two further initiatives on the same subject were launched. One of them aimed at laying down in the constitution the total number of foreigners allowed in Switzerland, the other aimed at limiting the number of aliens accepted for naturalization per year. The Swiss public again rejected both these initiatives, although the support given must not be underestimated.

In 1977 the 'Mitenand (side by side) Initiative' was launched, aiming at social security for foreigners and the right of entry to Switzerland for family members. Moreover foreigners were to be given the same freedom of domicile and free choice of workplace as Swiss nationals. Deportation was to be possible only for criminal offences and by order of a judge. However, the initiative also demanded legislation laying down that the number of entry permits for work purposes issued in any one year was not to surpass the number of working aliens who had left the country in the previous year. In 1981 this initiative was rejected in every canton, with 1.3 million voting against it and 250,000 for it. In 1983 the nation also voted against a parliamentary decision to facilitate naturalization for young aliens who had grown up in Switzerland, and for refugees and stateless persons. The most recent initiative on foreigners, launched in 1986, did not receive the necessary signatures before the deadline for submission was reached, although foreigners now account for some 25% of the population.

The vote held in 1986 on membership of the UN is not directly connected to Swiss policy on aliens, but its rejection by all cantons with a ratio of 3:1 against shows that the Swiss voter is suspicious of closer links to foreign countries and institutions.

The fear of too high a proportion of foreign nationals in Switzerland that has been apparent for many years springs from a general anxiety that a further increase of the foreign population could affect Switzerland's autonomy and identity. Freedom of movement for labour and the professions within the EC and the proposed freedom of domicile is also a relevant economic factor for Switzerland: it has full employment, and continuing high levels of unemployment in EC member states could affect this adversely.

Agricultural problems

The Swiss level of self-sufficiency taken as an average of all agricultural product groups is roughly 60% (50 to 55% after deduction of imported fodder). The level of self-sufficiency is above average for milk, meat, eggs and potatoes; for all other product groups it is below average. Some two-thirds of Swiss food imports are from the EC, to a value of some SFr. 4 billion per year. Of the Swiss exports, particularly cheese, some 50% or SFr. 1.2 billion are destined for EC member states.[41]

There is a wide gap between EC and Swiss producer prices. The current EC prices overall are 40 to 50% of the Swiss price level; approximately 70% for animals for slaughter, 55% for milk and between 30 and 40% for cereals. Even if agricultural products were to become cheaper through closer links between Switzerland and the EC, the Swiss farmer would have to reckon with a severe cut in income.

The report of the Federal Council points out that without income compensation of roughly SFr. 3 billion per year, there would be a substantial decline in production and a more rapid structural change towards larger production centres in Switzerland's Mittelland areas.

The decline and restructuring of Swiss agriculture anticipated as a result of closer links with the EC explain the strong opposition to European integration voiced not only by farmers but also by groups within the food industry and country-dwellers.[42]

The transport problem

In the past few years, as mentioned earlier. Switzerland has accommodated almost a quarter of the total north-south heavy traffic. The debate on transport issues has grown more lively because of the EC's programme to complete the internal market. According to a former head of the EC's cabinet for foreign relations and trade, future negotiations must take the potential size of the market into consideration. The small states 'should therefore be prepared to relegate their own special interests'.[43] Such comments are not individual statements but rather a basic EC approach, as shown by the planned negotiations on transit issues between the EC Council of Ministers and Yugoslavia, Austria and Switzerland. Even if the Council were to reject the European Parliament's demand for direct retaliation measures against Switzerland because of its 28 tonne limit, it was suggested that should major difficulties arise during the negotiations, the Council should 'either resort to measures based on the principle of reciprocity or locate the negotiations within the framework of overall relations between the Community and the countries concerned'.[44] (*NZZ* of 9.12.1988, no. 288).

Switzerland has to respond to the following demands: to increase the maximum weight allowed for goods transported by road from 28 to 40 tonnes; to lift the ban on night driving for lorries; to abolish the tax on heavy freight carriers; and to improve the construction of the north-south road network.

For environmental reasons, Switzerland cannot consider a 40-tonne corridor through its territory. All the roads lead through densely populated areas in the Swiss Mittelland. As an alternative, Switzerland has offered an additional rail link across the Alps (the location line has not yet been finally settled), but also demands the necessary infrastructure from its trading partners (that is, terminals) and priority for standardizing heavy transporters and containers.[45]

Prospects

The debate in Switzerland and the other European states during the past few years shows that there is no short-term solution to the problems facing them. Switzerland must ensure that its present good relations with the European Community and the other EFTA states are continued and developed.

As various statements from political and industrial circles show, the integration strategy initiated by the Swiss authorities has met with approval. According to Swiss industry, the 1972 free trade agreement between Switzerland and

Table 15.5 The Swiss population's willingness to integrate: poll results 1988

	*In per cent of the sample**	
	Willing	*Not willing*
Cooperation in R&D	72.9	6.1
Free movement of goods	50.1	27.7
Single passport	40.3	37.7
Free movement of labour	40.1	35.3
Integration into the EMS	31.4	36.3
Cutting agricultural subsidies	29.0	40.3
Introduction of VAT	19.4	51.8
Less federalism	13.7	53.1
Limiting neutrality	12.1	60.1
Less direct democracy (e.g. waiving right to referenda)	8.0	66.0

* Abstentions account for the differences between answers and total.

Source: Ruffieux/Thurler, 1988, p. 18.

the EEC has proved viable. The development clause included in the agreement is considered a practicable way of solving future problems. However, both political and industrial circles point out that Switzerland should not confine itself to one specific integration model. Various alternatives and procedures must be pursued simultaneously. Some problems should be approached bilaterally, others multilaterally and yet others through mirror legislation. It is also desirable to continue the development of European standards and regulations and to extend the pan-European research agreement.[46]

Table 15.5 sets out the results of a poll conducted by Roland Ruffieux and Anne-Lise Thurler of Lausanne University, which interviewed 1500 persons in the German-speaking and French-speaking parts of Switzerland. The poll showed that Swiss interest in economic and technical cooperation with the European Community is strong, but there is little readiness to give up traditional political rights.

Other polls held in Switzerland also conclude that the majority of the Swiss population currently rejects unconditional EC membership. This verdict would not apply if Switzerland were to be treated as a special case. Provided that typically Swiss features were taken into account, especially Switzerland's sovereignty and perpetual neutrality, many Swiss would be prepared to cooperate more closely with the other European states.

Notes

1. 'Bericht über die Stellung der Schweiz im europäischen Integrationsprozess', *Bundesblatt*, III, 1988, p. 379.
2. 'Botschaft des Bundesrates an die Bundesversammlung betreffend den Beitritt der Schweiz zu dem am 16.4.1948 in Paris unterzeichneten Abkommen über die europä-

ische Zusammenarbeit', *Bundesblatt*, II, 1948, p. 1182ff.
3. 'Botschaft der Bundesrates an die Bundesversammlung über die Teilnahme der Schweiz an der Organisation für Wirtschaftliche Zusammenarbeit und Entwicklung', *Bundesblatt*, I, 1961, p. 966.
4. 'Botschaft des Bundesrates an die Bundesversammlung über die Beteiligung der Schweiz an der europäischen Freihandels-Assoziation', *Bundesblatt*, III, 1960, p. 852ff.
5. GATT report, *Bundesblatt*, I, 1966, pp. 667, 742ff.
6. 'Die Entwicklung der europäischen Integrationsbestrebungen', *Bundesblatt*, II, 1971, p. 752ff.
7. *Bundesblatt*, III, 1988, p. 379.
8. *Bundesblatt*, I, 1960, p. 861.
9. *Bundesblatt*, III, 1988, p. 382.
10. *Bundesblatt*, I, 1960, p. 860.
11. *Bundesblatt*, III, 1988, p. 380; 'Die Schweizer Wirtschaft vor der Herausforderung des EG-Binnenmarktes 1992, Eine praxisorientierte Lageanalyse', *Vorort, Schweizerischer Handels- und Industrieverein*, Zurich 1988. p. 5ff.
12. *Neue Zürcher Zeitung (NZZ)*, no. 112, 18 May 1989, p. 21.
13. Ernst Thomke, 'Uhrenindustrie', in R. Senti (ed.), *Schweiz-EG, Stimmen der Schweizer Wirtschaft zur europäischen Integration* (Zurich, Neue Zürcher Zeitung, 1988), pp. 109–14.
14. Jakob Kellenberger, 'Die integrationspolitische Herausforderung aus schweizerischer Sicht', in *Vollendung des Binnenmarktes in der Europäischen Gemeinschaft* (Vienna, Österreichische Nationalbank, 1987), pp. 51–64.
15. Waldemar Hummer and Michael Schweitzer, *Österreich und die EWG: Neutralitätsrechtliche Beurteilung der Möglichkeiten der Dynamisierung des Verhältnisses zur EWG* (Vienna, Signum, 1987), p. 262ff.
16. *Bundesblatt* III, 1988, p. 380.
17. 'Die Schweiz und die europäische Gemeinschaft, Lage und Ausblick, Bericht der Arbeitsgruppe', *Vorort, Schweizerischer Handels- und Industrieverein* (mimeo), June 1987, p. 42.
18. Franz A. Blankart, 'Erwägungen zur Europapolitik der Schweiz', lecture in Lucerne (mimeo), 13 December 1986, p. 10.
19. Horst G. Krenzler, 'Zwischen Protektionismus und Liberalismus, europäischer Binnenmarkt und Drittlandsbeziehungen', *Europa Archiv*, vol 43, no. 3, 1988, p. 248.
20. *Vorort*, 1987, p. 31.
21. Blankart, 1986, p. 19.
22. Kellenberger, 1987, p. 54.
23. Willy Zeller, 'Ein verändertes Integrationspolitisches Umfeld, das Verhältnis der Schweiz zur europäischen Gemeinschaft', *Neue Zürcher Zeitung*, no. 146, 27/28 June 1987, p. 25. This is analogous to Waldemar Hummer and Michael Schweitzer, 'Österreich und die EWG: autonomer Nachvollzug – präinstitutionelle Zusammenarbeit – Beitritt unter Neutralitätsvorbehalt?', *Die Erste, Wirtschaftanalysen*, 2, Vienna, 1987; and Hummer and Schweizer, *Österreich und die EWG*, p. 262ff.
24. Zeller, 1987,
25. *Official Journal of the EC*, L 197, 18 July 1987, p. 33ff.
26. Willy de Clercq, speech at the EC-EFTA ministerial meeting (mimeo), Brussels 2 February 1988, p. 4; *EFTA Bulletin* 29, no. 1, Geneva, 1988, p. 10; Krenzler, 1988, p. 247.
27. Richard Senti, 'Für eine gesamteuropäische Zollunion, Gedanken zur Aussenhandlesstrategie der EFTA-Staaten', *Neue Zürcher Zeitung*, 11/12 October 1986, p. 17: and 'Ausbau der wirtschaflichen Beziehungen zwischen EFTA und EG (aus der Sicht der

EFTA-Staaten)', *Wirtschaftspolitische Mitteilungen der Wirtschaftsförderung*, vol. 4, Zurich, 1987.
28. Jan Herin, *Rules of Origin and Differences between Tariff Levels in EFTA and the EC*, EFTA Occasional Paper No. 13, Geneva 1986, Table 1.
29. Senti, 1987, p. 10.
30. M. Catinat, E. Donni and A. Italianer, *The Completion of the Internal Market: Results of Macroeconomic Model Simulations*, Commission of the European Communities Economic Papers, No. 65, 1988.
31. Rolf J. Langhammer, *Auswirkungen der EG-Binnenmarkt-Integration auf den Aussenhandel der Entwicklungsländer*, Kieler Staff Working Paper no. 369, May 1989.
32. *Vorort*, 1987, pp. 28–9.
33. Freisinnig-Demokratische Partei (FDP), *Positionspapier der Wirtschaftsauschusses der FDP der Schweiz zum Verhältnis Schweiz-EG* (mimeo), 27 April 1987.
34. Jürg Martin Gabriel, 'Neutralität – Probleme und Möglichkeiten', in J. Altwegg (ed.), *Horizont 92 – Die Schweiz im Zeichen der EG*, Sauerländer, 1988, p. 34ff.
35. Gabriel, 1988, p. 34.
36. *Bundesblatt*, III, 1988, p. 379.
37. *Bundesblatt*, III, 1988, p. 376.
38. Hans M. Mayrzedt and Hans C. Binswanger, *Die Neutralen in der Europäischen Integration* (Vienna and Stuttgart, University Press, 1970).
39. Hummer and Schweitzer, *Österreich und die EWG*, p. 284ff.
40. Gabriel, 1988, p. 37.
41. Bernard Lehmann, 'Landwirtschaft', in Richard Senti (ed.), *Schweiz-EG, Stimmen der Schweizer Wirtschaft zur europäischen Integration* (Zurich, Neue Zürcher Zeitung, 1988), pp. 42–3.
42. *Bundesblatt*, III, 1988, pp. 359–60.
43. Alexander Schaub, 'EG-EFTA-Beziehungen', *Euro Echo*, *Informationsbrief der EG*, 4, 1986, p. 4; Walter Meier, 'Freizügigkeit für Dienstleistungen, Kapital und Personen' in Willy Zeller, (ed.), *Europa 92 und die Schweiz* (Zurich, Neue Zürcher Zeitung, 1988), p. 25.
44. *Neue Zürcher Zeitung* no. 288, 9 December 1988.
45. *Neue Zürcher Zeitung*, no. 119, 26 May 1989.
46. Senti, 1988.

Part III
The Negotiations

16 EFTA and its Limits

Esko Antola

The historical perspective

The division of Western Europe into the 'Six' and the 'Seven' was made final in November 1958 when the former group, after two years of intensive negotiations, could not agree upon the establishment of a larger free trade area. For primarily political reasons, the founders preferred the newly established European Economic Community, with its far-reaching aims and legal obligations, to a much looser free trade area. As Uwe Kitzinger points out, those 'convinced' Europeans who saw the EEC as a vehicle for political union were afraid that a free trade area would detract from these aims.[1] Obviously, various national interests both in the Six and elsewhere also contributed to the same end. In particular the tension between France and Great Britain, which was to play such an important role in the later history of European integration, was a major factor in bringing the negotiations to an unsuccessful end.[2]

The 'Outer Seven' officially opened their negotiations for a new free trade arrangement in early 1959, after if became evident that a European economic association was beyond reach. Negotiations were concluded in a hurry and the Stockholm Convention was signed in autumn 1959, only a year after the final breakdown of negotiations on Great Britain's entry into the EC.[3]

In early 1960 EFTA came into operation. The creation of the new association had been facilitated by the preparatory work already done in the Maudling Committee. In Scandinavia negotiations for a Nordic Customs Union had been completed, and thus the basic framework for a free trade arrangement had also been identified there.[4] EFTA was thus created from principles and ideas developed for other purposes. There was no special EFTA identity: the Association was a combination of already tested ideas and new conditions laid down in the Stockholm Convention.

The role of the UK in the establishment of EFTA can hardly be overstated. British frustration at the process which resulted in the creation of the EEC gave fuel to the short and intensive process preceding the Stockholm Convention. The interest of the British government in establishing EFTA was primarily to use it as a tool to achieve what had not been achieved through the Maudling

Committee.[5] Internal discussion in the UK pointed to several other merits of a free trade area: EFTA could work as a pressure group vis-à-vis the EEC, parallel tariff reductions inside EFTA would make it easier to establish the larger European free trade area at a later date, and British industries could find at least some compensation for not being able to enjoy the advantages of the EEC.[6]

The motives of other EFTA members differed. The neutrals, Austria, Sweden and Switzerland,[7] preferred a solution which would keep them outside supranational decision-making structures, and both Denmark and Norway also had domestic reservations against supranationality. The Scandinavian countries had a common interest in achieving their aims through the Nordic free trade area negotiations. The EFTA solution guaranteed that, and secured their access to the British market which was of substantial importance for all of them.[8] The Scandinavian dimension and the British market were also the major motives for Finland's efforts to create a special relationship with EFTA.[9]

Against this background, it is no wonder that a standard view of the role of EFTA stresses that the organization was designed to be a bridgehead for a later expansion of the EEC. The members of EFTA did not see much future for their common enterprise. EFTA was, and has always been, a pragmatic organization, able to adapt itself to changes in the European integration arena. That EFTA was only a tool for achieving a larger European trading system is well illustrated both by its modest administrative structure and the policies of its members. EFTA's initial role is expressed in the preamble to the Stockholm Convention: 'determined to facilitate the early establishment of a multilateral association for the removal of trade barriers and the promotion of close economic cooperation between the Members of the Organization for European Economic Co-operation, including the Members of the European Economic Community. . . .'[10]

The early history of EFTA clearly points to the temporary nature of the organization. The member countries themselves understood it as a waiting-room for a better solution: this, for most of them, was the enlargement of the EC. As early as March 1961 the UK and Denmark applied for full membership: Austria, Sweden and Switzerland wanted association from December 1961; and Norway applied for membership in April 1962.[11]

The development of an EFTA view, 1960–1984

EFTA as a waiting-room, 1960–1966

In the early years the EFTA view, as expressed in the declarations of its ministerial meetings and reflecting its highest political authority, constantly referred to a Europe-wide market as the best solution for the continent. An important part of the argument was that EFTA was designed not to become an inward-looking economic block, since no restrictions on trade with third parties were introduced.[12] EFTA ministers pointed to the need to create a 'single European market'.[13]

The London ministerial meeting in June 1961 formulated for the first time the Association's policy on European integration. EFTA's point of departure was that the ultimate will of its member countries was to achieve the economic integration of Europe as a whole in the form of a single European market. They also pointed to the dangers which the split in Europe posed to the members of both organizations. Strategies to overcome this split presupposed the readiness of all concerned to modify policy.

This modification was obviously the key question for EFTA. The ministers noted in their London Declaration that changes in policy options must respect the basic political positions of both the participating nations and the European Community. At the end, however, the ministers noted: 'while some EFTA countries could not accept obligations of a political nature, all members of EFTA are willing to undertake, in order to achieve an integrated European market, obligations which go beyond those which they have accepted among themselves in the Stockholm Convention.'[14]

The major message of the statement was that EFTA was ready to go beyond the intentions of the Stockholm Convention. It also stressed that any solution should include effective institutions for implementation, a dimension which EFTA had so far lacked. An important part of EFTA policy was also the coordination of actions taken by the individual member countries. This policy of closer cooperation was expressed as follows:

> The obligations created by the Convention between the Members, and the momentum towards integration within the Association, would be maintained at least until satisfactory arrangements have been worked out in negotiations to meet the various legitimate interests of all Members of EFTA and thus enable them all to participate from the same date in an integrated European market.[15]

The aim of EFTA during the first round ot accession negotiations was clearly to act in a coherent way, to keep other member countries informed and to remain united throughout the negotiations, although these were carried out on a bilateral basis between each EFTA country and the Community. EFTA as an institution had no role. In the next few ministerial meetings the member countries reported on the progress made in their bilateral negotiations. Consultations were obviously fruitful and helped the member countries to coordinate their policies but no EFTA action was taken.[16]

A large and unified European market remained an EFTA goal after the breakdown of negotiations between the UK and the Community. EFTA assumed a somewhat more visible role in planning the future of free trade by asking its permanent representatives in Geneva to prepare a programme of action for the future.[17] EFTA was also gradually given a larger role in the collaboration between its members, for instance in preparations for the GATT negotiations.

During the mid-1960s EFTA ministers produced declaration after declaration on the need for a wider European trading system. Gradually a new approach was developed. Its emphasis was on the importance of bringing the EEC and EFTA closer to each other. A turning-point was the ministerial declaration issued in Vienna in 1965 calling for steps to bring the two institutions into closer and more continuous contact. The ministers also considered new ideas for increasing and strengthening cooperation between the EC and EFTA.[18] One proposal was for ministerial meetings between the two integration groups, an instrument which became a permanent element of the EC-EFTA relationship in the late 1980s.

Areas of cooperation proposed by the EFTA ministers included reducing obstacles to free trade, cooperation in research and development, harmonization of standards and the intensification of integration within EFTA. The strengthening of EFTA's internal integration, its role in external relations, in particular in relations with the Community, and its institutional aspects began to be studied by the EFTA Council.

The Vienna Declaration of 1965 was an important landmark in formulating EFTA's policy towards the Community. It initiated processes which further strengthened EFTA, indicated that the Association was assuming a more permanent role, and gradually delineated arrangements with the EC other than accession or association. The creation of a single European market still remained the final objective.

The bridge-building phase, 1967–1973

EFTA's internal integration was boosted considerably by the achievement of the free trade area in 1966. This achievement took place at a time when EC integration was in deep crisis. The resulting problems and delays in the EC made EFTA even more important for its members and the Association began to live a life of its own. The crisis of the EC made EFTA more cohesive, since it made EC membership less attractive, at least for the time being.[19]

The internal strengthening of EFTA had several aspects. First, ministerial councils worked out new interpretations of key questions on the functioning of a free trade area. These included interpretations of Article 15 on restrictive business practices (1965), Article 16 on the rights of establishment (1966), Article 14 on public undertakings (1966), and Article 13 on state aid (1968).[20] Another important step was the signing of the Pharmaceutical Convention, the first major convention negotiated inside the Association. In addition, EFTA was enlarged by the accession of Iceland in 1969. As a result of these developments member countries concluded that EFTA should be actively developed and expanded, even though some of them were again engaged in negotiations for membership of the Community.

During the latter part of the 1960s EFTA had twin goals. On the one hand it wanted to stress that it was active and alive and part of a single European market. The progress it had achieved was a sign of the determination which all EFTA pronouncements since the Vienna Declaration had affirmed. The other goal was to strengthen the internal market of EFTA. In fact the aims of the programme of action indicated that EFTA was moving from a mere free trade area towards a common market: a type of integration for which the proper functioning of trade was a vital element. Indeed, EFTA as a free trade area became economically significant for its members, in particular for the smaller economies.

However, the strengthening of EFTA was also directly linked to the continuing negotiations between the UK and the Community. EFTA was waiting for negotiations to be opened by the Community side. EFTA ministers declared at their meeting in London in 1967 that 'all EFTA countries should have the possibility to participate fully from the beginning in any negotiations for a trading arrangement which might follow'.[21] During the late 1960s EFTA members stressed the role of the Association as a negotiating body in their bilateral dealings with the Community. This function of the Association was repeated throughout the process of negotiations, though it played no role in the direct contacts between its member countries and the Community. However, EFTA's role as a forum for consultations between its members became even more important once it became evident that only some of its members were actually interested in membership of the Community.

Free trade area phase, 1974–84

To a great extent EFTA's bridge-building aims were achieved through the signing of the Free Trade Agreements (FTA). EFTA had lost two members, but in the process the Association had become more homogeneous: it consisted mainly of small, highly industrialized, neutral countries, which had common views on many questions of international economic relations. The persistent aim of a single market was also achieved, at least partially, in the form of a free trade area.

It quickly became evident, however, that it was in the interests of EFTA countries to develop further the FTAs signed by each individually with the EC.[22] During the first years of the operation of the FTAs there was no common EFTA strategy. Instead, its members expressed their views on the workings of free trade in their individual joint committees with the EC, and EFTA was used as a body for exchanges of information. This of course was the method which the Community offered. All the FTAs, except that between Finland and the Community, contain the so-called evolutionary clause, which expresses the interests of the parties in developing their relationship.[23]

A turning-point in the EFTA approach was the Declaration of Vienna in May 1977. The Council meeting was held at the level of prime ministers and in particular reviewed the progress of the FTAs, as well as calling for closer integration between the Community and EFTA. An additional reason for this high-level action was the economic crisis in Europe which threatened the liberal trading order and thus the achievements of free trade. The EFTA ministers proposed as areas of common interest between the Community and EFTA increased exchanges of information, closer consultation on economic questions and, where appropriate, coordinated efforts to secure free trade and to improve the general economic environment.[24]

The EFTA proposal actually went further in some respects than previous ones, but lacked certain other elements. The most important feature of the Vienna Declaration of 1977 was that the ministers started from the assumption that EFTA was a permanent element of Western European integration. The declaration argues:

> It [i.e. EFTA] will continue to be a useful and flexible instrument for the participating governments in the pursuit of their objectives regarding European free trade and economic cooperation. . . . They will make use of it as a forum for joint consideration

> of wider European and world-wide economic problems in order to make a constructive contribution to economic cooperation in international fora.[25]

The idea of EFTA as an instrument for its members touches core issues of strategy. The Vienna Declaration extended EFTA's role from a negotiating instrument into one for joint action, assuming that both EFTA and the EC were permanent elements of the European integration process. Their relationship was to be based on the notion of mutual interests and interdependency.

One indication of a concern to develop EFTA institutions was the creation of the Committee of the Members of Parliament. Thus institutionally EFTA, starting from a very modest framework in 1960, had by 1977 a structure which resembled that of the EC. Remarkable differences, however, still existed between the decision-making powers of the different bodies. It could plausibly be argued that EFTA had changed from association to community by adding channels of political support into its structure.

The years from the Declaration of Vienna to 1984 were marked by increasing determination on the EFTA side to develop a 'second generation' of integration. This concept envisage free trade as requiring more than the traditional aspects by which politicians had sought to establish free trade in Europe in the late 1950s. The concept of the second generation had two dimensions. First, it embraced those new areas of integration which became focal after the achievement of free trade in its initial definition. The aim here was to avoid the proliferation of new trade restrictions in areas not covered by the FTAs.

But, second, the concept had a more political connotation as regards the means by which EFTA countries should approach the new situation. In describing the challenges created by the new phase of integration, Franz Blankart has commented on the crucial question of EFTA strategy:[26] what role should be given to EFTA as regards the bilateral nature of the FTAs? In other words, should the EFTA countries first discuss among themselves this new phase in order to have a stronger position in their bilateral dealings with the EC, or should they first approach the Commission and only then try to find out common positions and strategies?

EFTA strategy in the 1980s

Answers to these questions have emerged gradually on the basis of four major elements. The first element is the notion that EFTA has a permanent place in the wider European liberalization of trade. In other words, EFTA has ceased to be regarded as a waiting-room for the EC by its members. Its role came to be seen in more active ways which stress its function as the most flexible and useful instrument for its members, with 'EFTA countries making increased use of the Association as a framework for consultations on subjects of common economic interest.'[27] EFTA also came to be seen as an instrument for negotiations on a multilateral basis with the EC wherever suitable. EFTA thus came to be seen not only as a body for multilateral dealings between its member countries but also as an active participant in itself.

A second element was the strong commitment to EC-EFTA cooperation. In the Declaration of Vienna it was argued that cooperation between the two bodies was fruitful because of interdependence. Later, the case was made more explicit by the articulation of the argument that EFTA and the EC are each other's most important trading partner.[28] This point was further emphasized by the argument that their relationship was stable in a period of economic turmoil.[29] These points served two purposes. Inside EFTA they convinced the member countries that development beyond the FTAs was in the interests of both partners. But they were primarily aimed at the Community, which had not reacted very positively or precisely to EFTA proposals.

The EFTA approach did not call for permanent institutional links with the Community. Instead, it stressed the flexibility of the relationship as advantageous. It was also willing to go beyond the limits of existing treaties in order to secure the future of the relationship:

> In order to secure and develop free trade, constructive and mutually satisfactory solutions have to be found in due time to problems wherever they arise. [Member countries] share the Community's view on the importance of increased economic cooperation within Western Europe, and suggest that possibilities and methods should therefore be explored, both individually and collectively, on a pragmatic and reciprocal basis, of enlarging it further both under the FTAs and in other fields not directly covered by them.[30]

In EFTA's approach, the areas of cooperation remained very much as defined in the Declaration of Vienna. In reviewing the situation of the FTAs and EFTA in May 1979 ministers distinguished between areas where common action was appropriate and those where exchanges of information were needed. Rules of origin, removal of technical barriers and trade-mark law were identified as issues where a common approach was needed, while monetary and economic policy matters were identified as areas for exchanges of information. Monetary issues and economic policy were new elements in the debate and marked an expansion of the EFTA view on the scope of free trade. The role of EFTA was increasing in these areas as its internal integration proceeded, thus making both possible and necessary an extended sphere of collaboration.

The third element of the EFTA approach was a policy of adjustment: a response to particular trends within the Community. EFTA countries found it increasingly important to adjust to the internal dynamics of the Community as regards, for instance, the strengthening of the internal market, the introduction of the European Monetary System and the research and technology programmes of the EC.

EFTA's initial reaction to the drive in the EC to complete the internal market was to hope that the special relationship between the two bodies could be recognized.[31] The establishment of the internal market was a potential threat to EFTA countries. Their reaction reflected the fear of new obstacles to trade. The call for a special relationship, together with readiness for cooperation in 'all fields of mutual economic interest', must be seen as a message to the Community.

Finally, the EFTA approach also implied that areas of mutual interest and action in the international economy should be discussed between the two bodies. Strategies could thus be proposed for overcoming the economic crisis in Europe or pursuing their common interests in the GATT, for example. Thus the rise of protectionism became a trigger for an EFTA approach.

EFTA's motivation for expanding its area of interest was twofold. The first factor was the increasing interdependency between it and the Community. The relationship had already clearly gone beyond the conventional bounds of free trade by the early 1980s. Second was EFTA's increasing sensitivity to the growing weight of the Community in the international political economy. The Community had begun to speak with one voice in a number of international forums and in many cases also in the name of Western Europe. It was only natural therefore that EFTA countries should want to make their views known to the Community.

The impact of the Luxembourg Declaration

A new phase in the EFTA-EC relationship began with the first joint meeting of ministers from both EFTA and EC countries in Luxembourg in April 1984. Such a meeting had first been proposed in the mid-1960s: the Ministerial Council of EFTA regarded it as 'desirable to seek to arrange meetings at ministerial level between the two groups at the earliest opportunity which offered prospects of a fruitful result'.[32]

The Luxembourg meeting was thus a logical step in the evolution of the West European free trade framework. Both parties had for several years stressed the need to go beyond the treaty framework in a large number of areas. The Commission had a list of twenty-five areas for the evolution of the FTAs. This evolution was a long-term aim of EFTA and a rather obvious one: the new phase of Community integration, characterized by the strengthening of the internal market and the deepening of political integration, was a potential threat to EFTA countries. EFTA wanted to have both a political commitment and a recognition of the special relationship from the Community's side.

EFTA was successful in both these aims. The idea of a special relationship between the Community and EFTA began to emerge in the Community in the early 1980s. The 1981 Annual Report of the Committe of Permanent Representatives (Coreper) on the EC-EFTA relationship strongly highlighted the importance of EFTA as a trading partner. The EFTA dimension was defined as a special relationship by the observation that among all preferential agreements concluded by the Community only those with EFTA countries granted it full reciprocity. This was regarded as all the more important since protectionist tendencies threatened to form barriers to free trade.[33] In subsequent Coreper reports the same view has been repeated. The joint EC-EFTA commitment to establish the European Economic Space (EES) is expressed in the Luxembourg Declaration.

EFTA's interpretation of the Luxembourg Declaration was given at the end of May 1984 in the Visby Declaration. In describing the evolution of the EES and EFTA, ministers used the term 'genuine West European home market for industrial goods' when announcing their support for both the Luxembourg

Declaration and progress towards the internal market of the Community.[34] Noting the great number of issues involved in the declaration, EFTA officials outlined a special EFTA work programme on the EES.

EFTA priorities were declared to be rules of origin and technical barriers to trade, along with border controls and trade documentation. These well illustrate the nature of the EES: it is a combination of traditional FTA issues and emerging new areas largely created by the intensification of integration in the Community. Since 1984 EFTA priorities have increasingly been defined as a function of progress in the EC internal market and in the High-Level Customs Group.

The Communiqué of the ministerial meeting in May 1987 talked of 'a homogeneous and dynamic European Economic Space'.[35] Four concrete areas of common interest were identified:

(1) an improvement of the INST procedure for the notification of new technical regulations by giving it a legally binding form;
(2) an extension to the EES of the system of mutual recognition of tests, inspections and certificates already operating in EFTA;
(3) transparency of government aids by notifying planned government aid measures in advance; and
(4) liberalization of public procurement on a reciprocal basis.

In all these areas EFTA can offer established regimes. It introduced the INST procedure as early as 1965. Renewed in 1984, it implies that governments have the duty to give notice of all new regulations in advance of their implementation. This notice should be given as early as possible and should contain essential information on the content of the new standard as well as explaining its relationship to other international standards.

Another example of an EFTA regime is the system of mutual recognition of tests, first tackled in 1971. Nine agreements, to which some EC member states have adhered, had been concluded by 1986. EFTA procedures may be used as models for cooperation in the EES as well.

The Delors factor

The speech given by Mr Jacques Delors, President of the EC Commission, in January 1989 gave a new impetus to the EC-EFTA relationship. Delors outlined a framework of 'more structured partnership with common decision-making and administrative institutions'.[36]

The Delors initiative was greeted with great interest by the EFTA governments, as was evident at the Oslo meeting in March 1989 of EFTA prime ministers. Their statement declared their readiness to 'explore together with the EC ways and means to achieve a more structured partnership with common decision-making and administrative institutions in order to make our co-operation more effective'.[37]

The EFTA approach to the EC internal market springs from traditional EFTA views but with new elements. EFTA is still very much an adaptive organization, its actions determined by the state of EC integration. This is only realistic: the EFTA economies are increasingly dependent on the dynamics of the internal market. The problem of adaptation is, however, increasingly complex. The pace of harmonization, the extension of the scope of the EC and the increasing importance of European Political Cooperation have changed the nature of the EC integration in ways which pose additional problems for the predominantly neutral EFTA countries.

The EFTA strategy continues to rely very much on the 'most important trading partner' argument, a persistent theme throughout the 1980s. The EC recognizes this in its own new approach to European non-members. Two other long-standing EFTA arguments have survived, also in changing conditions: EFTA is seen by its members as a permanent institution and a large European free trading area remains its major aim.

In attempting to adapt itself to the dynamics of the EC integration, the EFTA Council meeting in Oslo established a dual-track policy. On the one hand, this stresses the need to develop the Luxembourg process. On the other hand, EFTA has initiated a process of establishing its view on what the 'more structured relationship' could be. The maintenance and extension of the Luxembourg process retains a high priority, especially since many of the issues of common interest remain to be resolved. In May 1989 the Progress Report on EC-EFTA cooperation listed twenty-four areas of continuing discussion and negotiation, some items dating back to the 1950s.

The Luxembourg process has also produced some remarkable results. Among the most important agreements are the following: the Single Administrative Document Convention (1987); the Transit Convention (1987); the Lugano Convention on jurisdiction in civil and commercial matters (1988); the Convention for the Mutual Recognition of test results and proofs of conformity (1988); the simplification of origin rules (1988); and the association of EFTA countries with the TEDIS programme (1989).[38]

A new feature of this process has been the adoption of multilateral conventions. Increasingly, multilateralism is an expression of the emergence of new attitudes and the search for new models of cooperation. From the EFTA point of view multilateralism is a step into a new era, presenting it with new challenges.

As regards the new dialogue on the restructuring of the EC-EFTA relationship, discussions have moved forward both inside EFTA and in joint working groups with the EC. Exploratory discussions have taken place in the areas of the four freedoms, in which the EC Commission has asked EFTA countries to identify those elements in the relevant *acquis communautaire* which would cause problems. Institutional issues were debated in autumn 1989 by the High-Level Working Group, the 'Fifth Group', and had emerged by 1990 as critical issues in the EES debate.

In fact the EFTA approach also has a third track: discussions on the role and identity of the Association itself. Both the Luxembourg and the Delors processes have created demands for the revision of EFTA's internal working and decision-making methods. Traditionally, the EFTA philosophy has been based strictly on intergovernmentalism: by and large the member countries joined EFTA because they wanted to avoid supranational obligations. But the possible establishment of common decision-making institutions with the EC necessitates the strenthening of EFTA.

As an internal 'EFTA matter' the Association faces a level-of-commitment problem. To make the EES effective, EFTA countries have in many instances both to intensify internal integration and assume commitments which go beyond those accepted in EFTA. A similar problem is the lack of a history of collective action by EFTA, an aspect in which it is very different from the EC. Collective action, now increasingly agreed under the majority voting rule after the Single European Act, is the rule in the Community and the exception in EFTA.

The situation challenges the basic EFTA philosophy. It is doubtful whether EFTA can stay as it is – a purely intergovernmental organization – if its members really prefer the EES as an alternative. Common norms, the increasing openness of societies and the rise of multilateralism in the EES will influence the EFTA countries more than the Community. The advancement of the EES will therefore have remarkable political effects. The concepts of neutrality and political independence have to be taken into account. On the other hand, if EFTA countries can act together in a common framework with the Community they are guaranteed at least some influence on the relationship and its results.

The EC and EFTA are in no ways comparable in their capacities to participate in the work of common institutions. While the Treaty of Rome furnishes the Community with powers either to participate in international organizations or to be represented in their work, EFTA as an organization has no powers to speak for itself or for its member countries in other international institutions. However, EFTA maintains contacts with a number of international organizations. The normal procedure is that EFTA member countries confer with each other on matters of common interest that arise in various relevant international bodies. This has been the standard procedure in GATT negotiations as well as in the OECD. There are also contacts and exchanges of information between the secretariats of EFTA and OECD, between EFTA and the Council of Europe, and EFTA and the Nordic Council.

EFTA has entered into a more permanent relationship with some international bodies, in particular in the field of technology. For instance, it has observer status in the European Patent Organization (EPO). EFTA's representatives have begun to participate in a number of other bodies in this field, in particular since the EC intensified its quest for European standards in 1980; hence EFTA's interest in CEN and CENELEC.

There has also been a gradual increase of external policy elements in EFTA's international role. The most obvious example is the free trade agreement with Spain, signed in 1979. The cooperation agreement with Yugoslavia and the EFTA-Portugal Fund point in the same direction. These have now been complemented by the opening of dialogues with Czechoslovakia, Hungary and Poland, leading to initial declarations of cooperation.

It is quite obvious, however, that EFTA would need an internal structural reform in order to be able to meet the challenge of restructuring the EC-EFTA relationship, if this were to be based on an EFTA 'pillar'. EFTA would have to be able to speak with one voice. There seem to be basically two possibilities. EFTA might either strengthen the role of its secretariat or establish mechanisms of consultation, which would strengthen the position of the country in chair. A necessary precondition would be the introduction of majority decision-making. This would be to transform EFTA. It leaves EFTA members with a choice between ceding sovereignty to EFTA and ceding sovereignty to the EC. Neither option is easy.

Notes

1. Uwe Kitzinger, 'Europe: The Six and the Seven', *International Organisation*, XIV (1960), p. 30.
2. *The European Free Trade Association and the Crisis of European Integration* (London, Michael Joseph, 1968), pp. 174–7.
3. Emile Benoit, *Europe at Sixed and Sevens* (New York, Columbia University Press, 1961), pp. 69–82.
4. Franz Wendt, *The Nordic Council and Cooperation in Scandinavia* (Copenhagen, Munksgaard, 1959), pp. 97–8.
5. Miriam Camps, *Britain and the European Community 1955–1963*(London, Oxford University Press, 1964), pp. 217–18.
6. Uwe Kitzinger, *The Politics and Economics of European Integration* (New York, Frederick A. Prager, 1961), pp. 136–40.
7. On the position of neutrals, see Paul Luif, *Neutrale in die EG?* (Vienna, Austrian Institute for International Affairs, 1988), pp. 93–216.
8. See, for instance, Barry Turner and Gunilla Nordquist, *The Other European Community, Integration and Co-operation in Nordic Europe* (London, 1988,) pp. 109–22.
9. Esko Antola and Ossi Tuusvuori, *Suomi ja Lansi-Euroopan Integraatio* (Turku, Ulkopoliittinen Instituutti, 1983), pp. 131–7.
10. *The European Free Trade Association* (Geneva, EFTA Secretariat, 1987), p. 118.
11. On this phase of EFTA, see *European Free Trade Association and the Crisis of European Integration*, pp. 43–214.
12. *EFTA Bulletin*, 1 (2) (1960), p. 9.
13. *EFTA Bulletin*, 3 (2) (1961), pp. 8–9.
14. *EFTA Bulletin*, 2 (7) (1961), p. 8.
15. *EFTA Bulletin*, 2 (7) (1961), p. 9.
16. *EFTA Bulletin*, 3 (7) (1961), p. 9.
17. *EFTA Bulletin*, 4 (3) (1963), p. 4.
18. *6th Annual Report of the European Free Trade Association* (Geneva, EFTA Secretariat, 1966), pp. 40–1.
19. *European Free Trade Association and the Crisis of European Integration*, pp. 219–20.
20. *European Free Trade Association*, (Geneva, EFTA Secretariat 1987), p. 176.
21. *8th Annual Report of the European Free Trade Association* (Geneva, EFTA Secretariat, 1968), p. 47.
22. The simplification of origin rules were taken up in 1975 as an issue for the first time in a call for further development of the FTAs. See *15th Annual Report of the European Free Trade Association* (Geneva, EFTA Secretariat, 1975), p. 46.
23. Article 23 of the Free Trade Agreements reads: 'Where a Contracting Party considers that it would be useful in the interests of the economies of both Contracting Parties to develop their relations established by the Agreement by extending them to fields not covered thereby, it shall submit a reasoned request to the other Contracting Party. The Contracting Parties may instruct the Joint Committee to examine this request and, where appropriate, to make recommendations to them, particularly with a view to opening negotiations.'

24. *EFTA Bulletin*, 18 (5) (1977), p. 5.
25. Ibid.
26. Franz Blankart, 'Thoughts on the Second Generation of Integration Problems', *EFTA Bulletin*, 19 (1978), pp. 9–11.
27. *20th Annual Report of the European Free Trade Association* (Geneva, EFTA Secretariat, 1980), pp. 61–2.
28. *19th Annual Report of the European Free Trade Association* (Geneva, EFTA Secretariat, 1979), p. 62.
29. *23rd Annual Report of the European Free Trade Association* (Geneva, EFTA Secretariat, 1983), p. 59.
30. Ibid., p. 61.
31. Ibid., p. 56.
32. *6th Annual Report of the European Free Trade Association*, p. 40.
33. *Report of the Committee of Permanent Representatives to the Council of Ministers* (Brussels, Coreper, 1981), p. 1.
34. *EFTA Bulletin*, 2 (1984), pp. 1–3.
35. *EFTA Bulletin*, 2 (1987), p. 18.
36. Statement by Jacques Delors, President of the Commission, in Strasbourg, 17 January 1989, p. 32.
37. *EFTA Bulletin*, 2 (1989), p. 5.
38. Collected from various sources, see for instance *EC-EFTA Cooperation – Progress Report* (Geneva, EFTA Secretariat, 9 June 1989).

17 The Legal Issues
Friedl Weiss

The relationship between the EFTA countries and the European Communities lacks coordination of both policy objectives and institutional machinery. Although the Luxembourg Declaration of 1984 [1] envisaged the creation of a homogeneous and dynamic European Economic Space (EES), flexible cooperation going beyond the framework of the Free Trade Agreements (FTAs)[2] and consultations and exchanges of information, it failed to set up or even consider common institutional structures to service these developments. Instead, the EFTA countries devised a multitude of pragmatic procedural mechanisms for exchanges of views and contacts between the EFTA Secretariat, certain standing committees and the relevant Commission services, as well as *ad hoc* informal meetings of experts.[3]

Progress was slow and piecemeal, subordinated to the Community's priority of consolidating its internal market.[4] Most disappointingly to the EFTA countries, advances towards the EES never looked likely to parallel progress made within the European Community following the White Paper and the Single European Act (SEA).[5] However, the EFTA countries' main fear is that unless matched by measures of their own, the internal market will eliminate the EES and thus the present rough symmetry in access to all European markets. As the spectre of a European Economic Space *à deux vitesses* draws hauntingly closer, EFTA countries are beginning to examine their legal options on closer cooperation with the Community. This involves examination of the Community legal order, the EFTA regime and the FTAs. However, before moving on to the legal issues arising from this debate, a brief look at essential features of EFTA's structure and relations with the EC is necessary.

EFTA in European integration

EFTA's institutional set-up

EFTA's formal institutional structure is extremely simple and reflects both the drafters' pragmatism and their original conception of the organization as temporary.[6] The Stockholm Convention as a whole is characterized by brevity, simplicity and flexibility. It provides for only one organ, the Council, a permanent diplomatic body composed of government representatives, each with one vote. The Council has established several standing committees and other subsidiary bodies to assist it.[7] The most recent is the Group of Legal Experts, mandated to examine legal questions, notably those arising in cooperation between the EFTA countries and the European Community. While most EFTA bodies have had to shift their attention from purely internal matters to focus on those connected to the new dialogue with the Community, this new body is the clearest symbol of the fact that some 90% of EFTA's activities are now concerned with EFTA-Community relations and the foreign economic policies of its member governments. Intensified cooperation and negotiation with the Community require increasing consultation and coordination among EFTA countries. These at first found it useful to discuss together matters officially dealt with by the strictly bilateral joint committees set up in accordance with their respective FTAs. From there it was only a small step to common approaches on certain important matters of cooperation[8] and to the establishment of many procedural mechanisms for regular or *ad hoc* contacts between the EFTA Secretariat, various standing committees and experts from EFTA countries and the relevant Commission services. Since 1985 a High-Level Contact Group from the EFTA countries and the EC Commission has formulated mandates to joint experts' groups on the development of cooperation in their particular fields.[9] The institutional and procedural innovations of the SEA – majority Council decisions and executive powers of the Commission in respect of rules laid down by the Council (Art. 145, para. 3) – contrast sharply with EFTA's institutions and procedures. However, EFTA countries responded to Commission President Delors's call for an open and comprehensive dialogue on the scope and institutional framework needed for closer cooperation. Thus, at their Oslo Summit EFTA heads of government decided 'to strengthen EFTA's decision-making procedure and collective negotiating capacity' while continuing to follow up the Luxmbourg Declaration of 1984. In March 1989 the EEC and EFTA set up a High-Level Steering Group and five working groups with the objective of establishing throughout the EES the free movement of goods, services, capital and persons, as well as closer cooperation in areas going beyond the EC internal market.[10]

EFTA's main objectives

Since its creation in 1960 as a traditional intergovernmental organization, EFTA has assumed three main functions or objectives. The first, the establishment of free trade in industrial products between EFTA countries, was achieved in the late 1960s.

The second, the creation of a more comprehensive European free trade area, was set in train by the conclusion of the FTAs at the same time as two EFTA countries, the United Kingdom and Denmark, joined the EC. EFTA's third function is to develop trade and other economic cooperation between its members within the international framework of organizations such as the GATT and the OECD.

The first objective was realized in accordance with the Stockholm Convention[11] which remains of course the legal basis for relations between EFTA countries. Those of its provisions which were concerned with the establishment of free trade between member states are now outdated, and are of only historical or technical interest today.[12]

However, other provisions remain in force: the 'law-making' principles now relevant to EFTA activities, especially the rules governing competition,[13] and those concerned with EFTA's objectives, organizational structure and institutions, decision-making and the settlement of disputes.[14] Both sets of rules remain of central importance for EFTA internally as well as in relation to the EC. There are essentially two reasons for this, one economic and one institutional.

The first is connected to the new emphasis on the elimination of non-tariff barriers to trade (NTBs) such as state aids after the successful abolition of tariffs and quantitative restrictions. The second, more recent is principally related to the EFTA countries wish to assess their own legal instrumentation before attempting to coordinate their positions vis-à-vis the EC, even though, legally, relations are strictly bilateral. This latter development itself derives from two factors. First there is a tendency in Brussels, apparent at least since the Luxembourg Declaration, to develop free trade relations with the EFTA countries in the same manner, if not exactly in common, and to assume a certain degree of coordination between them. Second, following Jacques Delors's recent 'multilateral cuddle', EFTA countries may have to make up their minds to improve their own decision-making and system of legal remedies as a prelude to possible discussions with the EC on the creation of a multilateral institutional framework for their future relations.[15]

All this goes to show that while the operation of the EFTA free trade area may appear to have developed into a matter of uneventful routine, this function of EFTA is still important, perhaps even increasingly so.

As for the second function, EFTA's role as a centre for information, consultation and coordination on all matters of common interest did not of course cease with the conclusion of the FTAs. Since the FTAs are very similar, even identical in large parts, EFTA countries found it convenient to discuss together and even coordinate their positions vis-à-vis the EC. From a legal point of view the FTAs remain the central, albeit modest, plank in the EFTA countries' increasing network of bilateral treaties with the EC and an important peg for any further development. It is necessary, therefore, to examine their operation before considering in a more speculative manner alternative models for cooperation.

The Free Trade Agreements

Strcture and main content

It will be remembered that the free trade formula of the Stockholm Convention – free trade in industrial products, largely excluding agricultural products, with no obligation to harmonize – left EFTA countries' sovereignty over external economic relations unimpaired. The FTAs have a similar basis. They do not restrict the treaty-making powers of the contracting parties. This means that each EFTA country is free to pursue its own trade policy with no obligation to follow any particular line vis-à-vis third countries or other international organizations. However, since the FTAs are virtually identical, and since EFTA countries share a common interest in their effective functioning, patterns of coordination have emerged. Thus, common EFTA approaches have been adopted on rules of origin, technical barriers to trade, patents and trade-mark law and on economic and monetary questions.

The FTAs contain substantive procedural and institutional provisions, namely rules for the creation of bilateral free trade zones,[16] rules on competition[17] and safeguard clauses.[18] Joint committees administer the FTAs, through recommendations or unanimous decisions, and generally act as forums for consultations.[19] The FTAs have on the whole operated satisfactorily, at any rate with respect to the complete abolition of customs tariffs and QRs on industrial products. Thus by the end of 1983 EFTA's central ambition, the creation of a West European Free Trade Zone, was fulfilled.

The evolutionary clause and beyond

EFTA countries also make extensive use of the so-called evolutionary clauses contained in their respective FTAs. These allow for cooperation to be extended outside the trade area to fields not covered by the FTAs, where a contracting party considers it to be in the economic interest of both partners.[20] This clause has made it possible for a large number of bilateral agreements to be concluded, covering a whole range of second-generation 'post-EFTA' issues.[21] The resulting interlocking network of cooperation now constitutes the major part of the EFTA countries' relations with the EC. However, as will be shown in the next section, serious flaws in the implementation of the FTAs have developed, thus limiting their usefulness.

The uncertain status of the FTAs

The discussion of the FTAs' legal status, both in the constitutional and legal order of the contracting parties – the EC and the EFTA countries – and as instruments for establishing individual rights derived from them, has been prolonged and involved.

The main issue, which has attracted most analysis and comment, is the question whether the FTAs are directly effective, so that individuals may cite them in national courts, or whether they are binding only on the EFTA countries and the Community. This question appears dated in relation to Community law. Indeed, despite some confusing European Court of Justice (ECJ) case law, it can be regarded as settled both in EEC law and in international agreements concluded by the Community with third states. Accordingly, an obligation contained in a provision which is 'specific and not subject to any implied or express reservation on the part of the Community is 'capable of conferring on those subject to Community law the right to rely on it before the courts'.[22]

By contrast, the question whether the FTAs are directly effective in the municipal courts of Community and EFTA countries is still relevant today since case law of both the ECJ and the national courts in EFTA countries is insubstantial and inconclusive, as well as divergent in approach and result.

The ECJ for its part has proceeded cautiously. Since the aims and structures of the EEC Treaty are different from those of the FTAs, it at first discounted the possibility of extending its own criteria for the direct effectiveness of treaty provisions to the FTAs.[23] In only one case so far has the ECJ admitted such direct effectiveness, when it accepted the claim by a German importer of Portuguese port wine that Article 21 of the Portuguese FTA prohibits fiscal discrimination against imported spirits.[24]

The situation in the EFTA countries is very much less certain. The legal status of the FTAs depends on the position of international agreements in the national legal order of each EFTA country. The EFTA countries have neither a common court nor even a common official policy as to how to apply and interpret the FTAs. The Scandinavian EFTA countries have not incorporated the FTAs into national law, so no court cases have resulted from them.[25] Only Austria and Switzerland have made the FTAs 'the law of the land', but even there, very few cases have resulted and none of them in fact upheld the direct effectiveness of a provision in the relevant FTA or made even the slightest reference to the pertinent case law of the ECJ, (which accords greater importance to the FTAs than do its EFTA counterparts).[26]

This means a glaring imbalance between the decisions of the ECJ and of EFTA courts for which the FTAs as yet provide no corrective mechanism. The Joint Committees which operate under the FTAs cannot help as they function only as bureaucratic administrative organs whose decisions cannot be challenged before the ECJ by an individual.[27]

This judicial disequilibrium has profound economic implications. Traders established in the Community may more readily enlist the assistance of the ECJ to enforce provisions of the FTAs than those seeking redress before a national court of the EFTA countries. In practice this means that Community traders can attack trade barriers imposed by EEC countries on industrial goods imported from EFTA countries with a good probability of success. By contrast, corresponding measures taken by EFTA countries against imports from the Community cannot be challenged with any realistic chance of success, in those countries' courts. This 'judicial protectionism' amounts to a non-tariff barrier to trade.[28] EFTA enterprises continue to enjoy access to the large EEC market whereas Community enterprises may effectively be disbarred from access to the small EFTA market.

Proposals for a 'roll-back' of judicial protectionism

Various solutions have been proposed to overcome this intolerable situation, some of a political, others of a legal nature. The suggestion has been made that the supreme jurisdictions of the contracting parties should reach agreement on the interpretation of the FTAs. Another approach might rely on an authentic interpretation by agreement of the contracting parties. This raises intricate questions. In view of disparate court practice, what would be the scope of such an agreement? The Vienna Convention on the Law of Treaties recognizes as relevant subsequent practice 'agreement of the parties', that is, acceptance of a practice without requiring that every party must individually have engaged in the practice.[29] Since the FTAs are bilateral treaties, any such agreement could theoretically be pegged to the 'higher' Community or even any 'lower' EFTA country level of judicial protection. However, an agreement of that kind is inconceivable for several reasons. It would obviously be designed to bring about uniformity, not fragmentation, of standards of interpretation; a common approach by the EFTA countries might, however, be difficult to achieve. Even if a common standard could be established it would still not apply in EFTA countries which have not incorporated the FTAs into their domestic legal system.

The Community, on the other hand, would appear effectively estopped from agreeing to any practice or interpretation which could impair individual rights already declared by the ECJ or presumed capable of accruing under provisions of the FTAs. This argument can be supported by a double analogy. The Vienna Convention on the Law of Treaties precludes the revocation or modification of rights of third countries without their consent where this consent is an intended requirement.[30] While individuals cannot be regarded as associated with the process of subsequent interpretative practice in the same manner as third countries, it is at least debatable whether there is a presumption against the curtailment of individual rights by subsequent practice of contracting parties with respect to specific treaties such as the FTAs from which individual rights may be derived.[31] The second analogy relates to the case law of the ECJ whereby the practice of member states is disregarded if it contradicts the direct effect of provisions of the EEC Treaty.[32] The same practice would appear to be applicable to the FTAs. For all these reasons authentic interpretation of the FTAs is highly improbable and would probably be unworkable.

Another 'political' approach – and probably the most practical solution to the problem of the discrepancies in the interpretation of the FTAs – would be to make the FTAs, or at least some of their provisions, directly effective. Several steps would have to be taken to achieve the required uniformity in the national legal systems of EFTA countries.

First, with guidance from ECJ case law, agreement would have to be reached on which FTA provisions should be made directly effective. Second, these provisions would have to be incorporated into national law, so as to be directly applicable and directly effective if cited by individuals in court actions for the protection of their rights. Finally, these provisions would have to be entrenched so as to enjoy precedence over conflicting national law.

The EFTA countries have in fact begun to examine these questions more closely, notably how suitable provisions in the FTAs, particularly Articles 13 and 20, might be made directly effective: by additional protocols or interpretative guidelines? The same question is raised as to certain provisions of the Stockholm Convention, where equivalent provisions are directly effective under EEC law.[33]

Discussions between experts from the EFTA countries have concluded that the question of the direct effectiveness of treaty provisions in both the EC and the EFTA countries is one of general importance, extending beyond the FTAs to any future agreement, whatever its scope, on the EES.

Under traditional international law, agreements between states were presumed only to establish rights and obligations on the part of states. This presumption may be refuted where the contracting states have the manifest intention of conferring certain benefits directly upon individuals through such international agreements. It has been systematically and permanently reversed by the ECJ as far as Community law is concerned. This bold judicial innovation constituted the first successful common deregulation in the EC more than twenty years before the White Paper. It undoubtedly forms part of the legal *acquis communautaire* to which EFTA countries must adapt.

New machinery for the avoidance and settlement of disputes

Would a common mechanism for the settlement of disputes provide a practical alternative? It must be recalled in this connection that in the preliminary negotiations on the FTAs, the EFTA countries expressed a wish to include arbitration clauses. This request was rejected by the Community on the ground that it would interfere with the exclusive right of the ECJ to interpret all Community law. This means that even if EFTA countries could reach agreement among themselves on a common court or institution to interpret the FTAs, there would still be two jurisdictions and no guarantee for individuals affected by the FTAs as to which would apply.

The fact remains that the contracting parties to the FTAs have pledged themselves to refrain from 'any measure likely to jeopardize the fulfilment of the objectives of the Agreement and to take any general or specific measures required to fulfil their obligations under the Agreement':[34] a commitment which, as has been shown, has yet to be implemented.

The Luxembourg Declaration and beyond

Areas and method of cooperation

In the Joint Declaration of Luxembourg, ministers from the EFTA countries and the EC Commission agreed to 'continue, deepen and extend cooperation within the framework of and beyond the FTAs' and to create a 'dynamic European Economic Space'. EFTA ministers for their part decided 'to further consolidate free trade' and to promote 'progress in other areas of cooperation with the EC'. Thus, the bilateral relations of EFTA countries with the EC based on the FTAs and other bilateral arrangements acquired an additional multilateral flavour.

Cooperation was to be intensified in the 'classic' fields;[35] to these were added entirely new fields of intergovernmental cooperation such as research and development, transborder protection of the environment, consumer protection including product liability, and education. Other new areas were added to the list under the impulse of the EC's White Paper on the completion of its internal market.[36]

However, since the multilateral free trade system has no institutionalized organ of its own, a large number of informal procedures were set up for exchanges of views, and contacts between the EFTA Secretariat and some of its subsidiary bodies on the one hand, and the corresponding Commission services on the other; meetings between experts from EFTA countries and from the Commission were also provided for. The most important of these informal groups is the High-Level Contact Group, comprising high-ranking civil servants from the EFTA countries and representatives of the EC Commission; it normally meets twice a year and issues mandates and guidelines for the joint expert groups.[37]

Progress achieved

This is not the place to give a full account of all the work begun, in progress or completed. It must suffice to mention some of the more important results of cooperation[38] before considering certain legal aspects arising from it.

Regarding technical barriers to trade (TBTs), new European standards are being elaborated by CEN and CENELEC under joint EFTA-EC mandates. These bodies also assist in the formulation of new technical and safety requirements, so as to make compatible legislation possible throughout the European Economic Space. Negotiations were begun in September 1988 on an EFTA-EC agreement on the mandatory exchange of advance notification on draft technical regulations. Agreements on the reciprocal recognition of test results and certificates throughout the EC are being prepared.[39]

Since January 1989 new and simplified origin rules on cumulation have been in operation under the FTAs: these permit the use of parts or components originating in any country of the European free trade area. Three conventions must be mentioned here: the convention on the simplification of formalities in trade in goods which introduced the Single Administrative Document (SAD), replacing, from January 1988, some sixty different national documents used between the eighteen countries of the EES; the convention on common transit procedure; and the Lugano Convention of 1988 which created uniformity within the EES regarding the jurisdiction and enforcement of judgments of courts in civil and commercial matters.

In other areas EFTA internal rules are being revised, reinforced and adapted in preparation for specific agreements with the EC. This process will continue, piecemeal and slowly but steadily. EFTA ministers and the former EC Commissioner for External Relations recently reaffirmed the special relationship between the EC and the EFTA countries and the need to achieve further concrete results.[40]

However, such ringing exhortations cannot conceal the fact – indeed are probably indicative – of stagnation in cooperation and a widening gap between political declarations and concrete actions.

The changed outlook

The EC has moved on, invigorated by the White Paper, the Single European Act and, perhaps most importantly, the 'Cassis de Dijon' principle. EFTA countries, on the other hand, remain interested in negotiating parallel and synchronized measures for their relations with the EC to ensure access to a share of the benefits of the single market and to avoid discrimination in the event of a 'Fortress Europe' strategy by the Community. However, in the absence of a common commercial policy, any joint institutional framework for negotiations, and, it must be admitted, uniformity of purpose, EFTA countries have had to make do with their respective FTAs and a string of political expressions of intent and goodwill starting with the Luxembourg Declaration.[41] The limited value of these instruments became all too apparent and prompted EFTA countries to examine, jointly and individually, the whole range of options.

The EC showed an increasing tendency to warn EFTA countries that an enlargement of its cooperation with them could violate GATT undertakings. Already in its White Paper the Commission stated that 'the commercial identity of the Community must be consolidated so that our trading partners will not be given the benefit of a wider market without themselves making similar concessions'.[42] Moreover, according to a communication to the Council of July 1986 and a statement by Commissioner Willy de Clercq at the EFTA ministerial meeting at Interlaken in May 1987, the Commission has accorded absolute priority and unrestricted autonomy to Community integration and requested substantial reciprocity from EFTA.[43]

These EC guiding principles and the complex, cumbersome and slow follow-up to the Luxembourg Declaration as well as Mr Delors's initiative, prompted EFTA heads of government to declare at their Oslo meeting their 'readiness to explore together with the EC ways and means to achieve a more structured partnership with common decision-making and administrative institutions in order to make our cooperation more effective', while stressing their 'common resolve to progress in the present programme of cooperation'.[44]

Selected legal issues raised by the EES

Many legal questions arise in connection with matters on which there is matters at present no agreement among EFTA countries or between EFTA countries and the EC. However, only some of those questions which raise issues of principle or fundamental change will be considered here. Most of them may be classified roughly as procedural and institutional. The reason for this is that as far as the substance of the EES is concerned, EFTA countries, with few exceptions, are ready to accept as a starting-point for negotiations the content of the EC internal market as an *acquis communautaire*.

Selected legal issues

THE RELEVANCE OF ARTICEL XXIV, GATT

Article XXIV sets out the conditions under which customs unions or free trade areas may be exempted from the central GATT provision, the most favoured nation (MFN) obligation. It stipulates that members must eliminate duties and other restrictive regulations with respect to 'substantially all the trade between the constituent territories', and must not increase barriers to the trade of other contracting parties with such territories. During the examination of the FTAs in the GATT, some members of the working party expressed doubt as to whether

Article XXIV authorized a combination of customs unions and free trade areas as agreements between these were not explicitly envisaged in that provision. This challenge was then met by the counter-argument that since free trade agreements between different customs territories were permitted, an FTA between EFTA countries and the Community, each constituting a customs territory, must likewise be permissible. However, one of the reasons for the relative stagnation since the Luxembourg Declaration has been the suggestion put formally and informally by the EC that further measures to strengthen EC-EFTA cooperation would have to take account of the GATT, particularly Article XXIV.

It might be instructive to retrace the presumed line of reasoning with respect to a particular field of cooperation, namely public procurement. Government procurement in the GATT terminology is covered by one of the Tokyo Round MTN Codes, which provides rules for procurement by certain public institutions above a specified value threshold.[45] This code is applicable to the EC and EFTA with the exception of Iceland. EFTA-EC cooperation in this area necessarily aims at extending the liberalization of procurement beyond the scope of the GATT code as far as both institutions and value limits are concerned. The FTAs of EFTA countries do not contain any provision on public procurement.

The argument would appear to be that whereas Article XXIV of the GATT constitutes in respect of 'substantially all trade' an exception from the MFN requirement for the benefit of customs unions and free trade areas, no such exemption seems available for procurement since government procurement under the GATT is not subject to the MFN clause contained in Article I GATT. In principle, therefore, any liberalization of procurement practices beyond those agreed in accordance with the provisions of the code would have to be made available to the products and suppliers of any other party to the code. It would seem to follow that the exception to the MFN standard contained in Article XXIV cannot be cited to justify preferential liberalization of government procurement within a customs union or free trade area. Reasoning along those lines may have been the cause for the Commission's concern over narrow sectoral reciprocity apparently suggested by a document issued by the US Federal Communications Commission in 1987.[46] However, since the MFN obligation under Article II of the GATT code only extends to procurement 'covered' by the code, it would seem that any further liberalization agreed upon between EFTA countries and the EEC beyond that required by the code would not automatically become available to other parties not 'covered' by it.

It should also be noted that neither the US-Israel nor apparently the US-Canada FTA has been challenged in GATT as being in breach of its obligations even though they go beyond the code to some extent. It is difficult to imagine that similar steps in EC-EFTA cooperation would be treated differently in GATT.

THE ISSUE OF RECIPROCITY

A senior US trade official recently articulated some US concerns over EEC protectionism.[47] He pointed out that the EC Commission's proposed 'reciprocity' as a standard for granting third countries access to newly liberalized sectors outside the GATT, particularly in the banking and investment services directives, could be used in a discriminatory manner against US firms seeking entry to the EEC. He regarded reciprocity implying identical treatment in different countries as a troublesome retreat into protectionism, despite its superficial fairness and equitability. Instead he considered the right to national treatment the most effective means to avoid discrimination and to preserve open markets.

The Commission has taken the view that whereas third-country banks with subsidiaries in any EC country are considered Community undertakings upon their incorporation under the terms of Article 58 EEC and may benefit from the right of establishment and the freedom to provide services throughout the Community, this would not apply to third-country credit institutions. In respect of these institutions, therefore, Article 7 of the First Banking Coordination Directive provides that before an authorization can be given to a subsidiary of a non-EC bank to operate, or to a non-EC bank to acquire a share in an already established credit institution, the Commission is required to examine whether all credit institutions of the Community enjoy reciprocal treatment in the third country.[48] Article 7(5) of the Second Banking Directive originally also proposed 'reciprocal treatment': not absolutely identical but equivalent treatment, which is apparently favoured by the Commission in particular cases.[49]

The Commission attempted to allay these concerns when it revealed its official policy on external aspects of the single market on 19 October 1988.[50] It refuted the charge of a 'Fortress Europe' policy in line with the agreement of the Hanover European Council that 'the internal market should not close in on itself' and that the Community 'will seek to preserve the balance of advantages accorded, while respecting the identity of the internal market of the Community'.[51] A commentator recently remarked that what 'reciprocity' means 'is obscure and subjective and, in the end, may be determined simply by what is politically acceptable'.[52] Indeed, even the Commission reassurance appears opaque and it remains to be seen whether its notional reciprocity accords with the GATT definition of 'reciprocal and mutually advantageous arrangements'[53] or with its interpretative rendering now favoured, 'reciprocally advantageous arrangements'.[54] Still the Commission rejects the specific criticism that it favours 'sectoral reciprocity', in the sense of balanced trade in each sector between the Community and each of its partners. It claims that it insists on 'overall reciprocity' the technique used in multilateral negotiations to secure a mutually advantageous balance of benefits for all parties.[55] In June 1989 the Council of Ministers adopted the Second Banking Directive in which the reciprocity requirement had been replaced by a standard of national treatment. In this sector at any rate charges of protectionism have been laid to rest.

EXTENSION OF 'CASSIS DE DIJON' TO EFTA-EC RELATIONS?

In the EEC quantitative restrictions on imports – Article 30 – and exports – Article 34 – and measures having equivalent effect were prohibited from the end of the transitional period save on the grounds permitted under Article 36. Due to the direct effect given to Articles 30 and 36, the ECJ was given ample opportunity to circumscribe permitted exceptions restrictively, and in the 'Cassis de Dijon' case[56] the ECJ declared a minimum alcolhol content for spirits to be a 'measure with equivalent effect to a quantitative import restriction' which did not 'serve a purpose in the general interest, taking precedence over the requirements of the free movement of goods, which constitutes one of the fundamental rules of the Community'.

The Commission has summarized the principle resulting from the ECJ's 'Cassis de Dijon' judgment in a communication to the Council as follows: 'Any product lawfully produced and marketed in one member state must, in principle, be admitted to the market of any other member state'.[57] This amounts to the recognition by member states of the equivalence of national rules or practices governing the production, marketing and utilization of products.

In derogation from this principle, differences between commercial and technical national rules remain admissible – thus limiting the scope of the prohibition of measures of equivalent effect[58] – where they constitute mandatory requirements necessary for the protection of public health, fiscal supervision, the fairness of commerical transactions and the defence of consumers. These must be mandatory requirements, that is they must serve a compelling general interest, must be essential for the purpose to be attained and proportional to the aim to be achieved, and must give the least possible hindrance to trade. The 'Cassis de Dijon' principle is an alternative to, and only valid in the absence of, full harmonization of legislative and administrative provisions of member states which directly affect the establishment or functioning of the Common Market.

Harmonization proved to be a difficult and slow process due in particular to the unanimity requirement for directives envisaged under Article 100 EEC. To expedite matters in view of the 1992 deadline, the SEA introduced majority voting by virtue of Articles 100a and 100b while allowing member states to apply different national provisions even after the adoption of a harmonization measure on grounds of major needs referred to in Article 36, or the protection of the natural environment or the working environment. Thus protective measures which may be retained by member states are much more narrowly defined in Article 100a than those allowed by the ECJ in decisions on measures of equivalent effect under Article 30.

However, under Article 100b the Council may decide, on the basis of an inventory drawn up by the Commission during 1992, that certain 'opted-out' provisions in force in one member state must be recognized as equivalent to those applied by another member state. The 'Cassis de Dijon' principle, consequently, which is based on the ECJ's case law under Articles 30 and 36, will continue to apply in the absence of harmonization, pending and 'without prejudice' to a relevant Council decision.

EFTA products imported into the EC and those in 'free circulation' among EC member states[59] may become subject to the national marketing rules of EC member states. These, like those of the EFTA countries, would be prohibited by Article 13 of the FTAs only to the extent that they directly or indirectly hamper importation, or discriminate, openly or in a disguised way, against imported products in relation to domestic products.[60] Thus EFTA products once in free circulation enjoy the same status as EC products, so that measures which apply equally to domestic and imported products in a non-discriminatory manner would not appear to be prohibited under the FTAs.[61]

The 'Cassis de Dijon' principle, as has been mentioned, is an alternative to full harmonization of measures. But could it operate beneficially under the FTAs and between EFTA countries? The potential attractiveness of a solution encompassing the entire EES is not in doubt. However, there are numerous obstacles which are greater even than those that have led to the described judicial imbalance between EFTA courts and the ECJ regarding directly effective provisions of the FTAs. The 'Cassis de Dijon' principle is a flexible device in constant evolution. Even if it were possible to affix the growing bulk of case law in Articles 30 and 36 EEC onto the corresponding Articles 13 and 20 FTAs, this would achieve nothing so long as the FTAs do not have direct effect. So far at any rate the EC has not recognized the principle as applicable under the FTAs. Moreover, the 'Cassis de Dijon' principle, which is embodied in that case law, does not have stable and predictable contours, unlike the concept of direct effect.

Under these circumstances, acceptance of the ECJ's case law by EFTA countries is inconceivable. Furthermore, for the principle to apply in the EES as a whole, it would also have to be applied as between EFTA countries, either by means of an appropriate amendment of Articles 10 and 12 of the Stockholm Convention or by some agreed interpretation.[62] Models for additional protocols on the interpretation and implementation of Articles 13 and 20 FTAs and 10 and 12 Stockholm Convention have been disucssed by EFTA experts.

However, the formulation of an extended and legally binding EFTA-EC 'Cassis de Dijon' principle would have to overcome several technical problems. The principle itself is extremely volatile, a moving target in a sense. It would be necessary, yet immensely difficult, to define the scope of the 'mandatory requirements' (e.g. consumer, environmental protection) in view of their considerable policy content. It must also be remembered that in the EC the principle is a corollary of and interacts with harmonization and can be replaced by it.[63] Furthermore, it would appear unlikely that the essential effect of the principle under EEC law· (Articles 30, 36), which is to derogate national provisions, could be secured by agreed interpretations of the Stockholm Convention and of the FTAs. Even if agreement could be reached on agreed interpretations and on the direct effect of the provisions concerned, the question of how to achieve their uniform interpretation in national courts of EFTA countries as well as on the EES level remains open. One might recall the refusal of the ECJ to interpret identical provisions in an identical manner where the treaties concerned either differed in aim, purpose and structure (Kupferberg) or where, more pertinently, one of them lacked a comparable system for the progressive abolition of legislative disparities (Polydor).

In the absence of a common jurisdictional instance between EFTA countries and the EC, one existing but as yet untested device to bring about uniform interpretations might be mentioned here. Protocol No. 2 to the Lugano Convention on the jurisdiction, recognition and enforcement of judgments in civil and commercial matters requires contracting parties to pay 'due account' to the principles laid down by any relevant decisions of courts of other contracting parties, and establishes a system for the exchange of information on judgments of particular importance.[64] However, while such a device might provide a viable medium with respect to clearly defined sectoral agreements, it is doubtful whether it would be equally useful with respect to a vast and growing body of cases in the broad field of national marketing provisions.

In view of these difficulties, the status quo, however unpalatable, appears set to stay for some while yet, or may even be overtaken by a more ambitious, more general and broader approach towards establishing a future EES.

Towards a more structured EES

The Oslo Declaration by EFTA heads of government mapped out several elements of a future more structured partnership with the EC including 'common decision-making and administrative institutions', 'equally strong and reliable surveillance and enforcement procedures and common mechanisms for settlement of disputes' to ensure that treaty obligations receive 'harmonious and uniform application and interpretation throughout the whole of the EES'.[65] This covers a broad range of legal and institutional issues: the following discussion will concentrate on dispute settlement and common decision-making but will also briefly mention mechanisms for uniform interpretation throughout the EES.

DISPUTE SETTLEMENT

Unlike the EC, EFTA has no court of law. Under the FTAs with the EC, political bodies known as joint committees operate under governmental control. They are inaccessible to individuals. However, claims based on directly effective provisions are claims against governmental measures and are best entrusted to independent judicial bodies. Under the impulse of the 'direct effect' of provisions in a deeper, more extended and probably multilateral future cooperation, judicial methods of dispute settlement must be given serious consideration.

Since EFTA has not common court or equivalent body, surveillance and enforcement of agreements cannot be guaranteed to the same extent in EFTA countries as in the EC. A special ministerial-level meeting between the Community, its member states and EFTA states on the internal market obliquely agreed 'that cooperation should take into account the specific institutional and legal structures of the EC and EFTA countries' and that its evolution 'should aim at seeking a balance between benefits and obligations in the interests of all parties concerned'.[66]

Disputes arise when contracting parties adopt irreconcilable positions in fact and law. Any forum, procedure, measure or device which enables them to find a way out may be called 'dispute avoidance' and inevitably involves an element of negotiation. Any dispute settlement system which relies on a rule-oriented, coherent and predictable mechanism should be acceptable to countries which share rule-of-law concepts. Such a mechanism could involve, in descending order of stringency, binding judicial dispute settlement, binding arbitration, non-binding advisory opinions (as in the GATT Working Party and panel procedures) or an agreed practice for subsequent interpretation by the parties so as to secure uniformity. All these have been used variously and in different contexts. There is a great variety of dispute settlement methods in agreements concluded by the EC with EFTA countries and other third countries. While EFTA countries had failed to secure arbitration clauses in their FTAs and had to make do with the 'political' joint committees, some of them were able to obtain such clauses in other more limited agreements with the EC.[67]

Arbitration clauses are also to be found in EC agreements with other third countries, particularly in association[68] or cooperation agreements which either aim at institutional ties or at the establishment of a clearly defined sectoral regime.[69] Whatever the reasons for the EC's earlier refusal to accept arbitration under the FTAs, no principal objection appears currently valid. Indeed the recently initialled agreement with Switzerland on non-life insurance provides for binding arbitration. This certainly deserves careful examination as a possible model for inclusion in the exising FTAs or for multilateralization at the EES level.

The potential range is very broad indeed and could, in principle, be widened further by 'overseas' examples. All that can at present be said with certainty is that the present imbalances in the European free trade system between the EC and the EFTA countries in terms of individual judicial protection and enforcement of treaty provisions need to be eliminated in future negotiations on sectoral or comprehensive arrangements, be they bilateral or multilateral.

COMMON EES DECISION-MAKING?

In preparation for the much-heralded more structured EES, EFTA countries have begun to examine some fundamental principles which they would wish to see embodied in a common EES decision-making mechanism. It is widely assumed that the EES will eventually be largely based on identical substantive rules with respect to the free movement of goods, persons, services and capital, and that these rules will apply in the EC and between EFTA countries as well as in their relation to the EC. The content of the EES will in all probability consist of the *acquis communautaire*, modified in part to accommodate specific concerns of EFTA countries. However, EFTA countries wish to be involved on an equal footing with the EC in decisions on the further development of EES rules and will at least claim an equal right to initiate decisions as well as the right to block binding decisions which would be acceptable to the EC only. The EFTA Working Group on Legal and Institutional Questions has examined certain existing models drawn from a variety of European agreements but has apparently provisionally concluded that none completely satisfies all the principal EFTA conditions.

UNIFORM INTERPRETATION

With respect to the uniform interpretation of provisions, preliminary work is necessarily on surer, less speculative ground. The objective is clearly defined: avoidance of disparities in the application of EES rules and consequently of disputes within the EES. A variety of techniques may be used towards that end including 'direct effectiveness' of provisions and a 'pay due account' obligation imposed on national courts and administrative authorities to take into consideration relevant practice of the other contracting parties. Suffice it to mention just two recent examples of mechanisms to achieve uniformity of interpretation. One is provided by Protocol No.2 of the Lugano Convention[70] under which courts of the contracting parties have to 'pay due account' to each other's practices. Another is provided by the US-Canada FTA whereby the contracting parties may seek to intervene in the proceedings of a domestic court or administrative body where the interpretation of the FTA is at issue and may submit their own views.[71] On the other hand the EC Commission has tried and failed to obtain the right to intervene in national appeals proceedings to ensure compliance with the procedural rules governing the award of public supply and works contracts under the recently adopted Remedies Directive.[72] Uniform interpretation could also be attained by instituting a judicial organ at EES level for the purpose, primarily, of giving preliminary rulings, as under the EC's Article 177 procedure.

CUSTOMS UNION OR FREE TRADE OPTION

Essentially, two options would appear to be available to organize the trade policy of EES participants vis-à-vis third countries: a customs union or a free trade arrangement. Both solutions have found their advocates and detractors among both independent trade policy experts and EFTA governments. Senti, for example, argued in favour of an EFTA customs union as a first step towards the formation of an EFTA-EC customs union and thinks that the minimal tariff changes involved would not lead to significant deflection of trade in EFTA or loss of revenue.[73]

From a legal point of view, a customs union would have to conform to several GATT provisions. First and foremost, according to Article XXIV: 8(a), duties and other restrictive regulations of commerce would have to be eliminated with respect to 'substantially all the trade' between the members of the union who are required, moreover, to apply 'substantially the same' duties to third parties. Although, as is well known, the meaning of 'substantially all the trade' has never been defined in the GATT, it was also stated that this term had to be interpreted to mean free trade in all products,[74] and that the exclusion of a whole sector would be contrary to the spirit of both Article XXIV and the GATT. While past GATT practice was both lenient and inconclusive, a much more critical attitude has appeared recently. Thus, specific doubts were voiced with respect to the general and open-ended exception of agriculture in the Israel-US FTA.[75] Significantly, the Canada-US FTA covers the agricultural sector.

Contracting parties have also expressed different views on the interpretation concerning the assessment of the level of the common customs tariff (para. 5(a)) and on the procedure for compensation due to contracting parties following an increase in or withdrawal of bound duties (para. 6).

A customs union would have no rules of origin but would have a common external trade regime to avoid the deflection of trade. The different GSP schemes of the EC and EFTA countries would have to be aligned. In a customs union, under Article XXIV, other regulations of commerce applied to third parties should also be substantially harmonized. Quantitative restrictions and Voluntary Export Restrictions would need to be accepted by both the EC and EFTA countries. Differences in quotas would lead to the risk of circumvention and would prompt safeguard actions. Economic sanctions against third parties would likewise have to be adopted in common by both EFTA and the EC; otherwise they could be circumvented and corrective measures would have to be taken.

By contrast, in an EES based on a free trade relationship matters would be much simpler. The partners' autonomy over customs tariffs and external trade policy would be preserved while certain improvements, for instance of the rules of origin, would be permitted. Consultations on coordinated external policy matters might be found advantageous.

Negotiating a multilateral framework agreement

The above summary of selected legal issues has indicated some of the shortcomings of the Luxembourg follow-up. Two approaches have emerged in the attempt to avert or minimize the threat of growing marginalization: the private business initiative to purchase an 'admission ticket' and status within the Community; and the public governmental response, sometimes under more or less intense pressure from organized business pressure groups. The first is probably limited to larger business organizations; the latter is infinitely more complex. The present texture of EFTA countries' relations is a mixture of bilateral and multilateral agreements and arrangements. The former are usually in the form of international agreements; the latter in the form of some multilateral conventions[76] and an array of documents designed to provide an *ad hoc* legal structure for the results of the Luxembourg follow-up.[77]

The Joint Declaration of 19 December 1989 by the Community, its member states and the EFTA countries agreed on a radically new approach, namely a comprehensive framework agreement to create an EES.[78] This would be based on the *acquis communautaire* as regards the internal market programme, but would exclude the customs union, common trade policy and the common agricultural policy. EFTA's acceptance of the *acquis* is subject to requests for exceptions, some permanent, others temporary, to be settled in negotiations.

EFTA seeks genuine joint decision-making as regards future EES legislation, while the Community insists on preserving its autonomy. In theory both aspirations could be safeguarded by the conclusion of formal or informal international agreements in respect of *each* common EES measure. In practice this would be cumbersome and wholly unworkable. A new decision–making body might provide a solution, provided its operation was consistent with the EC Treaties.[79] The implementation of an EES agreement and the application of its provisions would require the primacy of EES legislation and its direct effect and uniform interpretation. One approach would be to extend the ECJ's jurisdiction; a separate EES tribunal composed of judges from the Community and EFTA countries, would be an alternative.

Notes

1. For the text of the declaration, see *EFTA Bulletin*, 25(2), (1984), p. 6.
2. Agreements between the EEC and (i) the Republic of Finland, OJ 1973 L 328; (ii) the Kingdom of Norway, OJ 1973, L 171; (iii) the Kingdom of Sweden, OJ 1972 L 300; (iv) the Republic of Iceland, OJ 1972 L 301; (v) the Republic of Austria, OJ 1972 L 300; (vi) the Portuguese Republic, OJ 1972 L 301; (vii) the Swiss Confederation, OJ 1972 L 300. See also Friedl Weiss, 'The Functioning of the Free Trade Agreements', in *L'Avenir du libre-échange européen: Vers un éspace économique européen?*, vol. 2, Collection de droit européen (Schulthess Polygraphischer Verlag AG, 1990), pp. 59–76.
3. Friedl Weiss, 'The European Free Trade Assoication after Twenty-five Years', *Yearbook of European Law: 5, 1985* (Oxford, Clarendon Press, 1986) p. 301.
4. At the meeting between EFTA ministers and the EC Commission in Interlaken on 20 May 1987, Mr Willy de Clercq, EC Commissioner for External Relations and Commercial Policy, outlined three guiding principles for EC-EFTA cooperation on the internal market: Community priority goes to its own integration; Community autonomy must not be restricted; there must be a balance of advantages and obligations. For the text of the joint conclusions see, *27th Annual Report of EFTA* (Geneva, 1987), p. 44. See also Club de Bruxelles, *The European Single Market* (Brussels, 1988).
5. White Paper on Completing the Internal Market, COM (85) 310 final, 14 June 1985, para. 219; SEA, OJ L 169, 29 June 1987. See also Emile Noel, 'The Single European Act', *Government and Opposition*, 24 (Winter 1989); N. Forwood and M. Clough, 'The Single European Act and Free Movement – Legal Implications of the Provisions for the Completion of the Internal Market', *European Law Review* 11(6), (1986), p. 383.
6. See Weiss, 'The European Free Trade Association after Twenty-five Years', pp. 301–17.
7. These are: the Consultative Committee, the Committee of Trade Experts, the Committee of Origin and Customs Experts, the Committee on Technical Barriers to Trade, the Economic Committee, the Budget Committee, the Committee of Members of Parliament of the EFTA Countries, the Joint EFTA-Yugoslavia Committee, the Working Group on the Liberalization of Trade in Fish, and the Group of Legal Experts. (Council Decision No.6 of 1987, 26 June 1987.)
8. Simplification of rules of origin, technical barriers to trade, patent and trade-mark law, border controls and customs documentation, anti-dumping practice, public procurement, research and development.
9. Mandates or guidelines covered the following areas: technical barriers to trade, rules of origin, public procurement, anti-dumping practices, quantitative export restrictions, R&D, environment, state aids, education, intellectual and industrial property rights, indirect taxation in cross-border traffic, product liability.
10. Working Groups on: the free movement of goods; the free movement of services and capital; the free movement of persons; the flanking and horizontal policies (R&D, environment, consumer protection, company law, economic and social cohesion, education, social policy aspects, citizens' Europe, tourism, small and medium–sized enterprises); legal and institutional questions.
11. Convention establishing the European Free Trade Association, vol. 370 United Nations Treaty Series 3; HMSO Cmnd. 906; for a detailed analysis, see Weiss, 'The European Free Trade Association after Twenty-five Years'.
12. Provisions on: (i) the elimination of customs duties and quantitative restrictions (Articles 3, 8, 10, 11); (ii) the definition of product origin and deflection of trade (Articles 4, 5).
13. To the extent that these measures frustrate the benefits of free trade, EFTA's rules of competition prohibit: (i) government aids (Article 13); (ii) discriminatory procure-

ment practices by public authorities and enterprises (Article 14); (iii) restrictive business practices (Article 15); (iv) restrictions on the establishment of enterprises (Article 16). With respect to all the 'rules of competition' the Council had adopted an agreed interpretation and procedures. For details, see Weiss, 'The European Free Trade Association after Twenty-five Years', pp. 300ff.

14. Articles 1, 2, 31, 32, 33.
15. Address by the Commission President to the European Parliament on 17 January 1989.
16. Articles 3, 6, 7, 13, 18, 19; subject, in a manner comparable to Article 36 EEC, to certain security and other exceptions laid down in Article 20 FTA; see Baldi, 'Das Verbot der Massnahmen gleicher Wirkung wie mengenmässige Einfuhrbeschränkungen in den Freihandelsabkommen EFTA-Staaten-EWG', in Koppensteiner (ed.), *Rechtsfragen der Freihandelsabkommen der Europäischen Wirtschaftsgemeinschaft mit den EFTA-Staaten* (Wien, Orac, 1987), pp. 159f; Articles, 6, 7 EFTA concern the same group of measures as Article 12 EEC; cf. Case 37 and 38/73, Social Fund for Diamond Workers, consideration 21, [1973] ECR 1623.
17. Article 23 FTA.
18. Article 21 permits measures which a contracting party considers necessary to protect its essential security interests, trade in military equipment or war materials, research and development, and production indispensable for defence purposes in time of war or serious international tension. Article 22 covers failure by a contracting party to fulfil its obligation under the Agreement; Article 24, problems caused by disparities of customs duties; Article 25, dumping; Article 26, serious sectoral or regional difficulties; Article 28, serious balance of payments difficulties.
19. Article 29 FTA. For a detailed analysis of these mechanisms, see P. Luif, *Österreichische Zeitschrift für Aussenpolitik*, 3–4 (1983), p. 139.
20. E.g. Article 32 of the Austrian FTA; only the Finnish FTA does not contain such a clause.
21. Relevant agreements are either formal or involve informal exchanges of information and views. Trade-related matters dealt with by way of bilateral agreement include: science and technology, research and development, transport, energy, industrial policy, protection of the environment, consumer protection, telecommunications, public procurement, state aids, insurance and trade in fish and agricultural products. For a discussion and classification of these agreements, see F. Blankart, *EFTA Bulletin*, 19(5) (1978), p. 9.
22. Case 87/75, Bresciani [1976] ECR 129, para. 25, 142.
23. Case 270/80, Polydor v. Harlequin Record Shops [1982] ECR 329.
24. Case 104/81, Hauptzollamt Mainz v. C.A. Kupferberg, [1982] ECR 3641.
25. Bernitz, 'Effects of the EEC FTAs from the viewpoint of the EFTA countries', in Sundstrom, Joutsamo, Sund, Loikkanen (eds), *EEC Law and Nordic Commerical Relations with the Communities* (Helsinki, 1985), pp. 317, 320.
26. 'Austro-Mechana', [1984] 2 CMLR 626–39; Adams v. Staatsanwaltschaft des Kantons Basel-Stadt, [1978] 3 CMLR 480–90; Bosshard v. Sunlight, [1980] 3 CMLR 664–75.
27. Case 53/84, Stanley George Adams v. Commission [1986] 1 CMLR 506.
28. Jacot-Guillarmod, 'Judicial Protectionism: Legal Fate or Political Challenge to Free Trade in Europe?', *EFTA Bulletin*, 4 (1985), pp. 8, 9.
29. Article 31(3) (b) of the Vienna Convention on the Law of Treaties.
30. Article 37(2).
31. Ress, 'Die Bedeutung der nachfolgenden Praxis für die Vertragsinterpretation nach der Wiener Vertragsrechtskonvention', European University Institue Colloquium Papers, Doc. IUE 125/86 (COL 64), 25.
32. Case 43/75, Second Defrenne Case, [1976] ECR 481.

33. Article 10 on quantitative import restrictions (cf. Article 30 EEC); Article 12 on exceptions (cf. Article 36 EEC).
34. Article 22 Swiss FTA.
35. Simplification of origin rules; liberalization of public procurement; the replacement of anti-dumping practices by competition rules; the prohibition of export restrictions; the elimination of trade distorting state aids; the protection of intellectual and industrial property rights and the creation of identical rules in EFTA and in relation to the EC to those in operation among EC countries by virtue of the 1968 Brussels Convention.
36. Other areas are: indirect taxation in cross-border traffic, financial services, a common EEC-wide transport policy. See generally, B. Hurni, 'EFTA-EC relations: aftermath of the Luxembourg Declaration', *Journal of World Trade Law* 20(5) (1986), pp. 497ff.
37. Weiss, 'The European Free Trade Association after Twenty-five Years', pp. 320–1.
38. For a detailed summary, see *EFTA Bulletin de Presse*, 3/89, 15 February 1989.
39. For further details see Friedl Weiss, *Yearbook of European Law: vol. 9, 1989* (Oxford, Clarendon Press, 1990).
40. Meeting in Geneva in November 1988, see *EFTA Bulletin de Press*, 3/89, 15 February 1989.
41. The Luxembourg Declaration – fn.1 – was followed by the Visby Declaration of Heads of EFTA Governments and Ministers of 23 May 1984, *EFTA Bulletin*, 25(2) (1984) p. 1; joint press communiqué of the meeting of EFTA ministers and the EC Commission in Vienna, 10 May 1985, *25th Annual Report*, March 1986, p. 49; Joint Conclusions of the meeting of EFTA Ministers with the EC Commission in Reykjavik, 5 June 1986, *26th Annual Report*, March 1987, p. 54; Interlaken ministerial meeting, 14–15 December 1987, *27th Annual Report*, March 1988, p. 47.
42. Para. 19.
43. See Note.4 above; the same theme was echoed in the Brussels Joint Declaration of 1989; see Note 66 below.
44. Oslo Declaration, para. 9 and *EFTA Bulletin, 15(2) (1989), p.4.*
45. *26 Basic Instruments and Selected Documents (BISD) 33 (1980).*
46. This document is entitled *Notice of Enquiry and Proposed Rule-making on Regulatory Policies and International Telecommunications*; see Green Paper on Telecommunications, COM (87) 290 final.
47. Club de Bruxelles, *The European Single Market*, 2.3., 2.4.
48. Ibid., 3.144; Directive 77/780/EEC of 12 December 1977, OJ L 322/30.
49. Proposals for a Second Banking Directive of 16 February 1989 amending Directive 77/780/EEC, COM (87) 715 final, OJ C84/1 (1988).
50. Club de Bruxelles, *The European Single Market*, 2.14.
51. Ibid., 2.16.
52. E. Dell, 'Of Free Trade and Reciprocity', *The World Economy* (1986), p. 125.
53. Preamble, para. 3.
54. D. Dicke, 'Non-reciprocal Treatment', in D. Dicke (ed.), *Foreign Trade in the Present and a New International Eonomic Order* (Fribourg, University Press, 1988), pp. 110, 111.
55. Club de Bruxelles, *The European Single Market* 2.18.
56. Case 120/78, [1979] ECR 649; for an excellent concise discussion, see Jacot-Guillarmod, 'How Far Should the 'Cassis de Dijon' Principle Developed in the Case Law of the European Court of Justice Be Introduced into EC-EFTA Relations?', in Mary Robinson and Jantier Findlater (eds), *Creating a European Economic Space: Legal Aspects of EC-EFTA Relations* (Dublin, Irish Centre for European Law, 1990), pp. 193ff.
57. Communication from the Commission concerning the consequences of the

judgment given by the Court of Justice on 20 February 1979 in Case 120/78, OJ C256/2, 1980.

58. Article 30 EEC Treaty.
59. Article 9(2) EEC; such products are 'definitely and wholly assimilated to products originating in member states'; cf. Case 41/76 Donckerwolcke v. Procureur de la République, [1976] ECR 1921, 1944; see also confirmation in Case 119/78 [1979] ECR 975.
60. Article 13 FTA is virtually identical in wording to Article 30 EEC and may yet not be interpreted in the same way; cf. Case 104/81 'Kupferberg', [1982] ECR 3641, paras 29, 30.
61. Articles 13 and 20 FTAs have not been interpreted in this way.
62. See the interpretations to various Articles of the EFTA Convention: Article 13 on governmental aids, *EFTA Bulletin*, 7(7) (1968) p. 17; 1966 Lisbon Agreement on Article 14 on the practices of public undertakings, *EFTA Bulletin*, 8(2), (1967) p. 2; two reviews of Article 15 on restrictive business practices of 1965 and 1968, *EFTA Bulletin*, 8(5), (1967) p. 4, *EFTA Bulletin*, 3(9) (1968) p. 8; Bergen Agreement, *EFTA Bulletin*, 7(8) (1966), p. 11; and see Weiss, 'The European Free Trade Association after Twenty-five Years', pp. 300, 301.
63. Articles 100, 100A EEC Treaty.
64. The Lugano Convention will apply between the EFTA countries and between the EC and EFTA countries. It is almost a replica of the Brussels Convention of 27 September 1968 on jurisdiction and the enforcement of judgments in civil and commercial matters, OJ C 97/2, 12 April 1983. See Ole Lando, 'Comparative Aspects of the Jurisdiction Rules of the Brussels and Lugano Conventions', in Robinson and Findlater (eds), *Creating a European Economic Space*, p. 117.
65. Oslo Declaration, paras 9, 14, *EFTA Bulletin*, 17(2) (1989), pp. 4ff.
66. Joint Declaration of Brussels, 2 February 1988, para.3, *28th Annual Report of EFTA* (1988), 31, 32.
67. E.g. The Fisheries Agreements between the EEC and Finland (OJ C 69/6, 13 March 1979), and Sweden (OJ L 226/2, 29 August 1980) but not that with Norway of the same day; cooperation agreements on thermo-nuclear fusion between EURATOM and Switzerland (OJ L 242/78, 4 September 1978) and Sweden (OJ L 162/76, 23 June 1976).
68. Under Article 67 of the former Association Agreement with Greece of 9 July 1961, the parties could agree to submit a case to the ECJ, any other court or an *ad hoc* arbitration court, OJ L 26, 18 February 1963; cf. also for a comparable provision, Article 25 of the Association Agreement with Turkey, OJ L 217, 29 December 1964.
69. See e.g. agreements with Algeria, Morocco and Tunisia, OJ L 263–265, 27 September 1978.
70. Convention on Jurisdiction and the Enforcement of Judgments in Civil and Commercial Matters, 16 September 1988, OJ L 319/9, 25 November 1988; see also Note 68 above.
71. Agreement of 2 Januray 1988, in force since 1 January 1989; Article 1808.
72. Europe, 17 June 1989. Council Directive 89/665/EEC on the coordination of the laws, regulations and administrative provisions relating to the application of review procedures to the award of public supply and public works contracts, OJ L 395/33, 30 December 1989.
73. R. Senti, *Ausbau der wirtschaftlichen Beziehungen zwischen EFTA und EG* (Zurich, Swiss Federal Institute of Technology, 1986), pp. 16ff.
74. See Working Party Reports in BISD 18S/164; 21S/79, 80; 27S/132.
75. 34S/58, para. 21.
76. The SAD Convention; the Convention on the Common Transit Procedure; the Lugano Convention on Jurisdiction and the Enforcement of Judgments in Civil and

Commercial Matters 1988; the EFTA Convention on the Mutual Recognition of Test Results and Proofs of Conformity as a basis for later EES-wide sectoral arrangements.

77. E.g. EFTA-EEC bridging arrangement on draft technical regulations; draft articles regarding export restrictions; revised EFTA draft rules on public procurement and bilateral transparency agreements; draft EFTA-EC agreement on combating counterfeit trade.
78. Cf. *EFTA Bulletin*, 4 (1989), 1 (1990), p. 5.
79. The limits of the Community's power to create such bodies have been spelled out by the European Court of Justice in the Opinion 1/76, *European Laying-up Fund for Inland Waterway Vessels*, [1977] ECR 741.

18 Conclusions

Helen Wallace and Wolfgang Wessels

The European Community (EC) and the members of the European Free Trade Association (EFTA) are caught in a dilemma. What had originally promised to be a rather useful but mundane process of gradual adjustment to consolidate the wider West European market has become charged with high politics. For the EC and its members a special deal with EFTA can no longer be kept insulated from either the EC's internal processes of political evolution or the new challenge of responding to its neighbours to the East. For the EFTA countries the dialogue about the European Economic Space (EES) was to have been a historic, but painless, reconciliation of their inhibitions about supranationalism with the realities of economic interdependence. Instead the ground has suddenly changed under their feet, since they face an EC that may be altering fundamentally in character and they risk being sidelined by the exciting developments elsewhere in Europe.

Neither group of countries was prepared for this dilemma and neither had a well-established set of conceptions from which to proceed. The EES negotiations were to have been straightforward in principle, however tricky on individual points of substance or procedure. Each side thought it had a fairly clear idea of the probable outcome, although of course individual participants had their own particular views on what could and should be agreed. The negotiations were to have been well under way by mid-1990 so that the EES could be in place by January 1993 and further enlargement of the EC deferred, with the possible exception of an accession negotiation with Austria. Instead, as we have seen, it has taken a long, long time to move from exploratory discussions and positioning to the heart of the 'real' negotiation. There have been uncertainties and confusion on all sides, with overall objectives and interests poorly defined, and, not surprisingly therefore, detailed strategies and key negotiating hands left in a muddle. The central question that has lain on the table, though barely articulated, has been whether the EES concept floated in the mid-1980s can hold up in the context of a Europe in flux and a process of secular transformation across the continent.

The production of this volume of essays has both suffered and benefited from these confusions. What started as a book with a rather tidy format, focused on the EES and its surrounding political and security context, has become a set of commentaries and reflections about a Western Europe and a range of West European countries struggling to adapt to the fluid dynamics of the continent in which they are located, while also coming to terms with a global economy which respects neither the borders of the EC nor the parochialisms of Europeans. The chapters on both countries and policy issues reflect this turmoil and can provide only interim assessments of the directions in which West European economic and political integration may be moving. However, in the course of this intellectual exercise all of the contributors have been forced to confront some old orthodoxies and to find many of them wanting. This has made the exercise interesting and at the same time frustrating.

This concluding chapter cannot resolve all of the underlying conundrums, nor can it proffer a clear set of unifying judgments. The analysis that follows seeks instead to draw out of the empirical and evaluative material earlier in the volume some reflections on how the EES debate has developed, what scope there may none the less be for recasting the EC/EFTA relationship, where the sensitive points lie for both EC and EFTA countries and what contribution a renewed partnership between them might make to the emerging constellation of the new Europe. One constant theme is the centrality of the EC, both economically and politically, to the redefinition of the transnational framework of that new Europe. Whether and when the EC enlarges its membership, and whether by full or by partial forms of membership, will be one of the crucial questions of the 1990s. The dialogue with the EFTA countries, both collectively and individually, provides a fascinating excursion into some very big issues about Europe, and not only Western Europe.

What are the stakes for EFTA?

The prior question, however, remains whether it matters or not if the EES succeeds or fails. As earlier chapters on both EFTA countries and some of the relevant policy issues make crystal clear, it matters greatly to *all* of the EFTA countries that some new form of accommodation is found with the EC. Their dependence economically on the EC as a partner and supplier is great and the alternatives are simply non-existent. Their vulnerability to the extraterritorial impact of EC legislation is beyond question, and the patchwork of free trade agreements (FTAs) and supplementary bilateral agreements cannot possibly keep pace with the volume or content of new EC rules. Although there is little evidence of deliberate intent by the EC authorities to discriminate against their EFTA partners, the intention does not have to be present for the impact to be felt. Much of that dependence on the part of the EFTA economies is hooked irretrievably to the fortunes of the German economy – a benign dependence that presupposes that the German economy will continue to perform well, but a dependence matched by little direct influence. Those EFTA-based companies that have the scale, resources and product-base to do so have already voted with their feet by establishing their presence within the borders of the EC as regards both local markets and the regimes to which they will be subject.

The dependency is not only economic. To participate on reasonably equal terms with EC economies implies wide-ranging policy convergence and thus bites into both domestic political autonomy and difficult choices about social and environmental values. It constrains economic policy vis-à-vis the rest of the world. No neat boundaries separate measures of economic liberalization and effective competition from the rest of the body politic. But the political impact of the EC goes much further. By and large the EFTA countries have been spectators only at the scenes of reform in Central and Eastern Europe, with the exception perhaps of Austria and Finland, where history and geography have preserved at least seats in the front row. Yet their future policies and political orientation are bound up with the reshaping of Europe and the refashioning of the Atlantic Alliance. The EC is a leading actor in the process. The governments of the EFTA countries (though not through the EFTA framework) have been involved at the margins and recruited as extras for the G-24 exercise in channelling economic aid; they have voices in the CSCE discussions. But no one else needs to know what their views are before acting. If they were more closely affiliated to the EC, there would be more chance to have a louder voice, to be routinely consulted and gradually to exercise a measure of influence on the outcome.

The asymmetry of power between the EC and the EFTA group is clear. It is not, however, new. Some within the EC already caustically observe that the members of the EFTA group have done very well out of being economic and political free-riders, pulled along in the slipstream of EC economic integration, yet able to maintain cherished national profiles and practices, and four of them (not Iceland and Norway, which are NATO members) secured by the political and military burdens undertaken by others. Indeed, for the four neutrals a key power and basis of sovereignty was precisely that possibility of opting out of the alliance structure and of maintaining a separate and neutral profile.

Whatever the force of such observations – and they would be contested vigorously within EFTA – opinion in the EFTA countries has become increasingly intolerant of the consequences of the asymmetry, especially in the business and financial communities. But it goes further: Iceland and Norway used to be able to derive political dividends from their positions as Alliance members in strategically important areas, but NATO is being recast and the Soviet threat is much reduced; the four neutrals used to be able to argue that their decisions to stand back from East/West confrontation benefited Europe as a whole, but neutrality policies seem so much less relevant now.

So the free-rider or go-it-alone option now looks much less relevant or appealing than it did. The risks of political and economic marginalization look much higher. The status quo of FTAs with the EC, supplemented by bilateral arrangements, is almost certainly inadequate, although the Swiss – with by far the most economic leverage among the EFTA group – may find it has a continuing appeal. The options available that would meet both the gaps in the old agenda of economic integration and the new agenda of political transformation of the continent boil down to a choice between something like the EES and applications for accession as full members of the EC.

What are the stakes for the EC?

The asymmetry outlined above makes it look as if all the arguments flow in one direction; that EFTA countries need accommodation with the EC much more than the EC needs to stretch its own thinking to devise a new and qualitatively different relationship with EFTA and its members. Indeed much of the evidence of the discussions between the two since that famous Luxembourg Declaration of 1984 would seem to reinforce such an analysis. But the assumptions need to be questioned a little more closely than that. The standard argument of the EFTA countries about their relevance to the EC rests on the large market and the positive trade balance that they provide. The argument is impeccable in substance, but weak in political cogency, since it would be unthinkable for the EFTA countries to deny market access on a systematic basis. Indeed their governments are in any case beginning to open up access even in many previously protected sectors (notably services) in response to global, as well as EC, pressures. It is hardly surprising, therefore, that so far the EC has not felt itself to be under real pressure from the EFTA camp.

So we need to look more widely. The most frequently deployed argument within the EC is that a new partnership deal with EFTA is infinitely preferable to an immediate queue of applications for accession from the EFTA countries. Indeed some of the initial EC, and particularly European Commission, enthusiasm for the EES had much to do with a desire to head off the Austrian application and to deter others. The strategy has not worked: the Austrians refused to be deflected; the Maltese and Cypriots have followed suit; there is an active and increasing constituency of support for membership applications in other EFTA countries; and the Czechs and Hungarians have signalled pretty clearly that their turns will follow soon. So enlargement is on the EC agenda whatever happens to the EES. The issues have perhaps become more of timing than of principle. An agreed EES now could almost certainly delay further membership applications from other EFTA countries and could perhaps obviate the pressures to open negotiations with Austria quickly. In other words, it would buy everyone time by a deliberate experiment in constructing a halfway house, more than an FTA-plus, but less than full membership.

Why does time need to be bought? The EC stands poised for an attempt at political and policy reinforcement, with Intergovernmental Conferences convened to debate economic and monetary union and political reforms, and it faces major responsibilities for underpinning German unity and aiding reforms in Central and Eastern Europe. An enlargement debate would be a distraction, but it would be more than that. It would require the EC and its members to take positions on the optimum size of the EC, on the core policy content – further security cooperation in or out? – and on the viability of its institutions for a much larger membership. These are not issues that are likely to be easily resolved by over-hasty responses. It may well be that the EC is condemned both to widen and to deepen, but not necessarily rapidly. Indeed it may not be in the interests of Europe, West or East, that the EC strain itself too far or too quickly to produce a definitive answer to so testing a question.

There are some signs too that attitudes within EC member states towards further enlargement and deepening of the EC are beginning to take shape. Mrs Thatcher has, for example, argued that a wider but looser EC would be desirable. Chancellor Kohl seems to favour some enlargement, but accompanied by the emergence of an inner hard-core group of really committed integrationists. French views on enlargement have been opaque. The Benelux countries have rather resisted any notion of early enlargement, wishing to protect the EC's identity. A Pandora's box of contentious views could very easily have its lid removed. But the status quo may no longer be an option for the EC either. Agreement on an EES would enable the EC to test the opportunities and the limits of a restructured partnership with the EFTA group, while also clarifying its thinking about the new relationships to be forged with Central and East European countries. There could be merit, too, in building into the partnership between the EC and EFTA a commitment to share ideas and resources as regards the short-to-medium term needs of those other Europeans.

There are other external reasons, too, for forging closer links between the EC and EFTA. The international regimes for managing the global economy are under severe test, as the final stages of the Uruguay Round have shown. The US administration is keen to develop new links with the EC, and the Japanese would like to broaden their relationship with Western Europe. EC and EFTA interests in the underlying issues of the international political economy are largely complementary, but have no collaborative focus. So far the emphasis of the EES debate has been on intra-European questions, whereas the external dimension remains to be explored. To the extent that the EC wishes to maximize its influence in wider international arrangements it could find helpful the buttress of EFTA alignment with its policy positions.

All of these points suggest that there may be more at stake for the EC in its dialogue with EFTA than has yet been admitted in the narrow and 'take-it-or-leave-it' attitude that it has so far adopted. The question is, however, whether so much is at stake that it may be worth the while of the EC to think outside the established orthodoxies of its relationships with other partners.

The Community's habits of partnership

In dealing with the EC, EFTA governments have to take into account the Community's record in developing an international profile, with a range of institutions, procedures and instruments for handling its relations with the outside world. Over the last thirty years the EC has created a variety of legal instruments and highly differentiated and complex procedures. Since the two Association Agreements with Greece and Turkey in the early 1960s the EC has moved on to become an international actor with a considerable range of activities and global relationships. The EC governments have also created European Political Cooperation (EPC), a framework for close cooperation on issues of general foreign policy, which is now tasked to develop into a 'European foreign policy' under the terms of the Single European Act (SEA) and perhaps to be reinforced by the Intergovernmental Conference. The EC governments have adopted declarations on all-important world events of the last twenty years. So far the hard-core security questions have been excluded, as distinct from the broad political and economic aspects.

EFTA countries need to take into account these established patterns as the relevant experiences and 'organizational memory' of the Community. The present *acquis* in external relations and European foreign policy-making is not a strait jacket that would determine all the possibilities, but it sets the basic orientation for any new relationships. By reviewing these experiences and history of these relationships, we can identify several institutional options for managing the EC/EFTA relationship.

A privileged partner?

The key question is whether there is a privileged place for the EFTA group, in whatever form the EES might take, with a role for EFTA as an organizational partner? Or whether an agreement would be struck essentially with individual EFTA governments? The spectrum of theoretical possibilities ranges from the status quo to EC enlargement. The EES concept rests on the assumption that neither extreme is a real option, or at least that it would be better to aim for an agreement that is deliberately at neither extreme. Much of the discourse on the EC side has focused on the challenge to EFTA to establish itself as a 'second pillar', able to act as a permanent interlocutor of the EC, not only to negotiate the EES, but also subsequently to share in managing it. Views within EFTA have varied from the widespread recognition that together the EFTA countries had more chance of winning a successful conclusion to the EES negotiation, to the protagonists of sustained EFTA solidarity, most insistently the Finns. We recall here the essence of each theoretical option, even though much of the debate has focused on a particular variant. But, since it is clear from those discussions (see further below) that the shape of a sustainable agreement has been hard to identify, some of the discarded options could some back into play.

Status quo plus

In a 'status quo plus' version of the EES the original legal framework and basic procedures of EC/EFTA relations would continue to exist. The need for more exchanges of information would be met by organizational improvements. The meetings of the High-Level Contact Group could be streamlined and perhaps more meetings could be held between the Commission and EFTA ministers. The number and quality of bilateral consultations between the Community and individual EFTA countries on specific areas of common iterest would also be increased. The process would be inductive, incremental, sectoral and reactive to what the EC does internally. This would in effect be to revert to the format set in train by the Luxembourg Declaration of 1984.

This option requires a degree of coherence within EFTA, but not a radical transformation. The approach could be fine-tuned to the needs of each EFTA country and might also look 'comfortable' and easy for the EC. The EFTA countries would broadly retain their decision-making autonomy, but continued dependence on EC bargaining and legislation would limit their influence. The issues embraced in the concept of an EES would almost certainly still not be dealt with adequately. Within the Community the debate about whether the EFTA countries were carrying a 'fair' share of the burden of responsibility for economic adjustment would be likely to increase and thus inhibit the willingness of the EC and some EC countries to go ahead in exploiting such a framework to the full.

A solemn declaration of partnership

This formula has been used by the EC in dealing with other regional groups. EFTA and the EC could combine to formulate common guidelines in the form of a political declaration, which would document their intention to improve cooperation. The internal legal procedures inside both groups would not be touched, but the degree of 'soft' cooperation in all phases of the decision-making and decision-implementation cycle would be increased. A summit of all EC and EFTA governments could conclude such a declaration – as a version of the Luxembourg Declaration with more political authority. Such a step could facilitate a more coherent enumeration of items to be addressed and the principles for tackling them. The issue of reciprocity, could, for example, be included; and cooperation could extend to subjects beyond strictly EC items to say EPC or monetary cooperation in the EMS context. The conclusion of such a declaration would need careful preparation and a clarification of objectives on both sides. The declaration might be valid for a certain period, say until 1992, and then 'renegotiated' for a further period of four of five years, or alternatively made into a more formal agreement.

As far as the procedures are concerned, the autonomy of each side would be respected, EC/EFTA meetings would be intensified, exchanges of information would become '*de facto*' mutual consultation and an informal 'regime of a common management' for the EES would emerge. EC relations with EFTA would become less and less an external affair. The declaration could include new procedures: regular meetings of the EFTA and EC Council presidencies to exchange views; informal or even formal EC/EFTA meetings at a ministerial level in different compositions (e.g. ministers responsible for the environment) to pursue sectors of common interest, thus establishing the sectoral councils envisaged in the FTAs; a 'committee for the management of the declaration' would be created at the highest official level, i.e. the members of COREPER for the EC and their EFTA equivalents, meeting frequently in order to monitor the implementation of the declaration; some form of arbitration for the settlement of disputes, based presumably on international law, rather than linked to the special character of Community law; a complementary formula might even be envisaged for EFTA consultations with EPC; and a joint EC/EFTA parliamentary committee could be created.

Agreements with individual EFTA countries would have still to be dealt with as now, but around a stronger collective role for EFTA. The merits of this approach are a stronger say for EFTA countries without too many legal strings attached. It would be necessary for EFTA countries to formulate coherent positions when the common declaration was being prepared *and* applied. The degree of internal coherence would have to be reinforced. The EFTA secretariat would also need broader mandates and additional professional staff.

Without 'legal obligations', this option might be pursued without precluding a more binding agreement at a later stage. Given the time constraints in the run up to 1992, this partnership declaration could still be a means of achieving a relationship at a higher level without having to complete negotiations on all the awkward points of substance, and without a long ratification process. By means of such a comprehensive approach it might be possible to find a 'fair' balance of mutual commitments. The EC and EFTA governments might in effect conclude a package deal, thus emulating a key feature of EC negotiating practice. For the EC, this kind of approach might be useful, since it could help to divert the pressures exerted by some EFTA countries. The EC would shows its 'good will' without reducing formally the autonomy of its actions. The experience of the EC with its group-to-group dialogues might be extended without major problems. Third countries outside the EC would have little reason to complain or to ask for similar treatment, which would be a risk with the subsequent options.

Association Agreement under Article 238

Relations with EFTA or EFTA countries could be put on a legal basis according to Art. 238 of the EEC Treaty, which covers association agreements. Art. 41.2 of the Stockholm Convention also permits EFTA as a whole to conclude association agreements, although such an association could be made by the EC with individual EFTA countries. A bilateral approach would have the effect of diffusing the EC's organizational resources and political attention considerably. For the EC bilateral Association Agreements would be only a minor part of its overall system of external relations. A multilateral Association would have a higher profile, but also increase the need for coherence within EFTA. An Association Agreement would need positive endorsement from the European Parliament with an absolute majority.

In effect, the exploratory negotiations about the EES have implied some such form of association, but in so far-reaching a form as to imply a novel form of privileged partnership. Certainly the EFTA group has had in view a formula that goes well beyond any association model yet found in the EC's relations with other partners. Nor have the Eftans simply been dreaming ambitiously. The language of Jacques Delors's invitation of 1989 to a new dialogue implied an innovative approach on the part of the EC and this has been echoed in some EC capitals.

But what would it mean in practice? It would establish a very close interconnection and interpenetration of the decision-making processes of both organizations, with areas of common interests jointly defined and pursued. A legal agreement between both sides, using Art. 238 on the EC side and Art. 41.2 on the EFTA side, would have to set up rules, rights and obligations over the areas of common interests. This 'hard' coordination would cover broad areas of common policies – the four freedoms and agreed corollary policies – and it could be open to progressive extension of shared management.

It could also though not necessarily, stretch to a customs union, as Jacques Delors hinted – no innovation for the EC, which has such an agreement in principle with Cyprus, for example. This would have the clear merit of being 'gattable', that is within the terms of Article 24 of the GATT. It is thinkable that a customs union might apply to goods and services, but not agriculture, as is already acknowledged in the EC/Cyprus Agreement. But it would also require accompanying coordination of external trade policies.

The basis of an EES of this kind would be a shared set of regimes, with common rules even collective legislation, applying in both EC and EFTA countries. This would provide the vehicle for systematically extending the rules of the single market of the EC to EFTA, to the extent that both sides so agreed. It could also provide an umbrella for other shared rules, e.g. for competition policy, and what have become known in the jargon as flanking policies, environmental, social, R&D and such like. Such an arrangement would, it could be argued, amount to quasimembership of the EC for the EFTA countries, but in only some, rather important, fields of activity.

Such far-reaching interpenetration would demand very special and effective institutional arrangements. These would need to apply across the range from policy formulation to policy implementation and enforcement, and to be accompanied by appropriate procedures of legitimation and accountability. Such arrangements might include:

- meetings of the EFTA and EC Council presidencies before each session of the European Council to set a common agenda;
- an EFTA involvement in various of the EC's procedures for legislative decisions, as well as trade-related and industrial cooperation;
- thus necessarily a Commission procedure to consult EFTA experts, as it consults experts from EC members, in preparing draft legislation, with proposals sent to EFTA at the same time that they go to the EC Council and Parliament;
- a fixed timetable for a common EFTA position to be transmitted to the Council and by the Council to COREPER, so that the position of EFTA would be part of the 'dossier' of the working groups of the Council;
- before the Council decision possibly a meeting of a common body, which might be called COREPER III, comprising ambassadors from the EC and EFTA countries, with consultative, but not binding, powers;
- for certain areas, such as trade policy under a customs union, a further element might even be an 'enlarged' Council of Ministers;
- a special mixed parliamentary assembly of the EP and the EFTA parliamentary committee with the procedural power to comment on the work of the EP in areas of common interest and to make statements at the first and second reading of proposals under Art. 149 or on enlargement and association agreements;
- for the control of implementation, special monitoring mechanisms between the Commission and the EFTA Secretariat;
- for binding enforcement and cross-jurisdictions – a major innovation and one of the most difficult elements in this package – either some kind of arrangement between the European Court of Justice and some special EFTA body or a new tribunal; and
- the application of relevant EC legislation in EFTA countries.

These questions have lain at the heart of the EES debate since the Delors-Oslo process was set in train in spring 1989. They are easy to identify in general terms, but have proved extremely hard to turn into concrete and textual form, as we shall see later. There are also two additional points to be made about the scope of such an arrangement. First, there has been some discussion of whether the EFTA countries should or could participate in some way in the resource transfer, thus budgetary, mechanisms of the EC, not least because the cohesion dimension to the internal market is so very important. If so, some budgetary formula would have to be found for which there is no precedent in the EC's history of dealing with associates, since in all previous cases there has been only a one-way relationship for aid from the EC through a financial protocol. Second, and probably more easily, there could be established for areas outside the EC treaty, like EPC or the Trevi Group for internal security, a regular procedure of consultation.

For EFTA, this model would have the advantage of offering a real opportunity to establish procedures for a kind of participation in those decisions that affect them, but without becoming at this stage members of the EC. It would, however, require a commitment from EFTA governments radically to reform EFTA and to adjust some of their own national processes, since the premise at the outset was that EFTA would become a kind of 'second pillar'. It implies an upgrading of the role of the EFTA Secretariat, a willingness to accept a tighter internal decision-making process and to achieve greater cohesion, the adoption of a more rapid response rate to take account of EC timetables, and the adaptation of EFTA and national provisions of an innovative legal character. Without these elements EFTA would not be able to be an effective partner of the EC on the extensive basis that this option presupposes.

Such a strengthening of EFTA would have to be founded on a strategic decision, rather than a pragmatic evolution from the current relationship with the EC. EFTA governments would have to weigh up carefully the pros and cons and carry public opinion at home with their preferred choice. A strengthened EFTA would impose much tougher disciplines and a greater collective identity, thus imposing costs as compared with the present, much looser, arrangements and the existing opportunities to follow bilateral, rather than multilateral, strategies. It would mean a reduction in formal autonomy and decrease the scope for individual room for manoeuvre. For some EFTA countries direct membership might be preferable to the strengthened EFTA concept, as this latter would establish an important *droit de regard*, but not equality in decision-making. EFTA would be the junior partner still and EFTA governments would be engaged in a two-layered process of interest aggregation, first in EFTA and then with the EC, in which necessarily some individual interests would be squeezed. For other EFTA countries such an outcome would be a means of squaring the circle of interdependence and supranationalism.

The benefits for the EC would be more effective and binding outcomes in negotiations with EFTA and a solidly based system of implementation and enforcement. The EC would also be 'rationalizing' an important area of its external relations. However, there would be additional costs: Community 'orthodoxy', so far strictly opposed to any blurring of the autonomy of EC actions and EC law, would have to be revised, and the obligation to joint procedures could slow down EC decision-making. Just conceivably, EC treaty revisions might be needed. There might also be increased pressures from other third countries to achieve a similar *droit de regard*. The Israeli government has said that it wants to match what EFTA achieves. More seriously the US government is after an intense and intimate partnership with the EC. It should also be noted that such an agreement would require some time to set in place. The European

Commission has worked on the basis that any agreement would be by the EC and not a 'mixed agreement' with EC member states as signatories, but much depends on the detailed substance. In any event EFTA countries would have to ratify the EES agreement and in some countries this could require a referendum as well as parliamentary approval.

Full membership of EC and EPC

For EFTA countries full membership is the most honest and clear option. They are able to identify the *acquis communautaire et politique* that they would have to adopt. It should, however, be stressed that to apply for membership is a difficult decision. EFTA countries would be confronted with major challenges, both in terms of substance and as regards the institutional and legal order into which they would have to be integrated. Finally there is an overall political commitment to make. In terms of the specific and concrete substance – especially as entry could take place only after 1992 – there would be rather far-reaching legal and economic adaptation to be achieved by any acceding member countries. Quite often these problems are underestimated in the debate, where it is sometimes assumed that EFTA countries could become EC members without any major problems. However, some of the impacts of 1992 on – let's say – the Federal Republic of Germany are already severe, in spite of its being a founder member of the EC. The adaptation would demand even more radical steps by countries without the experience of EC membership.

As for the institutional and legal impact, classical notions of sovereignty and international cooperation have to be adapted to EC membership. In terms of the overall political commitment implied by 1992, it is broadly understood by EC member governments and political forces in the Community that this is only one set of steps towards a 'European Union,' as endorsed by all Twelve in the preamble of the SEA. This is a vision to which the EFTA countries are much less attuned than even the least enthusiastic among the present EC members. Given the political processes already under way within the EC, with possible Economic and Monetary Union and some political upgrading in view, the threshold that EFTA countries need to reach could soon become much higher.

Then there is the neutrality issue, necessarily of vital concern for some EFTA countries. Already the remit of EPC and the trade policy commitments of the EEC raise difficulties. Any enhancing of EPC in the security domain would again raise problems for the neutrals, at least in principle. However much this may seem to have diminished in relevance over the period since mid-1989 it will not be easy for the EFTA neutrals to jettison a status to which they have adhered for so long and with such insistence. One possible 'solution' would be to permit accession to the EC without (immediate) participation in EPC, although partial versions of membership have never previously been contemplated by the EC.

The EES negotiations

How then have the negotiators from both sides coped in grappling with these options? The short answer is that it has all proved much more testing than either side had probably anticipated. The approach was to divide up the substantive and institutional issues, with different negotiating groups dealing with each cluster. The Commission spoke for the EC, with little direct involvement by the member states at the preparatory stages.The EFTA side made remarkable progress in developing a team approach, but, of course did not go so far as to obscure the profiles and preferences of individual EFTA governments, from the Austrian commitment to seek full membership, to the Swiss determination to ensure that any EES agreement provides demonstrable value-added both substantively and institutionally.

On the details of the four freedoms, EFTA members were asked to identify which parts of the relevant *acquis* would cause them problems and need detailed examination. Their careful efforts to do this meant that the EFTA countries were put through much of the work that would be required of candidates for full membership, not least because it is in practice so difficult to determine what is 'relevant'. In the process, a basic misunderstanding arose, since the problems identified by the Eftans were taken by some in the EC as a list of desired exemptions, rather than a list of topics for further negotiation. Among the most difficult, though not the most important, was the inevitable Icelandic claim for real guarantees of effective market access for its fisheries' products, an aim difficult to square with the Spanish determination to improve access for its huge fishing fleet to the Icelandic coastal seas. This risked becoming an issue of principle for the negotiation as a whole, even though common sense suggests that accommodation should be possible for what would after all elsewhere in Western Europe be treated as the local problem of a small community dependent on a single industry, such as a coal town or a steel town. The EC was also less than forthcoming in some areas, notably some of the 'people' issues that were sensitive within the EC.

The 'flanking' issues proved much more straightforward. The complementarities of interest were perhaps easier to define. The Eftans were increasingly reassured that the EES would not erode their on the whole higher standards of social and environmental provision. Transport issues were tough, because of the special problems of transit through Austria and Switzerland, but those issues would have been there anyway. One tricky point did emerge, namely that the EC rules of competition did not belong with the flanking policies but with the core of the 1992 programme, thus demanding full integration into the EES concept. This was fine in theory, but difficult in practice because of the very direct EC and Commission competence for operating those rules. The dog that kept on failing to bark was the issue of resource transfers: EFTA negotiators were ready to discuss a claim that the Commission seemed not to want to make, because it was too complex and apparently risky in institutional terms. Yet the Spanish government wanted also to ensure that cohesion would be built into the EES, a view in which they had support from the European Parliament.

Far and away the hardest nut to crack was the institutional framework. It had been easy to state at the beginning of the negotiation that each side recognized the 'autonomy' of the other. In practice the Commission, acting for the EC, found it very hard to identify a set of institutional arrangements that would neither erode the EC's autonomy nor be cumbersome and time-wasting. Nice formulas about EFTA access to decision-'shaping', but not decision-making, yielded vagueness and not the precision for which the Eftans had looked. Some of the

EC members were prepared to be more flexible, but it was the Commission's task to protect the overall Community interest on this point. In any case, as the negotiations proceeded, often fitfully, it became clear that many members of the European Parliament were greatly disturbed at any suggestion of an EFTA/EC level of consultation that might both follow and override their constitutionally derived influence on relevant legislation. MEPS supported the EES warmly in principle, but were much cooler when it came to the fine print.

As this book goes to press the real negotiations are due to start after the positioning, which has taken over a year. Whether an EES can emerge as a strong form of EFTA association with the EC remains unclear. The closer the crunch has come, the harder it has been to see the shape of a solution, especially on the institutional issues in which the Commission has been so reticent. What the EC may be able to offer as its maximum may yet prove below the bottom line of many EFTA countries, certainly the Austrians and probably the Swiss, who have consistently stressed the need for effective and not just decorative solutions, hence their repeated references to CEN and CENELEC in which there is a real EC/EFTA partnership that enables coalitions to be struck across the two groups.

It has been difficult to judge how far EFTA governments would be willing to go to accept a framework that would be essentially consultative, rather than one that included joint 'ownership' of shared EES legislation. But EFTA parliaments would have to endorse the EES as well and it has to be assumed that they would not do so lightly, especially if the concomitant requirement were to accept that EC legislation and jurisprudence would, via the EES, become embedded in their own legal systems.

The next steps

Whatever the outcome of this round of negotiations, the EES is not likely to be the end of the story. Far more probably it will prove to be a transition between the old Western Europe, with a robust and magnetic EC and a revived but constrained EFTA, and a subsequent round of reappraisal. A crucial flaw in the debate has been the notion that part of the answer lay in a long-term reinforcement of EFTA as such. The framework has proved remarkably useful to its members as a means of handling collectively a complex negotiation with the EC Commission, always a tough negotiating partner. It would be quite another matter to make EFTA a pale version of the EC. The persisting choices for EFTA members remain whether and when to opt for an application for membership, and whether they will do so individually or collectively. Of course the Austrians have taken their decision on Austrian – i.e. national – grounds, like the British, Danes and Protuguese before them.

If a solid EES proves negotiable and workable, the pressures will be off the campaigners for full membership within EFTA – or at least for a while. But for how long? It would probably have to be a very good agreement from an EFTA point of view for the membership lobbies to abate. Besides, it would only take one sign of EC readiness to open accession negotiations with almost any European country for other Eftans to be under renewed pressure to apply.

However, a solid EES could have a serious existence in the interim, and transitional solutions sometimes acquire durability.

If, on the other hand, the EES negotiations either fail outright or produce only sparse results, the queue of applicants for full membership can be expected to grow, but so too the agonizing. The complication of new links with Central and East Europeans really does make it so much more difficult to deal satisfactorily with the wider Western Europe. The notion that the Hungarians or Czechs could be negotiating EC accession within the next five years makes some of the EES debate look like an argument about how many angels can stand on the head of a pin. The technical substance, however important commercially, often seems a far cry from the rediscovery of a continent. It would be bizarre in the extreme for the EC to be enlarged to the East, but not to the North or to the Alpine heartland of Europe.

However, the temptation should be avoided to leave the EES issues on the sidelines of the debate about the new Europe. If the mundane and technical issues of the economy cannot be solved with partners that are so like the EC, then some scepticism is in order about the ease with which such questions could be addressed with partners only recently released from the shackles of inefficient central planning and forbidden market economics. Nor would any conceivable EES agreement with EFTA be directly transferable to the new democracies and their fragile new economies. The EES is made for sophisticated advanced economies with a sound technological base and a dynamic service sector.

Similar considerations apply to the institutional conundrums. There is no question as regards the EFTA countries about whether their legal and political systems could in practice deliver compliance with the emerging EC economic regimes or meet the accompanying environmental and social provisions. Indeed they are already well on the way to having congruent policies in place and, in some areas, setting the standards for the EC to follow. EFTA officials, politicians and entrepreneurs could, and already do, work closely with their EC counterparts. The issues are about a political envelope in which both groups can feel comforable. It is surely an illusion to imagine that the new democracies could do any of this more easily, however strong and passionate the statements of good intention on all sides.

So the difficulties of the EES debate should be taken as a serious indication of much greater difficulties to follow in constructing a viable partnership, let alone enlargement, to the East. But there is a difference. The new partnership to the East will be driven essentially by a political dynamic, and political determination can cut through the more mundane arguments of the technician. Indeed, political imagination is a prerequisite for solving otherwise impossible practical problems. Such imagination entered the EES negotiation only briefly at the time of Jacques Delors' brave call for a new relationship in January 1989. Both EC and EFTA governments then allowed the negotiations to relapse into the old and narrow mode of the past and, not surprisingly, found the going tough. The political question marks will remain for both sides and will have to be addressed. To marginalize the Eftans from the new process of European construction would be to fail to mobilize some of the important political and economic assets that the wider Western Europe has to offer.

Index